Friedrich Schiller

WALLENSTEIN
and
MARY STUART

The German Library: Volume 16
Volkmar Sander, General Editor

Friedrich Schiller

WALLENSTEIN
and
MARY STUART

Edited by Walter Hinderer

CONTINUUM · NEW YORK

PT
2473
.W3
1991
154702
Feb. 1992

1991

The Continuum Publishing Company
370 Lexington Avenue, New York, NY 10017

The German Library
is published in cooperation with Deutsches Haus,
New York University.
This volume has been supported by a grant
from the funds of Stifterverband für die Deutsche Wissenschaft.

Printed in the United States of America

Library of Congress Cataloging-in-Publication Data

Schiller, Friedrich, 1759–1805.
    [Wallenstein. English]
    Wallenstein ; and, Mary Stuart / Friedrich Schiller ; edited by
Walter Hinderer.
        p.   cm.
    Translation of: Wallenstein, and, Maria Stuart.
    ISBN 0-8264-0335-2. — ISBN 0-8264-0336-0 (pbk.)
    1. Wallenstein, Albrecht Wenzel Eusebius von, Herzog von
Friedland, 1583–1634—Drama. I. Schiller, Friedrich, 1759–1805.
Maria Stuart. English. 1991. II. Hinderer, Walter, 1934–   .
III. Title. IV. Title: Wallenstein. V. Title: Mary Stuart.
PT2473.W3   1991
832'.6—dc20   90-41477
                                                                      CIP

Contents

Introduction

When Friedrich Schiller arrived in Weimar in 1787, Goethe was still in Italy. He returned the following year, but the two best-known German writers of their day preferred to ignore each other's existence for some time. Goethe made no secret of his disdain for Schiller's dramatic production. Their historic meeting at the conference of the Society of Natural Science at Jena in 1794 marked the beginning of close collaboration between Goethe and Schiller and of the era of German classicism. The occasion of their rapprochement was a conversation on philosophy and science in which Schiller's idealistic arguments, based on Kant, deviated noticeably from Goethe's contemplative, morphological philosophy. In two letters written shortly thereafter, Schiller traced the origin of their two philosophies to divergent ways of thinking and diplomatically summarized Goethe's different, realistic existence. The substance of these letters is the basis for Schiller's typology of the writer and of mankind in his philosophical essay *On Naive and Sentimental Poetry* (1795–96).

After a lengthy interruption and intensive study of history and philosophy, Schiller closed down his "philosophical shop" in the fall of 1796 and began the *Wallenstein* trilogy, on which he worked for almost three years. Just as Schiller was constantly involved with Goethe's works, the two also discussed *Wallenstein* and related basic aesthetic issues. Early in 1796, they had begun to work together on the distichal epigrams, which they intended to be a critical confrontation with contemporary German literary life. The following year, they competed in a friendly fashion with a series of ballads. Schiller wrote four dramas in the few years that remained to him after finishing the *Wallenstein* trilogy, *Mary Stuart* (1800), *The Maid of Orleans* (1801), *The Bride of Messina* (1803), and *William Tell* (1804). Along with his poems and ballads, these plays made him for a time the most popular writer in nineteenth-century Germany. Schiller's last dramatic project, *Demetrius,* was still unfinished when the playwright died on May 9, 1805. Had he completed it, *Demetrius* would have been a complex, forceful historical drama that probably would have included a new entirely innovative concept of history and philosophy.

Two important early plays by Schiller, *Intrigue and Love* and *Don Carlos,* were published in volume 15 of The German Library. In the current volume, two of his most famous historical dramas, the *Wallenstein* trilogy and *Mary Stuart,* are presented in their entirety. The text of the *Wallenstein* trilogy is a new translation by Jeanne Willson. *Mary Stuart* is a revision of an older translation by Charles E. Passage. In addition, this volume includes notes on the historical background of both plays and a "List of Persons" in *Wallenstein* by Charles E. Passage.

1

Schiller's dramatic masterpiece, the *Wallenstein* trilogy, was written between 1796 and 1799. All three plays premiered in Weimar, *Wallenstein's Camp* on October 12, 1798, *The Piccolominis* on January 30, 1799, and *The Death of Wallenstein* on April 20, 1799. Schiller himself wrote with satisfaction about his work in a letter to Körner dated January 8, 1798: "It has become too rich an object, a small universe, and the exposition took me to astonishing length." In his *Essay on Schiller,* which appeared in 1955, Thomas Mann wrote: "I believe in the genial accuracy of Schiller's portrait of Wallenstein and do not share the opinion of those who say the 'real Wallenstein [was] different.' Historical and psychological intuition cleverly and unerringly preceded later investigation of the sources. . . ." Contemporary historical studies have confirmed Mann's belief and we are justified in reflecting anew on Schiller's productive fusion of fiction and history. Friedrich Schiller's work was an impressive combination of historiography, philosophy, and drama. The smallest detail of Wallenstein's personality that appears in Schiller's *History of the Thirty Years' War* (1791–93) recurs in the trilogy. In the play, however, the dark, saturnine traits of the historical Wallenstein are relieved by the fictional character of Max Piccolomini. For Wallenstein, Max embodies his own youth and the beautiful things in his life (*The Death of Wallenstein,* 5.3).

Wallenstein's power is represented on a number of levels from the viewpoint of the army in *Wallenstein's Camp* and in *The Pic-*

colominis. The existential dependence of the soldiers and officers on the commander is so strong, that the Austrian emperor's emissary, Questenberg, declares: "There is no Emperor here. The Duke is Emperor!" (*The Piccolominis*, 1:3). Different opinions in *Wallenstein's Camp* and in *The Piccolominis* are expressed by such characters as the first arquebusier, the Capuchin friar, Octavio, Thekla, and the Duchess of Friedland. The state of war prevents the return to life and humanity that Max longs for in *The Piccolominis* (1.4). The military, represented by Wallenstein's army, threatens the natural state of the farmers and the citizens. Schiller's legendary protagonist, hesitant to the last to betray the emperor, embodies the political alternative to "use violence or to suffer," of traditional and charismatic leadership, of military and civilian existence, and of war and peace. Schiller's judgment in the *History of the Thirty Years' War* also applies to the Wallenstein of the trilogy: "Wallenstein did not fall because he was a rebel; rather, he rebelled, because he fell."

The trilogy takes place during the Thirty Years' War of 1618–48, which delayed German development for many decades and divided the nation into many small states. More than a century later, Schiller represents this fateful period in the social and political history of his country as a lesson for his contemporaries. In the late eighteenth century, too, a new political order of authority and freedom was the issue. In a letter to the duke of Augustenburg dated July 13, 1793, Schiller defined his goal as the "monarchy of reason," the "greatest of all works of art." Schiller saw himself as a proponent of the age of enlightenment and believed in "the extraordinary case . . . when political legislation is subjected to reason, man is respected and treated as his own sole purpose, law is raised to the throne, and the foundation of the building of state is true freedom." Schiller's dramas as well as his historical and philosophical writings reflect this objective.

Schiller followed the French Revolution from the very beginning with great expectations, but recoiled in horror from the activities of the Jacobin reign of terror: "It was the best possible moment, but the members of this generation are spoiled and unworthy of it, knowing neither to respect nor to use it." For Schiller, political regeneration is now "nothing but a beautiful philosophical dream." Nevertheless, it remained the central concern of his dramatic and theoretical work as he tried to influence the character of his fellow citizens through aesthetic culture. In this way, he hoped to effect the change in their way of thinking that was a prerequisite for a state and a new constitution of freedom. In his fourth *Letter on Aesthetic Education,* Schiller defined "totality of character" as nothing less than the condition that allowed a "state of freedom." His disappointment in the outcome of the French Revolution changed his understanding of history. Schiller had believed that the "history of the world" reflected the "laws of nature" and that history had meaning, but now, aware of the discrepancy between idealistic expectation and reality, he saw "incomprehensibility" as the "standpoint of history." Schiller traces the historical action back to the protagonist and his character, as we see in the figure of Wallenstein.

Wallenstein is the creator and absolute commander of the camp, a separate empire that supposedly lives by its own laws, but he is also the subordinate of the emperor, who legitimates his power. Wallenstein vacillates between rebellion and obedience because the deposition imposed by the princes at Regensburg destroyed his trust in the emperor and in traditional authority. On the other hand, he is unable to free himself from the tradition that governs his reactions and cannot answer the higher call of his historical situation. As the genius of war, he might have become the European prince of peace and the patron of national unity. For this reason, Octavio Piccolomini, his supposed friend and representative of the old order, says: "He simply wants to bring peace to the Empire, / And since *this* peace is hateful to the Emperor, / He wants to—well, he wants to *force* it on him" (5.1). Octavio, who finally greatly weakens Wallenstein's power, accuses the duke of wanting "to satisfy all factions" in the hopes of receiving the Bohemian crown as a reward. The character of Wallenstein reflects the roles and potential for action that are represented in many of the minor characters. For instance, his struggle for power and his dream of leadership are illustrated in the characters of Illo, Terzky, and especially of the countess. She appears to understand Wallenstein best and finally persuades him to ignore his scruples concerning "responsibility and right." The words and the behavior of the duchess and of Gordon mirror Wallenstein's own loyalty to traditional authority. Max Piccolomini embodies the ideal aspects of existence and the national desire for freedom and unity that Wallenstein also sometimes yearns for, but Piccolomini seeks release from his conflicting duties in death.

The myth of the field commander Wallenstein is developed in *Wallenstein's Camp* colorfully and multifariously, only to be systematically destroyed in *The Piccolominis* and *The Death of Wal-*

lenstein. When political calculation advises action but astrology warns against it, Wallenstein waits for a more beneficial constellation of stars. Yet at the end, when his astrologer Seni warns him that the stars are not advantageous, Wallenstein disregards him entirely: when he should trust, he mistrusts and when he should mistrust, as in the case of Octavio, he trusts blindly. He plays with the possibilities, caught in the "double meaning of life" (*The Death of Wallenstein,* 1.4), in a fateful dialectic of thought and action, freedom and necessity. On the one hand, he presents himself as a solicitous father to the soldiers and treats Max as his son. On the other, he manipulates his subordinates, as the example of Buttler shows (*The Death of Wallenstein,* 2.6), and scornfully rejects Max as a son-in-law (3.4). His ruthlessness in dealing with others, his lasting feeling of being singled out, and his blind belief in his own greatness can be interpreted easily as syndromes of the "malignant narcissism" that seems to be characteristic of the infamous dictators of history.

In the *Wallenstein* trilogy, an astonishingly modern and complex drama, Schiller critically seeks the roots of the protagonist's false political and historical actions in his character. In this case study, he demonstrates how an advantageous historical moment was missed and elucidates the reasons why Wallenstein could not be the genial historical personality that could have established a new order in Europe and in Germany. In the trilogy, the victory ultimately goes to the reactionary powers and there is no evidence of any new hope. Thus, in 1800, the philosopher Hegel reacted with alarm to the tragedy: "Life against life; but only death opposes life, and unbelievably! horribly! death is victorious over life! This is not tragic, this is terrible! This tears the spirit, one can't jump out of this with a lightened heart!" Hegel obviously did not understand that Schiller intentionally had located the historical conflict in the person and character of the main figure. For Schiller, the point was a fundamental psychological and moral criticism of false historical greatness. It is not irrelevant that shortly before his death Wallenstein remembers Henry IV, the *bon roi,* for in Schiller's opinion, Henry truly was what Wallenstein might have been or become.

In spite of his criticism of the duke of Friedland, it should not be overlooked that Schiller undertook a slight transformation of the historical figure. When Wallenstein finally negotiates and signs an agreement with the Swedes, the events, helped along by his alleged friend, Octavio, and by his nemesis, General Buttler, have already conspired against him. In *Wallenstein's Camp*, Wallenstein is portrayed as a true child of fortune, but in *The Death of Wallenstein* and already to a certain extent in *The Piccolominis*, the previously omnipotent Wallenstein is presented in all his weakness and psychological trauma. He seeks protection from the "strangeness of life" in the stars and by toying with imagined possibilities, before finally coming to himself and decisively facing the battle ("Now I fight for my head and for my life," *The Death of Wallenstein*, 3.10). At the end, Schiller elicits the sympathy of the audience for the unsuspecting victim in the person of Wallenstein. Although Wallenstein does not change fundamentally, humane, touching traits in his character are betrayed in his mourning for his friend, Max Piccolomini, whom he had manipulated so cruelly, and in his generosity toward the servant (5.5). This is the reason that Goethe, in a letter of March 18, 1799, wrote that in the last part of the trilogy "the historical itself ... [is] only a veil through which purely human qualities" are glimpsed.

2

Schiller began his next historical drama, *Mary Stuart*, in 1799 and already had finished it on June 10, 1800. The premiere took place in Weimar on June 14, 1800. In *Mary Stuart*, both the poetic devices and the fictional character were stronger than in *Wallenstein*. In his letter to Goethe of July 19, 1799, Schiller wrote that he wanted to "create freedom" for the imagination "about and beyond history." In contrast to the *Wallenstein* trilogy, the dramatic action in *Mary Stuart* is strictly organized. Schiller speaks at this time of the "Euripidean method," and, in accordance with classical dramatic principles, the emphasis is on the acts, which are divided between the two competitors, the Scottish Mary Stuart (acts 2 and 5) and the English Elizabeth (acts 2 and 4). Their confrontation and the dramatic climax of the play occurs in the middle act (3). Their power struggle involves not only the hostility between papists and protestants, the consequences of political and religious convictions, and questions of legitimacy and authority, but also a beauty contest incited by Leicester. Mary Stuart certainly has brought guilt upon herself in the course of her dissolute, careless life, but she also possesses a legitimate claim to the throne. Elizabeth has led a morally blameless and ascetic existence, but she is well aware that her origins might be considered illegitimate. For this reason, Elizabeth calls Mary Stuart the "fury" of her life (4.10) and the "bad luck" that haunts her. She believes that the "doubts concerning her princely birth" can be laid to rest only with the death of Mary.

Here, as in *Wallenstein* and his early plays, Schiller seeks the causes of the figures' actions in their characters. He reveals in a subtle way how, quite apart from their different convictions, Mary and Elizabeth are both products of their upbringing, which calls for renunciation from both the Scottish sensualist and the English ascetic. Both women try to compensate for their deficiencies and both covet the advantages that the other has: femininity or political authority, the physical pleasure that derives from a sensual disposition or the intellectual sublimation that moral necessity requires. In Schiller's fictional account, when Mary and Elizabeth meet they react emotionally and not with the "magnanimity" prescribed by contemporary court rituals. Although Mary initially attempts to practice "meek resignation," Elizabeth responds to her rival with nothing but pride, disdain, and cold rejection. Neither is free to react. Mary, pressured by the passionate convert Mortimer, summarizes her problematic situation when she says, "Here is violence and within is murder" (3.6). She is confronted with the extremes of her earlier life, just as Elizabeth later must face her secret desires and the devices with which she has repressed them. These leave their traces in the dissatisfaction she feels with life and with authority (4.9). Just as Mary is a victim of her sensual passion, Elizabeth is the victim of the demands of the people and of political authority.

Elizabeth's complaints about the masculine demands made of her by political authority express in a modern manner the fate of women in a world dominated by men. Mary either is used by men as a sex object or degraded to a political instrument and Elizabeth, if not dominated, is at least manipulated by Burleigh, Leicester, and Shrewsbury. As a woman, Elizabeth truly stands alone "fighting against the world" and in addition must "hide the nakedness of her right . . . behind high virtue" (4.10). The weakness of which she often speaks is clearly expressed in her reluctance to sentence Mary to death. She does not want to go down in history as a murderess, although she believes she will only feel free when her rival is dead. However, it is Mary, the alleged sinner as opposed to the supposedly virtuous Elizabeth, who demonstrates the difference between outer and inner freedom. Mary overcomes her fear of death, thinking of her "nobler part," which Shrewsbury vainly petitions Elizabeth to save (5.15), and is united as "a beautiful transfigured angel . . . for eternity with God" (5.7). The more inner freedom Mary wins in the course of the drama (5.7,8), the more Elizabeth loses of morality and humaneness (5.14,15). In the tragedy *Mary Stuart,* the godly in mankind is transfigured. As Schiller defined it in his essay, *On Pathos,* it is a "representation of the metaphysical."

3

In the aforementioned *Essay on Schiller,* Thomas Mann wrote that Schiller's "personal theater idiom" was the "most brilliant, rhetorically powerful [idiom] that has ever been written in Germany and maybe in the world, a mixture of reflection and affect, so full of dramatic spirit, that ever since it has been difficult to speak of the stage without 'schillerizing.' " In nineteenth-century Germany, Schiller on the one hand and Goethe and Shakespeare on the other were the two major stylistic points of reference for writers and critics from Georg Büchner, Friedrich Hebbel, and Otto Ludwig to Ferdinand Lassalle, Karl Marx, and Friedrich Engels. Many playwrights adapted Schiller's theater idiom according to their own ideological-aesthetic philosophies (for example, Ferdinand Lassalle's drama of 1859, *Franz von Sickingen,* and Rolf Hochhuth's play of 1963, *The Deputy*), or decisively rejected it (Georg Büchner in the nineteenth and Bert Brecht in the twentieth century). As a dramatist, Schiller has never ceased to challenge directors and actors. His writing has influenced other countries and other branches of art. His philosophical works, of which a representative selection appears in volume 17 of The German Library, positively or negatively influenced the aesthetics of Wilhelm von Humboldt, Hegel, Hölderlin, Novalis, Friedrich Schlegel, Nietzsche, Georg Lukács, Bert Brecht, and Herbert Marcuse, and continue to be a source for contemporary aesthetic discussion. Through his theoretical and dramatic work, Friedrich Schiller remains a contemporary whose questions, posed in the eighteenth century, still concern us today.

W. H.

WALLENSTEIN
A Dramatic Poem

The Historical Background of *Wallenstein*

In 1618, one hundred and one years after the beginning of the Protestant Reformation, the smouldering fire of religious conflict burst into raging flame. At first it seemed as though the fire might be different neither in kind nor in degree from the four civil wars that had seared the history of France during that century, or from the intermittent disorders in England, in the Netherlands, or in German territory itself through the same period. Indeed, toward the year 1600 it looked as if Europe had, district by district, settled itself into fixed compartments according to the options of rulers and people either for the old Catholicism or for one of the new faiths. There were even signs, such as King Henry IV's Edict of Nantes in France, to suggest the grudging concession to coexistence of different faiths within a single dominion. The depth of latent fires, especially in central Europe, was underestimated. In 1618 such a conflagration developed as no one could control or stop, and it was to rage for thirty years.

It began in the German principalities, those three hundred and more sovereign and independent countries of assorted sizes and importance which nominally paid allegiance to the Holy Roman Emperor; specifically, it began in the Kingdom of Bohemia, the core of modern Czechoslovakia, which for long ages had formed one of the principal jewels in the crown of the Holy Roman Empire.

In 1609 (the year Hendryk Hudson discovered Manhattan Island), the aging Emperor Rudolf II had persuaded the Bohemians to elect his brother Mathias as their king, and in exchange had granted them—for all that he disapproved of such things—a charter that guaranteed religious toleration. As the years of Mathias's reign went on, however, Bohemian Protestants had more than one violation of the charter to complain of, and they complained in vain. When, in 1617, the childless Mathias persuaded his subjects to accept his nephew, Ferdinand II, as their king and then offered a renewal of the charter to sweeten the bargain, certain restive leaders, especially Count Thurn, determined to press for more effective guarantees for Protestants' rights. A Diet was summoned to deal with the issue. Ferdinand II forbade the Diet to meet. The Diet defied him, and in his absence from Prague, assembled on the fateful May 21, 1618. An angry deputation made its way to the Hradshin Palace, confronted the absent King's Regents, Martinitz and Slawata, and demanded to know precisely who had declared the Diet illegal. When no satisfactory answer was forthcoming, the furious delegates seized the two Regents, together with their secretary, and threw them out of one of the upper-story windows of the building. The three men personally survived their fall in this "Defenestration of Prague" but the grotesque incident was the provocation to a vast war.

Not satisfied with this step, the Diet next demanded that Ferdinand himself relinquish the kingship so that a Protestant might be put in his place. Ferdinand understandably refused. The Diet defied him further, chose a rival king, and invited the latter to appear in Prague forthwith. Their choice had fallen on Frederick V, who from his capital in Heidelberg ruled the area known as the Rhine Palatinate—at the opposite extremity of the Empire. Frederick saw the peril in accepting such an invitation but was inclined to take the risk. He consulted with his royal father-in-law, King James I of England, who urged him to decline the dangerous offer. Still Frederick leaned toward acceptance. The autumn of 1618 found him in Prague. Opinion held that he would be lucky if he lasted the winter. He did last the winter—and no more. Ignominiously fleeing from Prague the following spring, he bore with him the name of "the Winter King" into exile, for this grandfather of England's first King George was never again to enter either Prague or Heidelberg, and his existence was to be one long and sour peregrination with his consort and his large brood of children from one Protestant court of Europe to another, a superfluous guest to the end of his days.

The Catholic armies of the Emperor which now moved into Bohemia found Protestant defiance strong but Protestant generalship divided. A series of minor victories marked their cause, and then, on November 8, 1620 (the month and year when the Pilgrims landed at Plymouth Rock), in the battle of White Hill outside of Prague, they inflicted a major defeat upon the insurgents. For five years thereafter sullen guerilla warfare brought the Protestants total loss of Bohemia in the east and total loss of Frederick's Palatinate in the west. The war seemed all but over.

Meanwhile the conflict had been watched with mounting concern by the Protestant monarchs of northern Europe, yet none had ventured to intervene. By 1625, however, Christian IV of Denmark decided to come to the aid of his fellow religionists. With money supplied in part by England and the Netherlands he began raising an army with which to oppose the Emperor's undefeated General Tilly. Alarm seized the Imperial council in Vienna. The victories had cost the Empire dearly. Finances were strained. How was a huge new counterforce to be paid for?

Unexpectedly the dilemma was solved when a private individual made the Emperor a flabbergastingly generous offer. Albrecht Waldstein, or Wallenstein, titled master of the district of Friedland in Bohemia, himself a Catholic convert from Lutheranism, proposed to recruit 20,000 men, pay them out of his personal fortune, and put them at the Emperor's disposal. There was no alternative but to accept, chafe as the Emperor might at the embarrassment of being bailed out of his troubles by one of his subjects and chafe as the generals might at the prospect of a rival to their prestige. General Tilly in particular did not relish sharing his power with the upstart. Religious bigots questioned the good faith of the convert.

The legend of Wallenstein's wealth attracted more nearly 30,000 than 20,000 men, and by early spring of 1626 the man himself seemed to be showing ample justification of the command with which the Emperor had felt obliged to invest him. While Tilly faced the Danes in the north, Wallenstein attacked the Protestant General Mansfeld, drove him through Silesia, through Moravia, into Hungary, and there defeated him utterly in 1627. With each victory the Emperor had felt bound to reward him with new titles, new authority, and new grants of lands. Tilly's noteworthy but inconclusive victory over the Danes meanwhile seemed slight by comparison with the spectacular pursuit and annihilation of Manfeld's forces. Presently even that victory was eclipsed, for Wallenstein, heading north, joined Tilly, invaded Denmark itself, and conquered the whole country. In 1628 Wallenstein's opponents might gloat over his failure to reduce the independent seaport of Stralsund on the Baltic, which he had vowed to take, but the failure hardly dimmed the upstart's prestige. In 1629 the victors permitted Christian IV to resume his rule over Denmark on the condition of his solemn promise to interfere no further in the conflict. Again the war seemed all but over.

It was now the turn of Protestant Sweden to attempt what the Danes had failed to accomplish. In 1630 King Gustavus Adolphus, personally commanding a force of 12,000 Swedes, landed on the Baltic coast of the Germanies.

The entry of Sweden, however, was motivated by more than the defeat of their Danish friends. In the flush of victory over Denmark the Emperor, spurred on by the Catholic League, promulgated the Edict of Restitution, whereby all church lands lost since 1552—half a century before the war began!—had to be returned by the Protestants who had captured them. The Edict recognized the Lutheran faith, but, by ignoring the Calvinist minority, made the latter illegal and opened the way to its extermination. The Protestants thus had a fair idea of what would happen to them all in the event of total Catholic victory. As if this measure were not unwisdom enough, the Emperor proceeded to a second unwise act at the very moment of the arrival of the Swedish armies: he yielded to the jealous pressures of his advisors and dismissed Wallenstein from command. In fairness to the Emperor it must be said that the hapless monarch was forced to this step by desperate lack of money and by political forces completely beyond his control. Wallenstein, for his part, withdrew quietly to private life to await his inevitable recall, for the Swedes were fast advancing into the heart of Germany.

At first, Gustavus Adolphus, the Swedish king, sparred with General Tilly. Each took turns destroying a city held by his opponent and each sought to outdo the other in example-setting slaughter of civilians. In the sack of Magdeburg Tilly was estimated to have killed all but 5,000 of the town's 35,000 inhabitants. At last the two commanders met at Breitenfeld, near Leipzig, and in a battle which in retrospect could be identified as the turning point of the war, Tilly met disastrous defeat. It was the first real Protestant victory, and it brought into the war as active participants the Protestant states of Brandenburg, Saxony, and Weimar, as well as eliciting financial support for the Protestant çause from Catholic France! For Cardinal

Richelieu, the head of the French state in all but name, understood that total victory for Catholic Austria and the Empire would mean encirclement of France, as in the disastrous days of 1525, and possible annihilation, and he was determined to forestall that eventuality.

By October 1631 the Emperor's representatives were begging Wallenstein to resume command. Wallenstein declined. In November they urged anew, with the same result. In December a more urgent appeal was made to him at Znaim. Wallenstein agreed to raise a new army but refused to lead it. By April 1632 the magic of his name had attracted between 40,000 and 50,000 recruits. Still he refused to command them. The Swedes were now masters of something like a half of German territory and advancing toward the Catholic heartlands of Bavaria and Austria themselves. General Tilly, since his defeat near Leipzig, seemed unable to produce a victory. On April 15 he was killed in battle while resisting the Swedish thrust into Bavaria. Then a still more frantic appeal was addressed to Wallenstein. This time he accepted command, driving a hard bargain as he did so, and receiving powers as made him the equal of an independent sovereign. Little more than his personal word was left to make him responsible to the Emperor.

Immediately upon taking command of the new army Wallenstein recaptured Bohemia from the Protestant Saxons who had taken it the previous year. Next he marched against Gustavus Adolphus himself. To the amazement of everyone, he suddenly stopped short, avoided battle, and took up a strong defensive position near Nürnberg in northern Bavaria. Gustavus also halted. For nine weeks the two armies faced each other without making a move. On September 3 Gustavus attacked and lost heavily. Wallenstein, as if scorning to bother further with him, marched away toward Saxony, presumably to punish the Saxons for entering the war. In Saxony he directly captured Leipzig, the chief city. The Saxons urgently called for the Swedes, who had remained in Bavaria. The Swedes moved toward Saxony. On November 16 there was fought the appalling battle of Lützen with its immense losses in all the armies. Gustavus Adolphus himself was killed.

Wallenstein now proposed a general peace. The Emperor refused the principal concession of granting religious toleration, without which the Protestants would not budge. The Swedes also demanded territorial compensation in Germany which the Emperor refused to consider.

From this point onward Wallenstein's conduct becomes ambiguous. In May of 1633 he moved into Silesia, where Protestant forces of Brandenburg and Saxony were massed, but did not attack them. In a relatively small engagement at Steinau on October 11 he did defeat a Protestant army, but then took it upon himself to barter for the evacuation of the rest of Silesia by setting free the captured Protestant leaders, most particularly Count Thurn. When the Emperor urgently warned him that Protestant Prince Bernhard of Weimar was about to attack Bavaria, he claimed to be sure that Bernhard's real plan was to attack Bohemia; when Bernhard attacked Bavaria after all and captured the major town of Regensburg (Ratisbon), Wallenstein belatedly set out to attack him. The march, however, was halted midway and Wallenstein took up winter quarters at Pilsen in Bohemia without coming anywhere near Bernhard. It began to look as though Wallenstein were undertaking to conclude the war and make a European peace over the heads of all parties belligerent. The Emperor, having resigned to him all real power, could protest and plead with him, but he could do little more than to protest and plead. Catholic leaders were furious at what they considered outright betrayal of their cause.

Such was the situation in the winter of 1633–34, with Protestant armies holding the northeast, the north, and the southwest of German territory, with Catholic leaders having at their disposal no really effective instrument other than Wallenstein's army, and with Wallenstein deliberately refusing to move. With court approval he had been negotiating with the chiefs of certain Protestant states, but it was suspected and more than suspected that either he, or persons acting for him, was making secret bargains which the court would never approve. One rumor had it that he was planning a coup d'état to the end of becoming Emperor himself. In Vienna it became a fixed resolution to stop him at all costs, by assassination if necessary.

Schiller's drama opens at this point; it ends with the assassination of Wallenstein on February 25, 1634.

As for the war, fourteen years of its thirty-year course were yet to be run. Immediately after Wallenstein's murder events seems to justify the deed. Catholic armies led by the Emperor's son, the future Ferdinand III, retook Regensburg from Bernhard and elsewhere fought the Swedes and Saxons to a standstill. Peace was again discussed in May of 1635, but it was frustrated by the Emperor's refusal to grant religious toleration to the Calvinists.

It was now that Cardinal Richelieu determined to widen his policy from indirect support of states opposing the Empire to active intervention. Invasion eastward from France into the Rhine districts would sever the lines of communication between the Empire's staunch ally, Spain, and the Spanish Netherlands and simultaneously break the iron ring that the Empire held girt around France. Ultimately there might be realized the age-old dream of making the Rhine the eastern boundary of France. Thus the major battles of the second half of the war were fought most often in the west and south of the Germanies, the very areas hitherto relatively unaffected. Campaigns followed campaigns, years followed years. Many of the principal personages associated with the war died: Emperor Ferdinand II in 1637, Prince Bernhard in 1639, Richelieu in 1642. Armistice was discussed in 1643 and 1644. One by one, the Catholic leaders were conceding the necessity of making peace. Not so Maximilian of Bavaria, one of the few survivors from the heart of the events of 1618. French armies under Marshal Turenne invaded Bavaria in 1646 and for two years wrought such havoc in Maximilian's lands that even he agreed to come to terms. The signing of the Treaty of Westphalia in 1648 at last brought the weary conclusion. Lutherism and Calvinism were officially recognized, and a less stringent version of the Edict of Restitution established ownership of church lands as of 1624. The independence of the Netherlands was recognized. Sweden was accorded relatively small territorial compensation in northern Germany. Brandenburg—the future Prussia—received significant extension of boundaries. France gained Alsace. Imperial Austria gained almost nothing. Europe was now massively divided into Protestant north and Catholic south, each too powerful for the other to attack, each intensely hostile to the other. The Germanies were an economic, physical, and moral wreck.

CHARLES E. PASSAGE

PROLOGUE

*Spoken at the Reopening of the Theater in Weimar
   in October 1798*

The play of masks, both jesting and in earnest,
To which you often have lent ear and eye,
Most willingly surrendering your soul,
Unites us once again here in this hall—
But look! It is rejuvenated now,
By art adorned serenely as a temple,
And a high spirit speaks in harmony
To us from this array of noble columns
And animates the mind with festive feelings.

   And still this is the same old theater,
The cradle of such youthful vigor here,
The pathway of so much increasing talent.
We are the old ones still, who cultivated
Themselves before you with enormous zeal.
A noble master stood here on this spot,
Transporting you with his creative genius
Into the radiant heights of artistry.
Oh, may the worthiest be drawn into
Our midst by this new-fashioned worthy place,
And a dear hope that we have long embraced
May prove to be most splendidly fulfilled.
A great example wakens emulation
And gives more lofty precepts to opinion.
So may this circle, this new theater
Remain as proof of consummate achievement.
And where would these abilities prefer
To try themselves, to freshen and renew
Their strengths, than for a circle so select,
Which, stirred by every magic stroke of art,

With delicately versatile emotion
May catch the spirit in its fleeting presence?

   For quickly and without a trace the art
Of acting, wondrous art, has left the mind,
When products of the chisel or the songs
Of poets prosper for a thousand years.
Here magic dies when the performer's gone,
And as a sound grows fainter in the ear,
The swift creation of the moment fades,
And nothing that endures preserves its fame.
This art is difficult, its praise is fleeting.
Posterity will weave no wreaths for actors;
And so they have to make the most of now.
That moment that is theirs they must inspire,
Must make themselves the masters of their age
And, in the consciousness of the most worthy,
Create a living monument.—This way
They can anticipate their names' endurance.
For he who does the best in his own time,
He will have lived his life for every age.

   Today upon this stage an era of
Thalia's art begins, emboldening
The poet to relinquish his old course
In order to transport you from the narrow
Confines of everyday to nobler scenes,
Still worthy of the grandeur of the moment
In time, in which we move with aspiration.
For only great affairs will have the power
To stimulate mankind's first principles;
Thus in a narrow sphere the mind contracts,
But man grows great along with greater goals.

   So at this century's most solemn end,
When even what is real becomes a poem,
When we can see before our eyes the struggle
Of mighty natures for important ends
And for the great objectives of mankind
The battle for dominion and for freedom—
Now art may try upon its stage of phantoms

More elevated flight; indeed, it must
Or else be put to shame by life's own stage.

   The present time sees fallen into ruins
The old and solid form that once a hundred
And fifty years ago gave to the kingdoms
Of Europe welcome peace, the precious fruit
Of thirty miserable years of war.
Once more allow the poet's fantasy
To bring that dismal era back for you,
And look more cheerfully at what is present
And what the distant future promises.

   Now will the poet place you in the center
Of that war. Sixteen years of devastation,
Of plunder and of misery are past,
The world is restless with its cheerless masses,
No hope of peace is shining from afar.
The land, a place for martial exercises,
The cities desolated, Magdeburg
In ruins, trade and industry are gone,
The common man means nothing, soldiers all.
Unpunished insolence mocks the old ways,
And vulgar troops, grown wild in the long war,
Have been encamped upon the ravaged land.

   On this dark background of the times is drawn
An enterprise of daring arrogance
And an audacious character is sketched.
You know him—the creator of bold armies,
The idol of the camp and scourge of states,
His Emperor's support as well as dread,
Good fortune's daring son, who, elevated
Through favor of the times, most speedily
Ascended to the highest step of honor,
Unsatisfied and striving ever onward,
Became unchecked ambition's sacrifice.
Confused by party hate and party favor
Perception of his character is varied;
But now art will contrive to bring him nearer
To both your eyes and hearts as only human.

For *art*, which limits and unites all things,
Will always trace back each extreme to nature,
Will see a man caught in the stress of life
And lay the blame for more than half his guilt
On the misfortune of unlucky stars.

   It is not *he* who will appear today
Upon this stage. Still in the daring troops
That his command with strength directs, his mind
Inspires, his spirit will appear for you,
Until the shy muse dares to place the man
Himself before you in his living shape;
It is his power that has seduced his heart,
It is his camp that can explain his crime.

   Therefore forgive the poet if he does
Not hastily proceed *straight* to his plot's
Objective nor attempt a swift unfolding
Of his great subject now before your eyes,
As if it were a row of paintings only.
But may the play today prepare your ear
And your heart, too, for unaccustomed tones,
And may it take you to that place in time,
To that peculiar martial scene of action
That soon our hero will fill up with his
Activities.

   And if today the muse,
The goddess of both dance and poetry,
Demands, though modestly, the play of rhyme,
Her old most German right—do not find fault!
Yes, thank her that she can transmute that dismal
Portrayal of the truth into a realm
Of glorious art and openly destroy
Deceptions she herself has made and does
Not substitute illusion for the truth.
For life is grave, but art is glorious.

Wallenstein's Camp

CHARACTERS

CAVALRY SERGEANT ⎫
TRUMPETER ⎭ from a regiment of Terzky's carabineers
GUNNER
RIFLEMEN
TWO OF HOLK'S MOUNTED RIFLEMEN
DRAGOONS under Buttler
HARQUEBUSIERS from Tiefenbach's regiment
CUIRASSIER from a Walloon regiment
CUIRASSIER from a Lombard regiment
CROATIANS
LANCERS
A RECRUIT
LOCAL CITIZENS
A PEASANT
A PEASANT BOY
A CAPUCHIN MONK
A SCHOOLMASTER for the army children
A SUTLER (A WOMAN)
A WAITRESS
ARMY CHILDREN
OBOISTS

Outside Pilsen in Bohemia

Scene 1

*Sutler's tent, in front of it a stall with secondhand goods. Soldiers of
various allegiances and banners move around amongst each other;
all the tables are occupied. Croatians and lancers are cooking over a
charcoal fire, the sutler (a woman) is pouring wine, army children
are playing dice on a drum, from the tent comes singing.*

A peasant and his son.

PEASANT BOY: Father, there's bound to be some trouble,
   Let's stay away from that soldier rabble.
   Insolent are they, the way they treat us;
   I'll be surprised if they don't beat us.
PEASANT: Nonsense! They're not gonna eat us whole
   Though rashness and daring do take their toll.
   Look! Some new ones are coming in,
   Fresh from the Saal' and from the Main
   Bringing booty, the rarest pieces!
   Crafty we'll be so what's ours increases.
   One captain killed by another, he
   Left these lucky dice for me.
   I'll go and try to find out if they
   Still have the power they once had today.
   Stand and look in need of pity,
   Good-for-nothings'll treat you pretty.
   Love to be flattered and praised a lot,
   Soon as they get things, they lose what they got.
   Wholesale they take from us all that we own;
   Piecemeal we'll have it again when we're done.
   They use their swords in their gross behavior,
   But we will do fine as long as we're clever.

(There is singing, and sounds of celebration come from the tent.)

   Such carousing—may God be forgiving!
   Everything falls on the peasant's heads,
   Eight months long this swarm is living
   Here in our barns and in our beds.
   Far around in the countryside
   Not a feather or claw to hide,
   So we, from hunger and anguish and fear,
   Gnaw on the flesh and the bones of our hands.
   Wasn't a bit more difficult here
   Back when the Saxons roamed our lands.
   And Emperor's men they're supposed to be!
PEASANT BOY: Pa, from the kitchen a pair's coming, see?
   Don't look like there's very much to take from them.
PEASANT: Born in Bohemia, here's where they come from,
   Carabineers from the troops of Terschka,

Quartered here too long already.
These are worse than the others I've found
Strutting and swaggering all around,
Acting as if they were far too decent
To empty a glass with a mere peasant.
See the three riflemen sitting there
Just on your left around the fire?
Straight from the Tyrol they seem to be.
Emmerich, come! Let's go and see,
Talkative fellows, they're cheerful and funny,
Keep themselves clean and always have money.
(*Go toward the tents.*)

Scene 2

The former. Cavalry sergeant. Trumpeter. Lancer.

TRUMPETER: What's that peasant want? Move on! Away!
PEASANT: Sir, for a bite and a drink we pray.
   Haven't had anything warm and that's true.
TRUMPETER: Always need something to slurp and chew.
LANCER (*with a glass*):
   Nothing for breakfast? Here, pig, drink! (*Takes the peasant to
   the tent; the others come upstage.*)
CAVALRY SERGEANT (*to the trumpeter*):
   What is the reason, do you think,
   They allow double our pay today?
   Just so we'll live in a merry way?
TRUMPETER: The Duchess is coming today with her daughter,
   The princess—
CAVALRY SERGEANT: 'Tis just for appearance she's brought here.
   Troops from all the foreign lands
   Gather at Pilsen with all their bands.
   We are supposed to be luring them to us;
   Eating and drinking they are to see us,
   So that they're happy with what they've found,
   Firmer with us will they then be bound.
TRUMPETER: Yes, there is something brewing here!
CAVALRY SERGEANT: All of the generals and each top
   commander—
TRUMPETER: Nothing too good, that's pretty clear.
CAVALRY SERGEANT: All close together can be found here—

TRUMPETER: Not just to pass the time away.
CAVALRY SERGEANT: So many rumors and for the occasion—
TRUMPETER: Right you are!
CAVALRY SERGEANT: Here's Vienna's Great One,
  Seen around here since yesterday,
  Long golden chain around his neck,
  Bet they're planning something slick.
TRUMPETER: Wait and you'll see, it's another hound
  Sniffing his tracks on the Duke's own ground.
CAVALRY SERGEANT: They don't trust us. Mark what I said.
  Friedland's face is what makes them afraid.
  He has climbed far too high for them;
  They'd like to pull him back down again.
TRUMPETER: Oh, but we'll keep him right up there, we;
  If all think the same as you and me!
CAVALRY SERGEANT: Our regiment and with it will be
  Four under Terschka, the Duke's own kin,
  Most resolute in the camp they've been.
  We are most faithful to him and devoted,
  By him himself was our detail promoted.
  All the commanders were brought here by him,
  And him they belong to with life and with limb.

Scene 3

A Croatian with a necklace. A rifleman after him. The former.

RIFLEMAN: Croat, now where did you steal that necklace?
  Here, for these pisols I'll buy it from you.
  Come, let me have it! To you it's no use.
CROATIAN: Oh, no, you'll cheat me. You think I'm dumb, too.
RIFLEMAN: See here! I'll add this blue cap if you come through.
  Just won the thing on the roulette wheel.
  Take it and you'll have a fancy bonnet.
CROATIAN (*lets the sun play on the necklace*):
  Look how it glows when the sun shines on it!
  It's made of pearls and jewels that are real.
RIFLEMAN (*takes the necklace*):
  Here, I'll give you this canteen of mine.
  (*looks at the necklace*)
  I like it just for the beautiful shine.
TRUMPETER: Just take a look how he's cheating that Croat!

I'll take half just to keep me quiet.

CROATIAN (*has put the cap on his head*):
This cap of yours, I like it a lot.

RIFLEMAN (*beckons the trumpeter to him*):
These men are witness that I'm gonna buy it!

Scene 4

The former. A gunner.

GUNNER (*walks up to the cavalry sergeant*):
Carabineer, now how're things going?
How long'll we have to sit here on our hands
While the enemy's force in the field expands?

CAVALRY SERGEANT: Well, Brother Gunner, you must like to rove.
The roads are not fit now for us to move.

GUNNER: Not me. I'm happy with what I'm doing.
Still, there's a messenger come in here.
Regensburg's taken, it seems pretty clear.

TRUMPETER: Then soon enough we'll be sitting there.

CAVALRY SERGEANT: Just to protect the Bavarian's lair?
He's been no friend to the Duke, I'll vow,
And it's not likely that we're gonna care!

GUNNER: Ha! Is there anything you don't know?

Scene 5

The former. Two mounted riflemen. Later the sutler (a woman), army children, army schoolmaster, a waitress.

FIRST MOUNTED RIFLEMAN: Look! You'll see!
Here we'll find merry company.

TRUMPETER: What can the green jackets be on those two,
Coming in grandly and dressed like new?

CAVALRY SERGEANT: Those are Holk's gunners. The silver they wear
Is not something bought at the Leipzig Fair.

SUTLER (*comes with wine*):
Welcome, gentlemen!

FIRST MOUNTED RIFLEMAN: Well, I'll be!
If Gussie from Blasewitz's not who I see.

SUTLER: By golly, that's true, and you, I'd say,

Are Peter the Stilt from Itzehö,
Who squandered all of your father's gold
With our regiment—oh, what a sight—
At Glückstadt in one fabulous night—

FIRST MOUNTED RIFLEMAN: And got for my pen a shotgun to
    hold.

SUTLER: My, yes, we're friends from way back when!

FIRST MOUNTED RIFLEMAN: And meet in Bohemia wherever we've
    been.

SUTLER: Here today, Cousin, tomorrow I'm gone—
    One of those rough old war brooms, that's me,
    Sweeping my way from town to town,
    Meanwhile no telling where I might be.

FIRST MOUNTED RIFLEMAN: I can believe it! That's very clear.

SUTLER: All the way up to Temeswar
    I made the trip with the baggage wagon.
    That was when Manfeld's good luck was saggin'.
    At Stralsund when Friedland made his stand,
    I lost my shirt when I joined that band.
    Went with support troops to Mantua,
    Came out again with Feria,
    And with a Spanish regiment
    I took a side trip and went to Ghent.
    Now in Bohemia I'll cast my nets,
    Cash in on all of my old-time debts—
    See if the Duke will help pay the rent.
    And that over there is my sutler's tent.

FIRST MOUNTED RIFLEMAN: So you've got everything all together!
    Tell me, though, I am curious whether
    You're with that Scotsman you had before.

SUTLER: That rascal! He's gone, slipped out the door,
    Took off with everything he could grab—
    Everything I had managed to save.
    Left me with nothing but that fine laddy.

ARMY CHILD (*comes running*):
    Ma, are you talking about my daddy?

FIRST MOUNTED RIFLEMAN: Think nothing of it. The Emperor
    must feed them.
    To get a new army we have to breed them.

ARMY SCHOOLMASTER (*enters*):
    Off to the school now! Children, come!

FIRST MOUNTED RIFLEMAN: That's something to fear, that narrow
 room.
WAITRESS (*enters*): Auntie, they're leaving.
SUTLER: I'll be right there.
FIRST MOUNTED RIFLEMAN: Who is this charming little tease?
SUTLER: Her mother, my sister, sent her here.
FIRST MOUNTED RIFLEMAN: Aha, then she's your little niece?
                    (*Sutler exits.*)
SECOND MOUNTED RIFLEMAN (*holding onto the girl*):
 Stay here with us, my pretty one.
WAITRESS: I have people to wait upon.
                (*Extricates herself and exits.*)
FIRST MOUNTED RIFLEMAN: That girl's not bad, not bad at all.
 And her aunt! The boys in the regiment
 Have fought each other from tent to tent
 For the favor of such a pretty doll!—
 The people I've known wherever I went,
 And how time flies from event to event.—
 What else will there be that I'll have to recall!
(*To the cavalry sergeant and the trumpeter.*)
 Well, gentlemen, let's have a drink!
 If we can share this place with you?

Scene 6

Mounted riflemen. Cavalry sergeant. Trumpeter.

CAVALRY SERGEANT: We're glad to make room for you here, I
 think.
 Bohemia greets you—we do too!
FIRST MOUNTED RIFLEMAN: Here you sit warm, but there in the
 fight
Wretched was all the life we knew.
TRUMPETER: Can't tell it by looking you're so polite.
CAVALRY SERGEANT: In Meissen and down by the Saal' these days
 What you're likely to hear's not exactly your praise.
SECOND MOUNTED RIFLEMAN: Be quiet there now! Can he mean
 what he says?
 The Croats were something else to deal with—
 Left only the dregs to sharpen our zeal with.
TRUMPETER: You have a collar that's clean, I'll bet you,

And look how those trousers are made to fit you!
Your elegant linens, your hat with its feather!
Such an effect they do make together!
Seems you boys have all the good fortune.
Things like that are never our portion.

CAVALRY SERGEANT: But instead we're Friedland's regiment,
And respected and honored for the same.

FIRST MOUNTED RIFLEMAN: For us that's hardly a compliment,
It's as much our right to carry his name.

CAVALRY SERGEANT: Sure, you're just part of the multitude.

FIRST MOUNTED RIFLEMAN: Do you belong to some special
brood?
It all depends on the coat you're wearing.
With mine, I think, there's no comparing.

CAVALRY SERGEANT: Ah, Sir, it's a pity they need your presence
Out there in the country with the peasants.
But we who live near the General get
Good form and proper etiquette.

FIRST MOUNTED RIFLEMAN: Your lessons haven't helped you yet.
Watching him spit and watching him cough,
You've learned to mimic him well enough;
But the genius of such a man as he,
As troops on review, that's not what you'll see.

SECOND MOUNTED RIFLEMAN: Wherever you ask for us, good
Lord,
We're all of us Friedland's furious horde.
That name we honor as we go
Boldly through lands of friend and foe,
Crossing the country through wheat and corn—
They all know the Holkish hunting horn!—
In just one moment near or far,
Quick as the deluge, there we are—
Like a flash of fire in the black of night
Sweeps through the town with no one in sight.
There is no defense, no time for flight,
All is disorder and terrible fright.—
But war knows no mercy—the girl, with alarm,
Struggles, resisting my brawny arm—
I'm not just boasting—you ask around,
In Bayreuth, Westphalia, wherever we're found.
The children will tell it wherever we've been,

And their children's children will tell it again,
In a hundred or two hundred years they will
Tell the story of our troops still.

CAVALRY SERGEANT: With riotous living—you want to say
You can fashion a soldier in this way?
It's speed that makes him and comprehension,
It's sense and skill and good intention.

FIRST MOUNTED RIFLEMAN: It's freedom makes him! I don't know
   why,
I should talk to you or even try.—
Is that why I ran away from school,
That as a drudge I could play the fool,
In the army camp to meet my doom
Like a slave returned to his narrow room?—
I'll live a gay life and at my leisure,
And every day enjoy some new pleasure,
I'll trust what each moment has to give.
In the past or the future I'll not live.
I gave to the Emperor hide and hair
For a life completely free of care.
If into battle I should be tossed
As the Rhine's deep torrent must be crossed,
With a third of the men about to be lost;
I won't resist or hold a grievance.—
But please, that's it and nothing more,
I want no other inconvenience.

CAVALRY SERGEANT: Well, now, that's all that you're asking for?
You've everything there right under your jacket.

FIRST MOUNTED RIFLEMAN: What a bother it was and what a
   racket
With Gustav, the Swede, the plague of the people.
His camp was like a church with a steeple;
Prayers, by his orders, had to be
Said at retreat and at reveille.
And from his nag he'd preach and prate
If we were inclined to celebrate.

CAVALRY SERGEANT: He was a God-fearing gentleman.

FIRST MOUNTED RIFLEMAN: And girls?—You had to leave them
   alone
Or 'twas off to the church and a wife you'd own.
I couldn't stand it, so off I ran.

CAVALRY SERGEANT: It's different now than it was then.
FIRST MOUNTED RIFLEMAN: The League and its army began to
   prepare
   To take Magdeburg—and I joined them there.
   Now that was a lucky change for me!
   Everything there was merry and free,
   Drink and girls and games to play,
   Truly, such fun you never did see;
   For Tilly knew well the rules of command.
   He was hard on himself in his own way,
   But his soldiers lived a life quite grand.
   If it wasn't his own that he had to give,
   His motto was just to live and let live.
   But his good luck, it didn't last.
   When he failed at Leipzig, it was past.
   Nothing worked for him after that hour,
   And everything we tried turned sour;
   Now when we came and knocked on a door,
   We weren't welcomed as before.
   We had to slink from place to place;
   The old respect was gone with no trace.—
   Then I took the Saxons' pocket money—
   Thought that things might get quite sunny.
CAVALRY SERGEANT: You came in time so that you could
   Plunder Bohemia.
FIRST MOUNTED RIFLEMAN: It did no good.
   Discipline then was the rule of the day,
   To act like an enemy didn't pay,
   Had to watch over the Emperor's castles,
   Make lots of fuss and behave like vassals,
   Carried on war as if it were play,
   With halfhearted efforts went our way,
   Tried not to spoil things for anyone,
   We wanted glory, but we got none.
   Out of impatience I almost went
   Back home to my desk and all it meant.
   But all that happened exactly when
   Friedland arrived recruiting men.
CAVALRY SERGEANT: How long do you think that you'll last here?
FIRST MOUNTED RIFLEMAN: As long as *he's* in charge, I'm sure.
   I'll not be likely to run away.

Where could I have it better today?—
The war is now what the war should be,
It's done with style, as you can see,
And the spirit that rules the whole corps now
Stirs us with strength like the wind does the bough
Down to the lowest rider here.
Boldly I'll venture anywhere
And lord it over the men of the town
Like our general does to the princes now.
Things are done as they once were done,
When the blade was all the law that was known;
There's only *one* crime for which you'll pay:
If they give a command and you don't obey!
What is not forbidden, that you may do;
What you believe in, no one asks you.
Only two things that you have to know:
What is the army's and what is not.
And it's only these colors for which I fight.

CAVALRY SERGEANT: I like that! Now I think I can
Hear one of Friedland's stable of men.

FIRST MOUNTED RIFLEMAN:
It's not like a duty when he takes command,
Not like the power of the Emperor's hand!
He does not serve at the Emperor's whim—
What has the Emperor gained through him?
What has he, with all his might,
Done to improve the country's plight?
A kingdom of soldiers he wanted to found,
To set fire and inflame the world he was bound,
To venture all and to astound—

TRUMPETER: Be still! Who dares to talk that way?

FIRST MOUNTED RIFLEMAN: Whatever I think, that's what I'll say.
Our words are free, the General said.

CAVALRY SERGEANT: That's what he said, he really did,
Right next to me. "Our words are free,
Duty is blind, and action dumb."
He is the one I got this from.

FIRST MOUNTED RIFLEMAN: I can't remember what his words
were,
But things are just as he says, for sure.

SECOND MOUNTED RIFLEMAN: Though others foundered in his
position,

The fortunes of war will always be his.
Tilly outlived his reputation.
But under Friedland's banner I may
Be certain we will win the day.
The master of fortune is what he is.
When beneath his sign we fight,
We're given a peculiar might.
The whole world knows what people say,
That Friedland has a devil from Hell
Working for him and in his pay.

CAVALRY SERGEANT: That he can't be beat I know full well.
At Lützen in that bloody affair
When he rode with you in the fire-filled air
Up and down, his composure so great.
Though the balls flew by at a terrible rate
Piercing his hat in a dozen places
And his boots and doublet showed their traces,
They couldn't touch him in life and limb,
For the devil's salve protected him.

FIRST MOUNTED RIFLEMAN: What kind of a story is it you
Are telling! He wears a leather coat
That nary a bullet can go through.

CAVALRY SERGEANT: Oh, no, it's salve from the witch's pot,
Cooked and brewed with spells she's got.

TRUMPETER: There's something strange, I know that's true.

CAVALRY SERGEANT: They say that he can read in the stars
What will happen today and in future years,
But I know better how this is done.
A little gray man comes all alone
Through guarded doors in the dead of night;
The sentries have challenged him when he appears,
And always just after they've taken sight
Of the little gray cloak, something great occurs.

SECOND MOUNTED RIFLEMAN: He's given himself to the devil and
so
That's why our life is so merry, you know.

Scene 7

The former. A recruit. A local citizen. Dragoons.

RECRUIT (*comes from the tent, an iron helmet on his head, a wine
bottle in his hand*):

My respects to my father. Tell him and his brothers
I'm a soldier. We'll never again see each other.

FIRST MOUNTED RIFLEMAN: Look there, they're bringing in some
new quarry.

LOCAL CITIZEN: Oh, Franz, please listen! You're sure to be sorry.

RECRUIT (*sings*):
 Piping and drumming,
 A martial sound!
 Rambling and roaming,
 The world around.
 My charger I wheel
 With courage like steel
 My sword at my side,
 Away I will ride,
 Lively and free,
 Like the finch I will be,
 On bush and on vine,
 The heavens are mine!
What ho! I follow Friedland's banner!

SECOND MOUNTED RIFLEMAN: That he'll be a bold comrade I see
by his manner!

(*They welcome him.*)

LOCAL CITIZEN: Let him alone! He's got good kin.

FIRST MOUNTED RIFLEMAN: Do you think we're something they
just drug in?

LOCAL CITIZEN: I tell you, his family has property,
Just feel his coat—such quality!

TRUMPETER: The Emperor's coat is our specialty.

LOCAL CITIZEN: A cap-making business is what he'll inherit.

SECOND MOUNTED RIFLEMAN: A man's desire is what's of merit.

LOCAL CITIZEN: His grandmother's shop that's stocked with
notions.

FIRST MOUNTED RIFLEMAN: Who wants to deal in matches and
lotions?

LOCAL CITIZEN: His godmother's tavern he'll also get,
A cellar with twenty barrels of wine.

TRUMPETER: He'll want to share with his comrades, I bet.

SECOND MOUNTED RIFLEMAN: I want you to be a tentmate of
mine.

LOCAL CITIZEN: His girl he leaves sobbing because they must part.

FIRST MOUNTED RIFLEMAN: Quite right, it shows that he has a
hard heart.

LOCAL CITIZEN: His grandmother'll die of sorrow and care.

SECOND MOUNTED RIFLEMAN: The sooner he'll get to inherit his share.

CAVALRY SERGEANT (*steps forward gravely, laying his hand on the recruit's iron helmet*):
You thought it over as best you can,
And you're going to be an entirely new man,
With your helmet there and your sword belt on,
You want to join our worthy throng.
A noble spirit is now what you'll have.

FIRST MOUNTED RIFLEMAN: And your money is something you won't want to save.

CAVALRY SERGEANT: On Fortune's ship you'll take your stand,
The time to set sail is at hand.
The world is before you on every plain,
Who ventures nothing will nothing gain.
These stupid townsmen you see all around,
Like the dyer's nag, in their circle are bound.
Now every soldier can show what he's worth,
For war is at present the watchword on earth.
Look how with this coat in which I stand
I hold the Imperial staff in my hand.
All the world's power, as you must know,
Out from that staff is obliged to go.
And the very scepter a king holds here
Is only a staff, you must be aware.
And when a corporal's rank you've got,
You're climbing the ladder to power, no doubt,
And you can also reach that height.

FIRST MOUNTED RIFLEMAN: If you can only read and write.

CAVALRY SERGEANT: The way it happens I want you to know,
For I saw it first hand not long ago.
The corps of dragoons is in the command
Of Buttler, who once was a comrade of mine
Thirty years ago at Cologne on the Rhine,
As a major general you now see him stand.
He spread his own glory on every hand
Whene'er he excelled in some small way,
But all that I've done is unknown to this day.
Well, Friedland himself—you need only look here—
Our noble leader without a peer,
Who all he wishes will and can do,

Was once a simple nobleman, too,
And because he relied on the Goddess of War,
He attained greatness and even more,
And, after the Emperor, is the next man who
May gain still more before he's done.

(*slyly*)

For who can know what's yet to come.

FIRST MOUNTED RIFLEMAN: He started out small and is now so
  great,
But at Altdorf in his student days
He behaved, if I may use the phrase,
Quite boisterous, and in that state
He almost killed, the story goes,
His secretary. The gentlemen
Of Nuremberg wanted to lock him in
Their brand-new prison, no matter what.
A prisoner should name it—the very first one.
But how should he do it? He prudently put
The poodle before him and let it run.
It's been named for that dog from then till now;
He's someone to emulate, that I'll vow.
If I choose from the great deeds that this man has done,
The one I like best, this is the one.
(*The girl meanwhile has come to wait on the table. The second
mounted rifleman flirts with her.*)

DRAGOON (*steps between them*):
  Comrade, you better go on and steer clear.

SECOND MOUNTED RIFLEMAN:
  Who the devil is meddling here!

DRAGOON: This girl is mine, I want that known.

FIRST MOUNTED RIFLEMAN: He thinks this treasure is his alone!
  Dragoon, you must be out of your head!

SECOND MOUNTED RIFLEMAN: Wants something special in camp,
  he said.
  A girl's pretty face, just like the sun,
  In camp belongs to everyone! (*kisses her*)

DRAGOON (*pulls her away*):
  You won't get away with what you've done.

FIRST MOUNTED RIFLEMAN: Here come the boys from Prague!
  Whoopee!

SECOND MOUNTED RIFLEMAN: You want a fight? You can count
  on me.
CAVALRY SERGEANT: Peace there, gentlemen! Kisses are free!

Scene 8

*Miners step forward and play a waltz, at first slowly and then faster
and faster. The first mounted rifleman dances with the waitress, the
sutler with the recruit, the girl runs off, the rifleman after her and
grabs hold of the Capuchin monk who is just entering.*

CAPUCHIN MONK: Ho, ho, ho and heididdledee!
  It's lively here and that's for me.
  Is this an army of Christian men?
  Or Turks or Anabaptists then?
  Your conduct on Sunday's so shameful and bad,
  It's as if our Lord God really had
  The gout and couldn't stop it all.
  Is this the time for a drunken brawl?
  For banquets and a festival?
  Quid hic statis otiosi?
  What are you sitting with your hands in your lap for
  When there on the Danube the fury of this war
  Rages, Bavaria's ramparts are lost,
  And Regensburg's held by the enemy host,
  While here in Bohemia the army sits
  And feeds its face and never frets,
  While drinks are poured, forgets the sword,
  Makes plans to eat, not whom to beat,
  Chases the girls at every turn,
  Gobbles up oxen but not Oxenstirn.
  The Christian world mourns in sackcloth and ashes,
  The soldier grabs plunder that he carefully stashes.
  It's a time of wailing and misery,
  And omens and signs from the heaven's do fall,
  While from bloody red clouds it is plain to see
  The Lord God's warcloak is spread over all.
  He displays comets instead of his rod,
  As a threat from the window of heaven they're sent,
  The world as a whole is a house of lament,
  The ark of the Church is swimming in blood,
  The Roman *empire*—it's true I fear!

Ought to be labeled the Roman *dump here,*
The Rhine's not a *river,* but an agonized *shiver,*
The *nunneries* look like special *gunneries,*
Each *episcopate*'s now a *desert state,*
While the *abbies* and *seminaries*
Are now *shabbies* and *robbers' eyries,*
And each blessed German *land*
Is nothing more than *contraband—*
Now what did this come from? I'll gladly announce:
From your sins and vices in large amounts,
From the heathen life with its horrible deeds
That every soldier and officer leads.
For sin is that magnetic stone
That attracts the iron, as is well-known.
Are you Unjust? next in Vice you'll wallow,
As, given onions, tears will follow,
After U and V comes Woe,
In the ABC that's always so.
  Ubi erit victoriae spes,
Si offenditur deus? Where's the victory
If you skip the sermon and miss the mass,
If a tavern is where you're bound to be?
In the gospel we hear the story told
Of the woman who found her money again,
And Saul found his father's donkey again,
And Joseph his fine brothers then;
But among the soldiers you might as well save your
Effort in looking for good behavior,
And chastity's something you won't find either,
Though you light a hundred lanterns together.
In the desert to the preacher—
Here the evangelists are our teacher—
Soldiers went, and they returned thence
Fully baptized after penance,
Having asked: *Quid faciemus nos?*
What the way to Abraham's bosom was.
Et ait illis, he said, you will:
Neminem concutiatis,
Torment no one nor treat him ill.
Necque calumniam faciatis,
Malign no one with cruel intent.

Contenti estote, be content,
Stupendiis vestris, with what you've earned
And flee bad habits that you've learned.
The third commandment reads: The name
Of the Lord thou shalt not take in vain.
Here in Friedland's camp among the tents
The use of blasphemy is immense.
If for every swearword that's used here,
That pierces the air both loud and clear,
They rang the bells in the land around here,
There soon would be no sexton found here.
And if for every evil prayer
That leaves your mouths without a care,
They'd pull one hair from your head, then lo,
By morning that head would be quite bare,
Though the hair was as thick as Absalom's hair.
Still Joshua was a soldier we know,
And David killed Goliath with just one blow,
But where does it tell us that these men
Had such foul mouths as you have then?
It's just as easy, in my opinion,
To ask God's help as to be crude
And damn another by God's blood.
Fill a container and that, which is in it,
Is what will gush out of it every minute.
    The commandment says: Thou shalt not steal.
You follow that law to the word, you say,
For you openly carry your loot away;
But from your claws and vulture's clutch,
Your way of working and evil touch,
No money is safe as it lies in a chest,
The calf's not secure in the cow though it rest,
Along with the chicken the egg tastes best.
Contenti estote, the preacher said,
Be satisfied with your army bread.
But how can we judge the man below
When above is where the trouble doth grow!
As the limbs, so the head also goes!
In whom *he* believes, that no one knows!
FIRST MOUNTED RIFLEMAN: About us soldiers say what you will,
    But about our general, monk, be still.

CAPUCHIN MONK: *Ne custodias gregem meam!*
  An Ahab and Jeroboam, see him,
  And how the people from the truths they've learned
  To the worship of him false gods he's turned.
TRUMPETER AND RECRUIT:
  Don't say that again, you're hereby warned!
CAPUCHIN MONK: Such a braggart and such a bully.
  He'd take all the castles willy-nilly.
  With his wicked mouth thus he did rave
  That the city of Stralsund he would have,
  And if it were bound to Heav'n by a chain.
  But he shot his powder all in vain.
TRUMPETER: Shut his mouth!—he's got his gall.
CAPUCHIN MONK: Such a devil conjurer and King Saul,
  Such a Jehu and Holofernes in one,
  Denied his Lord as Peter had done,
  That's why he won't hear a rooster crow—
BOTH MOUNTED RIFLEMEN: Monk! you're really done for now!
CAPUCHIN MONK: Such a cunning fox like Herod—
TRUMPETER AND BOTH MOUNTED RIFLEMEN (*pressing in upon him*):
  That's enough! I warn you, you're dead.
CROATIANS (*interfering*): Stay here, monk, and never fear,
  Say your say and let us hear!
CAPUCHIN MONK (*shouting louder*):
  Such a Nebuchadnezzar, so haughty,
  The father of sin, a heretic so shoddy,
  The name he uses is *Wallenstein,*
  And he is, indeed, to us *all* like a *stone*
  That pounds upon us and angers us,
  While the Emperor leaves Friedland here
  In power, you'll have no peace to fear.
  (*He has gradually begun to withdraw with these last words that he speaks in a solemn voice as the Croatians keep the other soldiers away from him.*)

Scene 9

The former without the Capuchin.

FIRST MOUNTED RIFLEMAN (*to the cavalry sergeant*):
  What was he saying, how does he know

That the General can't bear it if the cock should crow?
Did he say it to scorn him and be rude, too?
CAVALRY SERGEANT: I can tell you this, that it's partly true.
The General's unusual, it would seem,
His ears are sensitive in the extreme.
If a cat meows, he cannot bear it,
And if the cock crows, he shudders to hear it.
FIRST MOUNTED RIFLEMAN: That is the case with the lion as well.
CAVALRY SERGEANT: All around him it must be quite still.
The watch may not allow a sound
Because his thoughts are so profound.
VOICES (*in the tent; uproar*):
Grab him, the lout! Use force and violence.
PEASANT'S VOICE: Help! Have mercy!
OTHER VOICES: Quiet! Silence!
FIRST MOUNTED RIFLEMAN: There's a fight in the tent. Let's take a
look!
SECOND MOUNTED RIFLEMAN: Just let me at 'em.
(*They run into the tent.*)
SUTLER (*comes out*): That dirty
crook!
TRUMPETER: Hey there, lady, what are you so mad about?
SUTLER: Thief and scoundrel, swindler and crummy lout!
Why did it have to happen to me now?
The officers will hear of it and cause a big row.
CAVALRY SERGEANT: Cuz, what is it?
SUTLER: What would it be?
They just caught a peasant in there with me,
His dice were crooked, it would appear.
TRUMPETER: His boy is with him; they're bringing them here.

Scene 10

Soldiers enter, dragging the peasant.

FIRST MOUNTED RIFLEMAN: They'll string him up!
RIFLEMEN AND DRAGOONS: Let's on to the provost!
CAVALRY SERGEANT: The order recently was sent out.
SUTLER: He'll hang in an hour, I have no doubt!
CAVALRY SERGEANT: For such bad business you get bad pay.
FIRST HARQUEBUSIER (*to another*):
They live in desperation's way.

They ruin them, and then in defeat
They learn the way to steal and cheat.
TRUMPETER: What's this? Excuses for his kind?
That dog! The devil has hold of you.
FIRST HARQUEBUSIER:
Well, peasants are people—sort of—too.
FIRST MOUNTED RIFLEMAN (*to the trumpeter*):
Enough! They're Tiefenbach's men, you'll find,
With families of shopkeepers left behind!
They were stationed in Brieg and both of them know
How things in a war are likely to go.

Scene 11

The former. Cuirassiers.

FIRST CUIRASSIER: Peace be! Now who's this peasant you've
caught?
FIRST RIFLEMAN: A scoundrel he is, whose dice were bad!
FIRST CUIRASSIER: I take it that you're the one he got?
FIRST RIFLEMAN: He took me for everything I had.
FIRST CUIRASSIER: How can this be? You're Friedland's man,
How can you face such ridicule
To gamble with a peasant like a fool?
Just let him go now while he can.
(*The peasant escapes, the others close ranks.*)
FIRST HARQUEBUSIER: He's resolute and makes short shrift
So that these people catch the drift.
He's not Bohemian. Where's he from?
SUTLER: You've got to respect him! He's a Walloon!
From Pappenheim's troops, a cuirassier.
FIRST DRAGOON (*joins them*):
Young Piccolomini leads them, I hear.
They made him a colonel on their own
In the battle at Lützen when it was known
That Pappenheim had fallen there.
FIRST HARQUEBUSIER: To do such a thing! How did they dare?
FIRST DRAGOON: This regiment is really elite;
It's always in front in every fight.
Its laws are its own, that's easy to see,
And Friedland loves it especially.

FIRST CUIRASSIER (*to another*):
  Where did you get this? Is this really right?
SECOND CUIRASSIER:
  From the colonel's own mouth, there is no doubt.
FIRST CUIRASSIER:
  We're not just their dogs to kick about.
FIRST MOUNTED RIFLEMAN:
  What's wrong with them? Just hear them cuss!
SECOND MOUNTED RIFLEMAN: Is it something, man, to do with us?
FIRST CUIRASSIER:
  It's not something meant for our greater enjoyment.
              (*Soldiers join them.*)
  The lowlands is where we'll be sent for deployment,
  Cuirassiers and riflemen and fusiliers,
  Eight thousand men all told, it appears.
SUTLER: What's this? We're off to Flanders you say?
  I got back from there just yesterday.
SECOND CUIRASSIER (*to the dragoons*):
  You Buttler men will be with those starting.
FIRST CUIRASSIER: And then we Walloons, of course, will go.
SUTLER: Oh, those are the best of the squadrons, we know!
FIRST CUIRASSIER: The man from Milan is the one we're escorting.
FIRST MOUNTED RIFLEMAN: That's very odd! The prince of Spain!
SECOND MOUNTED RIFLEMAN: That priest! They must think we're
  all insane!
FIRST CUIRASSIER:
  With Friedland we're supposed to part,
  Who was so generous to us all,
  And with that Spaniard to fight and fall,
  A skinflint we hate deep in our heart.
  No, that won't work! We'll disappear.
TRUMPETER: What in the devil should we do there?
  The Emperor bought us heart and hand
  And not that Spanish cardinal's band.
SECOND MOUNTED RIFLEMAN:
  On Friedland's word and reputation
  We joined up with the cavalry;
  If it weren't for Wallenstein's recommendation,
  We'd never have answered Ferdinand's plea.
FIRST DRAGOON:
  Wasn't it Friedland who put us here?

We'll follow his fortune anywhere.

CAVALRY SERGEANT: Now be advised and hear what I say.
This kind of talk won't save the day.
I can see farther than all of you,
And what I see is a trap here, too.

FIRST MOUNTED RIFLEMAN: Listen to wisdom! Quiet now!

CAVALRY SERGEANT: Cousin Gussie, I will allow
A glass of Melnecker for my digestion,
And offer my thoughts on the matter in question.

SUTLER (*pouring him a glass*):
Here you are, sergeant! You frighten me.
There's nothing wicked here certainly?

CAVALRY SERGEANT: Listen, gentlemen, it's all very well
To look to tomorrow as far as you can tell;
But the general says it's best, you'll find,
To keep the whole picture well in mind.
We all can call ourselves Friedland's men.
The townspeople have to find us a bed
And take care of us and feed us then.
The peasant's nag and oxen are led
To be harnessed up to our baggage train,
And it does no good for him to complain.
And if a corporal should be seen
With seven men in a little village,
He is the government therein
And as he pleases can loot and pillage.
They don't like us and in this case
They'd prefer the devil face-to-face
To the yellow coats that are worn by our band.
My God! Why not throw us out of their land?
There are more of them than us around;
We have our swords, but their clubs can pound.
Why should we be the ones to rate?
Because the sum of us is so great!

FIRST MOUNTED RIFLEMAN:
That's it! In the whole, strength will abide!
This lesson Friedland was to show,
When he brought the Emperor nine years ago
This enormous army from far and wide.
They wanted twelve thousand at first, they said.

He said he couldn't keep that many fed;
But sixty thousand men would never
Perish from starvation ever.
So we belong to Wallenstein.

CAVALRY SERGEANT: If you would take this hand of mine
And from five fingers that I own
Would cut away the little one,
It's just a finger, would you say?
Oh, no, you'd take my hand away—
It's just a stump and nothing more.
And these eight-thousand horses for
The war in Flanders, wanted sore,
Are like that finger to our force.
Take them away, and do you think
For that we're only one-fifth worse?
Here's news! The whole affair will sink.
The fear is gone, respect is, too,
The peasants put on airs anew,
And the government, as it used to do,
Writes out for us a requisition,
And we're beggars again on the road to perdition.
How long do you think it will last this way?
They'll remove our leader without delay—
His praises they're not wont to sing—
Now, that's the end of everything!
Who'll help us get our money then
And keep their bargains with the men?
Who has the brains, the strength to stand,
The ready wit, and the firm hand
To take this patchwork multitude
And make it one big brotherhood?
As an example—dragoon—say
Where you came from to join the fray.

FIRST DRAGOON: I come from Hibernia far away.

CAVALRY SERGEANT (*to the two cuirassiers*):
You're a Walloon, I know that by chance.
And your accent tells me you come from France.

FIRST CUIRASSIER:
Where do I come from? I don't know where,
When I was quite young, I was stolen from there.

CAVALRY SERGEANT: And this neighborhood could not be your
   home?
FIRST HARQUEBUSIER: Buchau am Federsee's where I'm from.
CAVALRY SERGEANT: And you?
SECOND HARQUEBUSIER: I'm Swiss. That's pretty far.
CAVALRY SERGEANT (*to the second mounted riflemen*):
   Well, rifleman, where might your country be?
SECOND MOUNTED RIFLEMAN:
   Near Wismar is where my parents are.
CAVALRY SERGEANT (*pointing to the trumpeter*):
   And Eger is home for him and me.
   Now who could tell by the looks of this throng
   That, blasted and blown in all kinds of weather,
   From north and from south we were driven together?
   Don't we look as if this is the way we belong?
   Don't we stand like a wall to the enemy
   So one solid front is all they can see?
   Don't we mesh like a grinder moving quickly
   At a word or a gesture, working slickly?
   Who is the one who has welded us so
   We are indistinguishable to our foe?
   It was Wallenstein and nobody but!
FIRST MOUNTED RIFLEMAN:
   You know, I never realized that
   This crowd fits together the way it does;
   I just went along the way I was.
FIRST CUIRASSIER:
   The sergeant's words get my applause.
   A loss of our strength they'd gladly cause.
   They'd like to see the soldiers cower
   So they alone could wield the power.
   It must be a conspiracy.
SUTLER: Conspiracy? Then God save me!
   How will the gentlemen pay me then?
CAVALRY SERGEANT:
   That's true. They'll be in bankruptcy.
   Generals and important men
   Had regiments that they underwrote
   To be recognized as people of note,
   Used up their wealth at a terrible rate,
   Thought their profit would be very great.
   Their money now will all be gone,

If the Duke should ever be overthrown.

SUTLER: O Christ! How cursed I'm going to be!
Half of the army's in debt to me,
Especially that Count Isolani,
He owes me a whole lot of money.

FIRST CUIRASSIER:
Well now, comrades, what's to be done?
There's a way to save us and this is how:
They can't do us harm if we act as one,
We all will represent *one* man now.
Let them send orders from near and far,
We'll plant our feet firmly where they are,
We will not march and will not yield,
To fight for honor we are steeled.

SECOND MOUNTED RIFLEMAN:
We won't let them shove us around these lands!
Just let them come and make their demands!

FIRST HARQUEBUSIER:
Gentlemen, you must consider with care,
The Emperor's wants and commands are there.

TRUMPETER: We'll bother about the Emperor a lot!

FIRST HARQUEBUSIER:
If you plan to repeat that, you'd better not!

TRUMPETER: But still, it's so, just as I said.

FIRST MOUNTED RIFLEMAN:
Yes, everybody understands
It's Friedland's right to give commands.

CAVALRY SERGEANT:
That's true, that was the pact he made.
Absolute power was given him
To make war or peace at his own whim,
Money and goods he can confiscate,
Have people pardoned or seal their fate.
He can make officers, goodness knows,
And signs of rank, he has all of those.
He got them, what's more, from the Emperor's hand.

FIRST HARQUEBUSIER:
The Duke is powerful, wise, and grand;
But he remains, however you will,
Like all of us, the Emperor's still.

CAVALRY SERGEANT:
Not like us all! Your knowledge is nil.

He can rule as free prince of the empire as good
As the one from Bavaria ever could.
Didn't I see with my very own eyes,
When I did guard duty there at Brandeis,
Didn't I hear when the Emperor said
He could keep his hat on his princely head?

FIRST HARQUEBUSIER:
That was the Mecklenburg equity
That the Emperor gave for security.

FIRST MOUNTED RIFLEMAN (*to the cavalry sergeant*):
When the Emperor himself was there?
That's very uncommon and very queer!

CAVALRY SERGEANT (*reaches in his pocket*):
If you don't believe what I'm telling you,
I'll show you something to prove it's true.
                    (*showing them a coin*)
Whose is that picture and stamp?

SUTLER: Let's see.
That's Wallenstein's coin as anyone knows.

CAVALRY SERGEANT:
There it is, what else do you want from me?
He's as sovereign a prince as any of those.
He mints his money like Ferdinand
And has his own people and his own land.
By the title of Highness he always is known,
And so his soldiers must be his own.

FIRST HARQUEBUSIER:
No one is going to argue with you,
But we owe the Emperor his due,
And the Emperor is the one who pays us.

TRUMPETER: I'll say straight in your face, that is not true.
The Emperor's the one who *doesn't* pay us!
It's been forty weeks, I know, since they
Promised us we would get our pay.

FIRST HARQUEBUSIER:
That's in good hands as everyone knows.

FIRST CUIRASSIER:
Gentlemen, peace! or you'll come to blows.
Is there anything here to quarrel about?
We're the Emperor's men, there is no doubt.

And just for that reason our wish is then
To fight for him as his cavalrymen,
To do him credit, but how can this be
When we're handed over to flunkies and priests
To be led around like a herd of beasts.
Is it not to a leader's benefit,
If his troops should think of themselves a bit?
Who but his soldiers make him so great,
Such a high and mighty potentate?
Whom but them does he have it from:
The biggest say in all Christendom?
Let them be the ones his yoke to bear
Who eat with him and whose food they share,
Who feast with him in his room of gold.
We know nothing of that but what we're told,
We have nothing for that but the trouble and grief
And what we derive from our own belief.

SECOND MOUNTED RIFLEMAN:
Every great tyrant and emperor
Thought this way and was wiser therefor.
They spoiled and ravished everywhere,
But they treated their soldiers with great care.

FIRST CUIRASSIER:
The soldier must feel his own worth is great.
Who would fight without a mind that's noble
Better save himself the trouble.
When I risk my life on the play of fate,
There must be something that I love more.
Or like the Croatians, I'd simply be slain,
And for myself I'd have naught but disdain.

BOTH MOUNTED CAVALRYMEN:
Yes, honor, that is worth dying for!

FIRST CUIRASSIER:
A sword is not a plow or a spade.
He's a fool who would try to farm with a blade.
No stalks for us blossom, no seeds will grow,
Without a homeland a soldier must go,
Fleetingly roving over the earth,
Never to warm himself at his own hearth,
He must leave behind the lights of the town,
Pass by the village's happy green,

The picking of grapes, the harvest crown,
As he wanders, is only distantly seen.
What does a soldier really own
But the honor he holds for himself alone?
Something must belong to him
Or he'll murder, pillage, burn at whim.

FIRST HARQUEBUSIER:

This wretched life I do deplore.

FIRST CUIRASSIER:

There's nothing I would change it for.
I've traveled around in the world a lot,
A bit of everything's what I've sought.
I served the Spanish monarchy,
The Republic of Venice, I served it, too,
And then the kingdom of Napoli;
But nowhere did my luck come through.
I've seen the merchants and the knights,
Artisans, Jesuits, and other sights,
And no other coat seems as good to me
As this iron doublet here can be.

FIRST HARQUEBUSIER:

No! That is certainly not what I'd say.

FIRST CUIRASSIER:

In this world if you aim to get somewhere today,
You've got to get moving and join in the fray.
If a person of rank and title you'll be,
Then bow to responsibility.
If you want to enjoy fatherhood,
With children and grandchildren in a brood,
Follow an honest occupation,
But I—I don't have that inclination.
I'll live and die free and on my own merit,
I'll never steal and never inherit,
And up on my horse I need not be aware
Of all the confusion beneath me there.

FIRST MOUNTED RIFLEMAN:

Bravo! That's what I like to hear.

FIRST HARQUEBUSIER:

It's more fun, I'm sure, for those in your stead
Who can trot away over anyone's head.

FIRST CUIRASSIER: The times are hard and it's true of late
  That justice no longer holds the sword's weight,
  But I hope no one will find fault with me
  That sword in hand is how I want to be.
  In war my humanity I can prove,
  But I won't be taken advantage of.
FIRST HARQUEBUSIER:
  Who but us soldiers is to blame
  That the peasants have gotten such a bad name?
  This loathsome war with its want and tears
  Continues nigh onto sixteen years.
FIRST CUIRASSIER:
  Not everyone at once will raise
  His heart to the Lord above in praise.
  One wants the sun, while another wonders why;
  One longs for moisture, the other wants it dry.
  When everything seems the worst to *you*,
  To *me* the sky appears bright blue.
  If the townsmen and peasants are in great need,
  Then I will be sorry for them indeed;
  But to change this nothing can be done,
  It's just like when a charge is run:
  The horses snort and start to go,
  Whoever's in their way, oh, woe,
  Though it should son or brother be,
  And his wailing rends the soul of me,
  I must ride him down without delay,
  And cannot carry him gently away.
FIRST MOUNTED RIFLEMAN:
  Oh, who has time for others today!
FIRST CUIRASSIER:
  And since for once, then, things are so
  That soldiers' fortunes seem to grow,
  Let's hang on tight with both our hands,
  It won't last long the way it stands.
  For peace is just around the bend,
  This state of affairs is bound to end;
  The peasant yokes up, our horses run free,
  In a flash things will be like they used to be.
  For now we're together in this land
  And presently still have the upper hand;

But if they should scatter us Lord knows where,
We'll never again get our fair share.
FIRST MOUNTED RIFLEMAN:
No, that shall nevermore be done!
We're one for all and all for *one*.
SECOND MOUNTED RIFLEMAN:
Let's make a pact here, listen now!
FIRST HARQUEBUSIER (*taking out a leather purse, to the sutler*):
Tell me, Auntie, what do I owe?
SUTLER: It's scarcely worth mentioning, I'll allow.
(*They figure it up.*)
TRUMPETER: If you want to leave, that's fine with me.
You're spoiling our society.
(*Harquebusiers exit.*)
FIRST CUIRASSIER:
Too bad about them! They're brave and true.
FIRST MOUNTED RIFLEMAN:
But that one thinks like soapmakers do.
SECOND MOUNTED RIFLEMAN:
So just between us now let's get back
To how we can stop this new attack.
TRUMPETER: What's that? We simply will not go.
FIRST CUIRASSIER:
Now, nothing against the rules, you know!
Each one of us goes back to his corps,
And with his comrades he will explore
The matter so they can understand.
We cannot withdraw far from this land.
I know my Walloons will all agree.
Each one is sure to think like me.
CAVALRY SERGEANT:
Terzka's soldiers, on foot or horse,
Will all agree with this, of course.
SECOND CUIRASSIER (*takes his place next to the first cuirassier*):
With the Walloons the Lombards will be.
FIRST MOUNTED RIFLEMAN:
We riflemen all aim to stay free.
SECOND MOUNTED RIFLEMAN:
Only with strength is freedom mine:
I'll live and die with Wallenstein.
FIRST RIFLEMAN: This man of Lorraine has already vowed

To stay with this large and lighthearted crowd.
DRAGOON: The Irishman follows his lucky star.
SECOND RIFLEMAN:
  By their sovereign's side the Tirolers are.
FIRST CUIRASSIER:
  So let's have every regiment
  Write a memorial clean and clear:
  That we'll all remain together here
  And never will be separated
  From Friedland, whom we all revere,
  No matter what tricks are perpetrated.
  We'll give it humbly when we're done
  To Piccolomini—the son—
  Who'll know how to get what we demand,
  For with Wallenstein he has a free hand.
  And both the Emperor and the King—
  So I've heard say—his praises sing.
SECOND MOUNTED RIFLEMAN:
  Then come! That's it! We all agree!
  Our spokesman is Piccolomini.
TRUMPETER, DRAGOON, FIRST MOUNTED RIFLEMAN, SECOND
CUIRASSIER, RIFLEMEN (*together*):
  Our spokesman is Piccolomini.
                    (*are about to exit*)
CAVALRY SERGEANT:
  First, one more glass raised to the skies!
                    (*drinks*)
  May Piccolomini's favor rise!
SUTLER (*brings a bottle*):
  This one's on me. There is no charge.
  I hope that your success is large!
CUIRASSIERS: Long may the military live!
TWO MOUNTED RIFLEMEN:
  Long may the peasants have to give!
DRAGOONS AND RIFLEMEN:
  May the army's prowess never quit!
TRUMPETER AND CAVALRY SERGEANT:
  And Friedland shall rule over it.
SECOND CUIRASSIER (*sings*):
  Come on, comrades, to horse, to horse!

To the field we'll ride to be free!
On the battlefield each man is a force,
    In the scales there his courage will be.
He cannot be helped there by anyone,
He depends on himself there alone.
(*Soldiers from the background approach during the song and
                    form the chorus.*)

CHORUS:
    He cannot be helped there by anyone,
    He depends on himself there alone.

DRAGOON:
    Masters and slaves are all we meet,
        Freedom's gone without a trace,
    Perfidy reigns here, and deceit,
        With this cowardly human race.
    He is free who does not fear to die,
    The soldier alone looks death in the eye.

CHORUS:
    He is free who does not fear to die,
    The soldier alone looks death in the eye.

FIRST MOUNTED RIFLEMAN:
    He casts off life's fears and anxiety,
        Need feel no alarm and no sorrow;
    Daring he rides to his destiny,
        If not today, then tomorrow.
    And if it's tomorrow, then come what may,
    We'll quaff to the dregs this precious day.

CHORUS:
    And if it's tomorrow, then come what may,
    We'll quaff to the dregs this precious day.
    (*The glasses are filled once again, they clink them and drink.*)

CAVALRY SERGEANT:
    His merry lot is Heaven's gift,
        He need not take pains to earn pleasure.
    The laborer digs and earth he sifts,
        He thinks that is where he'll find treasure.
    He shovels and digs through his life like a slave,
    And digs till he finally digs his own grave.

CHORUS:
    He shovels and digs through his life like a slave,
    And digs till he finally digs his own grave.

FIRST MOUNTED RIFLEMAN:

    The rider upon his horse so fine,
        He is an awesome guest,
    The lamps in the wedding castle shine,
        Uninvited he comes to the feast.
    The time to woo he can scarce afford,
    He takes by storm his love's reward.

CHORUS:

    The time to woo he can scarce afford,
    He takes by storm his love's reward.

SECOND CUIRASSIER:

    Why does the girl grieve so sorely and weep?
        Let him go, let him go away!
    There's no place on earth that's his to keep,
        With his true love he cannot stay.
    Fate drives him on at its rapid pace,
    There's no rest for him in any place.

CHORUS:

    Fate drives him on at its rapid pace,
    There's no rest for him in any place.

FIRST MOUNTED RIFLEMAN (*takes the hands of the two standing next to him, the others do the same; all of those who have spoken form a large half-circle*):

    So rein in your horses, prepare to bare
        Your breasts to the battle that's on!
    Our youth and our lives are now seething here,
        Come on! lest your spirit be gone.
    For to wager your life is what you must do,
    Or your life will never belong to you.

CHORUS:

    For to wager your life is what you must do,
    Or your life will never belong to you.

(*The curtain falls before the chorus has finished singing.*)

The Piccolomini

In Five Acts

CHARACTERS

WALLENSTEIN, duke of Friedland, imperial supreme commander in the Thirty Years' War

OCTAVIO PICCOLOMINI, lieutenant general

MAX PICCOLOMINI, his son, colonel of a regiment of cavalry

COUNT TERZKY, Wallenstein's brother-in-law, commander of several regiments

ILLO, field marshal, Wallenstein's confidant

ISOLANI, general of the Croatians

BUTTLER, commander of a regiment of cavalry

TIEFENBACH
DON MARADAS } Generals under Wallenstein
GOETZ
COLALTO

CAVALRY CAPTAIN NEUMANN, Terzky's adjutant

VON QUESTENBERG, member of the Council of War, sent by the emperor

BAPTISTA SENI, astrologer

DUCHESS OF FRIEDLAND, Wallenstein's wife

THEKLA, princess of Friedland, their daughter

COUNTESS TERZKY, the sister of the duchess

A STANDARD-BEARER

KEEPER OF COUNT TERZKY'S WINE CELLAR

FRIEDLAND'S PAGES AND SERVANTS

TERZKY'S SERVANTS AND OBOE PLAYERS

OTHER COLONELS AND GENERALS

ACT I

An old Gothic assembly room in the town hall at Pilsen decorated with flags and other warlike equipment.

Scene 1

Illo with Buttler and Isolani.

ILLO: You're late—but still you're here! Your journey's length,
   Count Isolan, excuses your delay.
ISOLANI: We also do not come with empty hands!
   At Donauwörth the word was brought to us
   A Swedish shipment was upon the road.—
   Six hundred wagons full of food supplies.
   This my Croatians seized upon with speed,
   We have it with us.
ILLO: Just in time it comes
   To feed this most distinguished gathering.
BUTTLER: It is already lively here.
ISOLANI: Oh, yes.
   The soldiers bed down even in the churches,
                   (*looking around*)
   And in the city hall I see you have
   Installed yourselves already. Well, a soldier
   Must help himself the best way that he can!
ILLO: So far, from thirty regiments there have
   Assembled here together all commanders.
   You will meet Terzky here, and Tiefenbach,
   Colalto, Götz, Maradas, Hinnersam,
   And son and father Piccolomini—
   You will be able to greet many friends.
   We're missing Gallas still and Altringer.
BUTTLER: Don't wait for Gallas.
ILLO (*startled*):   Why? Do you know what—
ISOLANI (*interrupts him*):
   Max Piccolomini? Oh, take me there.
   I still can see him—it was ten years past—
   When we were fighting Mansfeld there at Dessau,
   On his black horse he sprang off of the bridge
   And struggled through the Elbe's racing water

To help his father who was in distress.
His chin had scarcely down upon it then.
Now he must be a seasoned warrior.
ILLO: Today you'll see him. From Carinthia
He escorts Friedland's duchess and their daughter,
They should arrive here sometime before noon.
BUTTLER: And so the Duke has summoned wife and daughter?
He summons many here.
ISOLANI: So much the better.
I thought to hear of nothing else but marches
As well as batteries and troops and charges;
And only look! Our Duke has taken care
That something lovely will delight our eyes.
ILLO (*who has stood reflecting, to Buttler, whom he takes off to
the side a little*):
How do you know that Gallas will not come?
BUTTLER (*meaningfully*):
He wanted to keep *me* from coming too.
ILLO (*with warmth*): And you stood firm?
                              (*Presses his hand.*)
                                        You are my valiant Buttler!
BUTTLER: Because the Prince just recently was pleased
To raise me to—
ILLO: Oh, yes, to Major General!
ISOLANI: And that command the Prince has given him,
Is just the one, it's true I hear, in which
He rose in service from the rank of trooper.
This is a fact! And to the corps it acts
As an incentive when they see an old
Deserving warrior make his way.
BUTTLER: I do not know
If these congratulations are in order—
The Emperor has not confirmed it yet.
ISOLANI: It's yours for taking, since the hand that placed
You there is strong enough to keep you there
In spite of emperors.
ILLO: What if we all
Should be so very hesitant!
The Emperor gives nothing—everything
We have or hope for comes here from the Duke.

ISOLANI (*to Illo*):
　Well, sir, and have I told you yet? The Duke
　Is going to satisfy my creditors
　And will himself arrange my spending now,
　So he can make a proper man of me.
　And this is now the third time, only think,
　That he, so royally disposed, has saved
　Me from disaster and preserved my honor.
ILLO: If he could only do as he would like!
　He'd give both land and people to the soldiers.
　But in Vienna they cut short his reach
　And clip his wings whenever they are able!—
　These new demands, so nice and tidy, are
　Brought by that Questenberger here.
BUTTLER:　　　　　　　　　　　　　　I have
　Myself heard tell of these imperial
　Demands, but I can only hope the Duke
　Won't fail to hold his own in all respects.
ILLO: He won't give up his rights if only he
　Keeps his—command!
BUTTLER (*taken aback*): What's that? You frighten me.
ISOLANI (*at the same time*):
　We would be ruined, all of us.
ILLO:　　　　　　　　　　　　　Enough!
　Our man approaches over there; he comes
　With General Piccolomini.
BUTTLER (*shaking his head doubtfully*): I fear
　We won't leave here the way we came.

Scene 2

The former. Octavio Piccolomini. Questenberg.

OCTAVIO (*still at a distance*):
　Well, here are still more guests. Confess, my friend,
　It took a war as sorrowful as this
　To bring together in *one* camp's surroundings
　This gathering of heroes crowned with glory.
QUESTENBERG:
　No one should enter Friedland's army camp
　Who harbors ill will in regard to war.

I almost could forget its evil side,
In contemplating order's noble spirit,
By which it, devastator of the world,
Exists, beheld the greatness that it shapes.
OCTAVIO: Look there! a valiant couple who close up
　The ranks of heroes: the Count Isolan
　And Colonel Buttler.—Now, before our eyes,
　We have at once the total craft of war.
　　　　　　　　(*presenting Buttler and Isolani*)
　It's strength and swiftness, friend, that you see here.
QUESTENBERG (*to Octavio*):
　And in between the two comes seasoned counsel.
OCTAVIO (*introducing Questenberg to them*):
　This is the Chamberlain von Questenberg,
　Who brings imperial commands to us.
　The patron and protector of the soldier
　Is whom we honor in this worthy guest.
　　　　　　　　　　(*general silence*)
ILLO (*approaches Questenberg*):
　I think that this is not the first time, Sir,
　Our camp has had the honor of your presence?
QUESTENBERG:
　One other time I stood before these flags.
ILLO: And can you still remember *where* that was?
　Moravia it was, at Znaim, where you
　Appeared to represent the Emperor
　And beg the Duke to take on the command.
QUESTENBERG:
　To *beg*, sir? My instructions never went
　That far nor would, I'm sure, my zeal have done so.
ILLO: All right! To force him, if that's what you want
　To call it. I remember well—Count Tilly
　Was routed at the Lech—Bavaria
　Was open to the enemy—he could
　Advance into the heart of Austria.
　Then *you* appeared, along with Werdenberg,
　Importuning our leader with your pleas
　And threatening the Emperor's displeasure
　If he would not take pity on your plight.
ISOLANI (*joins them*):
　Oh, it's quite easy, sir, to understand

Why, with the errand that you have today,
That episode you'd rather not remember.

QUESTENBERG:
Why should I not! There is between the two
No contradiction! *Then* it was our aim
To save Bohemia from its enemy,
Today from its protectors and its friends.

ILLO: A fine job that! We shed our blood and drove
The Saxons from Bohemia, and now
As thanks they want to chase us from the land.

QUESTENBERG:
So that we don't exchange one evil for
Another only, that poor land must be
Freed from the scourge of friend and foe alike.

ILLO: Indeed! This year was good. The peasant has
Enough to give to us again

QUESTENBERG: If you
Would like to talk of herds and pastures, sir—

ISOLANI:
The war will live on war. If peasants fail,
The Emperor will then acquire more soldiers.

QUESTENBERG:
And lose an equal number of his subjects!

ISOLANI: His subjects? We are all of us his subjects!

QUESTENBERG:
With just this difference, Count! While those could fill
His coffers with their useful enterprises,
The others know the way to empty them.
The sword has made the Emperor a pauper.
The plow is what will make him strong again.

BUTTLER: The Emperor would not be poor, if—leeches
Weren't sucking at the lifeblood of the land.

ISOLANI: It cannot be so bad, for I can see
(*as he steps directly in front of him and examines his attire*)
Not all the gold by far has yet been minted.

QUESTENBERG: Thank goodness we have rescued just a bit
—So as to save it from Croatian fingers.

ILLO: There! Slavata and Martinitz, on whom
The Emperor, to the annoyance of
All good Bohemians, heaps charity—
Those who grow fat by plundering the people—

Who wax in this widespread corruption
And in this common misery still thrive—
In royal splendor scorn the suffering
Of all the land—it's *these* and others who
Are like them who can make war pay amidst
Destruction's flames, which they alone have kindled.

BUTTLER: These parasites, who always have their feet
  Beneath the table of the Emperor,
  Who hungrily snap up each benefit,
  Will take the soldier's bread while he still faces
  The enemy and put an end to him.

ISOLANI: I never will forget the day that I
  Came to Vienna seven years ago
  To ask for remounts for our regiment,
  And from one antechamber to another
  They let me shuffle back and forth among
  The hangers-on, left standing by the hour,
  As if I came to beg for charity.
  At last—they sent a Capuchin to me,
  I thought perhaps to save me from my sins.
  But no, he was the man with whom I should
  Conduct the business of my soldiers' mounts.
  And then I had to leave with no success.
  The Duke then got for me in three days' time
  What I could not accomplish there in thirty.

QUESTENBERG:
  Oh, yes, the item's charged to our account,
  I know, and that we have it still to pay.

ILLO: War is a violent and a brutal trade,
  And gentle measures will not ever work
  Nor will consideration. If one wished
  To wait till in Vienna they could choose
  The smallest evil out of twenty-four,
  One would wait long! —Quick action, that is best!
  Hurt whom it will! —For as a rule men do
  Know how to mend and patch and will adapt
  To what is necessary, though despised,
  Far better than they'll face a bitter choice.

QUESTENBERG:
  Yes, that is true! The Duke spares us that choice.

ILLO: The Duke is like a father to his troops,

We see the Emperor's intentions toward us.

QUESTENBERG:
  For every class he must have like esteem
  And cannot sacrifice one to the other.

ISOLANI: And so he drives us out amongst the wolves
  In order to preserve his precious sheep.

QUESTENBERG (*with scorn*):
  Well, Count, it's your comparison—not mine.

ILLO: But if we should be what the court supposes,
  It would be dangerous to give us freedom.

QUESTENBERG (*with gravity*):
  Freedom was taken, it was not bestowed,
  Now there is need to put a bridle on it.

ILLO: One could expect to find a horse that's wild.

QUESTENBERG:
  A better rider will soon calm it down.

ILLO: But it will carry only *him* who tamed it.

QUESTENBERG:
  If it is tame, it follows any child.

ILLO: They have, I know, picked out that child already.

QUESTENBERG:
  Concern yourself with duty, not with names.

BUTTLER (*who has until now stayed to one side with Piccolomini,
  but with obvious interest in the conversation, approaches*):
  Such splendid troops stand ready, Mister Chairman,
  To serve the Emperor in Germany,
  And thirty-thousand more are quartered here,
  Six-thousand men are in Silesia;
  Ten regiments are on the Rhine, the Main,
  And Weser, and in Swabia are six,
  While twelve are ready in Bavaria
  To face the Swedes, along with garrisons
  Protecting all the border fortresses—
  And all these men remain obedient
  To Friedland's officers, who all have had
  Their training in *one* school, been nourished by
  One milk, been animated by *one* heart.
  As foreigners they stand here on this soil,
  Duty alone is house and home to them.
  Their fervor is not for the fatherland,
  For thousands come, like me, from other places,

Nor for the Emperor, since half of them
Have come to us deserting other colors.
To them it is no matter if they fight
Beneath the lion, lily, or the eagle.
Still all of them are powerfully led
By just one man, who binds them all together
Through love and reverence into *one* folk.
And just as streaks of lightning always run
Directed safe and sure along a rod,
So he commands from that far distant guard
Who on the sand dunes hears the surging Belt,
Sees fruitful vales along the Adige,
Unto the sentinels who have raised up
Their boxes at the Emperor's front door.

QUESTENBERG:
What is the meaning of this long discourse?

BUTTLER: That the respect, the inclination, and
The trust that make us want to follow Friedland
Will not be given to the first best choice
They make at court and send us from Vienna.
It is still graven in our memory
How Friedland happened to receive command.
You think it was perhaps His Majesty
Who handed over an established army
And only sought a leader for his troops?
—There was no army there. First Friedland had
To make an army. He did not *receive* it.
He *gave* it to the Emperor. And not
That we were given Wallenstein as general.
It was not thus, not so! Through Wallenstein
Have we received the Emperor as lord,
We are bound to this flag through him alone.

OCTAVIO (*steps between them*):
Just to remind you, Councillor, you are
Surrounded here in camp by warriors.—
Their boldness and their freedom makes them soldiers.—
If they can act with daring, may they not
Speak that way too? —Where one is, is the other.—
The boldness of this worthy officer
                    (*pointing to Buttler*)
Who speaks perhaps a bit mistakenly,

Preserved—where nothing else but boldness could—
The Emperor's metropolis of Prague
From its rebellious garrison.
            (*Martial music can be heard from the distance.*)
ILLO: They're here!
    The watches are saluting them— This signal
    Informs us that the Duchess has arrived.
OCTAVIO (*to Questenberg*):
    Then my son Max is back. He met them in
    Carinthia and he has brought them here.
ISOLANI (*to Illo*):
    Well, shall we go together to receive them?
ILLO: Yes, to be sure, let's go. Come, Colonel Buttler!
                    (*to Octavio*)
    Remember that we'll meet these gentlemen
    Before the Prince while it is morning still.

Scene 3

Octavio and Questenberg, who remain behind.

QUESTENBERG (*showing signs of astonishment*):
    What have I heard here, my dear General!
    What boundless insolence! And such ideas!
    —If such a spirit is the common one—
OCTAVIO: Three-quarters of the army you saw here.
QUESTENBERG: Alas! Where will we find another army
    To stand guard over this one!—This man Illo,
    I think he is much worse than he appears.
    And Buttler, too, cannot conceal mean thoughts.
OCTAVIO: They're sensitive—their pride is hurt—that's all!—
    And Buttler, I've not given up on him.
    I know a way to exorcise this ghost.
QUESTENBERG (*restlessly pacing up and down*):
    No! This is bad, oh, so much worse, my friend,
    Than in Vienna we had ever dreamed.
    We only looked at it with courtiers' eyes,
    So dazzled by the glitter of the throne;
    But we had still not seen the General,
    Who is all-powerful here in his camp.
    Here it is different!

What's emperor? The Duke is emperor!
The walk I took just now here by your side
Throughout the camp discourages my hopes.
OCTAVIO: You see yourself now that a dangerous
    Affair it is you brought me from the Court—
    How dangerous the part I play here is.
    One slight suspicion of the General
    Would cost my freedom and my very life
    And would precipitate the start of his
    Audacious plan.
QUESTENBERG: What were we thinking when
    We put a sword into this madman's hand
    And trusted him with such authority!
    Too strong for such a heart, so unsecured,
    Was *this* temptation! Even in the case
    Of better men it would have been a danger!
    He will refuse, I tell you this straight out,
    To do the bidding of the Emperor.—
    He can and will.— His uncontrolled defiance
    Will demonstrate how powerless we are.
OCTAVIO: Do you believe that he has brought his wife,
    His daughter to the camp without good cause,
    Just now when we're preparing for a fight?
    That he removes the last security
    For his good faith from the imperial lands
    Should tell us that rebellion will soon come.
QUESTENBERG:
    Alas! How should we face this thunderstorm;
    This cloudburst threatens us from every side?
    Our enemy stands on the border and
    Controls the Danube, steadily gains ground—
    Within the land revolt's alarm rings clear—
    The peasant stands in arms—all is in ferment,
    And those whose help we would expect, the army,
    Seduced, grown wild, with discipline all gone—
    Torn from the state and from their Emperor,
    A fickle throng follows a fickle leader,
    A fearful instrument devoted to,
    And blindly following, the worst of men—
OCTAVIO: Let us not be discouraged, friend, too soon!
    For words are always bolder than deeds are,

And many who may seem determined now
In their blind eagerness to do their utmost
Will soon discover, when they give a name
To such a crime, that they still have a heart.
Besides—we are not wholly undefended.
Count Altringer and Gallas, you must know,
Maintain their little armies under oath,
And daily they grow stronger.—He cannot
Surprise us; for I have him, as you know,
Surrounded by my spies so thoroughly
That I know every step he takes at once—
And he discloses things to me himself.

QUESTENBERG:
It's inconceivable that he can't see
The enemy beside him there.

OCTAVIO: Don't think
I used deceitful tricks, the favors of
A hypocrite, to capture his affection,
Or nourished his reliance with false words.
Though my discretion and the duty I
Owe to the Emperor and land oblige
Me to conceal my sentiments from him,
I have not once pretended what was false.

QUESTENBERG:
It is quite clearly Heav'n's decree.

OCTAVIO: I do not know just what it is that draws
Him to my son and me and chains him to us.
Oh, we were friends, comrades in arms we were,
And habit and adventures that we shared
Soon brought us close together—still I know
The very day on which, quite suddenly,
He opened up his heart and trusted me.
It was the morning that we fought at Lützen—
A dream caused me to go in search of him
To offer him a different horse to ride.
Far from the tents, there underneath a tree,
I found him fast alseep, and after I
Awakened him and told him my concern,
He gazed at me at length and in surprise,
Then threw his arms around my neck and showed
More feeling than my little deed was worth.

So from that day his trust has followed me,
While to that same extent mine flees from him.
QUESTENBERG:
  Of course you've drawn your son into the secret?
OCTAVIO: Oh, no!
QUESTENBERG: What! Don't you want to warn him then
  About the evil of the hands he's in?
OCTAVIO: I must entrust him to his innocence.
  An open heart cannot dissimulate.
  His ignorance alone preserves his free
  Expression so the Duke will feel secure.
QUESTENBERG (solicitously):
  My worthy friend, I have the best opinion
  Of Colonel Piccolomini—but—if—
  Consider that . . .
OCTAVIO: I'll have to take my chances.—Hush! He's coming.

Scene 4

Max Piccolomini. Octavio Piccolomini. Questenberg.

MAX: Well, there you are yourself. So, welcome, Father!
  (*He embraces him. As he turns around, he notices Questenberg
  and steps back coldly.*)
  You're busy I can see. I'll not disturb you.
OCTAVIO: What's that, Max? Pay attention to our guest.
  An old friend certainly deserves politeness;
  Respect is due the Emperor's envoy.
MAX (*dryly*):
  Von Questenberg! You're welcome, if you bring
  Good news to us and our command.
QUESTENBERG (*has grasped his hand*): Don't pull
  Your hand away, Count Piccolomini.
  I do not grasp it for myself alone,
  Nor is my greeting something ordinary.
                    (*grasping the hands of both*)
  Octavio—Max Piccolomini!
  They're names to bless us, names with promise for us!
  Austria's fortune never will turn round
  As long as two such stars, so beneficial,
  Shall shine protectively above our hosts.

MAX: Well, sir, you're acting out of character;
    You are not here to praise us, that I know;
    You're sent to reprimand us and to scold—
    I do not want my share before the others.
OCTAVIO (*to Max*):
    He comes from court, where they are not as pleased
    With what the Duke has done as we are here.
MAX: What new thing is there then to blame him for?
    That he alone decides on things that he
    Alone can understand? Good! He is right,
    And that will be the end of it besides.—
    He simply is not made so tractable
    And able to accommodate to others,
    It is against his nature, he cannot.
    He has acquired the spirit of a sovereign
    And has been stationed in a sovereign's place.
    We're lucky it is so! There are so few
    Who know the way to govern, who can use
    Their judgment wisely. —For us all it is
    So good if there is only one who serves
    As focus for the thousands, a support,
    A solid column to which one may hold
    With pleasure and with constant confidence.
    Now such a one is Wallenstein, unless
    The court has someone better—such a one
    Alone avails the army.
QUESTENBERG: True! The army!
MAX: It is true pleasure how he can arouse
    And strengthen and enliven everything,
    How each ability is shown, each talent
    Becomes more evident when he is near!
    He draws out every strength of every one,
    Each individual strength, augmenting them,
    Allows each one to be just what he is.
    He takes care only that he'll always be
    At the right place, so he can utilize
    His men's capacities for his own purpose.
QUESTENBERG:
    Who can deny that he's a connoisseur
    Of men, can use them! Only he forgets
    Above the role of sovereign that of servant

As if he had been born to this estate.

MAX: And was he not? Was he not born with strength
For this, and so much strength that he can do
What truly is his nature and can win
The place of sovereign for his sovereign's talent?

QUESTENBERG:
So in the end what we are worth will be
Determined by his generosity!

MAX: Unusual men require unusual trust.
Give him the room, *he*'ll set himself the goal.

QUESTENBERG:
So we have seen.

MAX: That's how they are! They fear
At once if there is any depth, are only
Content where it is absolutely flat.

OCTAVIO (*to Questenberg*):
You might as well give up good-naturedly,
My friend, you never will be finished with him.

MAX: They call upon a spirit in their need,
And then they are afraid when it appears.
They want what is sublime to be the same
As everyday occurrences. But on
The battlefield the present moves us—what
Is personal controls, each eye must see.
He who commands needs greatness in his nature,
And he should also be permitted to
Exist on its great terms. The oracle
Within his inner self—that living thing—
Should be the object of his queries, not
Dead books, old regulations, moldy papers.

OCTAVIO: My son! Let us not give too little heed
To old, strict regulations. They are precious
And priceless weights that man in his distress
Has bound to his assailants' rash intent;
For action uncontrolled was always dreadful—
The path of order, though it may be crooked,
Is still direct. While straight ahead the path
Of lightning, of the cannonball, does go—
And by the shortest route arrives with speed
So, crushing, it can make a place to crush—
The road, my son, that men will travel over,

On which God's blessings are, this street will follow
The rivers' courses, valleys' open curves,
Will go around the wheat field and the vineyard,
And, honoring the borders of estates,
It will come later, certain, to its goal.

QUESTENBERG:
Oh, listen to your father. Hear a man
Who is both hero and a human being.

OCTAVIO: The camp's child speaks out of your mouth, my son.
A war of fifteen years has been your teacher,
And peace is something you have never seen!
But there are higher values than the warrior's;
In war itself, the war is not the end.
The great and sudden deeds of violence,
Amazing wonders of a moment's time,
Are not what will engender happiness,
Which quietly but mightily will last.
With haste and hurriedly the soldier builds
His trifling city out of canvas, where
There is a momentary stir and bustle;
The market comes alive, the streets and rivers
Are full of cargo and then business follows.
But still one morning suddenly you see
The tents are down, the troops have moved away,
While totally deserted like a graveyard
The land lies there, the trampled fields of corn;
And the whole harvest for the year is gone.

MAX: Oh, Father, let the Emperor make peace!
I'll gladly trade my bloody laurel wreath
For the first violet that March will bring,
The fragrant pledge of earth's rejuvenation.

OCTAVIO: What's this? Why are you suddenly so moved?

MAX: You say that peace is something I've not seen.
I've seen it, Father; just now I have come—
Just now from there—my way took me through lands
In which the war has never yet arrived—
Oh, Father, and the life there—it has charms
That we have never known. —We have but sailed
Along fair life's deserted shores just like
A band of robbers wandering astray
Who are confined in dank and narrow ships

And lodge with customs wild on a wild sea
And of the land know nothing but the inlets
Where they may dare to make a thief's assault.
What precious things the land conceals within
Its inner valleys, oh! of that—of that
On our wild voyage nothing has appeared.

OCTAVIO (*becomes attentive*):
And has this journey showed it to you then?

MAX: It was the first free time in my whole life.
Tell me, what is the aim and prize for work,
Painstaking work, that stole my youth from me
And left my heart so bleak and unrefreshed,
My spirit unadorned by education?
The loud, unruly tumult of this camp,
The horses' neighing and the trumpets' blare,
The clock of duty always set the same,
Commands and military exercises—
Those offer nothing to a longing heart.
This empty business has no soul. —There is
Another happiness and other joys.

OCTAVIO: You learned a lot on that short road, my son!

MAX: O lovely day, when soldiers finally will
Return to living and humanity
And fold their flags to join a happy throng,
While homeward bound the march of peace is sounding,
When every hat and helm is decorated
With greenery, the last spoils from the fields!
The cities' gates will open by themselves,
For no petard is needed anymore;
The walls will be filled up with joyous people
Who shout their greetings out into the air,
The peal of bells will ring from every spire
To toll the vespers of those bloody days.
From villages and cities there will stream
Rejoicing people who obstruct the troops'
Procession with their loving eagerness.
The old man, glad he's lived to see this day,
Will shake the hand of his returning son.
A stranger he appears on his own land,
Abandoned long ago; with its broad limbs
That tree will cover him on his return

That bent, a sapling only, when he left,
And bashfully a maiden comes toward him
Who, when he left, was at her nurse's breast.
Oh, happy he for whom a door is opened
While gentle arms embrace him tenderly—

QUESTENBERG (*moved*):
    If it were but tomorrow or today
    And not some distant time you speak about!

MAX (*turning toward him with vehemence*):
    And where but in Vienna lies the guilt?
    I will confess this freely, Questenberg,
    That when I saw you standing there just now,
    I was indignant to my very core.
    You are the ones obstructing peace, it's you!
    The soldier must bring it about by force.
    You make life bitter for the Duke, you make
    His very step a chore, you slander him—
    And why? Because the benefit of Europe
    Means more to him than a few hides of land
    That more or less belong to Austria.
    You call him an insurgent, and God knows
    What else besides, because he spares the Saxons,
    Tries to awaken our foes' confidence,
    Which surely is the only way to peace;
    For if the war does not desist from war,
    Where will peace come from? —Go away, just go!
    As I love goodness, so I do hate you—
    And here I solemnly declare that I
    Will shed my blood for him, for Wallenstein,
    The last of my heart's blood and drop by drop,
    Before I'll see you triumph at his fall!
                    (*He exits.*)

Scene 5

Questenberg. Octavio Piccolomini.

QUESTENBERG: Alas for us! Can it be so?
                    (*urgently and impatiently*)
    Friend, shall we let him go away from us
    With this delusion and not call him back

Straightway so we can open up his eyes
Here on the spot?

OCTAVIO (*coming to himself out of deep contemplation*):
      He opened *mine* for me,
And I perceive more than is pleasing to me.

QUESTENBERG:
 What can it be, my friend?

OCTAVIO: This cursed trip!

QUESTENBERG: But why? What is it?

OCTAVIO: Come along! I must
 Pursue forthwith these most unhappy traces
 And see with my own eyes. —Just come along—
      (*is about to lead him off*)

QUESTENBERG: But what? And where?

OCTAVIO (*urgently*): To her!

QUESTENBERG: To—

OCTAVIO (*corrects himself*):
 To him, the Duke! Let's go! I am afraid.
 I see the net that's been thrown over him,
 He has not come back to me as he went.

QUESTENBERG:
 If you would just explain—

OCTAVIO: Could I not see
 Ahead? Could I not act to stop this trip?
 Why did I keep it secret? —You were right,
 I had to warn him. —Now it is too late.

QUESTENBERG:
 What is too late? Try to consider, friend,
 That you are simply talking riddles to me.

OCTAVIO (*more composed*):
 Come now! We'll go and see the Duke. The time
 Approaches now that he appointed for
 His audiences. Come along!—
 And curséd, three times curséd, be that journey!
    (*He leads him off, the curtain falls.*)

ACT II

The Duke of Friedland's assembly hall

Scene 1

Servants are putting out chairs and spreading carpets. Immediately afterwards Seni, the astrologer, dressed like an Italian doctor in black and rather fantastically. He steps to the middle of the hall, a white rod in his hand, with which he indicates the points of the compass.

SERVANT (*walking around with an incense burner*):
    Let's go! Let's make an end of this! The watch
    Has called the men to arms. They'll soon be here.
SECOND SERVANT:
    Why did they cancel orders for the room above,
    The red one, where the lights are shining brightly?
FIRST SERVANT:
    Just ask the mathematicus! He says
    It's inauspicious.
SECOND SERVANT: That's tomfoolery!
    It's selling people bunk. A room's a room,
    What is significant about a place?
SENI (*with gravity*):
    My son, there's nothing insignificant
    In this whole world. But first and foremost is,
    Among all earthly things, the time and place.
THIRD SERVANT:
    Don't get mixed up with him, Nathanael!
    Our master even has to do his bidding.
SENI (*counts the chairs*):
    Eleven! A bad number. Put twelve here!
    Twelve signs are in the zodiac, and five
    And seven, sacred numbers, make up twelve.
SECOND SERVANT:
    What's bad about eleven? Tell me that.
SENI: Eleven stands for sins, and it exceeds
    The Ten Commandments.
SECOND SERVANT: Oh! Why do you call
    The five a sacred number?
SENI: Five stands for

The soul of man. Just as a man is mixed
Of good and evil, the first number made
Of odd and even is the five.
FIRST SERVANT:
    The fool!
THIRD SERVANT:
    Oh, let him be! I like to hear him talk,
    His words cause me to think of many things.
SECOND SERVANT:
    Let's go! They're coming! There, out that side door!
        (*They hurry out, Seni follows slowly.*)

Scene 2

Wallenstein. The Duchess.

WALLENSTEIN:
    Well, Duchess, in Vienna, then, were you
    Presented to the Queen of Hungary?
DUCHESS: And to the Empress, too. Both majesties
    Gave us permission there to kiss their hands.
WALLENSTEIN:
    How did they take it that I called my wife
    And daughter to the front in wintertime?
DUCHESS: I did as you directed and alleged
    You had decided for our child and wished,
    Before the campaign started, to allow
    Her future husband to set eyes on her.
WALLESTEIN: And did they speculate about my choice?
DUCHESS: They only wished, of course, no foreigner
    Or Lutheran gentleman would be your pleasure.
WALLENSTEIN: What do you wish, Elisabeth?
DUCHESS: Your wishes, as you know, were always mine.
WALLENSTEIN (*after a pause*):
    Now—how was your reception otherwise?
        (*The Duchess casts her eyes down and is silent.*)
    Hide nothing from me! — Tell me how it was.
DUCHESS: Oh, husband! —Things are not the way they used
    To be—there is a change that's taken place.
WALLENSTEIN: So? Were they lacking in their old respect?
DUCHESS: Not in respect. Their conduct was most seemly

And dignified—but there where once there was
A gracious and familiar courtesy,
There now was but a stiff formality.
And, oh, the tender care they showed me had
More pity in it than it had affection.
No, no! Duke Albrecht's royal consort or
Count Harrach's noble daughter, either one,
Should have—no, should not have been so received!

WALLENSTEIN: They did, of course, reproach my recent conduct?

DUCHESS: If they had only done so! I have long
Been in the habit of defending you,
Of satisfying their indignant minds.—
No, there was no reproach—they wrapped themselves
In such a heavy and oppressive silence.
This is no commonplace misunderstanding,
No incidental sensitivity—
But something sadly irreparable
Has happened—Once the Queen of Hungary
Was wont to call me her beloved aunt
And to embrace me when we left each other.

WALLENSTEIN: But now no more?

DUCHESS (*drying her tears, after a pause*):
                              She did embrace me but
'Twas only after I had taken leave,
Was going toward the door, she came to me
So quickly, as if she had just remembered,
And pressed me to her breast with an emotion
That was more sad than fond.

WALLENSTEIN (*takes her hand*): Compose yourself!—
And Eggenberg and Lichtenstein and all
Our friends—how were they then?

DUCHESS (*shaking her head*):   I saw not one.

WALLENSTEIN: And the ambassador of Spain, the one
Who gave me so much strong support before?

DUCHESS: He had no words to give you anymore.

WALLENSTEIN: *These* suns, it seems, don't shine for us today.
From now on our own fire must light our path.

DUCHESS: And was it, my dear Duke, because of what
Is whispered at the court, but in the land
Is spoken loud—what Father Lamormain
Has hinted—

WALLENSTEIN (*quickly*): Lamormain! What does he say?
DUCHESS: They charge you with presumptuous transgressions
   Of the authority to you entrusted
   And scoffing at the Emperor's commands.
   The Spaniards and Bavaria's proud Duke
   Will stand as plaintiffs and appear against you—
   A storm is gathering around you now
   That is by far more threatening than the one
   That overthrew you once at Regensburg.
   They speak, he says—oh, I can't say it—
WALLENSTEIN (*intent*):   Well?
DUCHESS: About a second—(*She falters.*)
WALLENSTEIN: Second—
DUCHESS: And a worse
   —Removal.
WALLENSTEIN: They say that?
        (*Intensely troubled, moving about the room*)
                     Against my will
   They will compel me, force me into it.
DUCHESS (*imploringly clinging to him*):
   Oh, husband, if there is still time! —If with
   Submission or with tractability
   You can prevent this thing—try to be yielding—
   Prevail upon your heart so proud; it is
   Your Lord and Emperor to whom you yield!
   Do not allow it to continue that
   Malicious spite should vilify your good
   Intentions with pernicious application.
   Rise up with the triumphal strength of truth,
   To shame the liars and the slanderers!
   For we possess so very few good friends,
   You know that! Fortune came so fast that we
   Are open to much hate—what will we be
   If the imperial favor turns away?

Scene 3

Countess Terzky joins them, leading the Princess Thekla by the hand.

COUNTESS: Already talking about business, Sister—
   And as I see, it is not very pleasant—

Before he can take pleasure in his child?
Now, this first moment should belong to joy.
Here, Father Friedland, here she is, your daughter!
(*Thekla approaches him shyly and is about to curtsy; he takes her
in his arms and remains for a time lost in contemplation of her.*)
WALLENSTEIN: Yes, all my hopes have risen now so fair.
I take her as a pledge of great good fortune.
DUCHESS: A tender child she was when you departed
To raise an army for the Emperor.
When you returned from Pomerania,
When the campaign was over, she was in
The Convent, where she's been till now.
WALLENSTEIN: And while
We sought upon the field to make her great,
To gain great worldly goods for her in battle,
Within the cloister walls, there Mother Nature
Has done her part and given the dear child,
Through voluntary kindness, godly gifts
And leads her, beautifully adorned, to meet
Her shining destiny and my fair hopes.
DUCHESS: (*to the Princess*):
Perhaps you did not recognize your father,
My child? You were but little more than eight
The last time that you gazed upon his face.
THEKLA: I knew him, Mother, at first sight. My father
Has not grown old. The image that I kept
Is just how he appears before me now.
WALLENSTEIN (*to the Duchess*):
The lovely child! Such observation and
Such prudence! I was angry with my fate
Because I was denied a son who could
Inherit both my name and my good fortune
And carry on, in a proud line of princes,
My own existence, all too soon extinguished.
I did fate an injustice. Here upon
This brow so fresh and virginal I wish
To place the laurels of my warrior's life.
I do not count it lost if one day I
Can place the wreath I've earned, now changed into
A royal ornament, on this fair head.
        (*He holds her in his arms as Piccolomini enters.*)

Scene 4

To the former, Max Piccolomini and soon thereafter Count Terzky.

COUNTESS: There comes the Paladin who was our guardian.
WALLENSTEIN: I welcome you, Max. You have always been
  The bringer of some special gladness for me,
  And, like each day's auspicious morning star,
  You bring the sunshine of my life to me.
MAX: My Lord—
WALLENSTEIN: Till now it was the Emperor
  For whom my hand rewarded you. Today
  You put this happy father in your debt,
  This obligation Friedland must repay.
MAX: My Lord! You made great haste to pay it off.
  I come ashamed and, yes, I come in sorrow;
  For scarcely had I reached this place and had
  Delivered wife and daughter to your arms
  Than from your stables there was brought to me
  A splendid hunting pair, so richly harnessed,
  To compensate me for my trouble. Yes!
  To compensate me. Was it trouble only?
  And only business, not the favor that
  I took it rashly for and came with heart
  So full to thank you— No, it was not meant
  My task should be my greatest happiness!
(*Terzky enters and gives the Duke letters, which he quickly breaks open.*)
COUNTESS (*to Max*):
  And if he pays you for your effort? He
  Rewards you for his joy. It suits you well
  To be so sensitive; it suits as well
  My sister's husband to be great and princely.
THEKLA: If this were so, I'd have to doubt his love,
  For his indulgent hands sent me adornments
  Before, with father's heart, he spoke to me.
MAX: Yes, he must always be a benefactor!
  (*He takes the Duchess's hand, with increasing warmth.*)
  How much I have to thank him for—how much
  I can express in this dear name of Friedland!
  For all my life I'll be the prisoner

Of this one name—in it shall flourish all
Good fortune and each lovely hope as well.
As if in an enchanted ring my fate
Holds me so firmly captive to this name.
COUNTESS (*who has meanwhile carefully watched the Duke,
notices he has become reflective over the letters*):
Our brother wants to be alone. We'll leave!
WALLENSTEIN (*turns around quickly, gets control of himself, and
says cheerfully to the Duchess*):
Once more, my Duchess, let me bid you welcome.
You are the hostess of this court. You, Max,
Will fill again your old position now
While we are occupied with our lord's business.
(*Max Piccolomini offers the Duchess his arm, the Countess
conducts the Princess off.*)
TERZKY (*calling after Max*):
Do not forget to be at the assembly!

Scene 5

Wallenstein. Terzky.

WALLENSTEIN (*in deep reflection, to himself*):
She saw things well. —That's how it is. It is
The same as all the other information—
There in Vienna they have formed their last
Resolve and have appointed my successor.
And Ferdinand, the king of Hungary,
The Emperor's young son, is now their savior,
The newly risen star. They think they are
Already finished with us here, and as
If we were dead, they make themselves our heirs.
There is no time to lose!
(*As he turns around, he notices Terzky and hands him a letter.*)
Count Altringer requests he be excused,
And Gallas, too—I am not pleased.
TERZKY: If you
Delay still more, the others will leave too.
WALLENSTEIN:
Count Altringer controls the Tyrol passes.
Then I must send him someone so that he won't

Allow those Spaniards from Milano in.
—Well, Sesin, that old intermediary,
Has shown himself around here once again.
What does he bring us from Count Thurn?

TERZKY: The Count says he
  Has gone to see the Swedish chancellor
  At Halberstadt where the assembly meets;
  He says, however, he is tired and does
  Not want to bother with you anymore.

WALLENSTEIN: And why?

TERZKY: Because you never speak in earnest,
  You only want to make fools of the Swedes,
  And to combine against them with the Saxons,
  And then dismiss them with some paltry bit
  Of money.

WALLENSTEIN: So! Perhaps he thinks that I
  Should leave this lovely German land as prey
  So that at last on our own ground and soil
  We are no longer masters? They must go,
  Away, away! We do not need such neighbors.

TERZKY: Just give them that small patch of land, it is
  Not part of your land after all! Why should
  You care, if you can win the game, who pays?

WALLENSTEIN:
  Away with them! —You do not understand.
  They'll not say I dismembered Germany,
  Betrayed it to the enemy so that
  By underhanded means I'd get my share.
  This land shall honor me as its protector,
  And proving I am worthy to be one,
  I'll sit down with the princes of the Empire.
  But in this land, no foreign power shall
  Take root through what I do, and least of all
  These Swedes, such needy wretches as they are,
  Who gaze upon our blessed German land
  With looks of envy, eager for the spoils.
  They are to aid me in my plans, but still
  In doing so they will not have their pick.

TERZKY: But with the Saxons will you not proceed
  More openly? They've lost their patience with you
  Because your methods are circuitous.

What are all these pretenses? Tell me, now!
Your friends suspect you, are disturbed by you,
And Oxenstirn and Arnheim—neither knows
How he should look upon your hesitation.
Then in the end I'll be the liar, for
It's all through me. I've nothing signed by you.

WALLENSTEIN: You know I won't put anything in writing.

TERZKY: But how shall they distinguish your intent
If deed is not to follow word—just say!
So far the things that you talked over with
The enemy might well have taken place
If you had wanted nothing better than
To get the best of them.

WALLENSTEIN (*after a pause, during which he looks closely at him*):
How do you know that I've not really gotten
The best of them? Or that I haven't gotten
The best of all of you? Do you know me
So well? I did not know I had disclosed
My inmost self to you. —The Emperor,
It's true, has used me badly! —*If* I wanted
I could do him much harm in recompense.
It gives me pleasure just to know my strength;
If I will really use it, *there,* I think,
You know no more than any other man.

TERZKY: You've always played a game with us this way!

Scene 6

Illo joins the former.

WALLENSTEIN: How does it look out there? Are they prepared?

ILLO: You'll find them in the humor that you want.
They know about the Emperor's demands
And rage.

WALLENSTEIN: Has Isolan declared himself?

ILLO: With soul and body, he is yours, since you
Are to support his faro game again.

WALLENSTEIN: How does Colalto act? Have you made sure
Of Deodat and also Tiefenbach?

ILLO: What Piccolomini does, they will do.

WALLENSTEIN: You think, then, I can take a risk with them?

ILLO: —If you can trust the Piccolominis.

WALLENSTEIN: I trust them as myself. *They'll* never leave me.

TERZKY: I only wish that you were not so quick
    To trust Octavio, that fox.

WALLENSTEIN: Will you
    Teach me to know my men? I've gone into
    The field already sixteen times with him.
    Besides, his horoscope was cast for me,
    Our births took place beneath the selfsame sign
    And briefly—
                 (*mysteriously*)
              That is where the matter rests.
    If you will answer for the others then—

ILLO: There is but *one* opinion held by all:
    They will not let you lay down your command.
    I hear they'll send a delegation to you.

WALLENSTEIN: If I am to commit myself to them,
    Then they must do the same to me.

ILLO: Of course.

WALLENSTEIN: They must give me their word, their oath, in writing,
    Without condition to be in my service.

ILLO: Why not?

TERZKY: *Without condition?* They will always
    Reserve the right to do their duty to
    The Emperor, that's clear.

WALLENSTEIN (*shaking his head*): Without condition
    Secure them and no talk of reservations!

ILLO: It just occurred to me—tonight Count Terzky
    Will give a banquet for us, won't he?

TERZKY: True,
    And all the generals are invited to it.

ILLO (*to Wallenstein*):
    Now tell me, may I have a free hand here?
    I'll get the generals' promises for you,
    Just as you wanted.

WALLENSTEIN: It must be in writing.
    But how you get it, that is up to you.

ILLO: And if I bring it to you, black on white,
    That all commanders who are present here

Deliver themselves blindly to you, then
Will you at last with your bold course of action
Pursue success?

WALLENSTEIN: Just get the written promise!

ILLO: Consider what you're doing! You cannot
　　Fulfill the Emperor's desires—you cannot
　　Allow the army to be weakened, or
　　The regiments be driven off with Spain's,
　　Unless you want to lose your power forever.
　　But then consider that you cannot scoff
　　At his commands and solemn orders either,
　　Not make excuses any longer or
　　Delay without a full break from the court.
　　Decide! Will you anticipate him with
　　Determined action? Or with hesitation
　　Await the worst?

WALLENSTEIN: That seems the thing to do
　　Till one can be quite sure what is the worst!

ILLO: Oh, make the most of time before it's gone!
　　So seldom does that moment come in life
　　That can be truly called momentous. Then
　　When a decision should be made, so much
　　Depends on luck and how things come together—
　　And individually and scattered do
　　The threads of fate appear, those moments that
　　Are brought together only at *one* time
　　In life, there to create a nodal point.
　　Look how decisively, how fatefully
　　All things are gathering around you now.
　　The army's leaders, all the very best,
　　Assemble here around their royal chief.
　　They only wait for you to give the sign—
　　Oh, do not let them go their ways again!
　　You never will bring them a second time
　　Together, so united in this war.
　　It is high tide that lifts the heavy ship
　　From off the strand—the feelings of each one
　　Will grow within the current of the crowd.
　　You have them now, just now! But soon the war
　　Will have dispersed them here and there again.
　　Their own small worries and their interests will

Divert their common spirit. Who today
Is carried by the current and forgets
Himself will be more sober when he is
Alone and feels his impotence and promptly
Will turn again into the old, well-worn
Pathways of common duty, only seeking
To bring himself to cover, safe and sound.

WALLENSTEIN: It is not time.

TERZKY: That's what you always say.
When will the time come?

WALLENSTEIN: When I say it's here.

ILLO: You'll wait upon the time set by the stars
Till earthly time escapes! You must believe
Your star of destiny lies in your breast.
Have faith in your own self, determination
Will be your Venus! And the only culprit,
The only thing that harms you, is your *doubt*.

WALLENSTEIN: That is the way you see it. Many times
I have explained it! —Jupiter, the god
Of light, was in descent when *you* were born;
You cannot look into *these* mysteries.
You only burrow in the earth in darkness,
As blind as that one who illuminated
You into life with his pale leaden shine.
The earthly, common things, these you may see,
You cleverly combine things that are near;
I trust you and believe in you for that.
But things of meaning moving secretly
And shaping in the very depths of nature,—
The spirit ladder that creates itself
Out of this sphere of dust and sends to that
Celestial sphere its thousand shoots on which
The heavenly powers wander up and down—
The circles in the circles drawing ever
More narrow all around the central sun—
These can that unsealed eye alone perceive
Of Jupiter's serene and bright-born children.
(*After pacing across the room, he stops and continues*)
The heavenly constellations make not just
The day and night, the spring and summer—not
The sower only sees through them the times

Of planting and of harvest. But the deeds
Of men are planting seeds of destiny,
Strewn on the dim-lit land of future time,
With hope, surrendered to the powers of fate.
So it is urgent that we learn the time
And ascertain the right celestial hour,
By searching in the *houses* of the heavens
And find out if the enemy of growth
And vigor lurks in *corners* causing harm.
So give me time! Do what you have to do!
I cannot say as yet what I will do.
I know that I will never yield. Not I!
Nor will I be removed by them. —On that
You can rely!

SERVANT (*enters*): The generals are here.
WALLENSTEIN: Let them come in!
TERZKY: Do you wish all commanders to be present?
WALLENSTEIN: That's not required. The Piccolominis,
    Maradas, Buttler, Forgatsch, Deodat,
    Caraffa, Isolani—these may come.
                    (*Terzky exits with the servant.*)
WALLENSTEIN (*to Illo*):
    Have you had someone watching Questenberg?
    Has he had words with anyone in secret?
ILLO: I've watched him carefully. He was with no one
    Except Octavio.

Scene 7

The former. Questenberg, both Piccolominis, Buttler, Isolani, Maradas, and three other generals enter. At the General's signal Questenberg stands directly opposite him, the others follow according to rank. A momentary silence reigns.

WALLENSTEIN:
    The substance of your mission, Questenberg,
    I have examined and weighed carefully,
    My mind is made up and cannot be changed.
    Yet it is right that all of my commanders
    Should hear from your own mouth the wishes of
    The Emperor. So will you please deliver

Before these nobles your commission now!
QUESTENBERG: I'm ready; still, I ask you to consider
  That the imperial authority
  Is speaking with my mouth, not my own boldness.
WALLENSTEIN: Spare us the preface.
QUESTENBERG: When His Majesty
  The Emperor, gave your courageous armies
  A leader, seasoned and with glory crowned,
  This in the person of the Duke of Friedland,
  'Twas done in happy confidence that it
  Would quickly change the fortunes of the war.
  In the beginning all seemed most propitious,
  For all Bohemia was purged of Saxons,
  The Swedish flush of victory was checked—
  These lands could draw an easy breath again,
  When Friedland drew from all of Germany's
  Great rivers scattered armies of the foe;
  Here on *one* single spot he laid upon
  The Rhine Count, Bernhard, Banner, Oxenstierna
  As well as the unconquered King himself,
  The charge that finally at Nuremberg
  The great and bloody contest be decided.
WALLENSTEIN: The point now, if you please.
QUESTENBERG: Another spirit
  At once was instituted by our leader.
  Blind rage no longer struggled with blind rage;
  In combat so refined, one could now see
  Stability resisting dash and daring,
  While prudence was exhausting gallantry.
  They try in vain to tempt him into battle,
  He only digs in deeper in his camp,
  As if he meant to found a dynasty.
  The King, at last despairing, will attack,
  And to the slaughter house he drags his troops,
  Who, ravaged by both hunger and disease,
  Are slowly dying in their corpse-strewn camp.
  Then through the abatis, behind which death
  Is lurking there upon a thousand shafts,
  He who has never yet been stopped attempts
  To break. There is a charge and a resistance
  Such as no happy eye has ever seen.

Then torn to pieces, finally the King
Leads his troops home, and not a foot of earth
Does he gain with this human sacrifice.
WALLENSTEIN: Spare us recitals from the daily news
  Of things we, shuddering, experienced.
QUESTENBERG: My duty and my mission are to charge you,
  It is my heart that lingers here in praise.
  The glory of the Swedish king was left
  In Nuremberg, on Lützen's plain his life.
  But who was not astounded when Duke Friedland,
  On this great day, like someone who is vanquished,
  Deserts the scene, flees to Bohemia.
  Meanwhile that young, heroic man of Weimar
  Was pressing forward to Franconia,
  And forced through to the Danube unrestrained.
  He rested suddenly at Regensburg
  To the alarm of all good Catholic Christians.
  Then in Bavaria their most just prince
  Cried out for swift assistance in his need.
  The Emperor sends seven riders to
  The Duke of Friedland carrying this plea
  And begs, where he as master can command,
  In vain! For in this moment what the Duke
  Can hear is only anger and resentment.
  The common good he sacrifices to
  Content his vengefulness on an old foe.
  And Regensburg is lost!
WALLENSTEIN: What does he speak of here, Max, I believe
  My memory has left me.
MAX: He must mean
  When we were in Silesia.
WALLENSTEIN: So! So! So!
  And what was it that we were doing there?
MAX: We had to rout the Saxons and the Swedes.
WALLENSTEIN: That's right! Because of his description I've
  Forgotten the whole war.
                    (*To Questenberg*)
                    You may proceed!
QUESTENBERG: Perhaps there on the Oder could be won
  What in disgrace was wasted on the Danube.
  It is remarkable what things we hoped

We would experience on this war's stage
With Friedland coming to the front in person.
The rival of Gustav Adolphus found—
An Arnheim and a Thurn before him. And
They were so close together that as friends
Or guests they could have entertained each other.
All Germany groaned under war's great burden,
But there was only peace in Friedland's camp.

WALLENSTEIN: Still many a bloody battle's fought for nothing
Because a young commander needs to win.
A proven leader has a great advantage
Because he does not need to fight just to
Convince the world he knows the way to win.
How little it would help me to make use
Of a success against someone like Arnheim;
But my restraint would profit Germany
If I were able to unbind those ties,
So ruinous, between the Swedes and Saxons.

QUESTENBERG: It did not work, and so began again
The bloody game of war. And here at last
The Duke could justify his reputation.
On Steinau's fields the Swedish army lays
Its weapons down, subdued without a blow—
And here, among the others, Heaven's justice
Hands over that established rabble-rouser,
Accursed as the torchbearer in this war,
Matthias Thurn, into avenging hands.
—These hands he fell into were generous;
Instead of punishment, rich gifts seemed to
Reward the Emperor's arch enemy.

WALLENSTEIN (*laughs*):
I know, I know—Vienna had already
Reserved the windows so that they could see
The cart with the condemned man tour the streets.
A battle lost would have brought mild abuse,
But never can the Viennese forgive
That I deprived them of their spectacle.

QUESTENBERG: Silesia was freed. It seemed the Duke
Must move into hard-pressed Bavaria.
Indeed, he does begin to march—and slowly
He goes the *long* way through Bohemia;

Before he sees the foe, he enters into
His winter camp. The Emperor's domain
Is burdened by the Emperor's own troops.
WALLENSTEIN: The army was so wretched. Every comfort
And each necessity was wanting—winter
Had come. What are troops to His Majesty?
Are we not human? Subject to the cold
And wet and each necessity of mortals?
Accursed is a soldier's fate! Wherever
He enters, people flee from him—and when
He leaves, they damn him! He must help himself;
They give him nothing; so he's forced to take
From everyone and is to each a terror.
Here stand my generals! Here's Caraffa!
Count Deodati! Buttler! Say how long
The troops have not been paid for what they've sold.
BUTTLER: It's been a year.
WALLENSTEIN: And what a soldier's sold
He must be paid for, that is what he's named!
QUESTENBERG: That sounds quite different from the things we
    heard
The Duke of Friedland say some years ago.
WALLENSTEIN: It's true, I have myself to blame, I know.
I spoiled the Emperor. Nine years ago
I gave him forty-thousand troops or more,
A mighty army, in the war with Denmark,
That cost him from his own resources not
A penny. Then throughout all Saxony
The rage of war advanced up to the cliffs
Of Belt and spread the terror of his name.
Those were the days! In all the Emperor's
Dominion no name was revered like mine,
And Albrecht Wallenstein was what they called
The third of three bright jewels in his crown!
But when the Diet met in Regensburg,
It was the end! Then it was made quite clear
Out of whose pocket I had kept things going.
What was the thanks they gave me that I had,
Like a true royal servant, taken on
Myself the people's curse—and let the princes
Support the war that made *him* only great?

Well? I was sacrificed to their complaints—
I was dismissed.
QUESTENBERG: Your Grace is well aware
That he was lacking every freedom at
That hapless meeting.
WALLENSTEIN: Hell fire and damnation!
What I *possessed* could have made freedom for him.
No, Sir! Since I was made to suffer when
I served the throne and charged it to the Empire,
I see the Empire in a different light.
Of course, the Emperor gave me this staff,
But now I bear it as the general of
The Empire, use it for the *common* weal
And not for the aggrandizement of *one*!
—Now to the point. What do they want of me?
QUESTENBERG: The first thing that His Majesty desires
Is that the army leave Bohemia.
WALLENSTEIN: This time of year? Where is it that they plan
For us to go?
QUESTENBERG: To meet the enemy.
His Majesty wants Regensburg to be
Purged of the enemy by Eastertime
So that in the cathedral there will be
No Lutheran preaching—loathesome heresy
Shall not befoul the feast's pure celebration.
WALLENSTEIN: Well, can that happen? Tell me, Generals?
ILLO: It is not possible.
BUTTLER: It cannot happen.
QUESTENBERG: The Emperor has ordered Colonel Suys
To move his forces to Bavaria.
WALLENSTEIN: And what has Suys replied?
QUESTENBERG: He did his duty.
He has advanced.
WALLENSTEIN: He has advanced! And I,
His chief, gave him express commands that he
Should not move from that place! Is that the state
Of my command! *That's* the obedience
That's owed me, lacking which no force in arms
Can be conceived of? So, my Generals,
I'll let you judge! What does the officer
Deserve who, oath forgotten, flouts his orders.

ILLO: To die!

WALLENSTEIN (*when the others remain contemplatively silent,*
   raising his voice):
  Count Piccolomini, what is
  His fate?

MAX (*after a long pause*): According to the law—to die!

ISOLANI: To die!

BUTTLER: The laws of war say he's to die!
    (*Questenberg rises. Wallenstein does likewise, and all rise.*)

WALLENSTEIN: It is the law condemns him here, not I!
  And if I pardon him, it is because
  Of the respect I owe my Emperor.

QUESTENBERG: If this is so, I have no more to say.

WALLENSTEIN: 'Twas on conditions I took this command;
  The first one was that no one have the right
  To contradict my handling of the army,
  And if it were the Emperor himself.
  If *I* must answer with my honor and
  My head for the results, I must be master
  Of what occurs. What made Gustav Adolphus
  Invincible and unopposed on earth?
  Just this: That he was *king* in his own *army!*
  A king, and one who really is a king,
  Is never beaten but by his own kind—
  Still, to the point. The best is yet to come.

QUESTENBERG: In spring the cardinal-prince is to proceed
  Out of Milan and lead a Spanish force
  Through Germany, advancing on the Lowlands.
  So that he may be certain of his way,
  Our monarch wants eight regiments of horse
  Out of this army to ride with him there.

WALLENSTEIN: I see, I see—eight regiments—that's good!
  That's well contrived, O, Father Lamormain!
  If it were not so damnably astute,
  One would be tempted to adjudge it stupid.
  Eight thousand horse! Well, well, it's really true,
  I see it coming.

QUESTENBERG: There is nothing here
  To see. It is good sense and necessary.

WALLENSTEIN: Well, Mr. Emissary, am I not
  Supposed to notice that they're tired of it

That might and sword hilt rest here in my hand?
That they are anxious and make this pretense,
And use the Spanish name to weaken me
And bring a new strong force into the Empire
That is not under me? I am as yet
Too strong indeed for you that I be cast
Aside. My contract stipulates that all
The armies of the Emperor are mine
As far as German is the language spoken.
Concerning Spanish troops and princes who
Are moving through the Empire as its guests,
The contract makes no mention—then they sneak
So quietly around behind their pact,
First make me weaker, then dispensable
Till they can make short shrift of me. —But why
Take all these devious approaches, Sir?
Straight out with it! The pact with me oppresses
The Emperor. He wants me to be gone,
And I will do that favor for him. That
Already was decided when you came.
        (*There is a commotion among the generals that becomes ever
                    greater.*)
I'm truly sorry for my officers.
I don't see how they'll get the money back
That they've advanced in payments well deserved.
New regiments bring in new men and then
All former services will quickly age.
So many foreigners serve in the army,
And if a man is good and capable,
I was not likely to inquire about
His ancestry or even his religion.
That will be different in the future, too!
Well—it does not concern me now.
                    (*He sits down.*)
MAX: My God,
    That it should come to this! —The army will
    Rise up in ferment, for the Emperor
    Has been misled; this simply cannot be.
ISOLANI: It cannot be, for all would fall in ruins.
WALLENSTEIN: And that it will, dear Isolani, all
    That we have circumspectly built, in ruins.

But anyway a general will be found;
An army surely will come running to
The Emperor when they can hear the drum.

MAX (*busily and fervidly running from one to the other and
    quieting them*):
Hear me, Commanders! Hear me, General!
Let me entreat you, Sir, not to decide
Until we can confer together and
Present our thoughts to you. So come, my friends!
I hope that everything can be restored.

TERZKY: We'll meet the others in the antechamber.
                       (*They exit.*)

BUTTLER (*to Questenberg*):
If you will listen to some good advice,
Be careful in the hours to come that you
Don't show yourself in public; scarcely can
Your golden key protect you from abuse.
             (*Loud commotion outside*)

WALLENSTEIN: That's good advice—Octavio, you are
Security to me for our guest's safety.
May all be well with you, von Questenberg!
         (*As the latter is about to speak*)
Now nothing more about this hateful matter!
You did your duty, and I know enough
To separate a person from his office.

(*As Questenberg is about to exit with Octavio, Goetz, Tiefenbach,
    and Colalto force their way in with several other officers fol-
    lowing them.*)

GOETZ: Where is the man who's said our general—

TIEFENBACH (*at the same time*):
What is this that we've heard, you want to take—

COLALTO (*at the same time*):
We want to live with you and die with you.

WALLENSTEIN (*with dignity, pointing to Illo*):
Field Marshal Illo knows about my wishes.
                   (*Exits*)

ACT III

A Room

Scene 1

Illo and Terzky.

TERZKY: Now, tell me how you mean to do your work
  Tonight at dinner with the officers?
ILLO: Just pay attention. We'll present a statement
  In which we pledge ourselves in writing to
  The Duke, our bodies and our lives are his,
  And our last drop of blood we'll shed for him.
  But still the oaths we've sworn that we will serve
  The Emperor will not be harmed. Note this!
  We will exclude *these* in a separate clause
  Expressly and thus save our consciences.
  Now listen! We will put this document
  To them before they eat, and no one will
  Have an objection to it. —But, what's more,
  When we have eaten and the wine's effect
  Has opened up their hearts and shut their eyes,
  We'll hand around a substituted sheet,
  In which that clause is missing, to be signed.
TERZKY: So? Do you think that they will feel they must
  Be bound by something that we have acquired
  Deceitfully through naught but trickery?
ILLO: We have them trapped forever. —Let them cry
  About our cunning, grumble all they want.
  At court their signatures will be believed
  Far more than their most sacred protestation.
  Once they are traitors, traitors they remain;
  They'll make a virtue of necessity.
TERZKY: Well, I like anything as long as something
  Occurs to move us from this spot at last.
ILLO: And then—it is not so important what
  Success we have with all the generals here,
  It is enough if we convince the Duke
  That they are his—then he will finally
  Behave with earnestness as if he had them.

Then they *are* his and they will follow him.

TERZKY: Sometimes I've almost given up on him.
He lends the enemy his ear and lets
Me write to Thurn and Arnheim, speaks against
Sesina freely with bold words, and talks
For hours with us concerning all his plans.
Then when I think I have him—all at once
He slips away; it seems as if he had
One thing alone to do: to stay right here.

ILLO: You think he would surrender his old plans?
I tell you that he, waking, sleeping, is
Concerned with nothing else; day after day
Because of this he asks the stars—

TERZKY: Are you
Aware that on this night that is now here
He'll shut himself up in the tower with
The doctor of astrology and they'll
Make observations? This night, I have heard,
Events both great and long awaited will
Occur in heaven above.

ILLO: If only they
Would happen here below. The generals are
Now eager and can be convinced they should
Do anything to keep their chief. You see!
We have the opportunity at hand
To form a close-knit league against the court.
Its character is harmless; what they want
Is only just to keep him in command.
But you know, in the heat of what will follow,
Beginnings will recede far out of sight.
I aim to plan it so the Duke will find
Them willing—and *believe* them willing, too—
For each bold stroke. The opportunity
Will soon seduce him. When that great step has
Been taken that Vienna can't forgive,
Then the necessity behind events
Will lead him ever further. It is just
The choice that makes it difficult. But when
He knows he must, he'll have the strength and vision.

TERZKY: The enemy is waiting just for that
To bring their army to us.

ILLO: Come! We must
  Accelerate our work in these few days
  More than it has progressed in years. —And when
  Things look auspicious here below, you'll see,
  The proper stars will also shine above!
  Now let us go to the commanders. We
  Must strike the iron while it is hot.
TERZKY: You go.
  I must await the Countess Terzky here.
  You know we've not been idle either, and
  If *one* rope breaks, another is prepared.
ILLO: Yes, Mistress Terzky has a crafty smile.
  Why is that?
TERZKY: It's a secret! Hush! She's coming.
             (*Illo exits.*)

Scene 2

Count and Countess Terzky, who comes out of a private room, afterwards a servant, and then Illo.

TERZKY: Will she be here? I can't detain him longer.
COUNTESS: She'll be here right away. Do send him in.
TERZKY: I must admit I'm not sure if our lord
  Will thank us for this. As you know, he has
  Not let his thoughts be known about this matter.
  You talked me into it, and you should know
  How far to go.
COUNTESS: I take it on myself.
          (*to herself*)
  Here no authority is needed. —We
  Can understand each other without words.
  I know why you required your daughter's presence
  And why you picked just *him* to bring her here.
  For this pretense of an engagement with
  A fiancé who's unidentified
  May fool the others! I can see through you—
  It is not fitting you should have a hand
  In this affair. Most certainly! It must
  Be left to my finesse. That's good! You shall
  Not be mistaken here about your sister.

SERVANT (*enters*): The generals!
                    (*Exits*)
TERZKY (*to the Countess*):   Take good care that you arouse
  Him, give him much to think about, so that
  When he comes to the table, he will not
  Consider long before he signs his name.
COUNTESS: Just take care of your guests! Go now and send him.
TERZKY: For all depends upon his signature.
COUNTESS: Go to your guests. Go now!
ILLO (*returns*):   Where are you, Terzky?
  The house is full, and everyone awaits you.
TERZKY: I'm coming!
                    (*to the Countess*)
                    See he doesn't hesitate—
  His father otherwise might be suspicious—
COUNTESS: No need to worry!
                    (*Terzky and Illo exit.*)

Scene 3

Countess Terzky, Max Piccolomini.

MAX (*looks in shyly*): Aunt, may I come in?
  (*Comes to the middle of the room, where he looks around
  uneasily.*)
  She is not here! Where is she?
COUNTESS: Just look there,
  See in that corner if she is concealed
  Behind the screen—
MAX: Her gloves are lying there!
  (*Reaches for them hurriedly; the Countess takes hold of them*)
  Why, unkind Aunt, you act against me now—
  I think that you enjoy tormenting me.
COUNTESS: That's thanks for all my trouble!
MAX: Oh! If you
  Just knew the way I feel! Since we are here—
  So to restrain myself, to weigh each word!
  I'm not accustomed to this!
COUNTESS: My fine friend,
  There's much you'll need to get accustomed to!
  Upon this proof of your obedience

I must depend, and only on *these* terms
Can I concern myself with this at all.

MAX: But tell me where she is, why she's not here.

COUNTESS: You'll have to leave things wholly in my hands.
Who could there be who had you more at heart!
And no one is to know, your father most
Of all!

MAX: There is no need to worry. There
Is no one here to whom I would express
How my enchanted soul affects me now.
—Oh, dear Aunt Terzky, are all things here changed
Or is it only me? I feel I am
Surrounded by strange people. Not a trace
Of all my former wishes and delights.
Where have they gone? Before I never was
Dissatisfied with this world as it is.
How dull things are now and how ordinary!
My comrades seem unbearable to me,
I don't know what to say to my own father,
My duties and my weapons are like toys.
So must a spirit, once departed, feel
Who, from the dwellings of eternal joy,
Returned to all his childlike occupations,
His preferences and fraternities,
To be again part of the human race.

COUNTESS: Well, still I'll have to ask you just to cast
A glance upon this very common world
Where now important things are happening.

MAX: There are things taking place around me here.
I see it in the strange, compulsive action;
When things are ready, I will surely hear.
Where do you think, dear Aunt, that I have been?
But do not tease! The tumult of the camp
Disturbed me, and the flood of pushy people;
The stale jest and the empty conversation,
'Twas too confined for me, I had to leave,
To seek some silence for my heart, so full,
An undefiled spot for my happiness.
Don't smile now, Countess! I was in the church,
There is a cloister here, the Gate of Heaven,
I went there and I found myself alone.

Christ's Mother hung above the altar there,
It was a wretched picture, but it was
The friend I looked for at this very moment.
How often I have seen Her glorious
And been unmoved by all the fervor of
Her worshipers, but suddenly it was
So clear, all their devotion and their love.

COUNTESS: Enjoy your happiness. Forget the world
  That lies around you. Friendship will take care
  Of you with vigilance, meanwhile, and act.
  But you must also take directions when
  The way to happiness is pointed out.

MAX: What has become of her? Oh, golden time
  When we were journeying, when each new sun
  Joined us again till night, when we were parted!
  No sand ran through the glass, no chimes rang out.
  Time seemed to me, as someone more than blessed,
  Completely stopped in its eternal course.
  Oh, he who thinks about the passing hours
  Has surely fallen from his Heaven above!
  The clock need never strike for one who's happy.

COUNTESS: When was it that you opened up your heart?

MAX: I only dared to speak a word this morning.

COUNTESS: What? Just today when there've been twenty days?

MAX: There at the hunting lodge that lies between
  Us here and Nepomuk, there where you fetched us,
  The last stop that we made on the whole journey.
  We stood there in an alcove and we gazed
  In silence out upon the empty field,
  And there before us the dragoons rode up,
  Sent to accompany us by the Duke.
  The fear of separation lay on me,
  And trembling I at last presumed to say:
  All this reminds me that today I must
  Be separated from my happiness.
  In just a little you will find a father
  And see yourself surrounded by new friends,
  And I will be a stranger to you then,
  Forgotten in the crowd. —"You'll have to speak
  With my Aunt Terzky," she broke quickly in,
  Her voice was trembling and I saw upon

Her lovely cheeks a glowing red appear,
And from the ground she slowly lifted up
Her gaze to mine—I could control myself
No longer—
(*The Princess appears at the door and stops, seen by the Duchess
but not Piccolomini.*)
                    boldly take her in my arms,
My mouth is touching hers—when there's a noise
Nearby that separates us.—It was *you*.
What happened then, you know.
COUNTESS (*after a pause, with a surreptitious look at Thekla*):
Are you so unassuming or perhaps
You have too little curiosity
To ask about *my* secret too?
MAX: Your secret?
COUNTESS: That's what I said! As I came in the room
Directly after you and found my niece,
And then as she in this first moment with
A heart that's taken unawares—
MAX (*briskly*):   Go on?

Scene 4

The former. Thekla, who steps forward quickly.

THEKLA: Just save yourself the effort, Aunt.
He'd better hear it from my lips.
MAX (*steps back*):   My Lady!
Aunt Terzky, you have let me say such things!
THEKLA (*to the Countess*): Has he been here for very long?
COUNTESS: He has, and now his time is almost gone.
Where have you been so long?
THEKLA: My mother's weeping so. I see her suffer
—And cannot change the fact that I am happy.
MAX (*lost in contemplation of her*):
I have the courage now to look at you.
Today I could not, for the shine of jewels
Around you then concealed my loved one from me.
THEKLA: You saw me with your eyes then, not your heart.
MAX: This morning, when I saw you in the circle
Of family and in your father's arms,

And saw myself a stranger in this circle,
I almost could not help myself that moment
From falling on his neck, from calling *Father!*
But in his stern appearance I could read
Him bid my seething sentiments be silent,
And then those diamonds frightened me away,
Encircling you just like a crown of stars.
Why, when he welcomed you, did he engage
To cast that spell around you, to bedeck
The angel for the sacrifice and cast
The burden of his rank on your glad heart!
For love can certainly strive after love,
But only kings dare to approach such splendor.

THEKLA: Be still about this masquerade. You see
How quickly I have thrown aside the burden.
                    (*to the Countess*)
He is not cheerful. Oh, why is he not?
You, Aunt, have made him difficult for me!
He was a different person on our journey!
Serenely bright! So eloquent! I wished
To see you always so and never different.

MAX: You found yourself, there in your father's arms,
Placed in another world that worships you;
'Twas novelty perhaps, but you were charmed.

THEKLA: There's much that charms me here, I'll not deny.
The colorful and warlike stage is charming,
Reminding me anew of something dear,
And binds for me again to life and truth
What had appeared to me to be a dream.

MAX: It made my happiness seem like a dream.
Upon an island in ethereal heights
I have been living in these recent days;
But now it has been lowered to the earth,
And so this bridge that brings me back again
To my old life divides me from my Heaven.

THEKLA: The game of life appears bright and serene,
If in one's heart one holds one's treasure safe,
And when I have surveyed it, I'll return
The happier to my own fine possessions.
                (*Breaking off and in a playful tone*)
What all I've seen that's new and scandalous

In this short span of time that I've been here!
But still all these must make way for the marvels
That secretly are locked within these walls.
COUNTESS (*reflectively*):
    What could they be? I too am quite familiar
    With all the gloomy corners of this house.
THEKLA (*smiling*): The spirits guard the way into this place,
    Two griffins keep a watch there at the door.
COUNTESS (*laughs*): The tower of astrology! How has
    This holy place, which is so strictly watched,
    Been opened to you in your first hours here?
THEKLA: A little, agéd man, his hair all white,
    His face so friendly, who bestowed his favor
    At once on me; he opened up the door.
MAX: That is the Duke's astrologer, named Seni.
THEKLA: He questioned me about a lot of things,
    When I was born, what day and month it was,
    If I was born in daytime or at night—
COUNTESS: Because he meant to cast your horoscope.
THEKLA: He also gazed upon my hand and shook
    His head reflectively, and it appeared
    The lines on it were not too pleasing to him.
COUNTESS: Now tell me how you liked it in that room.
    I've always looked around it hurriedly.
THEKLA: The feeling that I had was very strange,
    When I stepped in there from the light of day;
    For suddenly dark night surrounded me
    Illuminated weakly by strange lights.
    Around me on a semicircle there
    Were standing six or seven royal portraits,
    Their scepters in their hands, and on their heads
    Each one displayed a star, and all the light
    There in the tower seemed to emanate
    Just from these stars. They were the planets, said
    My guide, and they control your destiny;
    That is the reason why they're shown as kings.
    The last, an ancient man, morose and sad,
    Was *Saturn* with the cloudy, yellow star;
    The one with the red gleam across from him
    In military panoply was *Mars*,
    And both of them bring little luck to men.

But at his side there was a lovely lady,
The star upon her head was softly gleaming,
For this was *Venus,* planet of delight.
There on my left was wingéd *Mercury.*
And in the middle, shining silver bright,
A cheerful man with royal countenance,
My father's planet it was, *Jupiter,*
And *moon* and *sun* were standing at his side.

MAX: Oh, I will never find fault with his faith
In planets and the power of the spirits.
Not just the *pride* of men fills up the void
With spirits and with mystery-clad forces;
A loving heart finds ordinary nature
Too narrow, and a deeper meaning lies
In fairy tales told in my childhood years
Than in the truth that we are taught by life.
The world of wonders, so serene, alone
Can ever answer an enchanted heart,
Can open up its endless spaces to me;
A thousand boughs it stretches amply toward me
On which my drunken spirit rocks itself.
The fable is the native world of love;
It likes to live with fairies and with charms,
Believes in gods because it is divine.
The creatures of the fables are no more,
That charming race long since has gone away;
But still the heart requires a language, and
The old desire calls old names back again;
Now in the firmament they're seen to move,
Who wandered once as friends along life's way.
From there they signal down to those who love,
And all things grand are brought to us this day
By *Jupiter* and all things fair by *Venus.*

THEKLA: If *that's* astrology, then I will cling
Most happily to this serene belief.
It is a lovely and a friendly thought
That over us in those unbounded heights
The crown of love, when we first came to be,
Already was entwined from twinkling stars.

COUNTESS: But not just roses, Heaven has its thorns.
You're lucky if they do not harm your crown!

What Venus binds, the bringer of good luck,
Can Mars, misfortune's star, soon tear apart.
MAX: His gloomy reign will soon be at an end!
And blesséd be the ardor of our Prince;
He'll weave the olive branch into the laurel,
Presenting peace to a rejoicing world.
Then his great heart will have no more to wish for.
He will have done enough for his renown—
Can live life for himself and for his own.
He can retire and go to his estates,
At Gitschin he has such a lovely place,
And Reichenberg and Friedland both are fair;
His forests and his hunting reservations
Stretch to the foothills of the Riesenberg.
Then he'll be free and he can gratify
Great inclinations and superb creations.
As Prince he can encourage every art
And royally protect all that is grand,
Can build and plant and can observe the stars.
If his bold energy cannot be still,
Then he can struggle with the elements,
Divert the river, and break up the rock,
And open up an easy route for trade.
Our stories of the war will then become
The tales that we can tell on winter nights—
COUNTESS: Well, cousin, just remember I advised
You not to lay your blade aside too soon,
A bride like this is worthy, to be sure,
That you'd aspire to win her with a sword.
MAX: If only weapons were the way to win her!
COUNTESS: What's that? Did you not hear? I thought I heard
The sounds of fighting in the banquet room.
                    (*She exits.*)

Scene 5

Thekla and Max Piccolomini.

THEKLA (*as soon as the Countess is gone, quickly and secretly to
    Piccolomini*):
Don't trust them! Their intent is bad.

MAX: They could—
THEKLA: Trust no one here but me! I saw it right
  Away. They have a goal.
MAX: A goal! But what?
  What would they gain by letting us have hope—
THEKLA: That I don't know. Believe me, though, they don't
  Intend to make us happy, to unite us.
MAX: Then why these Terzkys? Have we not your mother?
  And does this gracious lady not deserve
  That, childlike, we should trust ourselves to her?
THEKLA: She loves you, treasures you above the others,
  But she would never have the courage to
  Conceal a secret like this from my father.
  For her own peace of mind the knowledge must
  Be kept from her.
MAX: Why everywhere are there
  These secrets? Do you know what I will do?
  I'll throw myself there at your father's feet.
  He shall decide my fate. He is sincere,
  He knows no subterfuge, and hates deception,
  He is so good, so noble.
THEKLA: So are you!
MAX: You met him just today. But I have lived
  Ten years already under his attention.
  Is this the first time he has done the rare
  Unhoped for thing? It would be very like
  Him to surprise us like a god. He must
  Forever act to charm and to surprise.
  Who knows but that he, in this very moment,
  Is only waiting for us to confess,
  To make us one? —You're silent, and you look
  With doubt. What do you have against your father?
THEKLA: I? Nothing—but he seems too occupied
  To ever have the leisure time to think
  About our happiness.
               (*Taking him by the hand tenderly*)
                    Take my advice!
  We'll not believe too much in other people!
  We will be thankful to the Terzkys for
  Their every favor, but we will not trust
  Them any more than they are worthy of,

And for the rest—we'll only trust our hearts.
MAX: Oh, do you think we ever will be happy?
THEKLA: Well, are we not? Are you not mine? Am I
    Not yours? —Now in my soul there does reside
    Great boldness that my love has given me—
    I should not be so open, I should hide
    My heart from you the way our manners dictate.
    But where could you then hope to find the truth,
    If you were not to find it on my lips?
    We've found each other, and we hold each other
    Thus tightly bound forever. And, indeed,
    That is a whole lot more than they desired.
    So let us keep it like some sacred plunder
    Protected at the bottom of our hearts.
    This came to us down from the heavenly heights,
    And we have only Heaven to thank for it.
    Still, it could work a miracle for us.

Scene 6

Countess Terzky joins the former.

COUNTESS (*urgently*):
    My husband sends to say it is high time
    He comes to dinner—
            (*When they pay no attention, she steps between them.*)
                    You must part!
THEKLA: Not yet!
    It can't have been a moment since I came.
COUNTESS: The time slips quickly by you, my Princess.
MAX: There is no hurry, Aunt.
COUNTESS: Now go! They miss you.
    Your father has inquired about you twice.
THEKLA: Indeed! His father!
COUNTESS: You must understand!
THEKLA: What should he do there in that company?
    They are not his acquaintances; they may
    Be worthy and deserving, but he is
    Too young and does not suit this company.
COUNTESS: You want to keep him for yourself alone?

THEKLA (*spiritedly*): That's right. That is exactly what I mean.
Yes, leave him here, and tell the gentlemen—
COUNTESS: Niece, have you really lost your mind? —You, Count,
You surely know the way things have to be.
MAX: I must obey, my Lady. Then farewell!
(*When Thekla quickly turns away from him*)
What do you say?
THEKLA (*without looking at him*):
                Just go!
MAX: How can I, when
You're angry with me—
(*He comes close to her, their eyes meet; they stand silently for an instant, then she throws herself on his chest and he embraces her.*)
COUNTESS: What if someone came!
I hear an uproar—voices drawing near.
(*Max tears himself from her arms and leaves; the Countess accompanies him. At first Thekla follows him with her eyes, then moves restlessly around the room and stands sunken in thought. There is a guitar lying on the table; she takes it up and, after she has played a few preliminary notes, she begins to sing.*)

Scene 7

THEKLA (*playing and singing*):
The clouds speed by; in the oaks it blows.
On the green of the shore the maiden goes.
The waves are breaking with all their might,
And she starts to sing in the dark of night,
For her heart with weeping is moved.

My world is empty, my heart is dead,
And all the desires I once felt have fled.
O holy one, call your child back home.
All earthly happiness I have known,
For I have lived and have loved.

Scene 8

The Countess returns. Thekla.

COUNTESS: What kind of thing was that, Niece? Fie! You throw
Yourself at him. It seems to me you should

Conduct yourself as if you were more dear.

THEKLA (*as she rises*):
  What do you mean, Aunt?

COUNTESS: You should not forget
  Just who you are and who he is. That has
  Not yet occurred to you, I think.

THEKLA: What's that?

COUNTESS: Remember that you are Duke Friedland's daughter.

THEKLA: So? And what else?

COUNTESS: How can you ask that question!

THEKLA: What we've become, *he* was when he was born.
  He comes from an old Lombard family.
  His mother is a princess.

COUNTESS: Are you dreaming?
  Indeed, we should politely ask him to
  Make Europe's richest heiress happy and
  Request her hand.

THEKLA: That will not be required.

COUNTESS: It would be best not to disclose yourselves.

THEKLA: His father loves him; Count Octavio
  Will not have anything against it—

COUNTESS: His father? His! And what about yours, Niece?

THEKLA: Well, I think that you fear *his* father, for
  From him—I mean his father—you conceal
  So very much.

COUNTESS (*looks at her searchingly*): You are deceitful, Niece.

THEKLA: Are you so sensitive, Aunt? Don't be cross!

COUNTESS: You think that you have won your little game—
  Do not rejoice too soon.

THEKLA: Aunt, don't be cross!

COUNTESS: Things have not gone so far.

THEKLA: That I believe.

COUNTESS: Do you believe he has devoted his
  Important life to military toil,
  Renounced each quiet bit of happiness,
  While from his couch he even banished sleep,
  And to such cares resigned his noble head,
  Just so you two could be a happy pair?
  At last to bring you from your convent and
  Convey to you in triumph just this man,
  Who finds acceptance in your eyes? —He could

Have gotten that much cheaper. But he did
Not plant this seed so that your childish hand
Could break the blossom for an ornament
And pin it on your breast!

THEKLA: What he did not intend for me, that could
With spontaneity bear fruit for me.
So if indulgent fate should be so kind
And from its awful, mighty presence it
Should want to make for me a life of joy—

COUNTESS: You act like nothing but a girl in love.
Just look around! Just think of where you are! —
You have not come into a house of pleasure,
The walls are not adorned to celebrate
A wedding, nor the guests with garlands. Here
The only glitter comes from weapons. Or
Perhaps you thought these thousands were brought here
To form their ranks just for your bridal feast?
You see your father's brow so deep in thought,
Your mother is in tears, and on the scales
There lies the destiny of our whole house!
Now leave the childish feeling of a maiden
Behind you with your petty wishes. Show
You are the daughter of a special man.
A woman's life is not her own possession,
An alien fate will keep her firmly bound.
She will fare best who willingly accepts
That which is alien within her heart
And cares for it sincerely and with love.

THEKLA: That's what they told me in the convent, too.
I had no wishes, only knew myself
To be the daughter of the mighty one;
The echoes of his life that reached me there
Gave me no other feeling than that I
Was destined to be sacrificed for him.

COUNTESS: That is your fate. Accept it willingly!
Your mother and myself are your examples.

THEKLA: But fate has shown me *one* I'll sacrifice
Myself for; I will gladly follow him.

COUNTESS: Your heart, you mean, dear child, and not your fate.

THEKLA: My heart is prompted by the voice of fate,
And I belong to him. His gift to me

Is this new life that I am living now.
He has a right to his creation. What
Was I before his beauteous love inspired me?
I do not want to think less of myself
Than my beloved does. One can't be small
Possessing what is priceless, and I feel
That strength is given me with happiness.
So life is earnest to the earnest soul.
I know that I belong now to myself
I am acquainted with my solid will,
Which is invincible here in my breast.
And I can stake it all on what is best.

COUNTESS: Are you about to act against your father,
If he's decided something else for you?
—You think you'll make him change his mind? You know
His name is Friedland.

THEKLA: That is my name, too.
He'll find that I most surely am his daughter.

COUNTESS: His Emperor cannot compel him, but
Still you, a maiden, want to fight with him?

THEKLA: What no one else would dare, his daughter can.

COUNTESS: Now, really! He is not prepared for this.
That he should overcome each obstacle
To have another struggle face him in
His daughter's strange intent? My child, my child!
Your father's smile is all that you have seen,
You have not seen him look at you in wrath.
Would your voice dare, this trembling one, in his
Vicinity to offer such resistance?
Well might you, when you are alone, propose
Great things while weaving flow'ry speeches and
Then arm your dovelike mind with lion's courage.
Just try it! Step before him while his eye
Intently gazes on you, and say no!
Like petals of a flower in the fire
Of sunshine, you'll succumb before him there.
—I do not want to frighten you, dear child!
I hope it will not come to these extremes—
Nor do I know his wishes. It may be
His purpose will concur with your desire.
Still, it can never be his will that you,

Proud daughter of his great good fortune, should
Behave like any other lovesick maid
And throw herself away on someone who,
If this reward be his, will have to make
The greatest sacrifice that love can give!
                    (*She exits.*)

                    Scene 9

THEKLA (*alone*):
  I thank you for the hint you've given me!
  It makes me certain of my premonition.
  So is it true, then, that we have no friends
  And not one single faithful soul is here—
  We have ourselves alone, and conflict threatens.
  O Love, divine one, give us strength for this!
  What she has said is true! These signs that light
  The union of our hearts are cheerless ones,
  This stage is not a place where hope can dwell.
  It is the muffled din of war we hear,
  And love itself, as if arrayed in steel,
  Steps forth prepared to battle to the death.
    A threatening spirit walks here through our house,
  And fate will quickly make an end to us.
  It drives me from my quiet sanctuary
  And dazzles me with its enchanting spell.
  It lures me with this heavenly appearance
  That hovers near and ever nearer me;
  It draws me onward with its force divine
  To the abyss, and I cannot resist.
          (*From the distance, dinner music can be heard.*)
  Oh, when a house shall vanish in the fire,
  Then Heaven drives together all its clouds.
  The lightning flashes from the heights serene,
  From craters 'neath the earth the flames appear;
  The raging god of joy now hurls the wreath,
  Ill-fated, in the burning edifice.
                    (*She exits.*)

ACT IV

Scene: A large, festively lighted hall, in the middle of which and placed toward the rear of the stage is a richly decorated table at which eight generals sit, among them Octavio Piccolomini, Terzky, and Maradas. To the right and left of it, more toward the rear, are two other tables, each occupied by six guests. Toward the front is the serving table. The whole front stage is left empty for the pages and waiters who are serving. Everything is in motion; musicians from Terzky's regiment move across the stage and around the tables. Before they have withdrawn entirely, Max Piccolomini enters; Terzky comes toward him with a paper, Isolani with a goblet.

Scene 1

Terzky. Isolani. Max Piccolomini.

ISOLANI: Well, brother whom we love! Where have you been?
  Go promptly to your place! It seems Count Terzky
  Has sacrificed his mother's noble wine—
  And things proceed as once in Heidelberg.
  You missed the best part. They are handing out,
  There at the table, all the princes' hats;
  And the estates of Eggenberg, Slavata,
  Of Liechtenstein and Sternberg are divided,
  And all the fiefs there in Bohemia.
  If you act quickly, you'll gain something, too.
  Come on! Sit down!

COLLALTO and GOETZ (*call from the second table*): Count
  Piccolomini!

TERZKY: We'll let you have him soon. —Just read this oath
  To see if you agree with what we've written.
  Each one of us has had a chance to read it,
  And each one here will sign his name thereto.

MAX (*reads*): *Ingratis servire nefas.*

ISOLANI: That sounds as if it is a Latin proverb—
  Well, Brother, tell us what it means.

TERZKY: No proper man will serve one who's not grateful!

MAX: "Inasmuch as our most high commander, His Highness,
  Duke of Friedland, because of the manifold wrongs he has
  received, has expressed the intention of leaving the Emperor's

service but upon our unanimous plea has let himself be
persuaded to remain with the army and not to part from us
without our consent, so we again bind ourselves in a body and
each for himself alone, instead of taking a verbal oath—also to
support him honorably and faithfully, to part from him in no
way whatsoever, and to commit to him everything that is ours,
down to the last drop of our blood, that is to say, as far as *the*
oath we have taken to the Emperor will allow. (The last words
are repeated by Isolani.) So also, if one or the other of us,
contrary to this alliance, should separate himself from our
common cause, we will declare him to be a traitor, deserting our
alliance, and be obliged to take revenge on his goods and
chattels and on him, life and limb. We testify to this by affixing
our names."

TERZKY: Are you disposed to sign your name to this?
ISOLANI: Whyever would he not? Each officer
  Of honor can—yes, must. Bring pen and ink!
TERZKY: When dinner's through there's time.
ISOLANI (*drawing Max away*):   Come on, come on!
          (*The two go to the table.*)

Scene 2

Terzky. Neumann.

TERZKY (*beckons Neumann, who has waited at the serving table,*
  and walks front stage with him):
  You have the copy, Neumann? Give it here!
  Can it be substituted easily?
NEUMANN: I've reproduced it line for line so that
  There's nothing missing but the part about
  The oath, just as Your Excellency said.
TERZKY: Good! Place it there and put this one into
  The fire at once. It's done what it should do.
  (*Neumann puts the copy on the table and walks again to the*
  serving table.)

Scene 3

Illo enters from the next room. Terzky.

ILLO: How does it look with Piccolomini?

TERZKY: I think all right. He mentioned no objections.
ILLO: He is the only one I do not trust,
   He and his father. —Keep an eye on both!
TERZKY: How are things going at your table? You
   Are keeping your guests warm, I hope?
ILLO: They are
   Extremely cordial now. I think we have them.
   And just as I predicted it would be,
   The talk now is not just how we can keep
   The Duke with honor. Now that they are all
   Together here, Count Montecuculi
   Proposes they present conditions to
   The Emperor and in Vienna. If
   It were not for the Piccolominis,
   We would not have to stoop to this deceit.
TERZKY: Now what does Buttler want? Be still!

Scene 4

Buttler joins the former.

BUTTLER (*coming from the second table*): Do not
   Disturb yourselves. I understand you well
   And wish you luck in what you do—and as
                    (*secretively*)
   For me, you can depend on me.
ILLO (*spiritedly*):   We can?
BUTTLER: With or without the clause. It's all the same.
   To me. You understand? Just tell the Duke
   To test my loyalty in any way.
   I aim to serve the Emperor as long
   As he is pleased to serve the Emperor,
   And I'll be Friedland's man as soon as he
   Decides it's time that he be his own man.
TERZKY: You make a good exchange. No skinflint he,
   No Ferdinand, to whom you pledge yourself.
BUTTLER (*sternly*): My loyalty is not for sale, Count Terzky,
   And I would not have given you advice
   Six months ago to bargain for a thing
   That I now offer voluntarily.
   Yes, with me I will bring my regiment

To serve the Duke, and the example that
I give will not, I think, lack for results.
ILLO: To whom is it not known that Colonel Buttler
Does shine as an example to the army?
BUTTLER: Well, do you think so, General? Then I won't
Regret my forty years of loyalty,
If my good name, so well preserved, should get
Its full revenge when I am in my sixties!—
Take no offense at what I say. It may
Be all the same to you *why* I am yours,
And you, I hope, do not expect that you
Distort my honest judgment with your game—
That fickleness or fervent temperament
Or any trifling reason should compel
A man of years to leave his path of honor.
Come! I am none the less determined, though
I clearly know just what I leave behind.
ILLO: Then tell us plainly what to take you for—
BUTTLER: Why, for a friend. Here, take my hand on it.
That I with all I have am wholly yours.
The Prince needs not just men but money, too.
While in his service I've acquired a lot.
I'll lend it to him, and if he survives
Me, it is his; he is my heir long since.
I stand alone here in this world and do
Not know the feeling that can bind a man
To a dear wife and to beloved children.
My name will die with me, my line will end.
ILLO: He does not need your money—but your heart
Weighs more than tons of gold, yes, millions, too.
BUTTLER: I came as a poor stable boy from Ireland;
To Prague I came, and there my master died.
From that low service in the stables I
Rose to this post of honor by some chance,
Unknowing toy of war's capricious luck.
And Wallenstein is also Fortune's child;
I love the pathway that resembles mine.
ILLO: All who are strong and brave are kindred souls.
BUTTLER: This moment is of vast import in time,
And favors one who's bold and resolute.
As small change goes from hand to hand, so towns

And castles make a quick exchange of owners.
The heirs of age-old houses emigrate,
Entirely new the coats of arms and names;
On German soil a northern people dares,
Unwelcome there, to make a lasting home.
The Prince of Weimar arms himself to found
A principality upon the Main;
And but a longer life was needed for
The man from Halberstadt and Mansfeld, too,
To gain lands for themselves with their sharp swords.
Still, who among these equals Wallenstein?
And nothing is so high that might has not
The right to place its ladder for a climb.

TERZKY: Those words you've spoken like a man!

BUTTLER: You make sure of the Spanish and the French!
    The Scotsman Lessley I'll take on myself.
    Come to the party now!

TERZKY: Where is the steward
    Who tends the wine? Bring up the best you have!
    The time is now, for our affairs look good.
               (*They go, each to his table.*)

Scene 5

The wine steward comes forward with Neumann. Servants move here and there.

WINE STEWARD: This precious wine! If my old mistress could
    Behold this unrestrained existence, she,
    His sainted Mama, would turn over in
    Her grave! —It's true, this noble house is surely
    Declining, and its excess knows no bounds!
    And this illustrious relationship
    By marriage with the Duke brings little blessing.

NEUMANN: May God forbid! Now it will surely flourish.

WINE STEWARD: You think so? Well, there's much that can be said.

SERVANT (*comes forward*):
    Some burgundy for table four!

WINE STEWARD: That is
    The seventieth bottle now, Lieutenant.

SERVANT: The German gentleman named Tiefenbach
    Is sitting there. (*Exits.*)

WINE STEWARD (*continuing to speak to Neumann*):
          They aim too high. They want
To rival even kings with all their splendor;
And where the Duke will venture, there the Count,
My gracious master, will not stay behind.
               (*to the servants*)
Here, don't just stand and listen! Now, get going!
Look to the tables and the bottles! There!
Count Palfy sits before an empty glass!

SECOND SERVANT (*comes forward*):
They want the special chalice made of gold,
Emblazoned with Bohemia's coat of arms.
My lord said that you'd know which one he meant.

WINE STEWARD: The one that Master William made, they say.
Especially for Friedrich's coronation?
The finest piece they took in spoils from Prague?

SECOND SERVANT: Yes, *that* one! They will use it for a toast.

WINE STEWARD (*shaking his head as he takes out the cup and rinses it out*):
Here's something else to tell them in Vienna!

NEUMANN: Let's see! That is a beauty of a cup!
It's made of heavy gold, and clever things
Are fashioned nicely on it in relief.
Right on that first small shield—now let me look!—
A stately Amazon rides on a horse.
She leaps across a bishop's staff and miters,
And on a pole she balances a hat
Next to a flag on which a cup is seen.
And can you tell me now what all this means?

WINE STEWARD: The woman on the horse there represents
The freedom to elect the ruler of
Bohemia. The round hat points that out
As well as the wild horse on which she rides.
The hat is man's adornment, and the one
Who, when with kings and emperors, cannot
Still wear his hat is not a man who's free.

NEUMANN: What does that cup mean there upon the flag?

WINE STEWARD: The cup shows freedom of religion in
Bohemia as in the days of yore.
Then in the Hussite War our ancestors
Won from the pope this special privilege
He never gave to laymen of the chalice,

The cup, which to the Hussites was supreme.
It is their precious treasure, and it has
Caused them to shed much blood in many battles.
NEUMANN: What does the scroll say that hangs over it?
WINE STEWARD: The charter of Bohemia is meant
  Thereby, the one that Rudolph had to grant.
  It is a precious parchment beyond price
  That gives the right to ring the bells and sing
  To our new faith as well as to the old.
  But since the man from Graz rules over us,
  All that has ended, and then after Prague
  Where Palatine Count Friedrich lost his crown,
  Our faith has had no pulpit and no altar;
  Our brothers have been forced to turn their backs
  On home and country, while the Emperor
  Himself cut up the charter with his shears.
NEUMANN: You know all that! Well, Steward, I can see
  You know the story of your country well.
WINE STEWARD: Because my ancestors were Taborites,
  And they served under both Prokop and Ziska.
  May their bones rest in peace! But still they fought,
  Supporting a good cause. —Take it away!
NEUMANN: First let me see the other little shield!
  Just look, that shows how at the castle there
  In Prague the Emperor's advisors were
  O'erthrown, both Martinitz and then Slavata.
  That's right! There stands Count Thurn commanding it.
                    (*Servant exits with the cup.*)
WINE STEWARD: Don't speak to me about that day. It was
  The twenty-third of May, the year we wrote
  One thousand and six hundred eighteen. It
  Seems like today, and with that fatal day
  It all began, our country's great affliction.
  And since that day—it has been sixteen years—
  There never has been peace upon the earth—
AT THE SECOND TABLE (*they call out*):
  The Duke of Weimar!
AT THE THIRD AND FOURTH TABLES:
                    Long may Bernhard live!
                    (*Suddenly the sound of music.*)
FIRST SERVANT: Such racket!

SECOND SERVANT (*comes running*): Did you hear? They gave a toast
    To Weimar!
THIRD SERVANT: He's the enemy!
FIRST SERVANT: A Lutheran!
SECOND SERVANT: Before, when Deodat proposed to toast
    The Emperor's good health, it was all quiet.
WINE STEWARD: When drinking, much can happen, but a servant
    Who's proper must not lend an ear to this.
THIRD SERVANT (*aside to a fourth*):
    Pay close attention, John, we know that Father
    Quiroga will be glad to hear from us;
    He'll give indulgences for this, I'm sure.
FOURTH SERVANT: I'll go and place myself by Illo's chair
    So I can do whatever's to be done;
    It is astonishing the things he'll say.
                         (*Goes to the tables.*)
WINE STEWARD (*to Neumann*):
    Who is that dark man there who wears a cross
    And chats so intimately with Count Palfy?
NEUMANN: He's also one of those they trust too much;
    He's called Maradas, and he comes from Spain.
WINE STEWARD: The Spaniards are no use, I'll tell you that:
    The Latins are all good-for-nothing.
NEUMANN: Oh!
    You should not talk thus, Steward, for among
    Them are the foremost of the generals
    Who are considered by the Duke to be the best.
    (*Terzky comes and takes the paper; there is a stir at the tables.*)
WINE STEWARD (*to the servants*):
    The Major General stands up. Now watch!
    They're breaking up. Go quick and move their chairs!
    (*The servants hurry toward the rear. Some of the guests come forward.*)

Scene 6

Octavio Piccolomini converses with Maradas, and they position themselves front stage to one side of the proscenium. Max Piccolomini steps to the other side, alone, lost in thought and taking no part in the rest of the action. The space between, but a few steps

farther backstage, is occupied by Buttler, Isolani, Goetz, Tiefen-
bach, Collalto, and directly thereafter Count Terzky.

ISOLANI (*as the crowd comes forward*):
    Good night! —Good night, Colalto! —Major General,
    Good night! Perhaps I should have said, "Good morning."
GOETZ (*to Tiefenbach*): Well, Brother, what a meal!
TIEFENBACH: It was a royal feast!
GOETZ: The Countess knows
    The way. Her husband's mother taught her how,
    God rest her soul! She was a real housewife!
ISOLANI (*about to leave*):
    A light! A light!
TERZKY (*approaches Isolani with the document*):
                  Wait just a minute. There
    Is something here for you to sign.
ISOLANI: What e're
    You want me to. Just spare me reading it!
TERZKY: I will not bother you. It is the oath
    That you have heard. A few strokes of the pen!
        (*as Isolani hands the document on to Octavio*)
    Whoever's next. There is no order here.
    (*Octavio glances through the document with apparent*
    unconcern. Terzky watches him from the distance.)
GOETZ (*to Terzky*): Allow me, Count, to bid a fond farewell.
TERZKY: Don't hurry so—let's have a nightcap! —Hey!
                  (*to the servants*)
GOETZ: I'm in no shape.
TERZKY: A little game.
GOETZ: Excuse me!
TIEFENBACH (*sits down*):
    Forgive me, gentlemen, it's hard to stand.
TERZKY: Feel free to make yourself at home, Commander!
TIEFENBACH: My head is clear, my stomach feels just fine,
    My legs, however, will not carry me.
ISOLANI (*pointing to his portliness*):
    You've made the burden for them far too great.
    (*Octavio has signed and hands the document to Terzky, who*
    gives it to Isolani. He goes to the table to sign.)
TIEFENBACH: The war in Pomerania must take

The blame, when we were in the ice and snow,
I never will get over it, that's sure.

GOETZ: Those Swedes cared not a bit about the season.

(*Terzky hands the paper to Don Maradas; he goes to the table to sign.*)

OCTAVIO (*approaches Buttler*):
I've noticed, Colonel, that you do not like
The feast of Bacchus any more than I.
It seems to me you would prefer the roar
Of battle to a banquet such as this.

BUTTLER: I must admit this is not quite my style.

OCTAVIO (*confidentially, stepping closer*):
Nor is it mine, of that I can assure you.
I am delighted, Colonel Buttler, that
Our way of thinking is so similar.
A half a dozen friends at most who are
Relaxed around a little table with
A glass of Tokay wine, an open heart,
And rational discourse, that's what I love!

BUTTLER: Yes, if it can be had, I like that, too.

(*The paper is given to Buttler, who goes to the table to sign. The proscenium is empty, so that the two Piccolominis, each on a side, stand there alone.*)

OCTAVIO (*after contemplating his son from the distance in silence for a time draws a little nearer to him*):
You were a long time coming in, my friend.

MAX (*turns quickly, embarrassed*):
I—was detained a while by pressing business.

OCTAVIO: And as I see, you still are not quite here.

MAX: You know such crowds will always make me quiet.

OCTAVIO (*comes a little closer*):
I may not know what held you up so long?
(*cunningly*) —But Terzky knows it.

MAX: What does Terzky know?

OCTAVIO (*meaningfully*):
He was the only one who did not miss you.

ISOLANI (*who has watched from the distance, approaches*):
That's right, old father, take him by surprise
With not a place to hide. It is not fair.

TERZKY (*comes with the paper*):
Is no one missing here? Have you all signed?

OCTAVIO: They all are there.

TERZKY (*calling out*):　　　　Well? Who still has to sign?

BUTTLER (*to Terzky*):
　Just count and see if you have thirty names.

TERZKY: Here is an X.

TIEFENBACH:　　　　The X belongs to me.

ISOLANI (*to Terzky*):
　He cannot write, but still his X is good
　And it is honored by both Jew and Christian.

OCTAVIO (*urgently, to Max*):
　Let's leave together, Colonel. It is late.

TERZKY: *One* Piccolomini alone has signed.

ISOLANI (*pointing to Max*):
　Look here, we lack this guest, who's made of stone,
　Who has been useless to us this whole evening.
　(*Max takes the sheet from Terzky's hand and stares at it
　thoughtlessly.*)

Scene 7

*The former. Illo comes from the back room. He has the gold cup in
his hand and is very excited; Goetz and Buttler follow him and
attempt to hold him back.*

ILLO: Let go of me now!

GOETZ and BUTTLER:　　Don't drink any more!

ILLO (*goes up to Octavio and embraces him, drinking*):
　Octavio, I'm bringing this to you!
　We'll wash away old grudges with this drink
　Of union. You have never loved me, nor
　Have I loved you—God punish me— Let's let
　What's past be past! I value you immensely.
　(*kissing him repeatedly.*)
　I'll be your dearest friend and, so you'll know it,
　Whoever dares to say you are a snake
　Will have to deal with me.

TERZKY (*in an undertone*):　Are you insane?
　You must consider, Illo, where you are!

ILLO (*guilelessly*):
　What do you want? We here are all good friends.
　(*Contemplating the whole circle with a look of satisfaction.*)
　There's not a rogue among us. I am pleased.

TERZKY (*to Buttler, urgently*):
  Take him away with you, I beg you, Buttler!
  (*Buttler takes him to the serving table.*)
ISOLANI (*to Max, who has till now looked fixedly but without
  thought at the paper*):
  Is it not time? Have you not read enough?
MAX (*as if awakening from a dream*):
  What is it I should do?
TERZKY and ISOLANI (*together*): Just sign your name.
  (*Octavio can be seen looking at him anxiously.*)
MAX (*hands it back*):
  I'll leave it for tomorrow! I am in
  No mood for *business*. Send me it tomorrow!
TERZKY: You should consider that—
ISOLANI: Come on! Just sign!
  You are the youngest at the gathering
  And certainly you won't maintain that you
  Arc smarter than the rest of us! Your father
  Himself has signed it too; we all have signed.
TERZKY (*to Octavio*):
  Give him advice now! Use your influence!
OCTAVIO: My son's of age.
ILLO (*has placed the cup on the serving table*):
                          What is the talk about?
TERZKY: He has declined to sign the document.
MAX: I only said that it could wait till morning.
ILLO: It cannot wait. We all have signed the sheet,
  And you must sign it, too; you simply *must*.
MAX: Good night now, Illo.
ILLO: No, you won't escape.
  The Prince will find out who his true friends are.
  (*All the guests gather about the two of them.*)
MAX: What I think of the Duke is known to him.
  And to you all and does not need these antics.
ILLO: That is the thanks the Duke will get for it
  That he gave preference to all the Latins!
TERZKY (*in the greatest embarrassment, to the commanders who
  are making an uproar*):
  The wine is speaking! Pay no heed, I beg you!
ISOLANI (*laughs*):
  The wine is not at fault. He's simply babbling.

ILLO: Whoever is not *with* me is *against* me.
  These tender consciences! They need to have
  The comfort of a loophole, of a clause—
TERZKY (*breaks in quickly*): He's raving now, pay no attention to
  him.
ILLO (*shouting louder*):
  They can relieve their minds with this same clause.
  What clause is this? The devil take this clause—
MAX (*becomes attentive and reads the document again*):
  What can there be here that's so dangerous?
  You make me want to take a closer look.
TERZKY (*aside to Illo*): What is this, Illo? You will ruin us!
TIEFENBACH (*to Colalto*): They read it differently before we ate.
GOETZ: I thought so too.
ISOLANI: Well, what is that to me?
  Where others' names are, mine can also stand.
TIEFENBACH: Before, there was a certain reservation
  Concerning duty to the Emperor.
BUTTLER (*to one of the commanders*):
  For shame, sirs! Think about the main thing here!
  The question now is whether we should keep
  The General or let him take his leave.
  We should not be so strict or so exact.
ISOLANI (*to one of the generals*):
  So, did the Duke attach conditions, too,
  When he allotted you your regiment?
TERZKY (*to Goetz*): Or when to you he made delivery
  Well worth a thousand gold coins in a year.
ILLO: Scoundrels they are, who make us into rogues.
  Who is not satisfied may speak! I'm here!
TIEFENBACH: We only mentioned it.
MAX: (*has read the paper and gives it back*):
                              So, till tomorrow.
ILLO (*stammering with rage and not in control of himself
anymore, holds the paper toward him with one hand and holds
his sword before him with the other*):
  Write—Judas!
ISOLANI: No, Illo!
OCTAVIO, TERZKY, BUTTLER (*together*):
                    Swords away!
MAX (*grabs his arm quickly and disarms him, to Count Terzky*):
                    Put him to bed!

(*He exits. Illo, cursing and scolding, is restrained by some of the commanders. The curtain falls amidst general departure.*)

ACT V

A Room in Piccolomini's Apartment. It Is night.

Scene 1

Octavio Piccolomini. A personal servant is lighting his way. Shortly thereafter, Max Piccolomini.

OCTAVIO: The minute that my son arrives, send him
  To me. What is the hour?
SERVANT: It's almost dawn.
OCTAVIO: Just leave your candle here. —We will not go
  To bed tonight, but you are free to leave.
  (*The servant exits. Octavio wanders meditatively around the room. Max Piccolomini enters, is not noticed by him right away, and looks at him for a few moments in silence.*)
MAX: You're mad at me, Octavio. God knows,
  I'm not the one who caused that hateful fight.
  —And certainly I saw that you had signed,
  What *you* approve of, that should be for me
  Agreeable—but still—you know—I must
  Behave according to my lights and not
  Another's in such matters.
OCTAVIO (*goes to him and embraces him*): Follow them,
  My dearest son! They guided you far better
  Than the example of your father did.
MAX: Explain yourself more clearly!
OCTAVIO: That I will;
  For after what occurred there, we must not
  Keep secrets from each other anymore.
  (*after they both are seated*)
  Max, tell me what you think about the pledge
  That was presented for our signatures.
MAX: It's something harmless, as I look at it,
  Although I hate formalities like that.
OCTAVIO: There was no other reason then that you
  Refused to sign when they would force you to?
MAX: The thing was serious—I was distracted—

The situation did not seem so urgent—
OCTAVIO: Be honest. No suspicion crossed your mind?
MAX: Why be suspicious! No, not in the slightest.
OCTAVIO: Then thank your angel, Piccolomini,
  He saved you, unaware, from the abyss.
MAX: I don't know what you mean.
OCTAVIO: I will explain:
  They wanted you to sully your good name
  And, with a knavish trick, make you renounce
  With one stroke of the pen your oath and duty.
MAX (*rises*): Octavio!
OCTAVIO: Just keep your seat! You have
  A lot to hear from me; you have for years
  Been living in incredible delusion.
  The blackest plot develops here before
  Your eyes; the power of the devil is
  Enveloping the brightness of your mind.
  I can be still no longer. I must take
  The blindfold from your eyes.
MAX: Before you speak,
  Consider well! If suppositions are
  What you will talk about—and I'm afraid
  It's nothing more—then save it. I
  Am not prepared to hear it quietly.
OCTAVIO: However great your reason not to hear,
  So much the greater mine is to explain.
  Before, I could quite calmly trust you to
  Your inborn judgment in your innocence;
  But now I see a snare made ready for
  Your heart that could be fatal—thus the secret
                    (*staring at him fixedly*)
  That *you* conceal makes me reveal *my own*.
  (*Max attempts to answer, falters, and drops his eyes in*
  embarrassment.)
OCTAVIO (*after a pause*):
  Then be aware! They are deceiving you—
  Play shamefully with you and with us all.
  The Duke pretends that he is planning to
  Forsake the army, while in this same hour
  Arrangements are begun to *steal* it from
  The Emperor and hand it to our foe!

MAX: I know this fairy tale told by the priests
    But hardly thought to hear it from your mouth.
OCTAVIO: The mouth from which you hear it presently
    Will guarantee it is no fairy tale.
MAX: What kind of madman would that make the Duke!
    If he imagined that he could entice
    These thirty-thousand seasoned troops, among
    Their leaders, too, a thousand noblemen,
    To break their oaths and leave their duty and
    Their honor to join in a villainy.
OCTAVIO: It's nothing so disgraceful and so vile
    That he desires—and what he wants from us
    Can bear a name that is more innocent.
    His wish is but to give the Empire peace;
    And since the Emperor disdains *this* peace,
    He wants to *force* him—force *him*—to accept it!
    He wants all parties to be satisfied,
    And in exchange for all his pains he wants
    To keep Bohemia, which he now holds.
MAX: Octavio, has he deserved it that
    We—*we*—should think so shamefully of him?
OCTAVIO: We are not talking about what we think.
    The facts speak here, the clearest evidence.
    My son, you are not unaware how bad
    Things stand for us at court—but you have no
    Idea of the intrigue and deceit
    That they are practicing to sow the seeds
    Of mutiny in camp. Unraveled are
    The ties that fasten to the Emperor
    Each officer and intimately bind
    Each simple soldier to civilian life.
    So, lacking law and duty, he is placed
    In opposition to the state he should
    Protect, about to turn the sword against it.
    It has progressed so far that at this time
    The Emperor is trembling out of fear
    Of his own army—is afraid to find
    The traitor's knife within the city, yes,
    Within the castle, stands prepared to save
    By flight his fragile grandsons—not from Swedes
    Or from the Lutherans but from his own troops.

MAX: That is enough! You shock and frighten me;
  For one may tremble from unfounded fears,
  But fake delusions can cause true misfortune.
OCTAVIO: It's no delusion. Civil war, the most
  Unnatural of all, is sure to come,
  If we do not go swiftly to the rescue.
  Commanding officers have all been bought;
  The loyalty of their subordinates
  Is wavering, as are whole regiments.
  The strongholds are assigned to foreigners;
  To Schafgotsch, that suspicious man, they have
  Entrusted all Silesia's troops and to
  Count Terzky five whole regiments on horse
  And foot; to Illo, Kinsky, Buttler, and
  To Isolan are handed all the best.
MAX: And to us, too.
OCTAVIO: Because they think they'll get us
  And plan to lure us with great promises.
  He's given me the principalities
  Of Glatz and Sagan, and I see the hook
  With which he means to catch you.
MAX: No! Oh, no,
  I tell you, no!
OCTAVIO: Just open up your eyes!
  What was the reason, do you think, that we
  Were called to Pilsen? To confer with us?
  Since when did Friedland need advice from us?
  We have been called here so we can be bought.
  If we refuse—we will remain here hostage.
  That is the reason Gallas stayed away,
  And you would not behold your father here,
  If higher duties did not hold him fast.
MAX: He's made no secret of it that we have
  Been called on his account—confesses that
  He needs our help now to maintain himself.
  He did so much for us, it is our duty
  To do what we can do for him.
OCTAVIO: So do
  You know what he would have us do for him—
  What Illo's drunken state betrayed to you?
  Consider what you heard and what you saw!

Does not the falseness of that document,
That very crucial clause that was left out,
Make clear that we are wanted for no good?
MAX: Tonight what happened with that document
Seems nothing but a wretched prank performed
By Illo. Such connivers as he is
Are always driven to extremities.
They see the Duke has broken with the court,
And they imagine that they're serving him,
If they enlarge the break till it cannot
Be healed. The Duke, I'm sure, knows nothing of it.
OCTAVIO: It pains me that I have to ruin your
Good faith in him, which seems so firmly based.
Still I cannot afford consideration—
You must take steps, and quickly; you must act.
—I will confess to you—that everything
I have confided to you now, that seemed
So unbelievable, I have it from
His own—the Prince's—mouth.
MAX (*with intense emotion*): That cannot be!
OCTAVIO: Yes, he confided in me—what I had
In other ways discovered long before—
That he would join the Swedes and at the head
Of a united army he would force
The Emperor—
MAX: He is impetuous,
The court offended him most grievously;
And in an angry moment—that may be—
He might quite easily forget himself.
OCTAVIO: He lacked all feeling when he told me this;
Because he saw my stupefaction but
Just thought I was afraid, he showed me letters
In confidence that came from Swedes and Saxons
Extending him the hope of certain help.
MAX: It cannot be! can *not* be! *can* not be!
You see that it cannot. You certainly
Would have been forced to show him your disgust.
He would have let you counsel him or else
You would not stand here living by my side!
OCTAVIO: Of course, I mentioned that I had my doubts.
Attempted to dissuade him earnestly;

—But my disgust, my innermost conviction,
I kept completely hidden.

MAX: How could you
Be so deceitful? That does not seem like
My father! I did not believe your words
When you spoke evil of *him;* how much less
Can I believe it when you wrong yourself.

OCTAVIO: I did not force my way into his secret.

MAX: His confidence deserved sincerity.

OCTAVIO: He was no longer worthy of the truth.

MAX: Less worthy of you was your own deceit.

OCTAVIO: Dear son, it is not always possible
In life to keep oneself so pure and childlike
The way our inner voices try to teach.
In constant self-defense against each trick
The honest heart itself does not stay true.
And there you have the curse of evil deeds,
That they continually create more evil.
I do not quibble here, I do my duty;
The Emperor dictates my conduct for me.
It would, of course, be better to obey
One's heart in everything, but one would be
Deprived that way of many good designs.
My aim here is to serve the Emperor,
No matter what my heart may say to it.

MAX: I cannot grasp you, cannot understand.
The Duke most honestly disclosed to you
His thoughts, which had a bad intent, and *you*
Claim to betray him with a good intent!
Desist, I beg you! —You have not deprived
Me of my friend! —May I not lose a father!

OCTAVIO (*suppresses his emotion*):
You do not know it all, my son! I still
Have something to reveal.

(*after a pause*)
                    The Duke of Friedland
Has made his preparations. He relies
Upon his stars. He thinks he will attack
Us unprepared—and with a hand that's sure
He thinks he has already grasped the crown.
He is mistaken—we have acted, too.

He'll grasp his evil, secret fate alone.

MAX: O Father, nothing rash! By all that's good,
Let me implore you! Take no hasty steps!

OCTAVIO: He crept in silence on this evil path;
So silently revenge crept slyly after him.
It stands unseen and ready, threatening behind him;
Just one step more and with a shudder he will touch it.
—You saw that Questenberg was here with me,
So far you only know his public face—
He brought a secret with him, when he came,
For me alone.

MAX: So—may I know it?

OCTAVIO: Max!
—I place the welfare of the Empire, yes,
Your father's life with these words in your hands.
You cherish Wallenstein deep in your heart;
The strongest bonds of love and of respect
Have joined you to him since your early youth.
You hold the hope—now I anticipate
The trust you hesitate to give to me—
You nourish the desire that you will be
Much closer.

MAX: Father—

OCTAVIO: I can trust your heart,
But am I certain of your self-control?
Will you be able to appear before
This man with face composed when I have told
You of his destiny in confidence?

MAX: When you confide in me about his guilt!
Octavio takes a paper out of his case and hands it to him.

MAX: What's this? A letter from the Emperor!

OCTAVIO: Now read!

MAX (*after he has cast a glance at it*):
                    The Duke is judged and is condemned!

OCTAVIO: That's so.

MAX: Oh, that goes far! Unhappy error!

OCTAVIO: Read on. Compose yourself!

MAX (*after he has read farther, with a look of astonishment at his
father*):
                              What's this? You are—

OCTAVIO: Just for the moment—and until the King

Of Hungary can come to join the army
The full command is given *me*—
Max: And do you think that you can snatch it from him?
You cannot think that—Father! Father! Father!
This charge you've taken is calamitous.
This paper here—you plan to make it valid?
Disarm the mighty in the middle of
His army with his multitudes around?
I know that you are lost—that we all are!
Octavio: I know what I must risk in doing this.
I rest in the Almighty's hand; He will
Protect the Emperor's most pious house;
He will demolish what the night has wrought.
The Emperor has loyal servants still.
In camp there are good men enough who will
Most cheerfully defend a cause that's good.
The faithful have been warned, the others watched;
I wait for his first move that I, at once—
Max: On only a suspicion you will act?
Octavio: The Emperor loves not the ways of tyrants!
The deed—not the intent—is what he'll punish.
The Duke still holds his own fate in his hands—
And if he does not carry out these crimes,
Then he will be relieved of his command;
He'll yield it to his Emperor's own son.
An honorable exile in his castles
Will be more kindness than a punishment.
However, should he make one open move—
Max: What would you think was such a move? He will
Not ever make a bad one, but you could
(As you have done) mistake a harmless one.
Octavio: However culpable the Prince's aims,
The steps that he has taken openly
Allowed a liberal interpretation.
I do not mean to use this sheet until
A deed is done that unequivocally
Attests to his high treason and condemns him.
Max: And who will be the judge of that?
Octavio: —You shall.
Max: Then you will never need this sheet at all.
I have your word on that: you will not act

Until I am myself convinced of it.

OCTAVIO: How can this be? Now—after all you know
  Can you still think that he is innocent?

MAX (*briskly*): Your judgment can be wrong, but not my heart.
               (*continuing, more temperately*)
  His mind cannot be grasped like every other.
  Just as he ties his fortune to the stars,
  So he is like them, too, in their most splendid,
  Mysterious, uncomprehended course.
  Believe me that you do him wrong. But all
  Will be resolved, and we will see him, pure
  And brilliant, wholly cleared of this suspicion.

OCTAVIO: I'll wait and see.

Scene 2

The former. The servant. Shortly thereafter, a courier.

OCTAVIO: What is it?

SERVANT: There's a courier to see you.

OCTAVIO: So early in the day! Where is he from?

SERVANT: He didn't want to tell me.

OCTAVIO: Bid him come in! Let no one know about him!
           (*Servant exits. Cornet enters.*)
  It's you, Cornet? You bring a letter from
  Count Gallas? Give it here!

CORNET: It is not written.
  He could not be so sure.

OCTAVIO: What is it then?

CORNET: He says to tell you— Am I free to speak?

OCTAVIO: My son knows all.

CORNET: We have him.

OCTAVIO: We have whom?

CORNET: His mediator! Sesin!

OCTAVIO (*quickly*):   And he's yours?

CORNET: In the Bohemian Woods two days ago
  By Captain Mohrbrand he was caught as he
  Left Regensburg for Sweden with dispatches.

OCTAVIO: And the dispatches—

CORNET: Were at once sent with
  The captive to Vienna by the General.

OCTAVIO: At last! At last! Oh, that is splendid news!
  For us *that* man will be a precious vessel
  That holds important things. —Did they find much?
CORNET: Six packets that were marked with Terzky's arms.
OCTAVIO: None in the Prince's hand?
CORNET: Not that I heard.
OCTAVIO: What of Sesin?
CORNET: He acted terrified
  When told that they would take him to Vienna.
  Count Altringer encouraged him, if he
  Would freely tell them everything he knew.
OCTAVIO: Is Altringer there with your lord? I heard
  That he was sick at Linz.
CORNET: Three days ago
  At Frauenberg he joined the General.
  That's sixty squads they have together now,
  Selected troops, and they want you to know
  That they are only waiting for your orders.
OCTAVIO: In just a few days very much may happen.
  When must you leave?
CORNET: I wait for your command.
OCTAVIO: Remain till dark!
CORNET: Good. (*is about to leave*)
OCTAVIO: No one saw you here?
CORNET: Not anyone. The Capuchins allowed
  Me to go through their little gate as always.
OCTAVIO: Go rest yourself and keep yourself concealed!
  Before it's night, I think I will dispatch you.
  Our business here approaches resolution.
  Before the day that in the heavens now
  So ominously dawns has passed away,
  A most decisive lot will have been drawn.
                    (*Cornet exits.*)

Scene 3

The two Piccolominis.

OCTAVIO: And now, my son? Now all will soon be clear,
  —For everything, I know, went through Sesin.
MAX (*who has been involved in a fierce inner struggle throughout the whole last scene, resolved*):

I'll take a shorter way to find the light.
Farewell!

OCTAVIO: Where? What?

MAX: I'll ask the Duke.

OCTAVIO (*alarmed*):   What's that?

MAX (*returning*): If you believed that I would play a role
  In your charade, then you miscalculated
  Concerning me. My course must be direct.
  I cannot be sincere in what I say
  And in my heart be false—not see that he
  Has confidence in me, his friend, and soothe
  My conscience with the thought he takes the risk
  Upon *himself* that I have not deceived him.
  What I am taken for, that I must be.
  —I go now to the Duke. Today I will
  Demand that he preserve his reputation
  Before the world, with one straightforward step
  To tear apart the web you have contrived.

OCTAVIO: You will do that?

MAX: I will. You need not doubt it!

OCTAVIO: I have miscalculated in you, yes.
  I thought I had a prudent son who would
  Heap blessings on me for my charity
  In drawing him away from the abyss—
  I find instead he is infatuated,
  Two eyes make him a fool and passion blinds
  So that in brightest day he cannot see.
  Go ask him! Go! Be indiscreet enough,
  Expose the secret of your father, of
  Your Emperor to him. Compel me to
  A public break with him before it's time!
  And now when Heaven, with a miracle,
  Protected till today my secret deeds
  And lulled suspicion's penetrating glance,
  I will be witness to it that my son
  Will rashly and insanely undertake
  To nullify the toil of statesmanship.

MAX: This statesmanship! profoundly I would curse it!
  You yet will drive him with your statesmanship
  To take this step; indeed, you could, because
  You *want* him to be guilty, *make* him guilty.
  Oh, that will never turn out well—whate'er

The end may be, this but forebodes the quick
Approach of a disastrous resolution.
This regal personage, if he succumbs,
Will rend the world around him in his fall,
And like a ship that suddenly, while in
The middle of the ocean, catches fire,
Explodes, and sends the men who were on board
Abruptly flying between heaven and earth,
Those of us who were bound to his success
He'll pull down with him in his headlong fall.
　　Look on it as you will, but grant to me
That I conduct myself in my own way.
Untarnished I will keep it between him
And me. It must be clear 'ere this day's end
If I shall lose a father or a friend.
　　　　　　　　(As he exits, the curtain falls.)

Wallenstein's Death

In Five Acts

CHARACTERS

WALLENSTEIN
OCTAVIO PICCOLOMINI
MAX PICCOLOMINI
TERZKY
ILLO
ISOLANI
BUTTLER
CAVALRY CAPTAIN NEUMANN
AN ADJUTANT
COLONEL WRANGEL, sent by the Swedes
GORDON, commandant of Eger
MAJOR GERALDIN
DEVEROUX ⎱
MACDONALD ⎰ Captains in Wallenstein's army
A SWEDISH CAPTAIN
A LEGATION OF CUIRASSIERS
MAYOR OF EGER
SENI
DUCHESS OF FRIEDLAND
COUNTESS TERZKY
THEKLA
LADY NEUBRUNN, lady-in-waiting ⎱
VON ROSENBERG, stable master ⎰   to the Princess
DRAGOONS
SERVANTS, PAGES, COMMONERS

The scene in the first three acts takes place in Pilsen, in the last two in Eger.

ACT I

A room furnished for astrological observation, supplied with globes, maps, quadrants, and other astrological instruments. A curtain has been opened that hangs in front of a rotunda in which the representations of the seven planets, each in a niche and strangely illuminated, can be seen. Seni observes the stars, Wallenstein stands in front of a large, black chart on which the aspects of the planets are drawn.

Scene 1

Wallenstein, Seni.

WALLENSTEIN: We'll let it be now, Seni. Come on down.
 The day begins to break. Mars rules the hour.
 It does no good to study anymore.
 We know enough.
SENI: Just let me look at Venus
 Awhile, Your Highness. Even now she rises.
 She shines just like a sun there in the east.
WALLENSTEIN: She is as close as she will come to earth.
 Her influence is felt in all its strength.
     (*observing the figures on the chart*)
 Most happy aspect! Finally we see
 The regal three stand fatefully together,
 And both the stars there are beneficent,
 Both Jupiter and Venus take the spiteful,
 Malicious Mars between them and compel
 That troublemaker to come to my aid;
 For he has long been hostilely inclined
 And shot, sometimes in quadrature and in
 Conjunction sometimes and oblique or straight,
 Onto my planets with his crimson fire,
 Disturbing their auspicious energy.
 Now they have overcome the ancient foe
 And bring him to me as a prisoner.
SENI: What's more, the two great lumina are not
 Unsettled by malefic aspects. Saturn,
 Disarmed, stands harmless *in cadente domo*.
WALLENSTEIN: Now Saturn's reign is over, he who rules
 The things that grow within the bosom of

The earth and in the depths of man's emotions
And governs everything that shuns the light.
No time is there to speculate and plan,
For Jupiter, the shining one, now reigns
And draws that deed, so darkly undertaken,
By force into the land of light. —Now we
Must act with swiftness and before that shape
Of fortune soars away above my head,
For constantly the vault of heaven changes.

(*There is a knock at the door.*)

A knock. Who is it?

TERZKY (*outside*):   Let me in!

WALLENSTEIN: It's Terzky.
What is so urgent? We are busy here.

TERZKY (*outside*): Put everything aside, I beg of you!
This cannot wait.

WALLENSTEIN: Go, Seni, let him in!

(*As Seni admits Terzky, Wallenstein draws the curtain in front of the figures. Seni exits.*)

Scene 2

Wallenstein, Count Terzky.

TERZKY (*enters*): You haven't heard? He has been taken captive,
Is handed to the Emperor by Gallas!

WALLENSTEIN (*to Terzky*):
Who's taken captive? Who is handed over?

TERZKY: The one who knows our secrets, knows about
All our discussions with the Swedes and Saxons,
And through whose hands our business all has gone—

WALLENSTEIN (*recoils*):
It's not Sesin? Tell me it is not he!

TERZKY: As he advanced toward Regensburg to see
The Swedes, a man sent there by Gallas, who
Had long been on his trail, took hold of him.
My packets sent to Kinsky and to Thurn,
To Oxenstirn, to Arnheim he was holding.
All that is in their hands, and now they have
Intelligence about all that has happened.

Scene 3

The former. Illo enters.

ILLO (*to Terzky*): You've told him?
TERZKY: Yes, he knows.
ILLO (*to Wallenstein*):   Do you suppose
  You can still make peace with the Emperor,
  Restore his faith in you? And even if
  You wanted to abandon all your plans,
  They know what you intended. You must go
  Ahead, for now you know you can't retreat.
TERZKY: They hold the documents against us and
  In handwriting that shows without a doubt—
WALLENSTEIN: Not in my hand. I give the lie to that.
ILLO: So do you really think what Terzky here
  Has been negotiating in your name
  Will not be charged by them to *your* account?
  You think the Swedes should take *his* word for yours
  And those who hate you in Vienna won't?
TERZKY: You gave me nothing written, but just think
  How far you went when speaking with Sesin!
  Will he keep still? If with your secret he
  Thinks he can save himself, will he preserve it?
ILLO: You didn't think of that yourself! Well, now
  They've been informed just how far you have gone,
  Say, what do you expect? You are no longer
  Secure in your command, but you are lost
  And past all help if you resign it now.
WALLENSTEIN: The army is my guarantee. The army
  Will not forsake me. So whatever they
  May know, the might is mine; they'll swallow that.
  —And if I place security for my
  Good faith, then they must surely be content.
ILLO: The army is still yours; now for the moment
  It is still yours; but you must fear the slow,
  The quiet might of time! The favor of
  Your troops protects you still today and on
  The morrow; but if you allow them time,
  Then unobserved they will corrupt the good
  Opinion on which you have placed your faith,

First one and then another slyly steal—
And when the mighty earthquake comes to pass,
The faithless, rotten structure falls apart.

WALLENSTEIN: It is unlucky chance!

ILLO: Oh, I would like to say that it is lucky,
  If it has the desired effect on you
  And causes you to act. —The Swedish colonel—

WALLENSTEIN: Has he arrived? Do you know what he brings?

ILLO: He only wants to talk to you alone.

WALLENSTEIN: Unlucky, yes, unlucky chance. —Indeed!
  Sesin—he knows too much and won't keep still.

TERZKY: He is a rebel from Bohemia,
  He's forfeited his neck, and if he can
  Save his own skin at your expense, will he
  Think twice? And if they put him to the torture,
  Will he, already weak, possess the strength?—

WALLENSTEIN (*lost in contemplation*):
  Their faith in me cannot be reestablished.
  It does not matter what I do, I will
  Remain for them a traitor to my country;
  And even if I should return to do
  My duty, honor bound, it would not help.—

ILLO: It would destroy you, for not loyalty
  But impotence is what they'll say it is.

WALLENSTEIN (*walking back and forth in severe agitation*):
  So! Shall I now in earnest have to do
  The things I only played with in my thoughts?
  Then cursed be he who trifles with the devil!—

ILLO: If this has been a game to you, I think
  That you will pay for it in deadly earnest.

WALLENSTEIN: If I must bring it to fulfillment, now,
  Now, while the strength is mine, it must be done.

ILLO: Before they have deliberated in
  Vienna and can get ahead of you—

WALLENSTEIN (*examining the signatures*):
  I have the pledges of these generals—
  Max Piccolomini is missing here.

TERZKY: It was—he thought—

ILLO: He thought, in his conceit,
  It was not needed between you and him.

WALLENSTEIN: It is not needed; he is right.—

The regiments don't want to go to Flanders,
So they have sent a paper to me, which
Speaks loudly for opposing the command.
The first step toward revolt has taken place.
ILLO: Believe me, you will find it easier
To lead them to our foe than to the Spaniards.
WALLENSTEIN: I want to hear now what the Swede has got
To say to me.
ILLO (*hurriedly*): You want to call him, Terzky?
He's just outside.
WALLENSTEIN: Wait just a little while!
I have been taken unawares—it came
Too fast—I am not used to having chance
Control me blindly, darkly lead me on.
ILLO: Just hear the man for now! Consider later!
(*They exit.*)

Scene 4

WALLENSTEIN (*talking to himself*):
Could this be true? Can I no longer act
As I would choose? no longer can turn back?
I must *complete* the deed because I *thought* it—
Did not dismiss temptation—and supplying
My heart with such a dream and, saving means
To reach a goal I was not certain of,
Had only meant to keep that doorway open?—
By that great God of Heaven! I was not
In earnest, it was never my resolve.
The fancy pleased me only in my mind;
'Twas freedom charmed me, possibility.
Was it so wrong in my imagination
To trifle with the hope of being king?
Was not my will here in my breast still free;
Could I not see the true path to the side,
Where my return was always kept secure?
Then where am I so suddenly conveyed?
My tracks are gone behind me, and a wall
Has been created by what I have done
That, towering, prevents my turning 'round.
(*He halts pensively.*)

I seem so guilty and I cannot shift
The guilt away, no matter how I try;
My ambiguity accuses me;
And though my deed comes from the purest source,
Suspicion lends a bad interpretation.
If I were what they take me for—a traitor—
Would I not strive to keep up a pretense,
Would I not pull a veil tight around me
And never show displeasure? Since I knew
The innocence of my intentions, I
Indulged my frame of mind, gave passion room—
My words were bold because they were not deeds.
But now with hindsight they will take as planned
What, lacking any plan, I perpetrated,
And those things I allowed myself to say
From anger or a surfeit of emotion
They'll make into an artificial fabric
From which they can create an accusation.
By which I am made speechless. Thus I have
Become entangled in a net I made,
And only deeds of violence can free me.
                    (*pausing again*)
How different when courageous impulse drove
Me to bold deeds that now necessity,
Self-preservation, will demand of me!
The aspect of necessity is grave.
The hand of man will never reach without
A shudder into fate's mysterious urn.
While in my breast, my deed was only mine;
But once released from that safeguarded nook
Within my heart that was its native soil,
Delivered to the foreign realm of life,
It then belonged to those malicious powers
That no man's skill can make him privy to.
(*He strides about the room with vehement steps, then he halts
again pensively.*)
And what was the beginning? Do you know
In honesty yourself? You want to shake
That might that safely and securely rules,
That in deep-rooted, sanctified possession
Rests firmly anchored in the common use,

That is attached with myriad stubborn roots
To what the people have believed since childhood.
This is not strength here striving against strength,
That would not frighten me. I'd challenge each
Opponent I can fix my eyes upon,
Who, full of courage, makes me bolder yet.
I fear the enemy I cannot see,
That can oppose me from within the breast
Of men where cowards' fears make me afraid.
Not what proclaims itself as powerful
Is dangerous and fearful, but instead
That which is common, the eternity
Of yesterday, which always was and will
Tomorrow be because it was today!
For from the commonplace mankind is made,
And in his cradle custom is his nursemaid;
So woe betide him who would touch those things
His ancestors have left behind for him!
The *years* exert a sanctifying strength;
As gray is for old age, so it is holy.
Be in possession and you're in the right
And solemnly the crowd will guard it for you.
                    (*to the page who enters*)
The Swedish colonel? Well, let him come in!
(*The page exits. Wallenstein fixes his gaze reflectively on the door.*)
It is still pure. The crime has not gone past
This doorstep—yet. —The border that divides
The two paths that a life can take is fine.

Scene 5

Wallenstein and Wrangel.

WALLENSTEIN (*after he has fixed him with a searching glance*):
Your name is Wrangel?
WRANGEL: Gustav Wrangel, colonel
Of Südermannland's fine Blue Regiment.
WALLENSTEIN: It was a Wrangel who at Stralsund caused
Me much displeasure, for his bold defense
Of it was why the seaport could resist me.
WRANGEL: The credit should go to the elements

With which you fought and not to me! The storm's
Authority defended it. Not just
One master should control both land and sea.

WALLENSTEIN: You tore the admiral's hat off of my head.

WRANGEL: I come to place a crown upon it now.

WALLENSTEIN (*motions to him to sit down and does likewise
    himself*):
You have been given full authority?

WRANGEL (*reflectively*):
There are so many questions to resolve—

WALLENSTEIN (*after he has finished reading*):
This letter is well done. It is a smart
And prudent man whom you are serving, Wrangel.
The chancellor has written that he will
Fulfill the dead king's own intent to help
Me win the crown and rule Bohemia.

WRANGEL: He speaks the truth. The late departed thought
Most highly of Your Grace's excellent
Intelligence and gifts of strategy
And liked to say that he who understood
The way to rule would ruler be and king.

WALLENSTEIN: That he might say.
                (*grasping his hand familiarly*)
In frankness, Colonel Wrangel—I was ever
Within my heart a Swede—at Nuremburg
And in Silesia you learned that well.
I had you often in my power and let
You always slip through some back door. That is
What in Vienna they cannot forgive;
It is what drives me to this step. —And since
Our mutual advantage will be served,
Let's also place our confidence in one
Another now.

WRANGEL: The confidence will come
As soon as each of us can feel secure.

WALLENSTEIN: The chancellor, I notice, does not trust
Me yet. I will admit—the game is not
Entirely in my favor. He believes
If with the Emperor who is my lord
I'd play this game, it's possible I'd do
It with the enemy, and *one* would be

Forgiven me as likely as the *other*.
Is that not what you think, too, Colonel Wrangel?
WRANGEL: I have a job to do and no opinion.
WALLENSTEIN: The Emperor has driven me to this
  Extremity. I can no longer serve him.
  For my security, in self-defense,
  I take a step my consciousness reproves.
WRANGEL: I can believe it. No one goes so far
  Unless he must.

(after a pause)
What Your Magnificence
Is moved to do against your Emperor
Is not for us to judge or to explain.
The Swede is fighting for his own good cause
With his good sword as well as his good conscience.
The circumstances of this opportunity
Are in our favor, and in war we take,
Unhesitating, all advantages;
And if the matter goes as we would wish—
WALLENSTEIN: What are you doubtful of? Of my intentions
  Or of my strength? I told the chancellor
  If he entrusted sixteen-thousand men
  To me, I'd match with eighteen thousand of
  The Emperor's—
WRANGEL: Your Grace is known to be
  The prince of warriors and you are hailed
  As an Attila and a second Pyrrhus.
  How you called forth an army years ago
  From nothing—it was inconceivable—
  And still—
WALLENSTEIN: And still?
WRANGEL: His Honor seems to think
  That it might be far easier to put
  An army in the field of sixty thousand
  Than cause a sixtieth of these—

(He pauses.)
WALLENSTEIN: Well, what?
  Just out with it!
WRANGEL: To alter their allegiance.
WALLENSTEIN: He thinks that? Well, he's thinking like a Swede
  And like a Protestant. You Lutherans are

In combat for your Bible and your cause;
You march behind your flag with your whole heart,
If one of *you* should join the enemy,
He'd have two masters he would have to break with.
There is no question of such things with us.
WRANGEL: Lord God in Heaven! Have you in this place
　No homeland, then, no fireside, and no church?
WALLENSTEIN: I'll tell you how that is with us—indeed,
　The Austrian—he *has* a fatherland
　And loves it and has reason, too, to love it.
　This host that calls itself imperial,
　That's quartered in Bohemia, has none;
　It is instead the refuse, the abandoned,
　Discarded men from other lands, and they
　Own nothing but the sun. And this land here,
　Bohemia, which we are fighting for,
　Lacks feeling for its Lord to whom it was
　Delivered by the sword and not by choice.
　They grumble at the tyranny of faith,
　Controlled by terror, they are not subdued.
　A glowing, vengeful souvenir lives on,
　The outrage that occurred upon this soil.
　How can a son forget that his own father
　Was forced to go to mass by packs of dogs?
　A people to whom *this* is done are dreadful
　Both if they take revenge or if they bear it.
WRANGEL: What of the nobles and the officers?
　For treason and such felonies as these
　Possess no precedent in world history.
WALLENSTEIN: Without condition they belong to me,
　You need not take my word; believe your eyes.
(*He gives him the paper with the oath. Wrangel reads it and then puts it on the table in silence.*)
　You understand now?
WRANGEL:　　　　　　　Who could understand?
　Well, Prince! I'll drop pretenses, for I have
　The full authority to make agreements.
　The Count is but a four days' march from here
　With fifteen-thousand men; he only waits
　For orders that he join his force with yours.
　These I will issue when we are agreed.

WALLENSTEIN: What does the Chancellor demand?
WRANGEL (*thoughtfully*):
  It means twelve regiments of Swedish troops.
  My head must answer for them. Everything
  Could be a trick.
WALLENSTEIN (*flaring up*): What, Swede!
WRANGEL (*continuing calmly*):   I must, therefore,
  Insist upon it that Duke Friedland break
  Irrevocably with the Emperor;
  For otherwise the Swedes will never trust him.
WALLENSTEIN: What is it you demand? Be short and sweet!
WRANGEL: Disarm the Spanish regiments that are
  Devoted to the Emperor, take Prague
  And yield that city and the Castle Eger
  As well to Swedish troops.
WALLENSTEIN: That is a lot!
  And Prague! Yield Eger maybe! Never Prague.
  I'll give you every guarantee that you
  Could ever rationally ask of me.
  But Prague—Bohemia—I'll guard myself.
WRANGEL: We do not doubt it. But for us it is
  Not only for defense. We do not want
  To have expended vainly men and money.
WALLENSTEIN: That's fair.
WRANGEL: And so until we are repaid,
  Prague stays a pledge.
WALLENSTEIN: You trust us then so little?
WRANGEL (*rises*):
  The Swede must be on guard against the German.
  They called us here across the Baltic Sea,
  We saved the Empire from complete destruction,
  And with our blood we sealed the freedom of
  Belief, the holy teachings of the Gospels.
  But now already they begin to feel
  The burden only, not the benefit.
  They look askance at all these foreigners
  And with a little money they would gladly
  Return us to our forests. No! We have
  Not left our king upon the battlefield
  For Judas money, tinkling gold and silver!
  The blood here shed by many noble Swedes,

That did not flow to bring us gold and silver!
And not with scanty laurels will we go
Back to our Fatherland, our pennons flying;
We will be *citizens* here on this ground
Where our king, falling, was a conqueror.

WALLENSTEIN: If you will help me hold our enemy,
　You will not lose the lovely borderland.

WRANGEL: And when our common enemy is crushed,
　What will then hold together our new friendship?
　We know, Duke—though the Swedes are not supposed—
　To know—you are negotiating with
　The Saxons now. What is our guarantee
　We won't be victim to these resolutions
　That you were careful to conceal from us?

WALLENSTEIN: The chancellor has chosen his man well,
　He could not send a more tenacious one.
　(*Rises*)
　Well, Gustav Wrangel, you must change your mind!
　No more of Prague!

WRANGEL:　　　　　My power ends with this.

WALLENSTEIN: Give up my capital! First I would go
　Back—to my Emperor.

WRANGEL:　　　　　　If there is time.

WALLENSTEIN: That still depends on me, now, at this hour.

WRANGEL: Some days ago perhaps, but not today
　—Not since Sesin was taken prisoner.
　　　　　(*as Wallenstein, taken aback, remains silent*)
　We think that you will act with honor, Duke;
　Since *yesterday* we're certain of it. —Now
　This paper guaranteeing us the *troops*
　Will not cause us to lose our confidence.
　We will not quarrel over Prague. The Old
　Town will suffice the Chancellor, and he
　Will let you keep the Radschin and the Small Side.
　But Eger must, above all, open to us
　Before we can begin to talk of union.

WALLENSTEIN: So, I should trust *you,* but you won't trust me?
　I'll have to think about your proposition.

WRANGEL: Don't take too long, for it has been more than
　A year we've carried on negotiations.
　If nothing happens now, the Chancellor

Considers them once and for all concluded.
WALLENSTEIN: You're pressing me too much. A step like this
Takes thought.
WRANGEL: Don't even think about it, Sir,
At all. It needs quick action to succeed.

(*He exits.*)

Scene 6

Wallenstein. Terzky and Illo return.

ILLO: You've settled it?
TERZKY: Are you agreed?
ILLO: The Swede
Went off quite satisfied. Yes, you've agreed.
WALLENSTEIN: Now, wait! It has not happened, and I think
That I would rather it did not.
TERZKY: What's that?
WALLENSTEIN: To function at the mercy of this Swede,
A man so arrogant? I could not bear it.
ILLO: Are you a fugitive who begs for help?
You bring them more than you will get from them.
WALLENSTEIN: How was it with that royal Bourbon who
Went over to his country's enemy,
The one who wounded his own fatherland?
A curse was his reward, disgust avenged
His most unnatural and wicked act.
ILLO: Is that *your* situation?
WALLENSTEIN: Loyalty
To each man is just like his dearest comrade;
He feels he was created to avenge it.
The enmity of sects, the rage of factions,
And jealousy and envy will make peace;
Whatever fury seems set on its own
Destruction will compose itself to chase
The *common* foe of man, the raging beast
That murderously breaks into the fold
Where man dwells out of danger—for he can
Not thrive on his intelligence alone.
Since nature has provided him with eyes
But on his forehead only, loyalty

Will guard for him his unprotected back.

TERZKY: Don't judge yourself worse than the enemy
    Who gladly gives you help to take this step!
    That Karl was not too sensitive when he,
    The ancestor of our fine Emperor,
    Received that Bourbon then with open arms;
    The world is ruled by what is advantageous.

Scene 7

Countess Terzky joins the others.

WALLENSTEIN: Who called you? We have no need here for women.

COUNTESS: I came to offer my congratulations.
    —Is it perhaps too soon? I hope it's not.

WALLENSTEIN: Be steadfast, Terzky! Tell her she must go.

COUNTESS: I gave Bohemia one king already.

WALLENSTEIN: He was not fit.

COUNTESS (*to the others*): Now, tell me what's the problem

TERZKY: The Duke will not.

COUNTESS: Will not do what he must?

ILLO: It's up to you to try. I'm finished with it
    When he tells me of loyalty and conscience.

COUNTESS: What's this? When everything was far away
    And when the road stretched endless there before you,
    Then you had courage and determination—
    But now, when dreams turn to reality,
    When they can be accomplished and success
    Is certain, then you start to hesitate?
    Are you courageous only in your plans,
    A coward in your deeds? Your enemy
    Is right! That's just what they expected of you.
    They gladly think you planned it; be assured
    That under hand and seal they'd say you did!
    But no one thought that it would come to deeds,
    Then they would have to fear you and respect you.
    So is it possible you've gone so far,
    And now the worst is known, now that the deed
    Has been accepted as already done,
    Will you withdraw and throw away the prize?
    A plan is nothing but a common crime,

When done 'tis an immortal enterprise;
And when successful, it can be forgiven
For with each ending God has made a judgment.
SERVANT (*enters*): The Colonel Piccolomini.
COUNTESS (*quickly*):   Can wait.
WALLENSTEIN: I cannot see him now. Another time!
SERVANT: He only asks you for a minute's time,
    He says he has some very urgent business—
WALLENSTEIN: Who knows what he will bring us. I will hear him.
COUNTESS (*laughs*): To *him* it's urgent. You can count on that.
WALLENSTEIN: What is it?
COUNTESS: You shall know it afterwards;
    Just now think how you're going to answer Wrangel.
                     (*Servant exits.*)
WALLENSTEIN: If only there were still a choice—a milder
    Alternative could be discovered—I
    Would choose it and avoid the worst.
COUNTESS: If that is all you want—there is a way
    That's obvious. Dispatch this Wrangel now!
    Forget your hopes of old and throw away
    Your former life, make up your mind you will
    Begin a new one. Virtue also has
    Its heroes just as fame and fortune do.
    Go to Vienna to the Emperor
    Right now, cash box in hand, explain to him
    You tested your officials' loyalties
    And only meant to show the Swedes as fools.
ILLO: It is too late for that. They know too much.
    He'd only put his head upon the block.
COUNTESS: No fear of that. They lack the evidence
    To try him and an arbitrary manner
    They will avoid. They will allow the Duke
    To take his leave. I see how it will be.
    The King of Hungary appears, and it
    Is understood the Duke will then depart;
    It will not even need to be explained.
    The King will have the troops swear loyalty
    And everything will stay just as it was.
    The Duke—in just one morning—will be gone,
    But at his castles things will be astir.
    There he will hunt and build and breed his mares.

His court will be established, golden keys
Distributed, and splendid banquets held;
He'll be a great king—though on a small scale!
And since he's smart enough to know his place,
Does not assert himself, they will allow
Him to appear as he may wish, he will
Appear to be a great prince till the end.
Oh, well, the Duke is, after all, just one
Of those new individuals who have been
Promoted by the war, who overnight
Are favored by the court which with the same
Display creates a baron or a prince.

WALLENSTEIN (*rises, intensely moved*):
Show me the way by which I can escape,
O forces of assistance! Show me *one*
That *I* may tread upon. —I cannot, like
An idle talker, chattering of virtue,
Console myself with wishes and with thoughts—
Not with a swagger say to Fortune when
It turns its back on me: "Who needs you? Go!"
If I no longer act, I am destroyed.
Not sacrifice, not danger will I shun
In order to avoid that last, worst step;
Still, rather than sink into nothingness,
To end so small who had begun so great,
To have the world mistake me for those wretches
Who are created and disposed of in a day,
I'd rather have this age and future ages
Pronounce my name with loathing, let it be
The watchword for each evil deed.

COUNTESS: What have we here that is unnatural?
I can find nothing, tell me what it is.
Do not allow that ghosts of superstition
Become the masters of your brilliant mind!
It is high treason they accuse you of—
If they are right or not is not the question—
If you do not avail yourself of power
That you possess, you will be lost—where is
The peaceful creature who will not defend
His life with his last bit of energy?
What act in self-defense is not excused?

WALLENSTEIN: This Ferdinand was once so kind to me.
  He loved me, and he valued me. I stood
  The closest to his heart. What prince is there
  Whom he has honored more? And to end so!
COUNTESS: You faithfully preserve each little favor
  And wipe great wrongs done to you from your mind.
  Must I remind you how at Regensburg
  You were rewarded for your faithful service?
  You had insulted everyone; to make
  Him great, you had accepted all the hate,
  The curses of the world upon yourself;
  In all of Germany you had no friend,
  Because you lived just for the Emperor.
  You clung to him alone at Regensburg
  When at the meeting that great storm arose
  That moved against you. There he let you fall,
  He simply let you fall, a sacrifice
  Made to that arrogant Bavarian!
  Don't tell me that the honor they gave back
  Made up for that most undeserved injustice.
  It certainly was not goodwill, it was
  The law of dire necessity that put
  You in a place they would have kept from you.
WALLENSTEIN: I know it is not their goodwill and not
  His liking I must thank for this position.
  If I abuse it, I abuse no trust.
COUNTESS: What trust? What liking? They had need of you!
  That urgent lady called *Necessity*,
  Who is not served with superficialities
  Or empty names, who will have *deeds* and not
  Appearances, who searches out the best
  And gives the rudder to him, even if
  She has to snatch him from the rabble—she
  Gave you this job and wrote out your appointment.
  As long as possible this family
  Relied upon the service of their venal
  Mercenaries and their puppet crew,
  But when they're driven to extremities,
  And empty pretexts will no longer do,
  Then nature takes things into her strong hands.
  It is a giant spirit that obeys

Itself alone, knows naught of treaties, and
Acts only on its *own,* not *their,* conditions.
WALLENSTEIN: That's true! They always saw me as I am.
I never did betray them basically;
It was not worth my effort to conceal
My bold, all-comprehensive disposition.
COUNTESS: But rather—you were always very awesome.
Not *you*—you always were true to yourself—
But *they* are wrong who were afraid of you
And still would put the power in your hands.
Each individual character is right
Who is in harmony with his own self;
There is no other wrong but contradiction.
Were you another person when eight years
Ago you drove through Germany with fire
And sword, lashed out at all the other lands;
Despised the way the Empire was arranged,
And showed the dreadful right that strength bestows,
While treading on each country's sovereignty
In order to extend your Sultan's might?
That was the time they should have tried to break
Your will and told you to stay in your place!
But pleasing to the Emperor was what
Was useful to him, and he put his seal
In silence on each outrage. What was then
Considered just, because you did it *for* him,
Today is shameful, since it now is aimed
Against him?
WALLENSTEIN (*rising*):
I never looked at it in just this way.
Yes, it is really so. This Emperor
Used me to carry out deeds in the land
That should not properly have ever happened.
The prince's mantle that I wear, I thank
That, too, to crimes that he calls services.
COUNTESS: Admit it then, between the two of you
The talk can never be of right and duty,
But just of strength and *opportunity!*
The moment now has come when you can draw
Upon the total of life's great account.
The signs appear triumphant over you.

The planets send their portents of success
And call out: "It is time!" Have you your whole
Life long for nothing plotted out the course
Of stars and drawn the quadrants and the circles?
—Have copied on your walls the zodiac,
The firmanent, and placed around you there,
As ominous though silent evidence,
The seven rulers of your destiny,
Just so you could pursue an idle game?
Does all this preparation lead to nothing
And is there nothing in this empty art
That counts for anything with you, that can
Affect you in this moment of decision?

WALLENSTEIN (*during this last speech has paced back and forth
with intense feeling and now suddenly stops, interrupting the
Countess*):
Call Wrangel to me and then saddle up
At once three messengers.

ILLO: At last, thank God! (*hurries out*)

WALLENSTEIN: It is his evil spirit and mine too.
Through me, the instrument of his ambition,
His will be punished, yet I do expect
The steel of vengeance aims too for *my* breast.
No hope has he who sows the dragon's teeth
To have a happy harvest. Every crime
Possesses its own angel of revenge,
It's evil expectation 'neath its heart.
    He cannot trust me now—and I cannot
Turn back. So let things happen as they must!
Our destiny preserves the right, for in
Our hearts is where its mandates are accomplished.
                    (*To Terzky*)
Bring Wrangel to me in my private chamber!
I want to send the messengers myself.
Send for Octavio!
    (*to the Countess, who is wearing a triumphant expression*)
                    Restrain yourself!
The jealousy of fate may have no measure.
Her rights are violated by our pleasure.
We put the seeds into her hand to sow;
If good or bad results, the end will show.
                    (*As he exits, the curtain falls.*)

ACT II

A Room.

Scene 1

Wallenstein. Octavio Piccolomini. Shortly thereafter, Max Piccolomini.

WALLENSTEIN: He sent me word from Linz that he was sick!
  But I have certain evidence that he
  Is with Count Gallas there at Frauenberg.
  Take them both prisoner and send them here!
  You then control the Spanish regiments,
  Make preparations that are never done,
  And should they urge you to advance on me,
  Agree with them but stay right where you are.
  I know that you prefer to have things so
  That you do not directly play this game.
  You hope you can keep up appearances
  And that your actions are not thought extreme,
  So I have picked this role for you to play;
  This time, by doing nothing, you will be
  Most useful. —In the meantime, if good luck
  Should favor me, then you know what to do.
            (*Max Piccolomini enters.*)
  Now, old man, leave! You must be gone tonight.
  Take with you my own horses! —Your son here
  I'll keep with me—be brief with your farewells!
  I'm sure we'll meet again most happily
  Before too long.
OCTAVIO (*to his son*): I want a word with you. (*Exits.*)

Scene 2

Wallenstein. Max Piccolomini.

MAX (*approaches*): My General—
WALLENSTEIN: That is not what I am,
  If you are in the Emperor's command.
MAX: It is true, then, you will forsake the army?
WALLENSTEIN: I've left the service of the Emperor.
MAX: Will you forsake the army?

WALLENSTEIN: Rather say
   I hope to keep the army closer, firmer.
                        (*He sits down.*)
   Yes, Max. I did not want to tell you this
   Until the moment of the deed had come.
   The happy feelings of the days of youth
   Assume the right so easily. It is
   A joy to test and use one's judgment when
   The problem has a genuine solution.
   But when from two undoubted evils one
   Must be assumed, when from the struggle over
   One's duty one cannot restore a heart
   That's *whole*, it is a benefit to have
   No choice; necessity becomes a favor.
   —The time is now at hand. Do not look back!
   It cannot help you anymore. Look forward!
   And do not judge! Prepare yourself to act!
   —The court decided I should be destroyed,
   I have a mind to get ahead of it.
   —We will combine our forces with the Swedes.
   They are a gallant people and good friends.
                (*Stops to wait Piccolomini's answer.*)
   You are surprised. You need not answer now.
   You need a moment to collect yourself.
(*He rises and goes toward the rear. Max stands for a long time motionless, suffering intensely; as he makes a movement, Wallenstein returns and stands opposite him.*)
MAX: My General! —Today you make me come
   Of age, for till today you spared me all
   The pains of choosing my own path myself.
   I followed you unquestioningly. I
   Had only to observe you to select
   The way. Today I must depend upon
   Myself, and you are forcing me to make
   A choice between your way and my own heart.
WALLENSTEIN: Fate rocked your cradle gently till today.
   You exercised your duties with great ease
   And satisfied each lovely inclination
   While acting with an undivided heart.
   This can no longer be, for hostilely
   The way divides and duty battles duty.

Now you must take a stand in this new war
That catches fire between your Emperor
And your good friend?

MAX: A war! Is that the word?
A war is frightful as the plagues of heaven,
Still like them it is good, like them is fate.
Is that a good war that you are preparing
Against the Emperor with his own men?
O God in Heaven, what a transformation
This is! Does it become me when I talk
This way to you, who always shone just like
The polar star to me as life's firm rule?
Oh, what a fissure in my heart you've torn!
The ingrown instinct of my veneration,
The sacred custom of obedience,
Shall I learn to deny these to your name?
No, do not turn your countenance toward me!
To me it always was a godlike face
And has not lost its power over me;
My senses are still bound to you, although
My soul, though bleeding, freed itself at once.

WALLENSTEIN: Max, listen to me

MAX: Please, don't do it, please!
Just look! Your pure and noble features still
Have no acquaintance with this grievous deed.
It is your thoughts alone that it has stained.
The innocence cannot be banished from
The grand appearance of your noble form.
Cast out this dismal stain, this enemy!
Then it is nothing but an ugly dream,
A warning to each steady virtue, for
It may be that mankind must have such moments,
But happy must the feeling be that triumphs.
No, you will not have *such* an end. That would
Discredit for all men each noble nature
And every mighty capability;
It would support that base delusion which
Does not believe in free nobility
And only trusts that which is powerless.

WALLENSTEIN: The world will judge me harshly, I expect it.
I've told myself each thing that you can say.

Who is there, if he had the chance, would not
Avoid the worst. But here there is no choice.
I must use force or I must suffer from it—
That is the case. No other way is left.

MAX: Well, do it then! Maintain yourself by force
In your command; defy the Emperor,
If it must be, then openly revolt.
I will not praise it, but I can forgive
And share with you what I cannot approve.
But—do not be a *traitor!* Now the word
Has been pronounced. A traitor you must not
Become! This is not simply a mistake,
Where courage errs, misled by its own might.
No, this is something else—it is so black,
Black as all hell!

WALLENSTEIN (*with ominous wrinkles on his brow, but
    temperately*):
Youth is soon ready with the hasty word
That wounds severely like a knife's sharp edge.
With its hot head it boldly ventures forth
To judge things that can only judge themselves.
To it all things are worthy or they're base,
They're bad or good—and what imagination
And fantasy put into obscure words
Is soon attributed to men and objects.
The *world* is *narrow* but the mind is *vast.*
Thoughts can exist so easily together,
But objects in a space will soon collide;
The place *one* fills is taken from *another,*
Who will not be dislodged must first dislodge;
Then strife ensues and only strength will win.
—One who can go through life without desires,
Exist without all purpose, he can live
Beside the salamander in the flame,
Be pure within the purest element.
But nature shaped me from much coarser stuff;
My eager longing draws me to the earth.
The earth belongs to evil spirits, not
To good. What we receive from those who are
Divine is held in common by us all;
Their light can comfort, but it brings no wealth.

In their domain no property is won.
A precious jewel or a golden treasure
Must be exacted from those guileful forces
That live in darkness evilly disposed.
Without a sacrifice they give no favors,
And no one is alive who walked away
From serving them and kept his spirit pure.

MAX (*meaningfully*):
Oh, fear them, fear them, all these untrue forces!
They do *not* keep their word; satanic liars,
Ensnaring you, they drag you in the pit.
You must not trust in them! Beware—you must
Return to paths of duty! Yes! You can!
Let me go to Vienna! Yes, let me
Make peace for you there with the Emperor!
He does not know you, but I know you well,
He shall now see you with my own clear eye,
And I'll restore his confidence in you.

WALLENSTEIN: It is too late! You do not know what's done.

MAX: And if it is too late—and gone so far
That only by a crime you'll save yourself
From falling, why, then fall, fall worthily
As you have stood! Lose this command! Retire!
Do this with splendor but with innocence!
—You've lived so much for others, finally
Live for yourself! I'll go along with you.
Your fate and mine will never be dissolved.

WALLENSTEIN: It is too late. While you are wasting all
These words, my couriers have put behind
Them milepost after milepost on their way
To carry my command to Prague and Eger.
—Submit to this! We do what we must do,
So let us handle it with dignity
And with decision. —What do I do that
Is worse than Caesar did, and his name still
Today is termed the greatest in the world.
He led the legions boldly against Rome
That Rome gave him to use for its defense.
Had he cast off his sword, he would have been
Done in, as I would be without my arms.
I feel some of his spirit in myself.

Give me his luck and I will bear the rest.
(*Max, who has stood in agonized conflict till now, exits quickly.*
Wallenstein looks after him astonished and disconcerted and
stands lost in deep thought.)

Scene 3

Wallenstein. Terzky. Thereupon Illo.

TERZKY: I see Max Piccolomini just left?
WALLENSTEIN: Tell me where Wrangel is.
TERZKY: He's gone.
WALLENSTEIN: So quick?
TERZKY: It was as if the earth had swallowed him.
   He had just left you when I followed him,
   I had to speak to him, but—he was gone,
   And no one who could tell me where he was.
   I do believe he really is the devil,
   No man can disappear so suddenly.
ILLO (*enters*): Can it be true you'll send the old man off?
TERZKY: Octavio? What are you thinking of?
WALLENSTEIN: He goes to Frauenberg, where he will take
   Command of both the French and Spanish troops.
TERZKY: May God forbid that you should do this thing!
ILLO: You will expose your men to his deceit?
   Just now allow us to lose sight of him,
   Now in the very moment of decision?
TERZKY: You cannot do this—not for anything!
WALLENSTEIN: You are peculiar men.
ILLO: Oh, just this once
   Pay heed to what we say! Don't let him go!
WALLENSTEIN: And why should I not trust him this *one* time
   When I have always trusted him? What has
   Occurred to rob him of my good opinion?
   Because of your caprice, not mine, should I
   Amend my old and proven view of him?
   Don't think I am a woman! And because
   I trusted him before, I'll trust him now.
TERZKY: Why must it be just *him*? Send someone else.
WALLENSTEIN: It must be him, because he is my choice.
   He fits the task, so it was given him.

ILLO: You value him because he is a Latin.

WALLENSTEIN: I know you never liked the two of them
    Because I love them, honor them, prefer
    Them over you, as they have merited.
    They are a thorn deep in your flesh! Your envy
    Has naught to do with *me* and my affairs,
    And that you hate them does not make them worse.
    So love or hate each other as you will,
    Each one of you may keep his own opinion,
    But still I know what each of you is worth.

ILLO: He will not go—if I am forced to smash
    His carriage wheels.

WALLENSTEIN: Control yourself, Illo!

TERZKY: And Questenberg, as long as he was here,
    They always seemed to have their heads together.

WALLENSTEIN: That happened with my knowledge and consent.

TERZKY: And I know, too, that secret messengers
    From Gallas come to him.

WALLENSTEIN: That is not true!

ILLO: You are so blind with your farseeing eyes!

WALLENSTEIN: You will not shake my confidence in him
    That's based upon a science so profound.
    If *he* is lying, then the stars are lies.
    Know this, I have a pledge from fate itself
    That *he* is the most faithful of my friends.

ILLO: Have you a pledge the pledge is not a lie?

WALLENSTEIN: The life of man has in it certain moments
    In which he comes close to the spirit of
    The world, and to one question fate will answer.
    Just such a moment was it in the night
    Before the fight at Lützen, when I had
    Been leaning on a tree in deepest thought
    And looked across the plain. So mournfully
    The campfire flickered through the bank of fog,
    The muffled sound of weapons and the call
    Of a patrol were all that broke the silence.
    And in this single moment my whole life,
    Both what had happened and what was to come,
    Passed through the vision of my inner eye.
    And that portentous spirit was to link
    The next day's fortune to the distant future.

Then I said to myself, "You have command
Of many men! They're guided by your star
And wager everything on your lone head
Like on a number in a game of chance.
They all have boarded fortune's ship with you.
But there will come the day when all of them
Are once more scattered distantly by fate,
And but a few will keep their faith with you.
I want to know who is most faithful of
All those who are within this camp's confines.
Give me a sign, O fate, and let it be
That one who first shall come to greet me in
The morning with a token of his love."
And as I fancied this, I fell asleep.
    And then my spirit was propelled into
The battle. Great was the distress. My steed
Was shot from under me, I sank, while horses
And riders passed above me unconcerned.
I lay there gasping like a dying man,
Crushed underneath the trampling of the hooves.
Then someone grabbed my arm to help me up.
It was Octavio—and I awoke,
The day had come—Octavio stood there.
He said, "My brother, do not ride today
Upon your piebald horse, but rather mount
A safer animal I've found for you!
Do this for me because of what I dreamed."
The swiftness of this animal allowed
Me to escape Bannier's pursuing band.
My cousin rode the piebald on that day.
I never saw him or his horse again.

ILLO: It was just chance.

WALLENSTEIN (*meaningfully*): There's no such thing as chance;
    What seems to us to be blind accident,
    Just that comes to us from the deepest source.
    I have it sealed and certified that *he*
    Is my good angel. Not another word! (*He starts to leave.*)

TERZKY: My comfort is that Max is here as hostage.

ILLO: And he will not depart this place alive.

WALLENSTEIN (*stops and turns around*):
    Are you not like old women who come back

Continually to where they started from,
When you have talked sense to them by the hour?
The deeds and thoughts of man do not begin
Like blindly swelling billows in the foam.
His microcosm and the world within
Create the source from which they ever come.
They function as the seed does to the tree,
And chance illusion cannot change that fact.
Once his heart's core is opened up to me,
I know what he will want and how he'll act.

(They exit.)

Scene 4

A room in Piccolomini's quarters.

Octavio Piccolomini ready to set out. An adjutant.

OCTAVIO: Is my detachment here?
ADJUTANT: It waits below.
OCTAVIO: You're sure they are trustworthy, Adjutant?
    What was the regiment you took them from?
ADJUTANT: From Tiefenbach's.
OCTAVIO: A loyal regiment.
    Have them wait patiently there in the rear,
    Let no one see them till you hear me ring!
    Then you will lock the house and guard it well.
    Each one you come across you must arrest.

(Adjutant exits.)

    Of course, I hope we will not need their help.
    I'm sure my calculations are correct.
    Our service to the Emperor's at stake.
    So better too much caution than too little.

Scene 5

Octavio Piccolomini. Isolani enters.

ISOLANI: I'm here now—so who else is coming still?
OCTAVIO (*mysteriously*):
    First just a word with you, Count Isolani.
ISOLANI (*mysteriously*):

Is it now time? The Duke will make his move?
I can be trusted. Put me to the test!

OCTAVIO: That may be done.

ISOLANI: Well, Brother, I am not
One of those people who is brave with words
But, when it comes to deeds, is far away.
The Duke has always been a friend to me,
God knows that's true! I owe him everything.
He can rely on me.

OCTAVIO: We shall soon know.

ISOLANI: Watch out! Not everyone is of his mind.
There are still many who hold with the court
And think that what they recently have signed,
Arranged through a deception, is not binding.

OCTAVIO: So? Name the gentlemen who think this way!

ISOLANI: The devil! That's what all the Germans say.
There's Esterhazy, Kaunitz, Deodat,
Who say now that we must obey the court.

OCTAVIO: I'm glad.

ISOLANI: You're glad?

OCTAVIO: The Emperor still has
So many friends and such stouthearted servants.

ISOLANI: Don't make a joke! They really aren't so bad.

OCTAVIO: Of course not! God forbid that I should joke!
I'm pleased in earnest to observe that this
Good cause is strong.

ISOLANI: The devil! What is this?
Are you not—? Why have I been summoned here?

OCTAVIO (*with dignity*):
In order plainly to declare if you
Oppose the Emperor or follow him.

ISOLANI (*defiantly*):
I will explain myself on that concern,
But just to him who has the right to ask.

OCTAVIO: That I am he this document will show.

ISOLANI: What's this? That is the Emperor's own seal.
                          (*reads*)
"So each and every officer within
Our army will treat all the orders of
Our loyal General Piccolomini
As if they were our own" —Well, well, I see!

I—my congratulations to you, General!

OCTAVIO: Will you submit to this command?

ISOLANI: I—well—
   You take me by surprise—I hope I will
   Be given time to think—

OCTAVIO: Two minutes' time.

ISOLANI: My God, this is a matter—

OCTAVIO: Clear and simple!
   You must declare if you want to betray
   Your master or to serve him loyally.

ISOLANI: Betray—my God—who's talking of betrayal?

OCTAVIO: That is the case. The Duke is now a traitor
   And gives the army to the enemy.
   You must declare yourself! Will you renounce
   The Emperor and join the enemy?

ISOLANI: What are you thinking of? Did I say that?
   Renounce His Majesty? When could I have
   Said that?

OCTAVIO: You have not said it yet. Not yet.
   I wait to see if you will say it now.

ISOLANI: Look here, I'm very glad that you yourself
   Are witness that I have said no such thing.

OCTAVIO: You say then that you will renounce the Duke?

ISOLANI: If he plots treason—treason breaks all bonds.

OCTAVIO: You have decided you will fight against him?

ISOLANI: He has been good to me—but if he is
   A rogue, God damn him! My account is cleared!

OCTAVIO: I'm glad that you submit to what is right.
   Tonight in silence you must break up camp
   With all of your light troops; it must appear
   As if the orders have come from the Duke.
   Our meeting place will be at Frauenberg.
   You will receive from Gallas further orders.

ISOLANI: It shall be done. Remember just how willing
   I was, when you speak to the Emperor.

OCTAVIO: I'll praise you highly.
                    (*Isolani exits, a servant enters.*)
                              Colonel Buttler? Good.

ISOLANI (*returning*):
   Forgive the brusqueness of my tone, old man.
   Lord God! how could I know how eminent

A person stood before me!
OCTAVIO: Let it be!
ISOLANI: I am a jolly fellow, and if I
    Have sometimes let a hasty little word
    Slip from my lips when I have drunk some wine,
    You know, of course, I meant no harm. (*Exits.*)
OCTAVIO: Do not
    Concern yourself about it. —That worked well.
    Good Fortune, be so kind now with the others!

Scene 6

Octavio Piccolomini. Buttler.

BUTTLER: I come as you commanded, General.
OCTAVIO: Be welcome as a valued guest and friend.
BUTTLER: The honor is too great.
OCTAVIO (*after both have seated themselves*):
    You don't reciprocate the sympathy
    With which I chose to greet you yesterday
    And have mistaken it for empty words.
    That wish came from my heart; I was in earnest
    Concerning you, for now the time has come
    When all good men should join in close communion.
BUTTLER: But only those who are like-minded can.
OCTAVIO: Still, all good men, I say, must be like-minded.
    And all I'll charge to any man's account
    Is just *that* deed to which his nature drives him;
    For blind misunderstanding has the strength
    To force the best man from the proper course.
    You came through Frauenberg. Count Gallas—did
    He speak to you? Tell me. He is my friend.
BUTTLER: On me the words he spoke were only wasted.
OCTAVIO: That I regret to hear, for his advice
    Was good; I had the same to offer you.
BUTTLER: Just save me the embarrassment of earning
    Your good opinion in this wretched way.
OCTAVIO: Now time is precious, let us speak right out!
    You know the way the situation stands.
    The Duke plans treason; I can tell you more;
    He has just carried out his plan, for he

Has made a firm agreement with the foe.
His couriers ride now toward Prague and Eger,
Tomorrow he will join the enemy.
But he deceives himself, the prudent are
On guard, the Emperor has faithful friends,
And their invisible alliance has
Great strength. By this intention he is outlawed,
And it releases from their obligations
The troops, and summons all right-minded men
To come together under my command.
Now you must choose if you will share with us
The good cause or with him an evil fate.

BUTTLER (*rises*):
  His fate is mine.

OCTAVIO: You're sure that this resolve
  Will be your last?

BUTTLER: It is.

OCTAVIO: You still have time
  To reconsider, Colonel Buttler. Here
  Within my breast the words you spoke will stay.
  Just take them back and choose the better side.
  You have not taken up the cause that's good.

BUTTLER: So have you further orders, General?

OCTAVIO: Consider your white hair and take them back!

BUTTLER: Farewell!

OCTAVIO: What? Do you really want to pull
  This good, brave sword in such a struggle? Want
  To turn to curses thanks that you have earned
  From Austria through forty loyal years?

BUTTLER (*laughing bitterly*):
  To them I'm thankful!
  (*He starts to exit.*)

OCTAVIO (*allows him to go to the door, then calls out*):
  Buttler!

BUTTLER: What's your pleasure?

OCTAVIO: What was that with the count?

BUTTLER: The count? How's that?

OCTAVIO: The title's what I mean.

BUTTLER (*flaring up furiously*): Death and damnation!

OCTAVIO (*coldly*):
  You tried to get one once. You were refused.

BUTTLER: You'll not sneer with impunity. Now draw!

OCTAVIO: Just sheathe your sword and tell me how it was.
  I'll give you satisfaction afterwards.

BUTTLER: May all the world know of this weakness that
  I'll never manage to forgive myself!
  —Yes, General, I do possess ambition.
  I never could endure it to be scorned.
  I was offended that one's birth and title
  Meant more than merit in the army's eyes.
  I wanted to be just as good as they,
  And so in one disastrous hour I let
  Myself be led to take that foolish step.
  But I did not deserve to suffer so
  For it. —They could refuse—but why did they
  Intensify it with so much contempt,
  And prostrate this old man, a faithful servant,
  By crushing him beneath their deep disdain,
  Remind him coldly of his origin,
  When for a moment he forgot himself?
  But nature gave the helpless worm a sting
  Whom reckless action trod on wantonly—

OCTAVIO: Someone has slandered you. Do you suspect
  An enemy who might have done this deed?

BUTTLER: Whoever it may be! The rogue is vile.
  A courtier, a Spaniard it must be,
  A country squire from some old family
  Whose way I'm in, a jealous scoundrel who
  Is irritated by the rank I've earned.

OCTAVIO: Now, did the Duke approve of your request?

BUTTLER: He urged me on and with the warmth of friendship
  He used his influence for me in this.

OCTAVIO: So? You are sure of that?

BUTTLER: I read his letter.

OCTAVIO (*with significance*):
  I too—but what it said was something else.
                    (*Buttler is perplexed.*)
  By chance I have that letter in my hand
  And can convince you, if you'll look at it.
                    (*He gives him the letter.*)

BUTTLER: Ha! What is this?

OCTAVIO: Well, Colonel, it would seem

That someone played a shameful game with you.
The Duke, you say, urged you to take this step?
Here in this letter he speaks with disdain
Concerning you and tells the minister
To punish what he calls your self-conceit.

(*Buttler has read the letter, his knees shake, he catches hold of a chair and sits down.*)

You have no enemy who bears a grudge.
This insult that you have received—ascribe
It to the Duke alone; his aim is clear,
To separate you from the Emperor—
Through your revenge he thought he would achieve
What he could never hope to gain from your
Well-tested loyalty on calm reflection.
He wanted a blind instrument to use
Contemptibly for his base purposes.
And far too well he has succeeded in
Enticing you away from that good path
On which you traveled these past forty years.

BUTTLER (*his voice trembling*):
Oh, can His Majesty forgive me this?

OCTAVIO: He can do more. He'll make up for this wrong
That happened to a worthy man unjustly.
For of his own accord he will confirm
The gift the Duke bestowed with bad intent.
The regiment that you command is yours.

BUTTLER (*starts to rise, sinks back. His feelings labor violently, he tries to speak and cannot. Finally he takes his sword from its sheath and extends it to Piccolomini.*)

OCTAVIO: What's this? Compose yourself!

BUTTLER: Here!

OCTAVIO: Stop! Consider!

BUTTLER: Here! Take it! I'm no longer worthy of it.

OCTAVIO: Receive your sword anew and from my hand
To wield it henceforth always for the right!

BUTTLER: I broke faith with my gracious Emperor!

OCTAVIO: Then make amends by parting from the Duke!

BUTTLER: Part from the Duke!

OCTAVIO: What? Do you hesitate?

BUTTLER (*bursting forth frightfully*):
Just part from him? Oh, he shall not survive!

OCTAVIO: Then follow me to Frauenberg where all
  The faithful go to Altringer and Gallas.
  The many others whom I have recalled
  To their commitment flee tonight from Pilsen.
BUTTLER (*has been pacing furiously up and down and advances towad Octavio with a determined look*):
  Count Piccolomini, may someone speak
  Of honor who himself has broken faith?
OCTAVIO: He who so earnestly regrets it may.
BUTTLER: Then let me stay here on parole.
OCTAVIO: But why?
BUTTLER: Just let me stay here with my regiment.
OCTAVIO: I trust you. Still I'd like to know your plan.
BUTTLER: The deed itself will tell. Ask me no more.
  Just trust me. And you can! God knows in me
  He'll find no guardian angel! —So farewell! (*Exits.*)
SERVANT (*brings a note*):
  A stranger brought it and then left at once.
  The horses of the Duke stand ready now. (*Off.*)
OCTAVIO (*reads*):
  "Make your escape. Your loyal Isolani."
  —Oh, that already I had left this town!
  So near the harbor will we run aground?
  Away, away! It is no longer safe
  For me here. But where is my son?

Scene 7

The two Piccolominis.

MAX (*arrives in the most violent state of agitation, his eyes roll wildly, his gait is unsteady; he appears not to notice his father, who watches compassionately from the distance. He passes through the room with great strides, then stops again, and at last throws himself into a chair, staring straight ahead.*)
OCTAVIO (*approaching him*):
  I'm leaving now, my son.
        (*When he receives no answer, he grasps his hand.*)
                          My son, farewell!
MAX: Farewell.
OCTAVIO: You'll follow me soon?

MAX (*without looking at him*):   Follow you?
  Your way is crooked, it is not my way.
              (*Octavio drops his hand and recoils.*)
  If you had only been sincere and honest,
  How different things would be—not as they are!
  He never would have done that dreadful thing;
  The good would have maintained its strength with him
  And he would not have fallen in these traps.
  Why should you lurk in secret, cunningly,
  Just as a thief and his accomplice do?
  Accursed falseness! Mother of all evil!
  This source of misery destroys us now!
  But truthfulness, so pure, it would have saved
  Us all, as it preserves the world. I can
  Not pardon you, O Father; I cannot.
  The Duke deceived me frightfully, it's true,
  But what you've done—it is not that much better.
OCTAVIO: My son, oh, truly I forgive your grief.
MAX (*rises, looks at him uncertainly*):
  Could it be possible then, Father, that
  You purposely forced things to come so far?
  You rise through his decline. Octavio,
  I would not find that pleasant.
OCTAVIO: God in Heaven!
MAX: Alas! My nature has become so changed.
  How has suspicion crept into my soul?
  Belief and faith and hope, they all are gone,
  For everything that I esteemed was false.
  No! No! Not everything! *She* still exists
  And she is just as true and sure as Heaven.
  While treachery is everywhere and sham
  And murder, malice, perjury, and treason,
  The one pure haven only is our love,
  The one place unprofaned amidst mankind.
OCTAVIO: Max! Come along with me; that will be best.
MAX: What! Leave before I've said good-bye to her?
  The last good-bye? —Oh, never!
OCTAVIO: Spare yourself
  The pain of parting that is bound to come!
  Come with me, Son!
                (*attempts to draw him away*)

MAX: No! By the living God!
OCTAVIO (*more urgently*):
  Come with me! I command it, as your father.
MAX: Command the possible. Here I will stay.
OCTAVIO: By order of the Emperor, Max, come!
MAX: No emperor can dictate to the heart.
  Will you remove the only thing that's left
  To me in my misfortune, her compassion?
  Must the inhuman come inhumanly?
  And shall I do that, which cannot be changed,
  Ignobly, and in furtive coward's flight,
  Like someone shameful, slink away from her?
  She shall see my distress, my agony,
  Hear the lament of my afflicted soul,
  And shed her tears for me. —Oh, they are cruel,
  These men, but she is always like an angel;
  And from this ghastly, raging desperation
  She will restore my soul and mournfully
  Dissolve these pangs of death with words of comfort.
OCTAVIO: You will not have the strength to break away.
  Oh, come away, my son, and save your virtue!
MAX: Don't bother to expend your words in vain!
  I listen to my heart, which I can trust.
OCTAVIO (*beside himself, trembling*):
  Max! Max! If that most dreadful thing occurred—
  If you—my son—my flesh and blood—I can
  Not think it—should be brought to sell your honor
  And with this stigma mark our noble house,
  The world should see a horrifying scene
  For then in monstrous combat a son's sword
  Would soon be dripping with his father's blood.
MAX: If you had only held a better thought
  Of man, you would have acted better, too.
  Damned be suspicion and unhappy doubt!
  For nothing is immovable and firm
  And all will waver when one's faith is gone.
OCTAVIO: If I have faith in your heart, then can you
  Be sure you have the strength to follow it?
MAX: You could not overcome my heart's advice;
  As little will the Duke be able to.
OCTAVIO: O Max, I never will see you again!

MAX: Unworthy of you, you will never see me.
OCTAVIO: I go to Frauenberg, but Pappenheim
  I'll leave to cover you, and Tiefenbach,
  Toskana, also Lothringen will stay.
  They love you and are faithful to their oath.
  They would prefer to fight and bravely fall
  Than to desert their leader and their honor.
MAX: You may depend upon it that I'll die
  In combat here or lead them out of Pilsen.
OCTAVIO (*as if to depart*):
  Farewell, my son!
MAX: Farewell!
OCTAVIO: What? Not one look
  Of love? No handclasp as we say good-bye?
  This is a bloody war that we are in;
  Uncertain and obscure is its result.
  We never parted in this way before.
  Can it be true? Do I not have a son?
  (*Max throws his arms around him, they embrace for a long
  moment, then they depart in different directions.*)

ACT III

The Duchess of Friedland's room

Scene 1

*Countess Terzky. Thekla. Lady Neubrunn. (The last two occupied
with ladies' handwork.)*

COUNTESS: Well, Thekla, is there nothing that you want
  To ask me? Not a thing? I've waited just
  To hear a word from you. How can you bear
  It for so long not once to speak his name?
  Am I no longer necessary then,
  And are there other ways than just through me?—
  Let's hear the truth, Niece! Tell me if you've seen him.
THEKLA: Today and yesterday I have not seen him.
COUNTESS: Nor heard from him? You mustn't hide it from me.
THEKLA: No word at all.
COUNTESS: And still so calm?
THEKLA: I am.

COUNTESS: Now, Neubrunn, leave us please.
  (Lady Neubrunn exits.)

Scene 2

Countess, Thekla.

COUNTESS: I do not like
  It that just at this time he is so quiet.
THEKLA: Just at this time?
COUNTESS: Now that he knows it all!
  This is the time he should declare himself.
THEKLA: Speak plainer, if I am to understand.
COUNTESS: It was for this I told her to withdraw;
  For, Thekla, you are not a child. Your heart
  Has come of age—you are in love, and love
  Is bold and daring. You have proven that.
  You have in you more of your father's spirit
  Than of your mother's. Therefore you can hear
  What *she* would not be able to endure.
THEKLA: I beg you, finish these preliminaries!
  Whatever it may be, then out with it;
  It cannot be worse than your prologue is.
  What do you want to tell me? Make it short.
COUNTESS: You must not be alarmed—
THEKLA: Just tell me! Please!
COUNTESS: It falls to you to do a service for
  Your father—
THEKLA: What? It falls to *me*? How can—
COUNTESS: Max Piccolomini adores you. You
  Can bind him to your father for all time.
THEKLA: What use am I? Is he not his already?
COUNTESS: He has been.
THEKLA: Why should he not still be now?
  Not always be?
COUNTESS: He is the Emperor's.
THEKLA: As duty and as honor have required.
COUNTESS: Instead of duty, what we now require
  Is proof of love. —His duty and his honor!
  These words mean different things, they are not clear.
  You shall interpret them to him. His love

    Can then explain his honor to him.

THEKLA: How?

COUNTESS: He shall part from the Emperor or you.

THEKLA: He would be glad to go with Father in
    Retirement. You yourself have heard him say
    How much he wished to lay aside his weapons.

COUNTESS: My meaning is, he shall not lay them down
    But draw them for your father.

THEKLA: He will give
    His blood, his life for Father joyfully,
    If some injustice should be done to him.

COUNTESS: You will not understand me—listen then!
    Your father quarreled with the Emperor.
    He is about to join the enemy
    Together with the army.

THEKLA: Oh, my mother!

COUNTESS: We need a good example for the army
    To follow, and the Piccolominis
    Are both respected by the troops. They can
    Control opinion and their actions are
    Decisive. We will win the father with
    The son. —You have a great deal in your hands.

THEKLA: Oh, what a deadly blow awaits you now,
    My wretched mother! —She will not survive.

COUNTESS: She will submit to what is necessary.
    I know her—what is distant and to come
    Alarms her timid heart; what can't be changed
    And is a fact she bears with resignation.

THEKLA: Such were my soul's presentiments! —And now—
    Now it is here, that chilling hand of dread
    Evoking shudders from my happy hopes.
    I knew it well—the moment I arrived
    My deep foreboding had already told
    Me my unlucky stars hung over me.—
    But why am I just thinking of myself?
    My mother! Oh, my mother!

COUNTESS: Calm yourself!
    Don't break forth in such vain complaints! Preserve
    A friend to help your father and a true
    Love for yourself, and all may still be well.

THEKLA: Be well? When we are parted now forever?

Oh, that is not the question anymore.
COUNTESS: He will not leave! He cannot part from you.
THEKLA: Oh, how unhappy he must be!
COUNTESS: If he does truly love you, his resolve
  Will soon be made.
THEKLA: That his resolve will soon
  Be made, there is no doubt of that. Resolve!
  Can there be a resolve?
COUNTESS: Compose yourself,
  I hear your mother coming.
THEKLA: How can I?
  Endure her look?
COUNTESS: Be calm!

Scene 3

The Duchess. The former.

DUCHESS (*to the Countess*): Who was that, Sister?
  I heard loud talk.
COUNTESS: It wasn't anyone.
DUCHESS: I am so nervous. Every sound proclaims
  The footstep of some messenger of doom.
  Could you not tell me, Sister, how things are?
  Will he obey the Emperor's commands
  And send the Cardinal his cavalry?
  Did he dismiss Von Questenberg to take
  An answer that was good?
COUNTESS: No, he did not.
DUCHESS: Then it is over, and the worst will come.
  They will remove him; it will be again
  The way it was at Regensburg.
COUNTESS: It will
  Not be that way this time. You can be sure.
  (*Thekla, intensely moved, rushes to her mother and embraces
  her, weeping.*)
DUCHESS: Oh, that unyielding man, so obstinate!
  What I have had to suffer and to bear
  In this unhappy bond of matrimony!
  For just as if I had been bound upon
  A fiery wheel that ever fiercely turns,

My life with him has been a fearful one;
He always brought me, reeling, with him to
The threatening edge of one more precipice.
—No, do not cry, my child! Do not allow
My suffering to be an omen to you,
To spoil the place that you have waiting for you!
There is no other Friedland; you, my child,
Need not fear you will share your mother's fate.

THEKLA: Oh, let us run away, dear Mother, now
And quickly. This is no place for us here,
When every fleeting hour here hatches out
Some new and terrifying apparition.

DUCHESS: Your lot will be more peaceful. Even we,
I and your father, saw some happy days,
And I still think of those first years with joy.
Then he was still a happy man with hopes;
Ambition was a mildly warming fire
And not that flame yet that with fury burns.
The Emperor still loved and trusted him;
Whatever he began would always prosper.
But since that fatal day at Regensburg
That plunged him from the heights that he had known,
A spirit, restless and unsociable,
Distrustful, gloomy, has come over him.
His peace had fled; he could not cheerfully
Trust to his old good luck and his own strength,
And so he gave his heart to those dark arts
That never yet have blessed their followers.

COUNTESS: That is the way you see things, but is this
The *proper* way to talk before he comes?
He will arrive soon, you should know. Should he
Find *her* in this condition?

DUCHESS: Come, my child,
And wipe away your tears; let's show your father
A happy face. —Look here, your ribbon is
Untied, and we must fasten up your hair.
Come, dry your tears! They mar the beauty of
Your lovely eyes. —Now what was I just saying?
Oh, yes, this Piccolomini, he is
A worthy nobleman and full of merit.

COUNTESS: Yes, Sister, he is that.

THEKLA (*to the Countess, anxiously*): Would you excuse
  Me, Aunt? (*Starts to leave.*)
COUNTESS: Where to? Your father will soon come.
THEKLA: I cannot see him now.
COUNTESS: He'll miss you and
  He'll ask for you.
DUCHESS: Why does she want to leave?
THEKLA: I really cannot bear to see him now.
COUNTESS (*to the Duchess*):
  She is not well.
DUCHESS (*concerned*): What ails the precious child?
  (*The two follow the girl and are engaged in detaining her.*
  Wallenstein enters in conversation with Illo.)

Scene 4

Wallenstein. Illo. The former.

WALLENSTEIN: It is still calm in camp?
ILLO: Yes, all is still.
WALLENSTEIN: A few hours hence and we will have the news
  From Prague that gives this city to us as
  Our capital. Then we can throw away
  The masks and give these troops the word about
  What we have done, along with our success.
  In such a case, example does it all,
  For man is, after all, an imitator.
  Whoever is the first, he leads the herd.
  The troops in Prague will know no better than
  To think the Pilsners have sworn homage to us,
  And here in Pilsen they will take the oath
  Because the men in Prague set the example.
  —You say that Buttler has declared himself?
ILLO: Yes, he came freely, and he offered you,
  Unasked, himself and all his regiment.
WALLENSTEIN: Not every voice, I find, can be believed,
  That sounds a warning deep within one's heart.
  Just to ensnare us, Satan will assume
  Oftimes a copy of the voice of truth
  To spread abroad deceptive oracles.
  I have a secret wrong that I should ask

This worthy Buttler to forgive me for;
A feeling that I am not master of—
I do not like to call it fear—creeps through
My senses with a shudder when he is
Close by and checks the happy stir of love.
This upright man, against whom I am warned,
Has offered me the first pledge of good luck.

ILLO: And his esteemed example, have no doubt,
Will win for you the army's choicest men.

WALLENSTEIN: Then go and summon Isolan to me.
Just recently I put him in my debt,
So I will make a start with him. Now go!
(*Illo exits; meanwhile the others move again toward the front.*)

WALLENSTEIN: Look here, a mother with her lovely daughter!
This once let's take a respite from our work.—
Come! I would like to pass a happy hour
Within the circle of my family.

COUNTESS: A long time's past since we've all been together.

WALLENSTEIN (*aside to the Countess*):
Can she accept it? Has she been prepared?

COUNTESS: Not yet.

WALLENSTEIN: Come here, my child, and sit by me.
A happy spirit hovers on your lips.
Your mother has commended much to me
Your skill; I have been told that you possess
A fine, melodic voice that can enchant
The heart, and such a voice is what I need
Just now to drive away those demons whose
Black wings are beating all around my head.

DUCHESS: Where have you put your zither, Thekla? Come
And let your father hear a sample of
Your artistry!

THEKLA: O Mother! O dear God!

DUCHESS: Come, Thekla, come, your father will be pleased!

THEKLA: I cannot, Mother—

COUNTESS: Niece, what's that you say?

THEKLA (*to the Countess*):
Oh, spare me—now—to sing—for him—with such
Anxiety that burdens my poor soul—
For him who sends my mother to her grave!

DUCHESS: What? Out of temper, Thekla? Shall your kind

And gracious father ask for this in vain?
COUNTESS: Here is your zither.
THEKLA: O, dear God, how can—
(*She holds the instrument in a trembling hand, her spirit is engaged in an intense struggle, and at the moment when she is about to begin singing, she shudders, violently, throws the instrument down, and exits quickly.*)
DUCHESS: My child—Oh, she is ill!
WALLENSTEIN: What ails her? Does she often act this way?
COUNTESS: Well, since she has betrayed herself, I will
   Not hold my tongue.
WALLENSTEIN: What's this?
COUNTESS: She is in love.
WALLENSTEIN: In love? With whom?
COUNTESS: With Piccolomini.
   Did you not notice it? Nor, Sister, you?
DUCHESS: Oh, was it this that has oppressed her heart?
   God bless you then, my child, you need not be
   Ashamed of such a choice.
COUNTESS: That trip—if you
   Did not intend it to be so, then you
   Have but yourself to blame. You should have picked
   Some other escort for her!
WALLENSTEIN: Is he aware?
COUNTESS: He hopes to win her.
WALLENSTEIN: Hopes
   To win her? —Is the man completely mad?
COUNTESS: Let her hear this herself!
WALLENSTEIN: He hopes to win
   The hand of Friedland's daughter? Well, the thought
   Is pleasant. It is not a humble one.
COUNTESS: Because you always favored him so much.
   He—
WALLENSTEIN: Thinks that he can also be my heir.
   It's true—I love him and I value him,
   But how does that concern my daughter's hand?
   Is it with daughters, with one's only children,
   That one attests to one's goodwill?
DUCHESS: His noble intellect and his fine manners—
WALLENSTEIN: Will win for him my heart but not my daughter.
DUCHESS: His rank and ancestry—

WALLENSTEIN: His ancestry!
   He is a subject, and I plan to seek
   My son-in-law upon the thrones of Europe.
DUCHESS: O my dear Duke, let us not strive to climb
   Too high lest we might have to fall too far!
WALLENSTEIN: Have I paid dearly so that I might rise
   To such a height, to tower over all
   The common heads of men, in order to
   Conclude the role of greatness I have played
   With low relationships? —Have I for this—
   (*Suddenly stops, collects himself.*)
   She is the only thing that will remain
   Of me on earth; I want to see a crown
   Upon her head or I don't care to live.
   You see, I have risked everything for *her*,
   To make her great—and at this very moment
   As we are talking—
   (*He stops to think.*)
                          Should I now, as if
   I were a tenderhearted father, just
   Relinquish simply all I have and love?
   And should I do that now, just now, when I
   Can place the crown upon my finished work?—
   Oh, no, she is my jewel, long put by,
   The last best piece of treasure that I have.
   I truly do not mean to bargain for
   One bit less than the scepter of a king—
DUCHESS: Oh, my dear husband, must you build and build?
   You build up to the clouds and past and do
   Not once consider that the ground cannot
   Support your reeling and unsteady work.
WALLENSTEIN (*to the Duchess*):
   Have you informed her of the place I've picked
   For her to live?
COUNTESS: No. Tell her that yourself.
DUCHESS: We're not returning to Carinthia?
WALLENSTEIN: No.
DUCHESS: Nor to somewhere else on your estates?
WALLENSTEIN: There you would not be safe.
DUCHESS: We'd not be safe
   Within the Emperor's domain and care?

WALLENSTEIN: The wife of Friedland may not hope for that.
DUCHESS: Oh, God, then you have carried things so far!
WALLENSTEIN: In Holland you will be protected.
DUCHESS: What?
  You're sending us into the Lutheran lands?
WALLENSTEIN: Duke Franz von Lauenburg will take you there
  And guard you on the way.
DUCHESS: Von Lauenburg?
  Who joined the Swedes against the Emperor?
WALLENSTEIN: Whose enemies are now no longer mine.
DUCHESS (*looks at the Duke and the Countess fearfully*):
  It's true, then, is it? You've been overthrown?
  You are deposed by his command? O God
  In Heaven!
COUNTESS (*aside to the Duke*): Let her rest in that belief.
  You see that she could never bear the truth.

Scene 5

Count Terzky. The former.

COUNTESS: Terzky! What can it be? What look of terror,
  As if he had beheld a ghost!
TERZKY (*drawing Wallenstein aside, secretively*):
  Did you command that the Croatians leave?
WALLENSTEIN: I did not.
TERZKY: Then we are betrayed!
WALLENSTEIN: What's that?
TERZKY: They all have gone, last night, the jaegers, too.
  The villages around are all deserted.
WALLENSTEIN: And Isolan?
TERZKY: You sent him on a mission.
WALLENSTEIN: I did?
TERZKY: Did you not send him and as well
  Send Deodat? They have both disappeared.

Scene 6

Illo. The former.

ILLO: Did Terzky tell you—
TERZKY: He knows everything.
ILLO: And that Maradas, Esterhazy, Goetz,

Colalto, Kaunitz, all have gone?

TERZKY: The devil!

WALLENSTEIN (*signals*):
Be still!

DUCHESS (*has been watching them anxiously from a distance,
joins them*):
                    What is it, Terzky? What has happened?

WALLENSTEIN (*about to leave*):
Let us depart.

TERZKY (*follows him*): Theresa, it is nothing.

COUNTESS (*holds onto him*):
It's nothing? Can't I see that all the blood
Has left your cheeks and turned you ghostly pale,
See that my brother's calm is only feigned?

PAGE (*enters*): An adjutant is asking for Count Terzky.
                    (*Exits. Terzky follows the Page.*)

WALLENSTEIN: See what he brings.
(*to Illo*)
                                        That could not have occurred
So secretly without a mutiny.
Who has the gate watch now?

ILLO: It's Tiefenbach.

WALLENSTEIN: Have Tiefenach relieved without delay.
Let Terzky's grenadiers mount guard. —Pay heed!
Have you had word from Buttler?

ILLO: He is here.
He's coming soon himself. He holds with you.
                    (*Illo exits. Wallenstein is about to follow.*)

COUNTESS: Don't let him leave you, Sister. Make him stay.
There is some mishap—

DUCHESS: God in Heaven, what?
                    (*She throws her arms around his neck.*)

WALLENSTEIN (*restrains her*):
Be calm! And leave me! Sister! Dearest wife,
We are in camp! That is the way it is,
Here storm and sunshine quickly alternate,
These forceful men are difficult to guide,
And leaders never have a peaceful time.—
Though I must stay here, leave; for women's tears
Are not in harmony with manly actions.
                    (*Is about to leave, Terzky returns.*)

TERZKY: Stay here. You must observe this from the window.
WALLENSTEIN: Go, Sister!
DUCHESS: Never!
WALLENSTEIN: I insist.
TERZKY (*draws her aside, with a significant gesture toward the Duchess*):
                        Theresa!
DUCHESS: Come, Sister, he commands us. (*They exit.*)

Scene 7

Wallenstein. Count Terzky.

WALLENSTEIN (*stepping to the window*): Now, what is it?
TERZKY: There is a lot of running and conferring
  By all the troops, and no one knows just why.
  And silently and with such secret stealth
  Each corps has drawn up underneath its flag.
  There Tiefenbach's men have such angry faces,
  And only the Walloons still stand apart,
  Remain in camp, let no one enter, and
  Retain their usual calm attitude.
WALLENSTEIN: Can Piccolomini be seen with them?
TERZKY: They've looked for him, but he cannot be found.
WALLENSTEIN: What did the adjutant report to you?
TERZKY: Those in my regiment dispatched him to
  Inform you they are loyal and await
  The summons to the battle with delight.
WALLENSTEIN: How did this uproar happen in the camp,
  Since everything was to be kept concealed
  Until we knew of our success in Prague?
TERZKY: If you had only listened when we all
  Implored you not to let Octavio
  And his intrigue out of the gates last night.
  Instead, you gave him horses for his flight—
WALLENSTEIN: The same old song! Once and for all, I want
  To hear no more of this absurd suspicion!
TERZKY: You trusted Isolani, too, and he
  Became the first one who deserted you!
WALLENSTEIN: Just yesterday I helped him in his need.
  Oh, well, I never counted on his thanks.

TERZKY: And so they all are, each one, like the other.
WALLENSTEIN: So, is it wrong that he abandons me?
  The god he serves he's worshiped all his life
  At gaming tables. He has made and breaks
  His pact with my good luck and not with me.
  What's he to *me* or I to *him*? I am
  The ship on which he's loaded all his hopes,
  With which he cheerfully has sailed the ocean.
  He sees the danger of the rocks approach
  And quickly rescues all his merchandise.
  He leaves me freely, as a bird will fly
  Off from the helpful branch where it has nested.
  No human bond between us has been torn.
  Yes, he deserves to see himself betrayed
  Who seeks a heart among the frivolous!
  On their smooth brows the images of life
  Are drawn with strokes that quickly are effaced,
  And nothing reaches deep within their breasts.
  Though merry spirits move their fickle humors,
  They have no souls to warm up their insides.
TERZKY: Still, I would rather trust a brow that smooth
  Than him whose forehead is so deeply furrowed.

Scene 8

Wallenstein. Terzky. Illo enters, raging.

ILLO: There's mutiny and treason!
TERZKY: Now what's this?
ILLO: When I gave Tiefenbach's troops orders to
  Retire, they—oh, they are such faithless scoundrels!
TERZKY: Well?
WALLENSTEIN: What has happened?
ILLO: They would not obey.
TERZKY: Then shoot them down! Go give the orders now!
WALLENSTEIN: Calm down! What reason did they offer you?
ILLO: That no one gave them orders now except
  Lieutenant General Piccolomini
WALLENSTEIN: How can that be?
ILLO: He left that word behind,
  And written in the Emperor's own hand.

TERZKY: The Emperor! —You hear that, Sir?
ILLO: And it
  Was he induced the others to desert.
TERZKY: You hear this?
ILLO: Montecuculi, Caraffa—
  Besides these there are six commanders whom
  He has persuaded to go off with him.
  He had received this from the Emperor
  In writing long ago, and recently
  He had discussed it with Von Questenberg.
  (*Wallenstein sinks onto a chair and covers his face.*)
TERZKY: If you had only trusted me!

Scene 9

Countess. The former.

COUNTESS: I could not stand this great anxiety.
  Just tell me, for the love of God, what's wrong!
ILLO: The regiments are all deserting us.
  We are betrayed by Piccolomini.
COUNTESS: I feared as much! (*She hurries from the room.*)
TERZKY: If you had trusted *me!*
  You see now how the stars have lied to you!
WALLENSTEIN (*rises*):
  The stars have not deceived me; *this* occurs
  In spite of what the stars and fate ordain.
  This art is honest, but *that* false heart would
  Bring lies and treachery to Heaven itself.
  A true prediction rests on truth alone:
  Where Nature breaks out of its boundaries,
  All knowledge easily can err. Was it
  Just superstition not to bring disgrace
  By such mistrust upon my fellow man?
  Oh, I will never be ashamed of this!
  Religion is innate among the beasts;
  The savage will not drink with his next victim
  When he intends to pierce him to the heart.
  That was no hero's deed, Octavio!
  You were not more intelligent than I.
  Your evil heart has triumphed over my

Sincere one in a shameful victory.
There was no shield to catch your deadly blow;
It fell on my unguarded breast. Against
Such ruthless weapons I am but a child.

Scene 10

The former. Buttler.

TERZKY: Look, here is Buttler. He is still our friend.
WALLENSTEIN (*goes toward him with outstretched arms and
    embraces him affectionately*):
Comrade in arms, I'll press you to my heart.
No better is the sunshine in the spring
    Than faces of one's friends at times like this.
BUTTLER: My General—I come to—
WALLENSTEIN (*leaning on his shoulder*): Have you heard?
He has betrayed me for the Emperor.
    What do you say to that? For thirty years
We suffered and enjoyed ourselves together.
We slept together on *one* army cot,
We drank out of *one* glass, and we divided
Each morsel; I relied upon him as
I now rely upon *your* loyal shoulder.
And in the moment when I trustingly
And with affection lean upon his breast,
He seizes the advantage, takes the knife,
And slips it slyly, slowly in my heart.
            (*He buries his face in Buttler's chest.*)
BUTTLER: Forget that false friend. Tell me what you'll do.
WALLENSTEIN: That is well-spoken. So, enough of that!
I am still rich in friends, is that not true?
And Providence still loves me; for just now,
As that dissembler's knav'ry is unmasked,
It has consigned a loyal heart to me.
No more of him! And do not think his loss
Is painful. 'Tis the treachery that hurts;
For I had loved and cherished both of them,
And Max—oh, Max, he truly loved me. He
Did not betray me, no, not he. —Enough,
Enough of that! Now for a remedy—

The courier Count Kinsky's sending me
From Prague could be here any moment now.
Whatever he may bring, we cannot let
Him fall into the hands of mutineers.
Dispatch a trusted messenger to bring
Him by concealed pathways here to me.
                    (*Illo is about to exit.*)
BUTTLER (*detains him*):
    Commander, who is it you're waiting for?
WALLENSTEIN: The messenger to bring me a report
    Of how things went in Prague.
BUTTLER: Hmmm!
WALLENSTEIN: What is wrong?
BUTTLER: Then you are not aware?
WALLENSTEIN: Of what?
BUTTLER: Of how
    This uproar started?
WALLENSTEIN: How?
BUTTLER: That rider—
WALLENSTEIN (*expectantly*):   Well?
BUTTLER: Has come.
TERZKY and ILLO: He's come?
WALLENSTEIN: My messenger is here?
BUTTLER: Some hours ago.
WALLENSTEIN: And I have not been told?
BUTTLER: The sentries took him.
ILLO (*stamps his foot*):   Damn!
BUTTLER: His letter has
    Been read and circulated through the camp—
WALLENSTEIN (*intently*):
    You know what it contained?
BUTTLER (*hesitating*):   Don't ask me that!
TERZKY: Alas! Then everything must have collapsed!
WALLENSTEIN: Conceal nothing! I can stand the worst.
    Has Prague been *lost*? It is? Be frank with me!
BUTTLER: It *has* been lost, and all the regiments
    At Budweis, Tabor, Braunau, Königingrätz,
    At Brünn and Znaym; they all forsake you and
    Pay homage to the Emperor, while you,
    With Kinsky, Terzky, Illo, are proscribed.
    (*Terzky and Illo display fear and rage. Wallenstein stands firm
    and composed.*)

WALLENSTEIN (*after a pause*):
   It is decided—well, that's good—right here
   I am relieved of all these doubts of mine;
   My heart is free again, my spirit clear,
   It must be night for Friedland's stars to shine.
   My spirit hesitated; when at last
   I drew my sword, it was reluctantly,
   Because I knew the choice was given me.
   Now it is necessary, doubt is past,
   And I am fighting for my life, you see.
                (*He exits. The others follow.*)

Scene 11

COUNTESS TERZKY (*enters from a side room*):
   Where are they? I can't stand it anymore.
   It's empty here. They've left me all alone—
   Alone with my anxiety. —I must
   Control myself before my sister and
   Seem calm and keep this agony shut up
   In my afflicted breast—I cannot bear it!
   —If we should fail, if he should have to join
   The Swedes, an empty-handed fugitive,
   Instead of as an honored ally with
   His army's strength behind him, if we should
   Be forced to wander as that count does from
   The Palatine, disgraced reminder of
   His former might— No! I'll not see that day!
   And if he could bear such diminishment,
   I could not bear to see him so diminished.

Scene 12

Countess. Duchess. Thekla.

THEKLA (*attempts to detain the Duchess*):
   O Mother, dear, remain outside with me!
DUCHESS: No, there must be some dreadful secret here
   That is concealed from me—why does my sister
   Avoid me? And why do I see her so
   Beset by anguish? Why are you afraid?
   What is the meaning of these silent gestures
   You have so secretly exchanged with her?

THEKLA: It's nothing, Mother!
DUCHESS: Sister, I must know.
COUNTESS: What does it help to make a secret of it?
  Can it be hidden? Soon or late she must
  Be told about it and endure it all.
  For now is not the time to yield to weakness.
  We must be brave and keep our spirits calm
  And learn to practice using all our strength.
  'Tis better that her fate be made quite clear
  With this one word. —They have deceived you, Sister.
  You think the Duke has been deposed—the Duke
  Was not deposed—he is—
THEKLA (*going to the Duchess*): You want to kill her?
COUNTESS: The Duke is—
THEKLA (*throwing her arms around her mother*):
                    Oh, you must be steadfast, Mother!
COUNTESS: The Duke is in rebellion. He had planned
  To join the enemy. His army has
  Deserted him, and everything has failed.
  (*During these words the Duchess totters and falls unconscious
  in her daughter's arms.*)

Scene 13

A large room in the Duke of Friedland's quarters.

WALLENSTEIN (*in armor*):
  Octavio, you have succeeded! —I
  Am as abandoned as at Regensburg
  When I went from the Diet of the princes.
  There I had nothing but myself—but what
  One man is worth, you soon experienced.
  You have denuded me of my fine boughs,
  I stand, a tree trunk stripped of foliage! But
  Within my bones lives my creative strength
  That, sprouting, bore a world out of itself.
  Time was, I meant more than an army did,
  Myself, alone. Your army had dissolved
  Before the Swedish might, and on the Lech
  Your last and greatest treasure, Tilly, fell;

Then Gustav like a swollen river gushed
Into Bavaria and in Vienna
The Emperor was trembling in his fortress.
Since soldiers mostly follow fortune, they
Were too expensive. —Then all eyes were turned
On me to help them in their need. Before
Me, sorely wronged, the Emperor put down
His pride. I was to say the word that would
Create an army in the empty camps.
I did it. Drums were sounded, and my name
Resounded like the God of War. The plow,
The workshop were deserted. Everyone
Came running to my long-known flag of promise.
—I think I am the same as I was then!
It is the spirit that creates the man,
And Friedland knows how to fill up his camp.
Confront me boldly with your thousands, they
Are used to winning under me, and not
Against me. —Separate the head and limbs
And then we'll see just where the spirit dwells.
(*Illo and Terzky enter.*)
Have courage, friends! We're not yet on the ground.
Five regiments of Terzky's we still have
And Buttler's gallant band—tomorrow we
Will join the sixteen-thousand Swedish troops.
I was no stronger when nine years ago
I took the field to conquer Germany.

Scene 14

The former. Neumann, who draws Terzky aside and speaks with him.

TERZKY (*to Neumann*):
  What do they want?
WALLENSTEIN: What's this?
TERZKY: Ten cuirassiers
  Of Pappenheim's come from the regiment
  To speak to you.
WALLENSTEIN (*quickly to Neumann*): Let them come in at once.
  (*Neumann exits.*)

This gives me hope. Pay good attention here.
They hesitate and still can be convinced.

Scene 15

Wallenstein. Terzky. Illo. Ten cuirassiers, led by a lance corporal, march in and, following commands, form ranks and salute the Duke.

WALLENSTEIN (*to the corporal, having measured them for a time with his gaze*):
I know you well. You are from Bruges in Flanders.
Your name is Mercy.
CORPORAL: I am Heinrich Mercy.
WALLENSTEIN: You were cut off while on the march, and your
One-hundred-eighty men, surrounded by
The Hessians, fought through their one thousand men.
CORPORAL: Yes, General, that's true.
WALLENSTEIN: What did you get
For this brave deed?
CORPORAL: I got the honor, Sir,
That I requested—service in your corps.
WALLENSTEIN (*turns to another one*):
You answered when I asked that volunteers
Step forth upon the Altenberg, who would
Go forth to seize the Swedish battery.
SECOND CUIRASSIER: That's true, Sir.
WALLENSTEIN: I cannot forget a man
With whom I ever have exchanged a word.
Well, tell me, what's your business?
CORPORAL (*gives the command*):   Present arms!
WALLENSTEIN (*turning to a third man*):
Your name is Risbeck. You come from Cologne.
THIRD CUIRASSIER: Sir, Risbeck from Cologne.
WALLENSTEIN: The Swedish colonel, Dübald—it was you
Who took him prisoner at Nuremberg.
THIRD CUIRASSIER: It was not me, Sir.
WALLENSTEIN: Yes, that's right. It was
Your older brother did it, and you had
A younger brother, too; where is he now?
THIRD CUIRASSIER: He serves the Emperor at Olmütz now.

WALLENSTEIN (*to the Corporal*): Now, I am listening.
CORPORAL: A paper from the Emperor has come
  That tells us—
WALLENSTEIN (*interrupts him*): Who chose you?
CORPORAL: Each company
  Drew lots for whom should come.
WALLENSTEIN: Your business then!
CORPORAL: A paper from the Emperor has come
  That tells us to renounce our oath to you:
  You are a traitor and an enemy.
WALLENSTEIN: And what is your resolve?
CORPORAL: Our comrades have
  Obeyed at Braunau, Budweis, Prague, and Olmütz
  Already, and Toskana's regiment
  And Tiefenbach's have followed their example.
  —But we do not believe it that you are
  An enemy and traitor, and we think
  It is a lie the Spaniards have made up.
                    (*frankly*)
  So you shall tell us what you have in mind,
  For you have always been sincere with us,
  And we have had the greatest faith in you.
  No foreigner shall push himself between
  A good commander and these, his good men.
WALLENSTEIN: Now I can recognize my Pappenheimers.
CORPORAL: So now your regiment requires to know:
  If your intention is but to maintain
  In your own hands the staff of power that
  The Emperor, quite rightly, gave to you
  To keep in Austria your just command,
  Then we will stand by you and will defend
  You on your good right hand against all men—
  And even if the other regiments
  All turn away from you, then we alone
  Will still be true and give our lives for you.
  That is our trooper's duty that we should
  Prefer to perish than to let you fall.
  But if the things the Emperor has said
  Are so, if it is true you want to lead
  Us as a traitor to the enemy,
  May God forbid, then we too will forsake

You and obey the Emperor's command.
WALLENSTEIN: Now listen, children—
CORPORAL: You need use few words.
   Say yes or no, we will be satisfied.
WALLENSTEIN: Just listen, for I know you're sensible,
   Think for yourselves, don't go where others lead.
   And that is why, you know, I always have
   Distinguished you among these waves of troops.
   The quick glance of commanders only can
   Perceive the companies, not single men,
   His orders must be strong and strict and blind,
   No single man can matter to the whole—
   But I have not, you know, done thus with you,
   As you began to comprehend your role
   In this raw craft, as from your foreheads there
   Appeared to shine such human purpose that
   I treated you as independent men
   And granted you the right to your own voice.
CORPORAL: You've always treated us with dignity
   And honored us, Sir, with your confidence
   And favored us above the other men.
   We do not follow with the rank and file
   As you have seen! We wish to stay with you.
   Just speak one word—your word will be enough—
   That says betrayal is not what you plan,
   You will not lead us to the enemy.
WALLENSTEIN: I, I have been betrayed. The Emperor
   Has sacrificed me to my enemies.
   I'll fall unless my brave troops rescue me.
   I will entrust myself to you—your hearts
   Will be my fortress! They are taking aim
   Here, at my breast, at this gray head! —This is
   The Spaniards' gratitude, that's what we get
   In payment for the bloody battle fought
   On Lützen's plain! It was for that we threw
   Our naked breasts against the wall of halberds;
   It was for that we made our beds upon
   The icy ground, the solid rock. No stream
   Was too swift and no woods too thick for us,
   We followed Mansfeld unrelentingly
   Through all the crooked windings of his flight;

Our life was nothing but one restless march,
And like the howling of the wind we rushed
Without a home throughout the warring world.
And now, when we have done this thankless task,
This most accursed exercise of force,
With tireless, loyal arms have turned aside
The burden of the war, shall now the peace
Be snatched by this imperial young man,
The olive branch, *our* well-deserved reward,
Be wound around his golden baby hair?

CORPORAL: That shall not happen if we can prevent it.
No one but you who gloriously waged
This war, this frightful war, shall finish it.
You led us out onto the bloody plain
Of death; you, no one else, shall lead us home
Rejoicing to those lovely fields of peace,
Shall share the fruits of our long enterprise—

WALLENSTEIN: So? Do you think when you are very old,
You will enjoy those fruits. It will not be!
You'll never live to see the fighting end.
This war will swallow up each one of us.
Well, Austria desires no peace, so I
Must fall, because *I* go in quest of peace.
What's it to Austria if this long war
Destroys the armies and lays waste the world?
It only aims to grow and gain more land.
You have been moved—I see the noble wrath
And how it flashes from your warrior eyes.
O, if my spirit could inspire you now,
As bold as when it led you into battle!
You want to stand by me on my right hand,
Defend me with your weapons—that is noble!
But do not think you will accomplish it,
One little army! All in vain you will
Have sacrificed yourselves for your commander.
                    (*confidingly*)
No, let us play it safe and look for friends.
The Swedes have promised help, so let us seem
To use it until we are frightening
To both and can control the fate of Europe,
Then from this camp to a rejoicing world

We will present a peace already crowned.
CORPORAL: Your compact with the Swedes is only show?
　Then you will not betray the Emperor?
　You will not make us Swedes? You see, it was
　Just that alone we needed to be told.
WALLENSTEIN: What are the Swedes to me? I hate them like
　The depths of Hell, and with God's help I hope
　To drive them back across the Baltic Sea.
　My aim is for the whole. You see, I have
　A heart, I have compassion for the German people.
　You are but common men, but still your thoughts
　Are not so common, and more than the others
　You rate a confidential word from me.
　The torch of war has burned for fifteen years,
　It never stops. The Swedes and Germans, Papists
　And Lutherans! Not one of them will yield
　To any other. Every hand is raised
　Against the other. Each one has his side.
　No one can judge. When will it end and who
　Untie the knot that endlessly adds to
　Itself? —It must be cut in pieces now.
　I feel I am a man of destiny
　And hope with your help to accomplish it.

Scene 16

Buttler. The former.

BUTTLER (*with passion*):
　It was not good to do this, Sir.
WALLENSTEIN: 　　　　　　　　What's this?
BUTTLER: And it will harm us with the loyal men.
WALLENSTEIN: What?
BUTTLER: 　　　　　To declare an open insurrection!
WALLENSTEIN: What do you mean?
BUTTLER: 　　　　　　　　Count Terzky's regiments
　Tore down the eagle of the Emperor
　And your insignia was raised.
CORPORAL (*to the cuirassiers*): Right face!
WALLENSTEIN: Accursed be this act and who advised it!
　(*To the cuirassiers, who are marching off*)

Stop, children, stop! —It is an error—stop!—
It will be strictly punished—hear me! Stay!
They will not listen.
(*to Illo*) Follow them, explain,
And bring them back, no matter what it takes!
                              (*Illo hurries out.*)
Now that will ruin us! Oh, Buttler! Buttler!
You are my evil demon, why did you
Announce this in their presence! —Everything
Was going well and they were half-convinced.
Those madmen with their most improvident
Desire to serve! Oh, cruel is the game
That fortune plays with me! It is my friend
Who ruins me and not the enemy.

Scene 17

The former. The Duchess rushes into the room. Thekla and the Countess follow her. Then Illo.

DUCHESS: O Albrecht! What is this you've done!
WALLENSTEIN: Now this!
COUNTESS: Forgive me, Brother! I did what I could;
    They know it all.
DUCHESS: Oh, what is this you've done!
COUNTESS (*to Terzky*): Are we now past all hope? Has everything
    Been lost?
TERZKY: Yes, everything. The Emperor
    Holds Prague. The regiments renew their oaths.
COUNTESS: The evil malice of Octavio!—
    Is Max gone, too?
TERZKY: Where would he be? He has
    Gone with his father to the Emperor.
    (*Thekla throws herself into her mother's arms and buries her
    face in her bosom.*)
DUCHESS (*enveloping her in her arms*):
    Unhappy child! And more unhappy mother!
WALLENSTEIN (*moves to the side with Terzky*):
    A carriage must be quickly brought into
    The rear, prepared to carry them away.
                              (*indicating the women*)

The loyal Scherfenberg can go with them.
He'll escort them to Eger; we will follow.
> (*to Illo, who is returning*)

You have not brought them back?

ILLO: You hear the crowd?
The whole corps of the Pappenheimers are
Approaching. They demand their Colonel Max
Be given back; they say that he is here
And they maintain you keep him here by force,
And if you do not free him, then they will
Know how to come and free him with their swords.
> (*All are astonished.*)

TERZKY: What shall we make of that?

WALLENSTEIN: I told you so.
Oh, my prophetic heart! He is still here,
And he has not turned traitor to me. He
Could not do that, I never doubted it.

COUNTESS: If he is only here, then all is well;
I know then what will always keep him here!
> (*embracing Thekla*)

TERZKY: It cannot be. Consider! The old man
Betrayed us, went to join the Emperor.
How could *he* dare to stay?

ILLO: I saw the horses
You gave him recently, as they were led
Across the marketplace a while ago.

COUNTESS: O Niece, he is not far away.

THEKLA (*her gaze fastened on the door, cries out with spirit*):
He's here!

Scene 18

The former. Max Piccolomini.

MAX (*stepping to the middle of the room*):
Yes! He is here! I can no longer bear
To sneak around this house with silent tread
And furtively to lurk and hope to find
A moment when—this long anxiety
Is more than I can stand.
(*Approaching Thekla, who has thrown herself into her mother's arms*)

Oh, look at me! Don't look away, sweet angel!
Confess it freely! Do not be afraid!
It matters not who hears; we love each other.
Why should we hide it now? A secret is
For happy people. Misery and those
Who have no hope no longer need pretend.
They act with freedom in the brilliant sun.
(*He notices the Countess, who is looking at Thekla with a
triumphant face.*)
Aunt Terzky, no! Don't look at me with hope,
Expectantly. I do not come to stay.
I come to take my leave. —'Tis over now.
I must forsake you, Thekla. —Yes, I must!
But I cannot leave knowing that you hate me.
Just grant me one last look of sympathy
Say that you do not hate me. Say it, Thekla!
　　　　　(*as he seizes her hand, intensely moved*)
O God! O God! I cannot leave this place.
I cannot—cannot let go of this hand.
Just tell me, Thekla, that you pity me,
That you know this is what I have to do.
(*Thekla, avoiding his glance, points to her father; Max turns
toward the Duke, whom he is aware of for the first time.*)
You here? —It was not you that I sought here.
I did not think to look on you again.
I am concerned with her alone. I want
To beg for absolution from this heart,
And nothing else is of importance now.
WALLENSTEIN: You think perhaps I'll play the fool and let you go,
　　Act out a scene of generosity?
　　Your father is a scoundrel to me now,
　　And you are nothing but his son. It shall
　　Not be for nothing you are in my power.
　　Don't think I'll honor our old friendship now
　　That he has wounded viciously. The days
　　Of love are gone, of tender care; and hate
　　And vengeance now will have their turn. I can
　　Be an inhuman creature just as he.
MAX: You'll do with me as you have power to.
　　But you know I do not defy your wrath,
　　Nor do I fear it. What it is that holds
　　Me here, you know!

(grasping Thekla's hand)
Just look! I wanted to owe everything
To you, and to receive this blessed prize
From your paternal hands. You have destroyed
It all. That does not interest you. You trample
The fortune of your loved ones in the dust.
The god *you* serve is never merciful.
Just like the elements, unfeeling, blind,
With whom no pact can ever be concluded,
You follow only your heart's fierce desire.
O, woe to those who trust in you, who leave
The shelter of their happiness to you,
Allured by your inviting form and manner.
Thus swiftly in the silence of the night
A seething grows within the fiery crater,
Erupting with a roar of violence,
And spews o'er all the settlements of men
That savage stream of frightful devastation.
WALLENSTEIN: You draw a picture of your father's heart.
What you describe is what you'll find within
His bowels, within his black dissembling breast.
I was deluded by the tricks of Hell.
The sliest creature, the most skilled in lies,
Was sent to me from the abyss and placed
Here at my side to be my friend. Who can
Withstand the blandishments of Hell? I took
The basilisk and held it to my bosom;
I nourished it with my heart's blood. It nursed
Its fill upon the breasts of my great love,
Toward him I never had an evil thought.
The gateway to my mind was open wide,
The key to caution I had thrown away,
And in the heavens I was searching, in
The universe, to find the enemy
Whom I held locked within my heart of hearts.
—If I had been to *Ferdinand* what this
Octavio has been to *me*, I would
Not be at war with him—I could not be.
He was my master only, not my friend,
He laid no trust in my fidelity.
We were at war already when he put

The staff of the field marshal in my hand,
For cunning and mistrust are ever warring;
Belief and trust alone engender peace.
Whoever poisons trust commits a murder
Upon those generations yet unborn!
MAX: I will not try to vindicate my father.
    O, woe is me that I cannot!
    Such grave unhappy things have come to pass,
    And each misdeed leads to another, so
    A tightly knitted chain of horrors forms.
    But why are *we* who bear no blame caught in
    This circle of misfortune and of crime?
    We've broken faith with no one! Then why must
    The double guilt of fathers and their wrongs
    Like serpents monstrously encircle us?
    Why must our fathers' unforgiven hate
    Rend us who love and separate us too?
    (*He embraces Thekla with fierce pain.*)
WALLENSTEIN (*fixing his eyes on him in silence and then
    approaching*):
    Max, stay with me! —Do not depart, O Max!
    When you came to the winter camp at Prague,
    They brought you to my tent, a tender boy
    Unused to German winters. In your hand,
    Grown stiff and numb, you held the heavy flag
    And bravely would not let it go. I picked
    You up that time, around you drew my cloak,
    I was your nurse, and I was not ashamed
    To wait on you. I tended you with all
    A woman's anxious industry until
    I made you warm again and on my breast
    Your young life once again was comforted.
    When have I changed the way I feel since then?
    I've made so many thousands very rich,
    Presented them with fine estates and posts
    Of honor—but to you I gave my *love,*
    My heart, myself, is what I gave to you.
    They all were strangers then to me, but *you*
    Were family—O Max, you cannot go!
    It cannot be and I cannot believe
    That Max will ever leave me.

MAX: O my God!

WALLENSTEIN: I cared for you, supported you since you
  Were but a child—what did your father do
  For you that I did not do even more?
  I wove a net of love around you here—
  Destroy it, if you can! —We are attached
  By those fine ties that bind our souls together,
  By every one of Nature's holy bonds
  That act to fasten men to one another.
  Go! Leave me! Go and serve your Emperor,
  And be rewarded with a chain of honor,
  Be decorated with the Golden Fleece,
  Because your friend, the father of your youth,
  And all these holy feelings count for naught!

MAX (*in intense inner struggle*):
  What else is possible? Must I not go?
  My oath—my duty—

WALLENSTEIN: Duty? Who are you?
  If *I* act wrongly to the Emperor,
  It is my fault, it is not yours. Do you
  Obey yourself? Are you your own commander?
  Do you stand free here in this world as I
  So that you are the author of your deeds?
  You spring from *me, I* am your emperor.
  To follow me, obey me, *that* is what
  Your honor is, your law of nature is;
  And if the star on which you live and breathe
  Moves from its course and burning hurls itself
  Upon another world, engulfing it
  In flames, you cannot choose if you will follow;
  It sweeps you up within its mighty flight
  Along with all its rings and all its moons.
  You carry little guilt in this affair;
  The world will not condemn you, it will praise
  You that your friendship meant the most to you.

Scene 19

The former. Neumann.

WALLENSTEIN: What is it?

NEUMANN: The Pappenheimers have dismounted and

Advance on foot; they are determined to
Invade their house, their swords held in their hands,
They mean to liberate the count.

WALLENSTEIN (*to Terzky*):   Then let
The chains be drawn and mount the cannon here.
They will be met with chain shot when they come.
                (*Terzky exits.*)
With swords they'll give me orders! Neumann, go,
And tell them that my order is they shall
Withdraw forthwith and *silently* in order
Await my pleasure.
      (*Neumann exits. Illo steps to the window.*)

COUNTESS: Oh, release him, please,
I beg of you, release him!

ILLO (*at the window*):   Death and devil!

WALLENSTEIN: What now!

ILLO: They're on the town hall roof, they've got
It open, with their guns they've taken aim
At us—

MAX: They're raving mad!

ILLO: They are prepared
To shoot us—

DUCHESS and COUNTESS: God in Heaven!

MAX: Let me go
Below to tell them—

WALLENSTEIN: Do not take one step!

MAX (*indicating Thekla and the Duchess*):
But their lives! Yours!

WALLENSTEIN: What can you tell us, Terzky?

Scene 20

The former. Terzky returns.

TERZKY: I bring news from our loyal regiments,
Their courage can no longer be restrained.
They beg you for permission to attack.
The Prague and Mill gates both are in their hands.
If you would only give the signal, they
Can seize the enemy now from behind.
When he is hemmed in, they can easily

Subdue him in the city's narrow streets.

ILLO: O, come, don't let their eagerness turn cold!
Since Buttler's troops are loyal to us still,
We have more men and we can vanquish them
And here in Pilsen finish this revolt.

WALLENSTEIN: This city would become a battlefield,
Fraternal discord with its eyes aflame
Would be set loose to rampage through its streets.
Shall the decision be committed to
This deadly rage that no command controls?
There is no room to fight here, just to slaughter;
The madness of the Furies, when let loose,
Cannot be called off by a leader's voice.
So it may be! I've long considered it.
That way, so quick and bloody, it could end.
(*turning to Max*)
How's that? You want to play this game with me?
You are at liberty to go. Array
Your men against me! Lead them in this fight!
You know the ways of war, for you have learned
From me. I will not be ashamed to have
You for my foe and never will you find
A better time to pay me back.

DUCHESS: Then has
It come to this. O Cousin, can you bear it?

MAX: The regiments that are assigned to me
I vowed to lead back to the Emperor,
And I will do this or I'll die. My oath
Requires no other thing for me. I will
Not fight against you, if it can be helped.
Your head, though hostile, still is sacred to me.
(*There is the sound of two shots. Illo and Terzky rush over to the window.*)

WALLENSTEIN: What's that?

TERZKY: He's falling.

WALLENSTEIN: Falling? Who?

ILLO: The followers
Of Tiefenbach have shot him.

WALLENSTEIN: Who?

ILLO: It's Neumann.
You sent—

WALLENSTEIN (*vehemently*): The devil take them. I will go—
(*He starts to exit.*)

TERZKY: To pit yourself against this fierce, blind rage?

DUCHESS and COUNTESS: O, God forbid!

ILLO: Commander! No, not
                                                now!

COUNTESS: O, hold him, hold him!

WALLENSTEIN: Let me go!

MAX: Don't do
   This now. Their bloody, hasty deed has put
   Them in a rage. Wait till they feel remorse—

WALLENSTEIN: Out of my way! I have delayed too long.
   They ventured to act so outrageously
   Because they could not see my face. They shall
   Now look upon my countenance and hear
   My voice. Are they not *my* own troops? Am I
   Not their commander and their awesome lord?
   We'll see if they can recognize this face
   That was a sun to them in darkest battle!
   I need no weapons here. I will appear
   Before these rebels on the balcony,
   And quickly tamed—you'll see—rebellious thoughts
   Will soon be bedded in obedience.
            (*He exits. Illo, Terzky, and Buttler follow him.*)

Scene 21

Countess. Duchess. Max and Thekla.

COUNTESS (*to Duchess*):
   When they lay eyes on him—there is still hope.

DUCHESS: What hope! I have no hope.

MAX (*who has stood apart during the last scene in obvious
   conflict, approaches*):
                                        I cannot bear this.
   My mind was firmly made up when I came,
   I thought that I would act above reproach;
   Now I stand here like one deserving hate,
   A brutish monster, laden down with curses
   And with the loathing of the ones I love;
   I see those dear to me severely pressed,

And I could make them happy with a word.
My heart revolts within me; there arise
Two voices that are struggling in my breast.
Within is darkness, how am I to choose the right?
O Father, what you said was all too true,
I was too confident in my own heart,
I waver and know not what I should do.

COUNTESS: You do not know? Your heart has told you nothing?
Then *I* will have to tell you!
Your father perpetrated treachery
Against us, did outrageous deeds against
His leader, plunged us into ruin, and
From this what you, his son, should do is clear:
Make up for the disgraceful things he did,
Establish an example of good faith,
So that the name of Piccolomini
Will not become obscene and be accursed
Within the house of Wallenstein.

MAX: Where is
A voice of truth that I can follow? We
Are moved by wishes and by passions. If
An angel would just come to me from Heaven
To fashion for me what is right and real
From that pure source of light with his pure hand.
                    (*as his gaze falls upon Thekla*)
Why am I searching for this angel still?
Is there another one?
        (*He approaches her and puts his arm around her.*)
                              Here on this heart,
Infallible, so pure and holy, I
Will put this question, I will ask your love
That only blesses those already blessed
And turns away from those cursed by some guilt
Can you still love me if I stay with you?
Declare to me you can, and I am yours.

COUNTESS (*with significance*):
Consider—

MAX (*interrupts*): No! Just tell me how you feel!

COUNTESS: Think of your father!

MAX (*interrupts*):   Friedland's daughter is
Not whom I ask, I ask the one I love!

There is no question here about a crown.
You might consider that with mind that's clear.
Your friend's peace is what counts, the happiness
Of all that multitude of valiant hearts
Who take his deeds as models for their own.
Shall I renounce the Emperor and shall
I aim the bullet of a parricide
At the encampment of Octavio?
For when the bullet leaves the barrel of
The gun, it is no lifeless thing; it lives,
It has a spirit; the Eumenides,
Avengers of great crimes, take hold of it
And guide it spitefully the meanest way.

THEKLA: O Max—

MAX (*interrupts*): No, do not answer hastily!
I understand you. To your noble heart
What is most difficult might first occur.
Not great but human should my actions be.
Think what the Duke has always done for me.
Think, too, of how my father has repaid him.
O, all those fine and free impulses of
His hospitality, of loyal friendship,
Create a true religion in the heart.
These are avenged by Nature's horror on
The base barbarian who ruins them.
Place everything there in the balance, speak
And let your heart decide.

THEKLA: Your heart has long
Ago decided. Follow what it told
You first—

COUNTESS: Misguided child!

THEKLA: How could *that* be
The right course which your tender heart did not
Immediately find and apprehend?
Go and perform your duty. Still I would
Forever love you. And no matter what
You choose, your would act nobly always and
Be true to your own self—but no regret
Shall now disturb your soul's tranquillity.

MAX: So I must leave you, I must part from you!

THEKLA: True to yourself, you will be true to me.

Fate separates us but our hearts remain as one.
A deadly hate will part eternally
The Friedlands and the Piccolominis,
But we are not part of these families.
—Away, and hasten, hasten to divide
Your noble action from our luckless one!
Upon our heads lies Heaven's curse, and we
Are dedicated to destruction. I
Will also walk the road to ruin with
My father's guilt. But do not grieve for me.
My fate will be decided soon.
(*Max clasps her in his arms, deeply moved. Behind the scene a
loud, wild, long-echoing cry of "Vivat Ferdinandus" can be
heard, accompanied by military instruments. Max and Thekla
embrace unmoving.*)

Scene 22

The former. Terzky.

COUNTESS (*to Terzky*):
   What was that? What's the meaning of that cry?
TERZKY: It is all over. Everything is lost.
COUNTESS: What? They were not moved by the sight of him?
TERZKY: No. It was all in vain.
DUCHESS: They're shouting "vivat."
TERZKY: Yes, to the Emperor.
COUNTESS: Such faithlessness!
TERZKY: They would not even let him say a word.
   When he began to speak, they interrupted
   By loudly playing military music.
   —He's coming now—

Scene 23

*Former. Wallenstein, accompanied by Illo and Buttler. Thereafter
the cuirassiers.*

WALLENSTEIN (*as he enters*):
   Where's Terzky?
TERZKY: Prince, I'm here.
WALLENSTEIN: Our regiments

Should be informed that we break camp today.
Before it's dark we will abandon Pilsen.
                    (*Terzky exits.*)
   Now, Buttler—
BUTTLER: Yes, Commander.
WALLENSTEIN: Write your friend
   And countryman who is in charge at Eger
   By courier that he should be prepared
   Tomorrow to receive us in the fortress.
   You follow us, you with your regiment.
BUTTLER: It shall be done.
WALLENSTEIN (*steps between Max and Thekla, who have clung to
   each other through this last exchange*):
                       Unhand each other.
MAX: God!
   (*The cuirassiers enter the hall with weapons drawn and
   assemble in the rear. At the same time from below can be heard
   a few passages from the Pappenheimer March, which seem to
   call to Max.*)
WALLENSTEIN (*to the cuirassiers*):
   He's here. He's free. I will not keep him now.
   (*He turns away and stands so that Max cannot come to him nor
   approach Thekla.*)
MAX: You hate me and in anger drive me forth.
   The bond of love between us shall be torn,
   Not gently loosened, and you want to make
   This painful wound so much more painful still.
   You know that I have not yet learned to live
   Without you—that it is a wasteland I
   Am entering, and everything that's dear
   To me, yes, everything is here. O, do
   Not turn away! Just one more time allow
   Me to look on your dear and honored face!
   Do not reject me—
   (*He tries to grasp his hand. Wallenstein draws it away. He turns
   to the Countess.*)
                       Is there no one here,
   No one to pity me? —Aunt Terzky, you—
   (*She turns away from him; he turns to the Duchess*)
   Most honored mother—
DUCHESS: Leave, Count, now, go where

Your duty calls you! —Then some day you can
Be our good angel and our faithful friend
Before the Emperor.

MAX: You give me hope.
You try to save me from complete despair.
Do not delude me with such hollow words.
My misery is certain; thanks to Heaven,
Who has presented me the means to end it!
(*The martial music begins again. The room gradually becomes
full of armed men. He sees Buttler standing there.*)
So, Colonel Buttler, you're here, too? —You will
Not follow me? May you be truer to
Your present master than your old one. Will
You promise, give your hand on it, that you
Will guard him and protect him from all harm?
(*Buttler declines to shake hands.*)
The Emperor has outlawed him and bared
His princely head to every cutthroat who
Hopes to gain profit from a bloody deed;
He will require the care of a good friend,
The faithful eye of love—and those I see
Around him as I leave—
(*Directing ambiguous glances at Illo and Buttler*)

ILLO: The traitors can
Be found in Gallas' and your father's camp.
Just *one* is here. Go now and free us from
This single hateful countenance. Depart!
(*Max attempts once more to approach Thekla. Wallenstein pre-
vents it. He stands irresolute, agonizing; meanwhile the room
becomes more and more crowded, and the bugles sound more and
more with an air of challenge and with ever shorter pauses.*)
MAX: Blow! Blow! If only these were Swedish horns
And I could go directly to the field
Of death, and all the swords I see unsheathed
Around me here would penetrate my breast!
What do you want? You come perhaps to drag
Me off? —O, do not make me desperate!
Don't do it! You could rue the day.
(*The room is completely filled with armed men.*)
Still more—such weight is added to the load
That its great size alone can drag me down.

Think! This is nothing pleasant you begin
By choosing me to lead as I despair.
You snatch me from my happiness, well then,
I give your souls to Vengeance for her care!
You've made a choice that you will not survive;
Who goes with me will not come out alive!
(*As he turns toward the rear, there is a swift movement on the
part of the cuirassiers; they surround him and escort him with
wild tumult. Wallenstein stands motionless Thekla sinks into
her mother's arms. The curtain falls.*)

ACT IV

In the house of the Mayor of Eger

Scene 1

BUTTLER (*who is just arriving*): He's here. His destiny is guiding
   him.
Behind him the portcullis has been dropped,
And as the drawbridge that he trod came down
And then rose up, suspended in the air,
Each means of rescue was cut off for him.
"So far, Duke Friedland, and no farther," say
The fates. Your meteor, so much admired,
Rose from the earth there in Bohemia,
Raced splendidly across the sky, and must
Fall at the border of Bohemia!
—You have renounced the standards that you bore,
And now, deluded, trust to your old luck!
You have equipped your sacrilegious hand
To fight the Emperor within his realm,
To overturn the holy household gods.
Take care—since you are driven by revenge—
That it is not revenge destroys you!

Scene 2

Buttler and Gordon.

GORDON: It's you? How much I need to talk to you.
   The Duke is called a traitor! O my God!

And is a fugitive, his royal head
Proscribed! I beg you, tell me in detail
How all of this has come about at Pilsen!

BUTTLER: Did you receive the letter that I sent
Ahead to you express by courier?

GORDON: And I have faithfully done as you asked;
Without reserve I opened up to him;
The letter from the Emperor commands
Me blindly to submit to all *your* orders.
Forgive me, though; when I saw him arrive,
Then I began again to have some doubts,
Because the Duke of Friedland did not come
Into this city like a man proscribed.
A sovereign's majesty shone from his brow
As always, claiming our allegiance here;
And he, serenely as in ordered days,
Accepted my account of duty done.
Misfortune breeds familiarity,
And guilt and fallen pride will bend the knee
And fawningly make up to lesser men;
But sparingly, with dignity, the Prince
Weighed every word of praise as does a lord
Who lauds his servant for a job well done.

BUTTLER: Just as I wrote you, that is how it was.
The Prince has sold his army to the foe
And aimed to open Prague and Eger to him.
When this report was heard, his regiments
Deserted him, except for five; and these,
The ones that Terzky leads, have followed him.
He has been excommunicated and
To hand him over, dead or living, is
The bounden duty of each faithful servant.

GORDON: A traitor to the Emperor—and such
A lord! So gifted! What is greatness now?
I always said that could not end well, for
His greatness and his strength would be a snare,
As well as his obscure, unsteady power.
A man will seek to gain more for himself;
You cannot trust his moderation. He
Is kept in bounds by careful laws alone
And by the deeply trampled track of custom.

The war's dominion was unnatural,
A new variety in this man's hands;
It made him equal to the Emperor,
And his proud spirit had forgotten how
To bow. It is a pity, for I think
There is no man who could stand where he fell.
BUTTLER: Spare your laments till he needs sympathy;
He is still powerful and must be feared.
The Swedes are marching against Eger now.
They soon will be united, if we do
Not quickly hinder it. That cannot be!
The Prince shall never leave this place of his
Free will, for I have pledged my honor and
My life that here I'll take him prisoner,
And it is your support I'm counting on.
GORDON: Would that I'd never lived to see this day!
It was from his own hand I have this rank;
This castle he entrusted to me that
I now am asked to turn into his prison.
Subordinates have no will of their own;
A free man must be someone powerful,
For he alone can bow to human feeling.
But we are hirelings of inhuman law,
Obedience is what the virtue's called
For which we baser men seek to compete.
BUTTLER: That limited capacity should not
Be painful. Where there's freedom, there is error;
The narrow path of duty is secure.
GORDON: You say that everyone's deserted him?
By him the happiness of thousands was
Begun. His spirit was so regal and
His hands were always full of gifts to give—
                    (*with a sidelong glance at Buttler*)
So many men he rescued from the dust
And elevated them to rank and honor;
Did that not buy one friend for him, not *one*,
To keep his colors in this time of need?
BUTTLER: He has one here whom he did not expect.
GORDON: I have enjoyed no favors from his hands.
I almost doubt that in his greatness he
Has thought about this friend from his young days.

My service kept me far from him, his eye
Lost sight of me within these fortress walls
Where I, untouched by all his kindnesses,
Preserved in quietness a heart that's free.
But when he placed me in this fortress, he
Held earnestly to duty; I will not
Betray his trust if loyally I guard
What he entrusted to my loyalty.

BUTTLER: Just say if you will execute the ban
On him and lend your help to take him captive.

GORDON (*after a thoughtful silence, sorrowfully*):
If it is so—if things stand as you say—
If he betrayed his Emperor and sold
The army and the strongholds of the land
To aid the Empire's enemy, well, then
There is no saving him. Still, it is hard
That, from them all, fate chooses me to be
The implement that causes his destruction.
At Burgau we were pages at the court
Together, but I was the older one.

BUTTLER: I know of that.

GORDON: 'Twas thirty years ago. That spirit bold
Already strained within the youth. His mind
Was serious beyond his twenty years
And aimed alone at great and valiant things.
He moved among us quietly and was
His own best company; he was not moved
By childish pleasures like the other boys;
But often, suddenly, he was possessed,
And from his breast so secretive there came
A flash of thought, significant and bright,
So that we were amazed and did not know
If madness or a god's voice spoke from him.

BUTTLER: And there he fell two stories to the ground
When he was sleeping in a window's bow,
And he got up again and was unharmed.
From that day on, they say, one could detect
Some slight attacks of madness in his ways.

GORDON: It's true he did become more thoughtful. He
Turned Catholic. The miracle of his
Escape did change him strangely. Now he thought

That he was favored and exempt from danger.
He ran upon the swaying rope of life
As daring as a man who cannot fall.
Then we were led by fate far, far apart;
With hasty step he boldly trod the path
To greatness—giddily I saw him go—
Was count and prince and duke and then dictator,
And now that is too small for him, he will
Reach out his hands to grasp a crown and then
Will plunge into immeasurable ruin.

BUTTLER: He's coming! Quiet!

Scene 3

Wallenstein in conversation with the Mayor of Eger. The former.

WALLENSTEIN: You were an independent city once.
 I see the eagle halved is in your seal.
 Why just the half?
MAYOR: We were the subjects of
 The Empire till two-hundred years ago
 The city bowed down to Bohemia.
 Our coat of arms thus bears the eagle halved.
 The lower part has been crossed out until
 The Empire shall again redeem us.
WALLENSTEIN: You
 Deserve your freedom. Just be good and give
 No ear to agitators. Is your tax
 Set high?
MAYOR (*shrugs his shoulders*): We scarcely can afford to pay;
 We also must support the garrison.
WALLENSTEIN: You shall receive relief. Now tell me, are
 There any Protestants within the city?
                     (*The Mayor hesitates.*)
 Now, now, I know it. Many still are hidden
 Within these walls—confess it freely now—
 I think you are yourself?
 (*Stares fixedly at him. The Mayor is alarmed.*)
                     Don't be afraid!
 I hate the Jesuits—I wish they were
 Banned from the Empire—mass or Bible is

The same to me—I've proved this to the world.
In Glogau I myself allowed a church
To be constructed for the Lutherans.
—Now listen to me, Mayor—what's your name?
MAYOR: Pachhälbel, my most noble Duke.
WALLENSTEIN: Now listen—but do not repeat what I
Reveal in confidence.
(*Laying his hand on the Mayor's shoulder, with some
solemnity.*)
                              The time has come
When it shall be fulfilled, so know this, Mayor,
The mighty ones will fall, and then the lowly
Will be raised up—but keep this to yourself!
The double sovereignty of Spain draws to
A close, and now a new arrangement of
All things will come. Just recently you saw
Three moons up in the heavens?
MAYOR: With great dread.
WALLENSTEIN: And two of these contracted and were changed
Into the shape of bloody daggers. One
Alone, the middle one, stayed pure and bright.
MAYOR: we thought that it concerned the Turks.
WALLENSTEIN: The Turks!
Two empires in the east and in the west
Will perish with much bloodshed, this I say,
And what remains will be the Lutheran faith.
                    (*He notices the other two.*)
There was a lot of shooting in the night
On our left hand as we were on the way.
Were you aware of that here in the fortress?
GORDEN: We heard it, General; the sound was brought
Here by the wind as it blew from the south.
BUTTLER: It seemed to come from Neustadt or from Weiden.
WALLENSTEIN: The Swedes approach us now from that direction.
How many men are here?
GORDON: One-hundred-eighty,
Prepared to fight; the rest have been disabled.
WALLENSTEIN: How many are in Jochimsthal?
GORDON: I sent
Harquebusiers, two hundred of them, there
To fortify that post against the Swedes.

WALLENSTEIN: I must applaud your care. They're building, too,
  Outside the walls I saw as I arrived.
GORDON: Because the Rhine Count is so near to us,
  I had them quickly build two bastions.
WALLENSTEIN: You serve the Emperor most certainly.
  I'm satisfied with you, Lieutenant Colonel.
                    (*to Buttler*)
  The post in Jochimsthal shall be dissolved,
  Along with all who stand against the foe.
                    (*to Gordon*)
  Commander, in your faithful hands I leave
  My wife, with her my child and sister, for
  I cannot stay here longer; I expect
  Some letters, then I'll leave the fortress at
  The earliest with all the regiments.

Scene 4

The former. Count Terzky.

TERZKY: Here's good intelligence and happy tidings!
WALLENSTEIN: What do you bring?
TERZKY: A battle has been fought
  At Neustadt, and the Swedes are victors there.
WALLENSTEIN: What's that you say? Where have you heard this
  news?
TERZKY: A farmer brought it here from Tirschenreit,
  The battle started after sundown, when
  A troop of men who serve the Emperor
  Arrived from Tachau, broke into the camp,
  And then the shooting lasted two hours long.
  The Emperor has lost a thousand men,
  Their colonel with them; that was all he knew.
WALLENSTEIN: How did the soldiers of the Emperor
  Reach Neustadt? Altringer must have grown wings.
  He was still fourteen miles off yesterday,
  And Gallas groups his men at Frauenberg;
  They are not yet together. Could it be
  That Suys has ventured so far out in front?
  That is not possible.
                    (*Illo enters.*)

TERZKY: We'll find out now;
  In haste but in good spirits here comes Illo.

Scene 5

Illo. The former.

ILLO (*to Wallenstein*):
  A mounted soldier wants to speak with you.
TERZKY: Has he confirmed the news of victory?
WALLENSTEIN: What does he say? Who does he come from?
ILLO: From
  The Rhine Court, and I'll tell you what he says.
  The Swedes are camped five miles away from here.
  At Neustadt, Piccolomini threw all
  His cavalry against them. After that
  The quantity of bloodshed there was frightful.
  The greater numbers overcame at last,
  And all the Papenheimers, even Max
  Who led them there, lie dead upon that place.
WALLENSTEIN: Where is the rider? Take me there!
  (*Is about to exit. At this the Lady Neubrunn rushes into the
  room; she is followed by some servants, who run across the
  room.*)
NEUBRUNN: Oh, help!
ILLO and TERZKY: What's this?
NEUBRUNN: My lady!
WALLENSTEIN and TERZKY: Knows?
NEUBRUNN: And wants to
                                          die.
  (*Rushes out. Wallenstein follows her with Terzky and Illo.*)

Scene 6

Buttler and Gordon.

GORDON (*astonished*): Can you explain to me what all that
  meant?
BUTTLER: She has just lost the man she loves. It was
  Max Piccolomini who perished there.
GORDON: Unhappy lady!
BUTTLER: You heard the news that this man Illo brought.
  The Swedes approach victorious!

GORDON: I heard.

BUTTLER: They have twelve regiments, and there are five
  Nearby whose job is to protect the Duke,
  While we have just my single regiment
  And not two-hundred men here in the fortress.

GORDON: That's true.

BUTTLER: It is not possible with so few men.
  To keep a prisoner of state like him.

GORDON: I understand.

BUTTLER: That multitude would soon be able to
  Disarm our band and free him.

GORDON: This I fear.

BUTTLER (*after a pause*):
  Know this, that I have vouched for the results,
  And I must answer for his head with mine.
  My word must be preserved, no matter what.
  If I cannot take care of him alive,
  At least—if he is dead, he's safe.

GORDON: Do I hear right? Oh, gracious God! You could—

BUTTLER: He shall not live.

GORDON: You could do that?

BUTTLER: You or else I. He's seen his last day break.

GORDON: You want to murder him?

BUTTLER: That is my plan.

GORDON: He trusts your loyalty.

BUTTLER: That's his bad luck.

GORDON: He is your sacred leader.

BUTTLER: Once he *was*.

GORDON: What he once was, no crime can change. Without
  A verdict?

BUTTLER: Execution is the verdict.

GORDON: That would be murder and not justice done,
  Even the guiltiest must still be heard.

BUTTLER: His guilt is plain, the Emperor has judged,
  And we must only execute his will.

GORDON: One should not do a deadly deed in haste,
  You can take back a word, but not a life.

BUTTLER: But kings seem to be pleased by hasty deeds.

GORDON: No one of noble mind will play the hangman.

BUTTLER: No man who's brave can blanch at a brave deed.

GORDON: The brave may risk their lives but not their conscience.

BUTTLER: Should he go free to light anew the flame,

So inextinguishable, of this war?

GORDON: Just take him captive, only do not kill him.
Do not prejudge God's mercy with his blood.

BUTTLER: I would have let him live, if they had not
Laid low the army of the Emperor.

GORDON: Why did I ever let him enter here!

BUTTLER: His fate and not this place puts him to death.

GORDON: I would have died well in a fight for these
Walls of the castle of the Emperor.

BUTTLER: A thousand worthy men would perish, too.

GORDON: For duty—that gives honor to a man;
But nature does despise an act of murder.

BUTTLER (*holding out a paper.*):
Here is the proclamation that requires
We seize him. It was sent to you as well
As me. Will you accept the blame, if he
Gets to the enemy because of us?

GORDON: I who am powerless? —O, God!

BUTTLER: Take on yourself the consequences then,
Whatever comes, I put the blame on you.

GORDON: O God!

BUTTLER: Do you know any other way
To carry out the Emperor's intent?
I wish to overthrow him, not to kill him.

GORDON: I see what must be, just as clear as you.
But in my breast my heart says something else.

BUTTLER: This Illo and this Terzky, too, they can
Not be left living when the Duke is dead.

GORDON: I am not sorry for these two. 'Twas not
The stars that drove *them,* but their evil hearts;
They were the very ones who sowed the seeds
Of wicked passion in his peaceful heart,
Gave nourishment to this unhappy fruit
By their accursed industry—may they
Reap evil for the evil they have sown.

BUTTLER: It's best if they should die before he does.
It is arranged already, and tonight,
While at their dinner, we were going to seize
Them still alive and keep them in the castle.
It takes less time this way. I'm going now
To take care of the necessary orders.

Scene 7

The former. Illo and Terzky.

TERZKY: Now things will soon be changed. The Swedes will come
　　Tomorrow with twelve-thousand gallant men.
　　Then next, Vienna! Hey, old man, be glad!
　　No sour faces with such happy news!
ILLO: Now it will be our turn to make the laws
　　And take revenge on all those wretched men,
　　Those shameful ones, who left us. One of them
　　We know has paid, Max Piccolomini.
　　May all of those who wish us ill fare thus!
　　How hard the blow will be on that old head!
　　Throughout his life he toiled so that at last
　　He'd be a duke where he was only count,
　　But now he'll bury first his only son.
BUTTLER: But it's too bad about that noble youth.
　　It grieved the Duke himself. That one could see.
ILLO: Just listen, friend, that's what I never liked
　　About our lord, it always made me mad
　　That he preferred those Latins over us.
　　And even now, I swear it on my life,
　　He'd gladly see the rest of us all dead,
　　If that way he could bring his friend to life.
TERZKY: Be quiet! Nothing more! The dead may rest.
　　Today what matters is who'll drink the most.
　　Your regiment is set to entertain,
　　And we will have a merry carnival.
　　Let night be day, and with our glasses full
　　We will await the Swedish forward guard.
ILLO: Yes, let us keep our spirits high today,
　　For things will soon be hot and heavy now.
　　This sword of mine will not be still till it
　　Has wallowed in the blood of Austria.
GORDON: For shame! What kind of talk is this? Why do
　　You rage so fierce against your Emperor?
BUTTLER: Don't hope too much from this first victory.
　　You know how fast the wheel of fortune turns.
　　The Emperor is still a mighty force.
ILLO: The Emperor has soldiers, but he has

No leaders. Ferdinand of Hungary
Knows naught of war—and Gallas has bad luck
And always was the ruin of his army.
And this sly serpent, this Octavio,
Can wound, it's true, in secret from behind,
But not against the Duke in open battle.

TERZKY: Believe me that we cannot fail. Good luck
Will never leave the Duke, and Austria,
It's clear, can only win with Wallenstein.

ILLO: The Prince will soon have gathered such a host
Together; everyone will rush in here,
They're drawn here by the glory of his standard.
I see the days of old returning now.
He'll be again the great man that he was.
Those fools who have deserted him just now—
Such injury they will have done themselves.
These lands he will bestow upon his friends
And faithful service royally reward,
But we will be the first ones in his favor.
                    (*to Gordon*)
He will remember you as well and will
Remove you from this hole and find a post
In which your loyalty can better shine.

GORDON: I'm satisfied; I do not wish to have
A higher place; with heights go also depths.

ILLO: There is here nothing further you can do;
The Swedes will take the fortress on the morrow.
Come, Terzky, it will soon be time to eat.
What do you think, should we light up the town
In honor of the Swedes, and anyone
Who doesn't is a Spaniard and a traitor?

TERZKY: No more of that! It will not please the Duke.

ILLO: What's that? We're masters here, and where we are,
Let no one say he's for the Emperor.
—Good evening, Gordon. For the final time
You are in charge. Send watches on the rounds;
The password can be changed for safety's sake.
At ten o'clock you'll hand the Duke the key.
Then you are finished as the keeper here;
The Swedes will take the fortress on the morrow.

TERZKY (*as he leaves, to Buttler*):

You'll come this evening?
BUTTLER: At the proper time.
(*Illo and Terzky exit.*)

Scene 8

Buttler and Gordon.

GORDON (*looking after them*):
    Those miserable wretches! How they rush
    In their elation at their victory
    All unsuspecting toward the trap that's set.
    I have no pity for them, for this Illo,
    This rogue so bold and arrogant, who wants
    To wallow in the blood of Austria.
BUTTLER: Do just as you were told. Send out patrols,
    Care for the fortress's security.
    I'll lock the castle when they've all gone up,
    So nothing will be heard around the town.
GORDON (*anxiously*): Don't hurry so. First tell me what—
BUTTLER: You
        heard,
    All will be Sweden's on the day that dawns.
    Tonight alone is ours; they have been quick,
    But *we* will be still quicker! —Fare-thee-well!
GORDON: Alas, your look bodes nothing good to me.
    Just promise me—
BUTTLER: The sun's light has gone down.
    A most portentous evening now descends.
    Their self-conceit makes them feel safe, and they
    Are handed to us by their evil star.
    Amidst their drunken dreams of great success
    This blade will quickly carve their lives to shreds.
    The Duke was always very good at figures;
    He always did know how to calculate.
    Men were to him as pieces on the board,
    To set up at his pleasure and to move.
    He did not hesitate to gamble with
    The honor and respect of other men.
    He calculated on and on, but now
    That calculation finally is wrong;

He will have reckoned his life in, and like
Another once, will fall amidst his figures.

GORDON: Oh, don't be mindful of his failings now!
Think of his greatness and his benefactions,
On all his traits so worthy of your love,
On all the noble actions of his life,
And let them as entreating angels, who
Do beg for mercy, stay your lifted sword!

BUTTLER: It is too late for me to feel compassion,
And bloody thoughts are all that I may have.

                    (*grasping Gordon's hand.*)

But, Gordon, it is not my hate—I do
Not love the Duke and have no reason to—
But it's not hate makes me his murderer.
It is his evil fate. Misfortune drives
Me, and the hostile union of all things.
A man may think that he is free to act—
In vain! He is naught but the plaything of
Blind force that quickly turns the thing he chose
Into a frightening necessity.
What help is it to him, if in my heart
I'm moved for him—I'll have to kill him still.

GORDON: If your heart cautions you, obey its warning.
God's voice is in your heart; the works of man
Are artificial judgments of what's wise.
What happiness can come to you from such
A bloody deed? No good will come from blood!
Will it provide you with a step to greatness?
Do not believe it! —Kings take pleasure in
A murder, but not in the murderer.

BUTTLER: You do not understand. Why must the Swedes
Be winning and approaching with such speed!
I'd gladly leave him to the Emperor,
Not take his blood on me. No, he could live.
But I intend to keep my word of honor,
And he must die or—listen now and know!—
I am dishonored, if the Duke escapes.

GORDON: To rescue such a man—

BUTTLER (*quickly*):   What's that?

GORDON: Is worth a sacrifice. Be generous!
Your heart, not your opinions, honor you.

BUTTLER (*cold and proud*):
    He is a great man, is a prince—but I
    Am just a little chief, you mean to say.
    And if the lowly born are honored or
    Disgraced, you think what is it to the world
    As long as the nobility is saved?
    —Each man can fix his worth himself. How high
    I estimate myself depends on me.
    No one upon this earth is placed so high
    That next to him I must despise myself.
    A man's *will* fashions him both great and small,
    And I am true to mine, so he must die.
GORDON: Oh, I've aspired to move a mountain here!
    You are not human and begot by man.
    I have no way to stop you; only may
    Some god protect him from your awful hand.
                (*They exit.*)

Scene 9

A room in the Duchess's chambers.

*Thekla in an armchair, pale, with closed eyes. The Duchess and
Lady von Neubrunn busy themselves about her. Wallenstein and
the Countess in conversation.*

WALLENSTEIN: How did she learn so quickly?
DUCHESS: She appeared
    To sense misfortune. When a rumor came
    About a battle where a colonel of
    The Emperor was killed, she was alarmed.
    I saw it right away. She rushed to find
    The Swedish courier and quickly got,
    Through questioning, the hapless secret from him.
    Too late we noticed she was gone; we followed
    And found her lying senseless in his arms.
WALLENSTEIN: Oh, that this frightful blow should strike her so
    Unready! My poor child! —Is she reviving?
             (*turning toward the Duchess.*)
DUCHESS: Her eyes are open.
COUNTESS: She's alive.
THEKLA (*looking around*):   Where am I?

WALLENSTEIN (*goes to her, takes her in his arms*):
Come to yourself now, be my own strong girl;
Just see your loving mother standing there,
Your father's arms that are supporting you.

THEKLA (*straightens up*):
Where is he? Has he gone?

DUCHESS: Who do you mean?

THEKLA: The one who spoke those words of woe—

DUCHESS: Don't think of that, my child! Just chase that thought,
Try to erase that picture, from your mind!

WALLENSTEIN: No, let her sorrow speak! Let her lament!
Let your tears mingle with the tears she sheds!
This is great pain that she is suffering;
But she will overcome it; Thekla has
Her father's strong, unconquerable heart.

THEKLA: I am not sick. I have the strength to stand.
My mother's crying. Have I frightened her?
It's over, and I am myself again.
(*She has gotten to her feet and looks searchingly around the room.*)
Where is he? Do not try to hide him from me.
I want to hear him, and I have the strength.

DUCHESS: No, Thekla, such a messenger of grief
Will never set foot in your sight again.

THEKLA: O, Father—

WALLENSTEIN: My dear child!

THEKLA: I am not weak,
And I will soon recover even more.
Grant me just one request.

WALLENSTEIN: You've but to speak.

THEKLA: Give your permission that this foreigner
Be called and that I be allowed to talk
To him alone and question him.

DUCHESS: No! Never!

COUNTESS: O, no! That is not good. Do not allow it!

WALLENSTEIN: Why do you want to talk to him, my child?

THEKLA: I would be calmer, if I knew it all.
I do not want to be deceived. My mother
Intends to spare me. I will not be spared.
What is most dreadful has been said. I can't
Hear anything more dreadful now.

COUNTESS and DUCHESS (*To Wallenstein*): Don't do it!

THEKLA: My fear and horror took me by surprise;
   My heart betrayed me with that foreigner;
   He was a witness to my weakness, yes,
   I sank into his arms—I am ashamed.
   I must restore myself in his esteem,
   And so I need to talk to him, so that
   The foreigner will not think falsely of me.

WALLENSTEIN: I feel that she is right and am disposed
   To grant her this request. Tell him to come.
   (*Lady Neubrunn exits.*)

DUCHESS: But I, your mother, want to stay with you.

THEKLA: I'd rather speak to him alone. I will
   Be able to behave with more composure.

WALLENSTEIN (*to the Duchess*):
   Let it be so. let her have words with him
   Alone. Some suffering is such that one
   Can only help oneself; a heart that's strong
   Will only trust itself to its own strength.
   In *her* own breast, not on another's, she
   Must gather strength to overcome this blow.
   She is my own strong girl. I'll have her used
   Not like a woman, but a heroine. (*He starts to exit.*)

COUNTESS (*holding on to him*):
   Where are you going? I heard Terzky say
   Tomorrow you intend to leave this place,
   But we must stay behind.

WALLENSTEIN: Yes, you remain,
   Entrusted to the care of these brave men.

COUNTESS: Oh, take us with you, Brother! Do not leave
   Us here alone and mournful, to await
   With anxious spirits what the end will be.
   Misfortune that is here can be endured,
   But the uncertainty and torment of
   The wait for far-off things grows so much greater.

WALLENSTEIN: Who says misfortune? You must change your
   words.
   I hope for something very different.

COUNTESS: Then take us with you. Do not leave us in
   A place with such a melancholy air.
   Within these battlements my heart grows heavy.

It has the feeling of a sepulcher.
I cannot tell you how I loathe this place.
Take us away. Come, Sister, beg him, too,
To take us with him. Help me, my dear niece.
WALLENSTEIN: I'll change the evil omens of this place.
It shall be here my treasures are preserved.
NEUBRUNN (*returning*): The Swedish gentleman.
WALLENSTEIN: Leave them
alone.
(*Exits.*)
DUCHESS (*to Thekla*):
Just look how pale you've grown! Child, you cannot
Converse with him. Come with your mother now.
THEKLA: The Lady Neubrunn may remain with me.
(*The Duchess and the Countess exit.*)

Scene 10

Thekla. The Swedish captain. Lady Neubrunn.

CAPTAIN (*approaching respectfully*):
Princess—I—want to beg you for forgiveness:
My thoughtless and imprudent words—how could I—
THEKLA (*with noble demeanor*):
You saw me in my suffering, and through
This most unfortunate coincidence,
From stranger you became my confidant.
CAPTAIN: I fear that you must hate the sight of me.
It was my tongue that spoke those mournful words.
THEKLA: It was my fault. I drew those words from you.
They were the voice of my own destiny.
My terror interrupted the report
You had begun. I ask you now to finish.
CAPTAIN (*doubtfully*): Princess, it will renew your suffering.
THEKLA: I am prepared for that—I will be calm.
How did the battle start? Complete the tale.
CAPTAIN: We were encamped at Neustadt and were not
Expecting an attack and only slightly
Entrenched. It was toward evening when a cloud
Of dust came from the woods. Our guard rushed in
The camp and cried, "The enemy is here."

We only had the time to throw ourselves
With haste upon our horses when there broke
At a full gallop through the abatis
The Pappenheimers, and then quickly, too,
These stormy troops had jumped their horses o'er
The trench that had been dug around the camp.
But recklessly their courage had contrived
To drive them far ahead; the others came,
The infantry, far back; the Pappenheimers
With boldness followed their bold leader—
(*Thekla makes a motion. The Captain stops for a moment until
she gives him the sign to continue.*)
In front of them, and from the sides, we set
Upon them then with all our cavalry.
And forced them backwards to the trench, and then
The infantry, drawn up with haste, had formed
A wall of lances that confronted them.
They could not go ahead, could not move back,
They were wedged in this close and frightful place.
The Rhine Count then called to their leader that
He could surrender in this fight with honor;
But Colonel Piccolomini—
(*Thekla, swaying dizzily, takes hold of a chair.*)
                              his plume
Gave him away and his long hair that had
Been loosened by the swiftness of his ride—
He signals toward the trench and himself jumps
His noble horse across; the regiment
Is plunging after him—but—then it happened!
His horse, pierced through by one of his command,
Rears frantically and hurls its rider off,
Then there goes over him the full force of
The horses who no longer heed their reins.
(*Thekla, who has attended the last speech with all the signs of
increasing anxiety, lapses into a violent trembling; she seems
about to collapse; Lady Neubrunn hurries to her and takes her
in her arms.*)
NEUBRUNN: My dearest lady—
CAPTAIN (*moved*):   I will take my leave.
THEKLA: It is all over—make an end to it.
CAPTAIN: The troops, when they perceive their fallen leader,

Are seized with fiercely raging desperation.
Not one of them thinks now of his escape,
They fight like savage tigers and excite,
By their inflexible resistence, ours;
The battle does not have an end until
We have destroyed the last one of his men.

THEKLA (*with trembling voice*):
And where—where is—you have not told me all.

CAPTAIN (*after a pause*):
We buried him this morning. He was borne
By twelve young men of the most noble lines;
Our entire host accompanied his bier.
A laurel was placed on his coffin, and
The Rhine Count laid his victor's sword upon it.
There was no lack of tears for his sad lot,
For there are many with us who have known
His generosity and friendliness.
His fate has moved them all. The Rhine Count would
Have gladly saved him, but he brought all his
Attempts to naught; they say he chose to die.

NEUBRUNN (*moved, to Thekla, who has covered her face*):
My dearest lady—please—look up at me!
Ah, why were you determined to endure this?

THEKLA: Where is his grave?

CAPTAIN: He was interred within
A Neustadt monastery until they
Can find a way to get word from his father.

THEKLA: What is the cloister's name?

CAPTAIN: Saint Katherine's.

THEKLA: How far is it?

CAPTAIN: It's seven miles away.

THEKLA: How does one get there?

CAPTAIN: Go to Tirschenreit
And Falkenburg past our first posted guards.

THEKLA: Who has command?

CAPTAIN: It's Colonel Seckendorf.

THEKLA (*steps to the table and takes a ring out of a jewel case*):
You saw me in my suffering and you
Have shown compassion for me—please accept
              (*as she gives him the ring*)
A small remembrance of this hour. Now go.

CAPTAIN (*dismayed*): Princess—
   (*Thekla motions to him in silence that he should go and moves
   away from him. The Captain hesitates and is about to speak.
   Lady Neubrunn repeats the gesture. He exits.*)

Scene 11

Thekla. Neubrunn.

THEKLA (*throws her arms around Neubrunn's neck*):
   Now, Lady Neubrunn, demonstrate the love
   That you have always pledged and prove that you
   Are my companion and my faithful friend!
   —We have to leave this very night.
NEUBRUNN: Leave, and go where?
THEKLA: Go where? There is but *one* spot on this earth!
   Where he lies buried, where his coffin is!
NEUBRUNN: Why do you want to go there, precious one?
THEKLA: Why there? Unhappy lady, for you would
   Not ask if you had ever loved. There, there
   Is everything that is still left of him,
   That single spot to me is all the world.
   —Do not detain me. Come, let us prepare
   And think of ways we can escape from here.
NEUBRUNN: Have you thought fully of your father's wrath?
THEKLA: It does not matter who is angry now:
NEUBRUNN: The world's disdain? The harsh words of reproach?
THEKLA: I look for someone who is here no more.
   In his arms will I—O, my God—I want
   To go but to the grave of my beloved.
NEUBRUNN: We too alone, two frail and helpless women?
THEKLA: We'll arm ourselves, I will be your protector.
NEUBRUNN: In deepest darkness?
THEKLA: Night will be our shelter.
NEUBRUNN: On this cold stormy night?
THEKLA: Was it for *him*
   An easy bed beneath his horse's hooves?
NEUBRUNN: O, God! The enemy has many sentries.
   They will not let us through.
THEKLA: They are still men.
   Misfortune can move freely through the world.

NEUBRUNN: The distance—

THEKLA: Does the pilgrim count the miles,
    When on his travels to the shrine he seeks?

NEUBRUNN: How is it possible to leave this town?

THEKLA: With money we'll get through the gate. Just go!

NEUBRUNN: If we are recognized?

THEKLA: No one will look
    For Friedland's daughter in a fugitive.

NEUBRUNN: Where will we get the horses for our flight?

THEKLA: My cavalier will get them. Call him now.

NEUBRUNN: Dare he do that without his master's knowledge?

THEKLA: He will. Just go now. Do not hesitate.

NEUBRUNN: Oh, what will ever happen to your mother,
    If you should disappear?

THEKLA (*reflecting and gazing painfully in the distance*):
                O my dear mother!

NEUBRUNN: She has already borne so much, your mother.
    Must this last frightful blow now strike her, too?

THEKLA: I cannot spare her this. Just go now, go!

NEUBRUNN: You must consider still what you are doing.

THEKLA: I have considered all that's to consider.

NEUBRUNN: When we are there, what will become of you?

THEKLA: Once there, a god will grant my soul release.

NEUBRUNN: Your heart is so uneasy now, dear Lady,
    But this is not the way that leads to peace.

THEKLA: To that deep peace that he has also found.
    O, hurry! Go! Do not say one word more,
    For I am drawn, by what I cannot say,
    But I cannot resist it, to his grave.
    There, instantly, I will feel easier,
    The bands of pain that suffocate my heart
    Will be dissolved—my tears will start to flow.
    O, go! We could be on the road already.
    I'll have no peace until I have escaped
    These walls—they are collapsing over me—
    Some strange dark power drives me forth from here—
    Oh, what a feeling that is! All the rooms
    Here in this building are filled up for me
    With pallid, faint, and shallow apparitions—
    I have no place here—there are always more!
    I who am still living am compelled,
    By this atrocious swarm to leave these walls.

NEUBRUNN: You frighten me, my Lady, make me anxious,
    So that I would not dare to stay here now.
    I'll go forthwith and summon Rosenberg.
                    (*Exits.*)

Scene 12

THEKLA: It is his spirit calling me. It is
    The faithful ones, who gave themselves as his
    Avengers, charging me with base delay.
    They did not want to let him go in death,
    Who was their leader while they lived. They could
    Act thus with their coarse hearts and *I* should live?
    —O, no! That laurel wreath that rested on
    Your bier was also made for me to share.
    What is a life, when love's bright glow is gone?
    Discard it, for there is no value there.
    I found you, loved you, and it was so rare,
    The life we had then. There before me lay,
    All shining, a new golden day.
    I dreamed of those short hours divinely fair.
        I set foot in the world so timidly
    From cloistered walls, and what I saw was you.
    A thousand suns shone brightly—I could see
    That my good angel put you there for me,
    To take me from my childish joys up to
    The pinnacle of life that I then knew.
    I was divinely happy from the start,
    For my first glimpse was of your *heart!*
    (*She falls into a state of reflection here and then with a start
    takes on the appearance of terror.*)
    Then fate steps in, and it is rude and cold.
    It reaches out, my friend's shape to enfold,
    And casts him where those hooves beat him to earth—
    The world's reward for those of greatest worth!

Scene 13

Thekla. Lady Neubrunn with the Stable Master.

NEUBRUNN: He's here, my Lady, and he'll do it, too.
THEKLA: You'll get the horses for us, Rosenberg?
STABLE MASTER: I'll get them.

THEKLA: Will you go along with us?
STABLE MASTER: My Lady, to the world's end.
THEKLA: But you
  Cannot come back here to the Duke again.
STABLE MASTER: I'll stay with you.
THEKLA: You'll be rewarded and
  Commended to another master. Can
  You help us leave the fortress secretly?
STABLE MASTER: I can.
THEKLA: When can I leave?
STABLE MASTER: Within the hour.
  Where do we go?
THEKLA: To—tell him, Lady Neubrunn.
NEUBRUNN: To Neustadt.
STABLE MASTER: Good. I'll go take care of things.
  (*Exits.*)
NEUBRUNN: My Lady, there's your mother.
THEKLA: O, dear God!

Scene 14

Thekla. Neubrunn. The Duchess.

DUCHESS: He's gone. I find you are much calmer now.
THEKLA: I am, dear Mother. —Now you must allow
  Me to retire with Lady Neubrunn near.
  I need the rest.
DUCHESS: And you shall have it, Thekla.
  I'll leave now comforted, for I can set
  Your father's mind at rest.
THEKLA: Good night, dear Mother.
  (*She embraces her mother with great emotion.*)
DUCHESS: My daughter, you are not completely calm.
  You're trembling so severely, and your heart
  Beats audibly upon my own.
THEKLA: It will
  Be soothed by sleep. —Good night, my dearest mother.
  (*As she disengages herself from her mother's arms, the curtain
  falls.*)

ACT V

Buttler's Room

Scene 1

Buttler. Major Geraldin.

BUTTLER: Select a dozen big and strong dragoons,
Provide them all with lances, for no shot
Is to be fired. Conceal them there beside
The dining hall, and when dessert is served,
You force your way in and cry out, "Who is
The Emperor's?" —I'll turn the table over—
You hurl yourselves at them and strike them down.
The castle is locked tight, and watch is kept
So that no hint of this will reach the Duke.
Now go! —Has Deveroux been summoned with
MacDonald?
GERALDIN: They will be here right away.
(*Exits.*)
BUTTLER: We must not hesitate. The townsmen, too.
Declare themselves for him; I do not know
What kind of craziness has seized the place.
They think the Duke will be the prince of peace
And bring about a new and golden age.
The council hands out weapons, and there have
Been hundreds who have volunteered to stand
Guard over him. Therefore we must be quick,
For enemies are outside and within.

Scene 2

Buttler. Captain Deveroux and MacDonald.

MACDONALD: We're here now, General.
DEVEROUX: What is the password?
BUTTLER: The Emperor!
BOTH (*stepping back*): What's that?
BUTTLER: And Austria!
DEVEROUX: We swore allegiance to the Duke of Friedland!

MACDONALD: Are we not here to act in his defense?

BUTTLER: We should defend a traitor to the Empire?

DEVEROUX: You were the one we followed in his service.

MACDONALD: And you were with him when he came to Eger.

BUTTLER: I did it all the better to destroy him.

DEVEROUX: Oh, well!

MACDONALD: That's something else, then.

BUTTLER (*to Deveroux*):   You poor
   wretch!
  You will so easily desert your flag?

DEVEROUX: The devil, Sir! I followed your example.
  If you're a scoundrel, I can be one, too.

MACDONALD: We don't consider. That's for you to do.
  You are the general and can command,
  We'll follow you though you lead us to Hell.

BUTTLER (*appeased*): Good then! We know each other.

MACDONALD: I agree.

DEVEROUX: We're his who offers most, for we are soldiers
  Of fortune.

MACDONALD: Yes, that's just the way it is.

BUTTLER: I aim to keep you honest soldiers now.

DEVEROUX: We're glad to be that, too.

BUTTLER: And make your fortunes.

MACDONALD: That's better still.

BUTTLER: Now listen.

BOTH: That we will.

BUTTLER: The Emperor has made his wishes known,
  That Friedland shall be caught alive or dead.

DEVEROUX: That's what the letter says.

MACDONALD: Alive or dead!

BUTTLER: And fine rewards in money and in goods
  Are waiting for the one who does the deed.

DEVEROUX: That sounds good, just as everything that comes
  From them sounds good. Yes, yes! We know, we'll get
  A golden decoration or perhaps
  A crippled horse, a noble's patent, or
  Some such. —The Duke pays better.

MACDONALD: Splendid pay!

BUTTLER: He's finished now. His lucky star has set.

MACDONALD: You're sure of that?

BUTTLER: *I'm* telling you.

DEVEROUX: His luck
  Is over?
BUTTLER: Yes, it's over now forever.
  He's just as poor as we are.
MACDONALD: Poor as we are?
DEVEROUX: Well, then, MacDonald, we'll be leaving him.
BUTTLER: Already twenty-thousand men have left him.
  We must do more, my countrymen. In short—
  We have to kill him.
  (*Both recoil in surprise.*)
BOTH: Kill him?
BUTTLER: I said, kill him.
  And I have picked you two for this.
BOTH: Picked us?
BUTTLER: I've picked you, Deveroux, and you, MacDonald.
DEVEROUX (*after a pause*):
  Pick someone else!
MACDONALD: Yes, pick some other man!
BUTTLER (*to Deveroux*):
  It frightens you, you coward. Why is that?
  Already thirty souls are on your head.
DEVEROUX: Lay hand on our commander! —Such a thought!
MACDONALD: When we have given him our sacred oath?
BUTTLER: Your oath was void when he himself broke faith.
DEVEROUX: Commander, that seems horrible to me.
MACDONALD: That's true. We have a conscience, after all.
DEVEROUX: If only it were not our chief who has
  Commanded us so long and earned respect.
BUTTLER: Is that the problem?
DEVEROUX: Yes, *whomever* else
  The Emperor desires, be it my son
  Himself, I'll pierce his innards with my sword—
  But, listen, we are soldiers, and to *kill*
  The *army's leader,* that's an outrage and
  A sin that no confessor can absolve.
BUTTLER: I am your priest—and give you absolution.
  Decide at once!
DEVEROUX (*reflecting*): I cannot.
MACDONALD: No, I can't.
BUTTLER: Well, then, dismissed—and—send me Pestalutz.
DEVEROUX (*taken aback*): Send Pestalutz!

MACDONALD: What do you want with
him?

BUTTLER: If you reject the job, there are enough—

DEVEROUX: No, if he has to die, then we can earn
The prize for it as good as any man.
—What do you think, MacDonald?

MACDONALD: Yes, if he
Has got to die and should, and it *must* be,
I don't want Pestalutz to be the one.

DEVEROUX (*after some thought*):
When must he die?

BUTTLER: Today, this very night,
Because the Swedes will be here by tomorrow.

DEVEROUX: And you will answer for the consequences?

BUTTLER: I'll answer for it all.

DEVEROUX: Is this the true
Will of the Emperor? He may desire
The murder and condemn the murderer.

BUTTLER: These orders stated: either dead or living.
Alive it cannot be; look here yourselves—

DEVEROUX: Well, dead then.—But how do we get to him?
The city is alive with Terzky's men.

MACDONALD: And we must deal with Terzky and with Illo—

BUTTLER: We'll start with those two, that is understood.

DEVEROUX: What's that? They must die, too?

BUTTLER: They must go first.

MACDONALD: Well, Deveroux, this evening will be bloody.

DEVEROUX: Have you the man for that? Charge *me* with that.

BUTTLER: That will be left to Major Geraldin.
Tonight is Carnival. A dinner will
Be given at the castle. There we will
Attack them while at table, lay them low—
Both Pestalutz and Lessley will be there.

DEVEROUX: Oh, listen, it can't matter, General,
Now listen—let me switch with Geraldin.

BUTTLER: The lesser danger will be with the Duke.

DEVEROUX: Sir, what the devil do you take me for?
It is the Duke's eye, not his sword, I fear.

BUTTLER: His eye can't do you harm.

DEVEROUX: The devil says!
You know me—that I am no filthy coward;

But look here, it has not been eight days since
The Duke presented me with twenty pieces
Of gold to buy this coat that I have on.
And if he looks at me when I stand with
This lance and sees this coat—you see—well—well—
The devil take me, I am not a coward.

BUTTLER: And so Duke Friedland gave you this warm coat,
And now, poor creature, you will hesitate
To take your sword and run him through with it.
Well, there's a coat that was still warmer that
The *Emperor* gave *him*, his royal cloak.
How did he thank him? With this treachery!

DEVEROUX: Yes, that's true, too. The devil take my thanks!
I'll—kill him.

BUTTLER: If you want to ease your conscience,
You only need to lay your coat aside;
Then you can do the deed quite cheerfully.

MACDONALD: But there is something else to keep in mind—

BUTTLER: What else is there to keep in mind, MacDonald?

MACDONALD: What use are all our weapons against *him*?
He can't be overcome, he is *protected*.

BUTTLER (*flaring up*): What is it he—?

MACDONALD: Against each shot or blow!
He's *frozen* solid, captive of the devil.
His body is impervious, you see?

DEVEROUX: That's right. In Ingolstadt there was a man
Like that. His skin was strong as steel; they had
To take their gun butts to him in the end.

MACDONALD: Here's what I'll do!

DEVEROUX: Well, tell us!

MACDONALD: I know that
There's a Dominican, a monk, here who
Is from our homeland, and I'll have him dip
My sword and lance into the holy water
And say a good, strong blessing over them;
That's tried and true, it works with any spell.

BUTTLER: Do that, MacDonald. Now, though, you must go,
Pick twenty, maybe thirty, stalwart men
Of yours and swear them to the Emperor.
Then, when eleven strikes and when they've made
The first rounds, you will lead them silently

Up to the house—I will not be far off.
DEVEROUX: How do we pass the guards and archers, too,
    Who will be standing watch within the yard?
BUTTLER: I've learned about the possibilities
    Around here, and I'll take you through a gate
    That's in the rear, where *one* man guards alone.
    My rank and station give me access to
    The Duke at any time. I will go first,
    And quickly, with a dagger in his throat,
    I'll pierce that archer and make way for you.
DEVEROUX: Then, when we are upstairs, how do we reach
    The bedroom of the Duke and still not wake
    His servants, who will raise a row? He is
    Accompanied by plenty of attendants.
BUTTLER: His servants all are in the right wing, for
    He hates the noise and keeps the left himself.
DEVEROUX: If it were only done, MacDonald!—I
    Feel very strange at this, the devil knows.
MACDONALD: Me, too. He is much too important, and
    We will be taken for two dreadful villains.
BUTTLER: With honor and abundant gifts, you can
    Laugh at the rumors and the bad opinions.
DEVEROUX: If it is certain we will get the praise—
BUTTLER: Don't worry. You are saving crown and Empire
    For Ferdinand. Your payment can't be small.
DEVEROUX: His plan is to dethrone the Emperor?
BUTTLER: That's right. To rob him of his life and crown.
DEVEROUX: The executioners would have him, if
    We took him to Vienna still alive?
BUTTLER: There is no way he could escape that fate.
DEVEROUX: We will preserve respect for his command.
    He'll die with honor at his soldier's hand.
    (*They exit.*)

Scene 3

A room from which there is access to a gallery that stretches into the distance.

Wallenstein sits at a table. The Swedish captain stands before him. Directly thereafter, Countess Terzky.

WALLENSTEIN: I send your leader my regards. I share
  In his good fortune, and if you do not
  Observe that I seem quite as pleased as this
  Report of victory should well require,
  Believe me, it is no lack of goodwill,
  For now our fortunes are as one. Farewell.
  Accept my thanks for favors done. The fortress
  Will open wide tomorrow, when you come.
  (*The Swedish captain exits. Wallenstein sits deep in thought,*
  looking ahead blankly, his head resting on his hand. Countess
  Terzky enters and watches him unnoticed for a moment; finally
  he makes a sudden movement, notices her, and quickly
  composes himself.)
  Is she recovering? What is she doing?
COUNTESS: Her mother says she's calmer since she had
  The interview, and now she's gone to bed.
WALLENSTEIN: Her grief will lessen soon and she can cry.
COUNTESS: You, too, are changed from what you were, my
    brother.
  With such a victory you should be glad.
  Oh, keep your strength, maintain your courage now,
  You are the light and sunshine for us all.
WALLENSTEIN: Don't worry. I'm all right. Where is your husband?
COUNTESS: Illo and he are at a dinner party.
WALLENSTEIN (*rises and walks about the room a bit*):
  It's dark night now—you must go to your room.
COUNTESS: Don't make me go; oh, let me stay with you.
WALLENSTEIN (*has moved to the window*):
  The heavens are so full of agitation.
  The tower flags are windswept, and the clouds
  Flock swiftly by; the crescent moon dissolves
  And reappears, and strange lights pierce the darkness.
  —No constellation can be seen. That faint
  And single light comes from Cassiopeia,
  And over there is Jupiter—but now
  He's hidden by the black and stormy sky.
  (*He becomes thoughtful and stares straight ahead.*)
COUNTESS (*who has watched him in sadness, takes his hand*):
  What are you thinking of?
WALLENSTEIN: If I could see him, I would be content.
  He is the planet who controls my life.

The sight of him is strangely strengthening.
(*Pause*)

COUNTESS: You will see him again.

WALLENSTEIN (*has again become preoccupied; he rouses and turns quickly to the Countess*):
See him?—No, nevermore.

COUNTESS: What did you say?

WALLENSTEIN: He's gone—he's dust!

COUNTESS: Whom are you speaking of?

WALLENSTEIN: He is the lucky one; he is fulfilled.
For him there is no future, and fate can
Play no more tricks on him—his life lies there
Spread out without a wrinkle, shining bright,
No blemishes remained behind on it,
No hour strikes for him that brings distress.
He has escaped desire and fear and is
Not captive of the vacillating planets—
He is well off! But who can know what these
Next darkly shrouded hours hold for us.

COUNTESS: You speak of Piccolomini. How did
He die? The messenger left as I came.
(*Wallenstein gives her to understand, with a gesture of his hand, that she should be silent.*)
You must not turn your gaze into the past.
Let us look forward to a brighter time.
Enjoy the victory, forget its cost.
Your friend was taken from you not today;
He died for you when he took leave of you.

WALLENSTEIN: I will survive this blow, I know, for what
Is there that man cannot survive! From greatest
To meanest, he learns to accept it all,
For he is conquered by almighty time.
Still, I know well what I have lost in him.
The blossom has been wrenched out of my life,
And cold and pale I see it lie before me.
He stood beside me like myself in youth;
He made reality seem like a dream
And wove the golden perfume of the dawn
Around the common evidence of things.
The flame of loving sentiment he bore
Exalted for me, to my own surprise,

The shallow character of everyday.
—Whatever I may strive for and attain,
What's fair is gone, and it will not return.
A friend is better than all happiness,
For he creates it and increases it.

COUNTESS: Do not despair of your own strength. Your heart
Is rich enough to elevate itself.
You love and praise the virtues in him that
You planted and developed there yourself.

WALLENSTEIN (*going to the door*):
Who comes to bother us this late? —It is
The commandant. He brings the fortress keys.
Leave us now, sister. It is very late.

COUNTESS: Today it is so hard for me to leave
And I am sorely frightened.

WALLENSTEIN: Frightened? Why?

COUNTESS: You could ride off tonight most suddenly,
And then when we awoke, we would not find you.

WALLENSTEIN: Imagination!

COUNTESS: Oh, my soul has been
So troubled lately by such sad misgivings,
And when awake I fight them, they assail
My anxious heart with melancholy dreams.
—Last night I saw you sit at table with
Your first wife, and you both were finely dressed.

WALLENSTEIN: That is a dream that presages good things.
That marriage was the start of my good fortune.

COUNTESS: And then today I dreamed I went into
Your room to look for you, but then it was
Instead the monastery of Carthusians
That you established once at Gitschin, where
You have expressed the wish to be entombed.

WALLENSTEIN: Your mind is occupied with things like this.

COUNTESS: Well, do you not believe that warning voices
Can speak to us forebodingly in dreams?

WALLENSTEIN: Such voices do exist—there is no doubt.
But I would never call *those* warning voices
That only tell of the *inevitable*.
Just as the sun's shape is reflected on
The atmosphere before it rises, so
The spirits of great fates proceed them, too;

So that today tomorrow walks abroad.
I've always had peculiar thoughts about
Tales of the death of Henry, called the fourth.
The King could feel the spirit of the knife
Within his breast before Ravaillac, who
Would murder him, possessed it. His repose
Evaded him, he had to leave his Louvre
And go outdoors; the coronation of
His consort seemed a death knell to him, he
Could hear the tread of feet, so ominous,
That searched for him through all the streets of Paris.

COUNTESS: Do your presentiments not speak to you?

WALLENSTEIN: No, not a word. Rest easy.

COUNTESS (*lost in gloomy thought*): Once before
I hurried after you, you ran ahead
Down a long corridor, through spacious rooms,
There was no end to it—doors were slammed shut.
They crashed, and gasping I pursued you, but
I could not reach you. Suddenly I felt
A cold hand take hold of me from behind.
And it was *you*. You kissed me, and it seemed
A coverlet of red was over us—

WALLENSTEIN: That is the crimson carpet in my room.

COUNTESS (*regarding him*):
If it should come to this, if you who stand
Before me in the fullness of your life—
(*Weeping, she falls upon his breast.*)

WALLENSTEIN: The Emperor's proscription frightens you.
Words cannot hurt, and he will find no hands.

COUNTESS: But should he find them, then I know what I
Will do—I have my consolation with me.
(*Exits.*)

Scene 4

Wallenstein. Gordon. Thereupon servants.

WALLENSTEIN: Is it all quiet in the town?

GORDON: It is.

WALLENSTEIN: I hear some noisy music, and there are
Lights everywhere. Who are the happy ones?

GORDON: A banquet is in progress in the castle—
 For the Field Marshall and Count Terzky, too.
WALLENSTEIN (*to himself*):
 It is the victory. This type of man
 Cannot rejoice except with food and drink.
 (*He rings. His personal servant enters.*)
 Help me undress. I want to go to bed.
 (*He accepts the keys.*)
 We are protected from each enemy
 And are encircled by our trusted friends.
 I must be much mistaken or a face
 Like this (*looking at Gordon*) cannot disguise a hypocrite.
 (*The servant has removed his coat, his ruff, and his ceremonial belt.*)
 Be careful! What was that?
SERVANT: Your golden chain has cracked and come apart.
WALLENSTEIN: It lasted long enough. Hand it to me.
 (*As he looks at the chain.*)
 The Emperor's *first* favor—as archduke—
 Presented in the Battle of Friaul.
 From habit I have worn it till today.
 —From superstition, if you like. It was
 Supposed to be a talisman as long
 As I devoutly wore it on my neck.
 First casual favor of his approbation,
 To bind me for my life. —Well, let it be!
 From this time forth we start our luck anew,
 For this one's charm is finished.
 (*The servant departs with the apparal. Wallenstein rises, takes a few steps around the room, and finally stops in meditation before Gordon.*)
 How close the old times seem to me just now.
 I see myself as I was at the court
 Of Burgau, where together we were pages.
 We often quarreled; you meant good by me
 And were accustomed to play moralist.
 You reprimanded me because I strove
 Excessively for higher things, believed
 In my bold dreams. You praised the middle way.
 —Your wisdom has preserved you poorly though.
 It changed you to a man whose life was done,

And if I did not intervene with all
My lucky stars, it certainly would have
Let you die calmly in some wretched corner.
GORDON: My Prince! The fisherman, with simple courage, can
Tie up his little boat in its safe harbor,
If in a storm he spies a great ship wrecked.
WALLENSTEIN: So, old man, are you safe in harbor now?
Not I! My undiminished spirit drives
Me fresh and grand upon the wave of life.
I still can call upon hope as my goddess,
My spirit is still young. If I compared
Myself with *you*, I certainly might boast
That fleeting years have powerlessly passed
Above the chestnut locks upon my head.
(*He walks about the room, taking long strides, and stops on the
    opposite side from Gordon.*)
Who says that fortune's false? It's true to me.
It raised me up out of the ranks of men
With love and carried me through all life's stages
Within its gentle, strong, divine embrace.
And there was nothing common in fate's course
For me, nor in the creases of my palms.
Who could explain my life in human ways?
It's true, just now I seem to be cast down,
But I will rise again; high tide will soon
Appear and with its swells replace this ebb—
GORDON: And yet that proverb creeps into my thoughts:
One should not praise the day till it is done.
I do not want to gather hope from long good luck,
For hope is sent to us in our misfortune.
Fear should be hovering o'er fortune's head,
The scales of providence are bound to waver.
WALLENSTEIN (*smiling*): The Gordon of the past is speaking now.
—Well do I know that earthly things may change,
That evil gods may come to claim their toll.
The ancient heathen peoples knew of that
And therefore chose some trouble for themselves,
So that they could appease the jealous gods
With human sacrifices to Typhoeus.
(*After a pause, earnestly and quietly.*)
I've sacrificed to him—my dearest friend

Was lost to me and lost because of me.
I cannot now rejoice in fortune's favor
Since this blow pained me so. —The envy of
My fate is satisfied. It will accept
This one life for another, so upon
This pure beloved head the lightning struck
That should instead have felled me violently.

Scene 5

The former. Seni.

WALLENSTEIN: Is that not Seni? And beside himself!
    What brings you here so late tonight, Baptist?
SENI: I fear for you, Your Highness.
WALLENSTEIN: Now, what's this?
SENI: Before it's daylight, flee, Your Highness! Do
    Not trust the Swedes.
WALLENSTEIN: What are you thinking of?
SENI (*his voice rising*):
    You must not trust the Swedes!
WALLENSTEIN: What do you mean?
SENI: Do not wait for the coming of the Swedes!
    Approaching danger threatens from false friends.
    The signs are there, most dreadful; near, so near
    The network of destruction closes round.
WALLENSTEIN: Baptist, you're dreaming, and your fears delude
    you.
SENI: Oh, do not think I am deceived by fear.
    Come, read it for yourself there in the stars:
    Misfortune threatens you through your false friends.
WALLENSTEIN: All my misfortune comes from my false friends.
    Your warning should have come to me before;
    I do not need the stars to tell me now.
SENI: Oh, come and witness it with your own eyes.
    A dreadful sign rests on the House of Life,
    A nearby enemy, a monster, lurks
    Behind your planet's rays—this is a warning!
    Do not submit yourself to disbelievers,
    Those who make war upon our holy Church!
WALLENSTEIN (*smiling*): Is *that* the reason for this oracle?

Now I remember you were never pleased
By this alliance with the Swedes. —Baptist,
Just go to bed! I do not fear these signs.

GORDON (*who has been severely affected by this exchange, turns to Wallenstein*): My royal liege, allow me a few words,
For often useful words come from poor mouths.

WALLENSTEIN: Speak freely!

GORDON: My Prince, what if it is no empty sign
And if God's providence were making use
Of *this* mouth to preserve you wondrously.

WALLENSTEIN: You're talking in a fever, both of you.
How can misfortune be brought by the Swedes?
They sought to join with me in their own interest.

GORDON: However, if the coming of the Swedes
Was just exactly what accelerated
Those who will bring destruction on your head—
(*Throwing himself at his feet.*)
There is still time, my Prince—

SENI: Oh, hear his words!

WALLENSTEIN: Still time? For what? Arise—I order you!

GORDON (*rises*): The Rhine Count is still far away. Command
It and this fortress will be closed to him.
Will he lay siege to us? —Just let him try!
I'll tell you this: He'll perish there before
These walls, with all his troops, much sooner than
He will exhaust our courage and our spirit.
He will discover what such heroes can
Perform, inspired by a heroic leader
Who means to make up for a wrong he's done.
The Emperor will be appeased by this;
His heart is happy when it can be kind.
And Friedland, who returns repentant, will
Stand higher in his favor than the one
Who never failed him ever could have done.

WALLENSTEIN (*looks at him with consternation and surprise and remains silent for a time, showing strong inner emotion*):
The heat of passion, Gordon, leads you on;
A friend of youthful days can be so free.
But, Gordon, blood was shed. The Emperor
Cannot forgive me. Could he do so, I
Could not allow myself to be forgiven.

If I had known the things that would occur,
That it would cost me my beloved friend,
And if my heart had spoken then as now—
Maybe I would have hesitated—maybe,
But maybe not. What use would there be now?
It is too serious to end in nothing,
So let it run its course!
(*Walking to the window.*)
Look, night has come; there in the castle all
Is quiet now. —Come, light the lamps for us.
(*The servant, who has entered meanwhile and has been
standing at some distance, taking an obvious interest, steps
forward, intensely moved, and throws himself at the Duke's
feet.*)
You, too? Still, I am sure I know just why
You want my peace made with the Emperor.
Poor creature! In Carinthia he has
A little farm, and he's afraid they'll take
It, since he is with *me*. Am I so poor
That I cannot have someone take his place?
Well, I will not compel you. If you think
That my good luck has left me, you may leave.
Today you may undress me one last time
And then go over to your Emperor.
Then, good night, Gordon.
I think that I will sleep a long, long time,
For these last days have been a trial to me.
Take care you do not wake me up too soon.
(*He exits. The servant lights the way. Seni follows them.
Gordon remains behind in the darkness, following the Duke
with his eyes until he disappears from the gallery in the
distance; then he expresses his grief with appropriate gestures
and leans sorrowfully on a column.*)

Scene 6

Gordon. Buttler (at first offstage).

BUTTLER: Be quiet here until I give the sign.
GORDON (*with a start*): He and the murderers are here.
BUTTLER: The lights

Are out, and everyone is fast asleep.

GORDON: What shall I do? Shall I attempt to save him?
Shall I wake up the house and call the guards?

BUTTLER (*enters from the rear*):
A light is shining from the corridor.
That's where the Duke's room is.

GORDON: Would I not break
My oath made to the Emperor? Should he
Escape to aid the enemy, would I
Not bring dire consequences on my head?

BUTTLER (*coming somewhat nearer*):
Be still! What do I hear?

GORDON: Oh, it is best
I leave it all to heaven. Who am I
That I should dare to do so great a deed?
I have not murdered him, if he should die;
But if I rescue him, it is *my* deed,
And I must bear the grievous consequences.

BUTTLER (*coming front stage*):
I know that voice.

GORDON: Here, Buttler.

BUTTLER: Gordon! You!
Why are you here? Why did the Duke dismiss
You at so late an hour?

GORDON: Your hand is bandaged?

BUTTLER: Yes, I was wounded. Crazy Illo fought
Just like a madman until we at last
Could lay him low—

GORDON (*shuddering*): Are they all dead?

BUTTLER: It's done.
—Is he in bed?

GORDON: Oh, Buttler!

BUTTLER (*urgently*):   Is he? Tell me!
What we have done cannot be hidden long.

GORDON: He shall *not* die. Not by your hand, for heaven
Does not accept it. See, it has been wounded.

BUTTLER: It does not need *my* hand.

GORDON: The guilty ones
Are dead; enough is done for Justice now.
This sacrifice can be atonement to her!
(*The servant comes from the passage with his finger on his lips
to request silence.*)

He's sleeping. Do not murder holy sleep.
BUTTLER: No, he shall die awake.
   (*Starts to leave.*)
GORDON: His heart is still
   Devoted just to earthly things. He is
   All unprepared to step before his God.
BUTTLER: God is All-merciful.
   (*Starts to leave.*)
GORDON (*holds him back*): Grant him this night.
BUTTLER: One moment more and we can be found out.
   (*Attempts to go.*)
GORDON (*holds him back*):
   Give him one hour!
BUTTLER: Unhand me! What can such
   A little time avail him?
GORDON: Oh, time is
   A wonder-working god. In just an hour
   How many thousand grains of sand will run
   As quickly as the thoughts of man can move.
   In just one hour—*your* heart could be attuned
   To *his*—some information might arrive—
   Or else some beneficial happening
   Occur, decisive, rescuing, from Heaven—
   What all can happen in an hour.
BUTTLER: You make
   Me think how precious minutes are.
   (*He stamps on the floor.*)

Scene 7

MacDonald, Deveroux enter with halberds. Thereupon the servant. The former.

GORDON (*throwing himself between Buttler and the others*): You
     brute!
   You'll do it over my dead body; for
   I'll not survive to see this monstrous deed.
BUTTLER (*thrusting him away*):
   Old man, you're crazy.
   (*Trumpets can be heard in the distance.*)
MacDONALD and DEVEROUX: Those are Swedish trumpets!
   The Swedes have got to Eger. Let us hurry.

GORDON: My God!

BUTTLER: Go to your station, Commandant!
(*Gordon rushes out.*)

SERVANT (*hurries in*):
Who dares to make such noise? The Duke is sleeping.

DEVEROUX (*in a loud and frightening voice*):
Now is the time to make a noise!

SERVANT (*crying out*): Help! Murder!

BUTTLER: Dispatch him!

SERVANT (*run through by Deveroux, falls at the entrance to the gallery*):
Jesus! Mary!

BUTTLER: Quick! Break down the doors!
(*They step over the body and proceed down the passageway. In the distance the sound can be heard of two doors being broken down, one after the other. —Muffled voices—the sound of weapons—then suddenly utter silence.*)

Scene 8

COUNTESS TERZKY (*with a lamp*):
Her bedroom is deserted. She cannot
Be found, and Lady Neubrunn, who was told
To watch her, is gone, too. Where can she be?
Where can she have run off to? We will have
To hurry after her—start right away!
How will the Duke receive this frightful news?
I only wish my husband had come back
From this big banquet. Is the Duke awake?
I thought I heard some voices and some steps.
I'll go inside and eavesdrop at the door.
But listen! Someone's running up the stairs.

Scene 9

Countess. Gordon. Thereupon Buttler.

GORDON (*rushing in breathless*):
You are all wrong—it's not the Swedes who came.
Do not continue—Buttler—Oh, my God!
Where is he?

(*Noticing the Countess.*)
> Countess, tell me—

COUNTESS: You've come here from the fortress. Where's my
husband?

GORDON (*horrified*):
> Your husband? —Oh, don't ask me that! Go back
> Inside—
> (*Starts to leave.*)

COUNTESS (*takes hold of him*): I will not till you tell me what—

GORDON (*with extreme urgency*):
> The whole world is dependent on this moment!
> Please, for the love of God, go back! While we
> Are talking—God in Heaven!
> (*Crying out loudly.*)
> > Buttler! Buttler!

COUNTESS: He's over in the castle with my husband.
> (*Buttler appears, coming from the gallery.*)

GORDON (*catching sight of him*):
> You were all wrong—it's not the Swedes who came—
> The Emperor's own forces have arrived—
> I'm sent by General Piccolomini.
> He'll be here soon— Do not continue with—

BUTTLER: He comes too late.

GORDON (*sinks against the wall*): Oh God All-merciful!

COUNTESS (*full of misgivings*):
> What is too late? Who's coming right away?
> Octavio has penetrated Eger?
> It's treachery! It's treachery! Where is
> The Duke?
> (*Rushes toward the passageway.*)

Scene 10

*The former. Seni. Then the mayor, page, chambermaid. Servants
run across the stage in fright.*

SENI (*who comes from the gallery exhibiting all the signs of
horror*):
> O bloody, most atrocious deed!

COUNTESS: What have
> They done here?

PAGE (*coming from the passageway*): Oh, the sight is piteous!
  (*Servants with torches.*)
COUNTESS: What is it, for God's sake?
SENI: You still must ask?
  The Duke lies murdered here. Your husband has
  Been killed there in the fortress.
  (*The Countess stands as if paralyzed.*)
CHAMBERMAID (*rushes in*):
  Help! Help the Duchess!
MAYOR (*enters, frightened*): What are these loud cries
  Of lamentation that have waked this house?
GORDON: Your house is cursed into eternity!
  Here in your house the Duke lies murdered.
MAYOR: Pray God that is not so! (*rushes out*)
FIRST SERVANT: Run! Run! They'll kill
  Us all!
SECOND SERVANT (*carrying silver utensils*):
          This way! The halls below are taken.
BEHIND THE SCENE (*a shout is raised*):
  Make way! Make way for General Piccolomini!
  (*At these words the Countess recovers from her paralysis, gets
  control of herself, and exits in haste.*)
BEHIND THE SCENE: Control the gate and keep the people back!

Scene 11

*The former, except for the Countess. Octavio Piccolomini enters
with his retinue. Deveroux and MacDonald, with their halberds,
come forward together. Wallenstein's body, wrapped in a red carpet, is carried across the stage in the rear.*)

OCTAVIO (*entering quickly*):
  It cannot be! It has not happened! Buttler
  And Gordon! Tell me it is not the truth.
GORDON (*without answering, gestures with his hand toward the
  rear. Octavio looks and is horrified.*)
DEVEROUX (*to Buttler*):
  Here is the Golden Fleece, the Prince's sword.
MACDONALD: You tell the chancellery—
BUTTLER (*pointing to Octavio*): Here is the man
  Who can alone tell it to anyone.

(*Deveroux and MacDonald step back respectfully; everyone disperses quietly until only Buttler, Octavio, and Gordon remain.*)

OCTAVIO (*turning to Buttler*):
Was that your meaning, Buttler, when we parted?
Dear God of righteousness! I wash my hands
Of this. This awful deed cannot be blamed
On me.

BUTTLER: Oh yes, your hands are clean. You have
Made use of mine for this!

OCTAVIO: You vicious man!
You had to take advantage of your lord's
Command to drag the Emperor's own name
Into a gruesome, cruel assassination?

BUTTLER (*calmly*): I carried out the Emperor's own verdict.

OCTAVIO: Oh, curse of kings that animates their words
With independent life and quickly turns
A passing thought into the deed itself
In its irrevocable consummation!
Should it have been obeyed so swiftly? Could
You not grant to the merciful the time
For mercy? Time is man's bright angel, and
Quick execution of a verdict can
Be proper only for a changeless God.

BUTTLER: Why reprimand me? What has been my crime?
I have performed a beneficial deed;
I've freed the Empire from a fearful foe,
And I lay claim here to my just reward.
The only difference that exists between
Your deed and *mine* is that you set the bolt
And I discharged it. You have planted blood
And are dismayed to see the blood has grown.
I always knew what I was doing, so
I am not terrified by my success.
Have you no other mission here for me?
I ride posthaste straight to Vienna now
To lay my bloody sword before the throne
And seek the favor of the Emperor,
Which quick and punctual obedience
Can always count on from a righteous judge.
(*Exits.*)

Scene 12

The former, except for Buttler. Countess Terzky enters, pale and drawn. Her voice is weak, and she speaks slowly, without emotion.

OCTAVIO (*opposite her*):
O Countess Terzky, has it come to this,
These consequences of disastrous deeds?
COUNTESS: It is the fruit of what you did. —The Duke
Is dead, my husband too, the Duchess now
Fights for her life, my niece has disappeared,
This house of splendor and of glory has
Been devastated, and through all the gates
The servants, terrified, are rushing off.
I am the last one here; I locked it up
And put the keys into your hands!
OCTAVIO (*suffering greatly*):   O Countess,
My house is devastated, too!
COUNTESS: Who else
Will have to die? Who else will be abused?
The Duke is dead; the Emperor can be
Content with his revenge. But spare the old
Retainers, faithful to their love and trust,
So that they are not charged with any crime.
Fate overtook my brother far too fast;
He had no time left to consider them.
OCTAVIO: No talk of vengeance, Countess, or abuse!
Grave guilt has been atoned for gravely and
The Emperor appeased. Naught will reflect
From father to his daughter but his fame.
The Empress honors your misfortune and
Will open her maternal arms to you.
So no more fear! You may be confident
That you can place yourself with hope into
The Emperor's hands.
COUNTESS (*lifting her gaze toward Heaven*):
                    I give myself into
The hands of someone greater. —Tell me where
The body of the Duke will find a grave
In Gitschin at the monastery that
He founded lies the Countess Wallenstein.

In thanks he wished to slumber next to *her*
From whom his first good fortune was derived.
Allow him to be buried there with her.
And for my husband's body I would ask
This favor, too. The Emperor now owns
Our castles; he will surely not begrudge
A grave there where our fathers have their graves.

OCTAVIO: You tremble, Countess— You grow pale— Dear God!
What meaning should I read into your words?

COUNTESS (*summons her last show of strength and speaks with
spirit and nobility*):
You surely estimate me higher than
To think I would survive my family's fall.
We did not feel we were too small to lift
Our hands and reach out for a royal crown—
Though it was not to be—we *think* like kings
And must regard a free, courageous death
As worthier than a dishonored life.
—I've taken poison. . . .

OCTAVIO: Help! Oh help!

COUNTESS: It is
Too late. Just moments and my fate will be
Fulfilled.
(*She exits.*)

GORDON: Oh, house of murder and of dread!
(*A courier arrives, bringing a letter.*)

GORDON (*goes to meet him*):
What's this? It carries the imperial seal.
(*He reads the address and hands the letter to Octavio with a
look of reproach.*)
It's for *Duke* Piccolomini.
(*Octavio recoils and looks in sorrow heavenward.*)

Translated by Jeanne Willson

List of Persons

Names are given first as they occur in the play; the alternate spellings freely used by Schiller are given in capital letters; common or more accepted spellings are given immediately after in parenthesis.

ALTRINGER, ALTRING (Aldringen, Altringen), Count Johann, a Catholic general. Distinguished himself as Dessau, 1626, and at the siege of Mantua. After Tilly's death he became general of the Catholic League, operating in southwestern Germany in 1633 in conjunction with the Duke of Feria. Killed in battle a few months after Wallenstein.

Referred to: *Picc.* 21, 338, 806, 809, 2578, 2580; *Death* 664, 1171, 2656.

ARNHEIM (Arnim), Johann Georg von, a Saxon noble and distinguished general. Served successively under Sweden, Poland, and Austria. Became intimate with Wallenstein and was made field marshall in 1628. Unable to secure his pay from the Emperor, he entered the service of the Elector of Saxony and was the negotiator with Gustavus and Wallenstein until the latter's death. He took part in the battle of Breitenfeld and captured Prague in 1631. Mistreated by the Swedes, he again entered imperial service. Died 1641.

Ref.: *Picc.* 850, 1096, 1107, 1337; *Death* 51.

ATTILA, the famous "Scourge of God," King of the Huns, who was defeated at the battle of Chalons in 451.

Ref.: *Death* 287.

BANNIER, BANNER, one of the chief Swedish generals after the death of Gustavus, with a record of many victories and scarcely any defeats. Died 1641.

Ref.: *Picc.* 1034; *Death* 940.

THE BAVARIAN—see MAXIMILIAN.

BERNHARD, Prince of Saxony-Weimar, one of the greatest generals of the war. Born 1604, he served under various Protestant leaders but submitted in 1628 to the Emperor. On the arrival of Gustavus, however, he joined the Swedish king, rose to high rank, and at age 29 helped to win the battle of Lützen after the death of Gustavus. At the time of Wallenstein's death Bernhard was in command of the Swedish forces that were to join Wallenstein. This portion of his career is assigned in the play to the Rhinegrave in order not to give offense to the court of Saxony-Weimar, where the drama was presented, by representing one of their ancestors in the quality of a traitor.

Ref.: *Picc.* 1034, 1068, 2022, 2119.

BOURBON, Charles of, Constable of France, deserted his king, Francis I of France, and entered into a league with the king's enemies, Charles V of the Holy Roman Empire and Henry VIII of England, whereby he was to receive a throne. He was killed in the siege of Rome in 1527.

Ref.: *Death* 419, 442.

BURGOMASTER PACHHÄLBEL, one of the burgomasters of Eger, but not in 1634.

Appears: *Death* IV, 1; V, 2. Ref.: *Death* 2602.

BUTLER (Butler), Colonel Walter, one of Wallenstein's commanders. He directed the assassination of Wallenstein, but not for the motives alleged in the play. As far as is known, he was motivated by greed for reward and by devotion to the Catholic faith. His reward came in the form of a Count's title.

Appears: *Picc.* I, II, IV; *Death* II, 2; III, 1, 2; IV, 1; V, 1, 2. Ref.: *Camp* 440 ff.; *Picc.* 94, 273, 282, 285, 1005, 1147, 2374; *Death* 1440, 1580, 1821.

CARAFFA—see KARAFFA.

CARDINAL INFANTE, Don Fernando of Spain. His brother, Philip IV of Spain, desired to send him in 1663 to the Netherlands via Germany, and to furnish him an escort Wallenstein was directed to detach six regiments.

Ref.: *Camp* 697; *Picc.* 1226, 1250; *Death* 1370.

CHARLES V, the great Emperor in the first half of the sixteenth century, during whose reign the Empire included the largest territory ever brought under the control of a single individual in the course of European history.

Ref.: *Death* 440.

CHRISTIAN, Duke of Brunswick-Wolfenbüttel and administrator of the Lutheran bishopric of Halberstadt, a commander in the first period of the war. His warfare was particularly irregular, leading to the nickname "The Mad Halberstädter." He fought in conjunction with Mansfeld, and died June 1626.

Ref.: *Picc.* 2024.

CONTE AMBASSADOR OF SPAIN, Count Oñate, special envoy to Vienna to secure the escort for the Cardinal Infante, and finally one of the most vigorous workers against Wallenstein.

Ref.: *Picc.* 682.

DEODAT (Deodati), an Italian, joined the counter-conspiracy against Wallenstein, entered Pilsen after Wallenstein's withdrawal and directed Gordon to admit him to Eger. This part is assigned to Buttler in the play.

Ref.: *Picc.* 879, 1005, 1147, 2122; *Death* 989, 1565.

DEVEROUX, an Irish captain, the actual assassin of Wallenstein. Appears: *Death* V, 1.

DÜBALD (Duwall), a Swedish colonel who was captured at Steinau with Thurn.

Ref.: *Death* 1846.

EGGENBERG, Duke of, a member of the imperial council in Vienna and of the faction friendly to Wallenstein: Wallenstein's second wife was a sister of Eggenberg's son-in-law. In December 1631 it was Eggenberg who finally persuaded Wallenstein to resume command of the imperial forces. His part is taken by Questenberg in the drama.

Ref.: *Picc.* 680, 1919.

ESTERHAZY, name of an ancient Hungarian family of many branches; one member of it was Palatine of Hungary in the third decade of the 17th century. No member of the family took a conspicuous part in the war.

Ref.: *Death* 989, 1567.

FERDINAND II, Emperor of Germany 1619–1637, called from his birthplace (Gratz), "der Grätzer." a mild-mannered man, fond of hunting, having no executive ability. Only in matters of religion did he have a fixed purpose, which may best be seen in his own words: "Better a desert than a land full of heretics."

Ref. (among many others): *Picc.* 1022 ff, 1970, 2094; *Death* 549 ff., 645 ff.; 2119, 3378, 3532, 3647.

FERDINAND III, the King of Hungary 1625 and Emperor of Germany 1637–1657, son of Ferdinand II. He became commander-in-chief of Wallenstein's army after the latter's assassination and, through 1634–1635, until the active intervention by France, won important victories.

Ref.: *Picc.* 208 (as "the child"), 800; *Death* 501, 504, 1934, 2792.

FERIA, Duke of, commander of the Spanish regiments which came in 1633 from Italy, intended as escort for the Cardinal Infante. Died Jan. 1634.

Ref.: *Camp* 144.

FORGATSCH (Forgach), Palatine of Hungary in 1618; not known to have been in the conspiracy. In one draft of the drama Esterhazy stood in stead of Forgatsch.

Ref.: *Picc.* 1005.

FREDERICK V—see PALATINE.

FRIEDLAND, "the FRIEDLANDER," Wallenstein's title from his estate of Friedland in Bohemia. See WALLENSTEIN.

GALLAS, Count Matthias, important general under and succeeding Wallenstein. He served throughout the war and with fair ability. His most brilliant performances were at the taking of Mantua, 1630, for which he was ennobled, and the battle of Nördlingen, 1634, won over Bernhard of Weimar. Among Wallenstein's generals Gallas was the one on whom the court depended. He received Friedland as his reward for Wallenstein's death. Died 1647. Much of his real role is in the play assigned to Octavio Piccolomini.

Ref.: *Picc.* 21, 40, 338, 807, 2387, 2560; *Death* 41, 48, 666, 889, 1036, 1064, 1171, 2410, 2668, 2793.

GERALDIN, Buttler's sergeant-major who conducted the assassinations of Illo, Terzky, Kinsky, and Neumann.

Appears: *Death* V, 1. Ref.: *Death* 3305.

GOETZ, served first in the Protestant cause but joined Wallenstein's army in 1626. Infamous for his atrocities in the sack of Pasewalk, 1630. The most important part of his career followed Wallenstein's death.

Appears: *Picc.* II, IV. Ref.: *Picc.* 18; *Death* 1568.

GORDON, a Scotch soldier of fortune, lieutenant-commander of Eger.

Appears: *Death* IV, 1; V, 2. Ref.: *Death* 3461.

THE GRÄTZER—see FERDINAND II.

GUSTAVUS ADOLPHUS, born 1594, King of Sweden 1611–1632. From 1630 his deeds were an essential part of the war. Killed in the battle of Lützen, Nov. 16, 1632. (Before writing *Wallenstein,* Schiller had contemplated a work with Gustavus as hero.)

Ref.: *Camp* 256; *Picc.* 1035, 1063, 1095, 1220; *Death* 239, 241, 367, 374, 1800.

THE HALBERSTÄDTER—see CHRISTIAN.

HARRACH'S DAUGHTER, Wallenstein's wife, the Duchess of Friedland. Count Harrach was a leading intriguer at the Austrian court, being connected with Eggenberg and Wallenstein. He often served as deputy to Eggenberg. He died 1628.

Ref.: *Picc.* 660.

HENRY, King of Navarre, subsequently King of France, assassinated 1610 by the Catholic fanatic Ravaillac.

Ref.: *Death* 3491.

HINNERSAM (Henderson), one of Wallenstein's commanders, of Scotch birth. He is mentioned as one of the committee of officers that visited Wallenstein Jan. 12, 1634 to urge him not to lay down his command.

Ref.: *Picc.* 18

HOLK, General von, an imperial commander famous for the brutality of his warfare. Devastated the Voigtland in 1632.

Ref.: *Camp* 121, 216, 230.

HUSS, Jan, founder of Bohemian Protestantism, burned at the stake at Constance by order of the Council of Constance, 1415.

Ref.: *Picc.* 2082.

ILLO (Ilow), one of Wallenstein's generals, a native of Brandenburg. He was apparently the ringleader of the conspiracy, especially at the officers' meeting of January 12, 1634.

Appears: *Picc.* I, II, III, IV; *Death* I, II, 1; III, 1, 2; IV, 1. Ref.: *Picc.* 281, 2129, 2374, 2396, 2403; *Death* 1739, 2680, 2740, 3300, 3520, 3699.

ISOLANI, ISOLAN, one of Wallenstein's commanders.

Appears: *Picc.* I, II, IV; *Death* II, 2. Ref.: *Camp* 826; *Picc.* 93, 875, 1006, 2374; *Death* 1458, 1563, 1617, 1640.

KAUNITZ, an Austrian family. A Count Kaunitz married Wallenstein's daughter, but took no prominent part in the war. Like Esterhazy, the name Kaunitz may have been introduced by Schiller less for historical reasons than from familiarity with them from his own time.

Ref.: *Death* 989, 1568.

CARAFFA, Prince Geronimo, member of a distinguished Italian family. Fought in the battle of White Hill, 1620, was made Prince and Vice-King of Aragon. Died at Genoa, 1633. His enumeration among Wallenstein's generals is an error.

Ref.: *Picc.* 1006, 1146; *Death* 1665.

THE KING OF HUNGARY—see FERDINAND III.

KINSKY, Count William, a Bohemian noble, a leader in the insurrection of 1618, and an active intriguer for Wallenstein with the French, whether authorized or not is uncertain. He was with Wallenstein at Pilsen and at Eger and was murdered together with Illo and Terzky. His wife was Terzky's sister and the original of the Countess Terzky of the play.

Ref.: *Picc.* 2374; *Death* 50, 1716, 1739.

Kolalto (Colalto), a native of Mantua, became one of Wallenstein's generals in 1625, President of the War Council in 1627. Led 20,000 troops to Italy and took Mantua in July, 1630; died a month later.

Appears: *Picc.* II, IV. Ref.: *Picc.* 18, 878; *Death* 1568.

Lamormain (French corruption of Lämmermann), a Jesuit priest, confessor of Ferdinand II and actual director of the latter's policies; an active intriguer against Wallenstein.

Ref.: *Picc.*; 689, 1233.

Lauenburg, Duke Franz Albert von, a Saxon field marshal, was engaged in negotiations between the Elector of Saxony and Wallenstein.

Ref.: *Death,* 1549.

Lessley (Lessly), a Scotch soldier, Lieutenant-commander of Eger; a friend of Buttler; represented as having taken part in the murder of the officers.

Ref.: *Picc.* 2032; *Death* 3309.

Liechtenstein, Prince Karl von, made prince in 1618 by Ferdinand II, a member of the imperial council, and friendly to Wallenstein. He is one of the precious jewels (Steine) in the Emperor's crown, along with Dietrichstein and Wallenstein, and is thus indirectly referred to in *Picc.* 1164.

Ref.: *Picc.* 680, 1919.

Lorraine, Duke Charles of, who, persecuted by Richelieu, joined the imperial army. After Tilly's death he even aspired to the chief command.

Ref.: *Death* 1267.

MacDonald, confederate of Deveroux.

Appears: *Death* V, 1, 2.

Mansfeld, Ernst von, a natural son of Count Peter Ernst von Mansfield. Reared a Catholic, he was driven into the Protestant opposition by the ingratitude of Archduke Leopold, but fought as a free-lance during the first period of the war till, in 1625, he raised an army as general of the Palatine. He attacked Wallenstein at the Dessau Bridge, but was defeated and pursued through Silesia till he joined Bethlen Gabor in Hungary. The latter making peace, Mansfeld set out for Venice, but died on the way, 1626.

Ref.: *Camp* 140; *Picc.* 2024; *Death* 1926.

Marádas (Marradas, Marrados), a Spaniard and loyal imperial general, commander in Bohemia and later Silesia.

Appears: *Picc.* II, IV. Ref.: *Picc.* 18, 1005, 2135; *Death* 1567.

Martinez, Jaroslas von, a prominent Bohemian noble, member

of the Committee of Regency; one of the three men "defenestrated" at Prague in 1618. (see SLAWATA.)

Ref.: *Picc.* 151, 2109.

MAXIMILIAN, Duke and Elector of Bavaria, leader of the Catholic League, the rival and determined enemy of Wallenstein. As the Emperor's son-in-law he had great influence at court, and with that influence combined the qualities of statesmanship and generalship which Ferdinand II wholly lacked. Along with General Tilly, Maximilian bore the primary responsibility for the dismissal of Wallenstein at the meeting of the Diet at Regensburg in July 1630. Again in 1633 he urged the replacement of Wallenstein by Aldringen, and when Wallenstein failed to save Bavaria from the invasion of Bernhard of Weimar in the autumn of that year, he exerted such pressure upon the Emperor as to precipitate the actions leading directly to Wallenstein's assassination. Maximilian was the last of the Catholic leaders to agree to a peace, and only the major campaigns against Bavaria by the French marshal Turenne in 1646–1648 forced him to consent to the Treaty of Westphalia which brought the war to its conclusion in 1648.

Ref.: *Camp* 858; *Picc.* 694, 1073; *Death* 565.

MOHRBRAND, must be a careless or deliberate alteration of Mohra, who was Lieutenant-commander of Prague when Schlief was captured.

Ref.: *Picc.* 2566.

MONTECUCULI (Montecuccoli), Count Ernst, an Italian and friend of Wallenstein, chief of ordnance. He was killed in Feria's campaign in 1633. Uncle of the more famous Count Raimund Montecuccoli.

Ref.: *Picc.* 1953; *Death* 1665.

NEUMANN, historically Wallenstein's secretary; in the play, Terzky's adjustant.

Appears: *Picc.* IV; *Death* III, 2. Ref.: *Death* 2381.

OXENSTIRN (Oxenstjerna), Swedish Chancellor and Regent after the death of Gustavus Adolphus. A shrewd and successful diplomat, but lacking in the military ability of Gustavus.

Ref.: *Camp* 502; *Picc.* 815, 850, 1034; *Death* 51, 238, 258, 282, 291 ff., 336, 384, 406.

THE PALATINE, THE COUNT PALATINE, Frederick V, "the winter king." See Introduction. Died 1632.

Ref.: *Picc.* 2058, 2096; *Death* 448, 1759.

PAPPENHEIM, General, arrived at the battle of Lützen, Nov. 16,

1632, just in time to save the day for the imperial armies. He was killed in that same battle.

Ref.: *Camp* 677; *Death* 1266.

PALFFY, Stephen von, distinguished himself in wars with the Turks. Made Count in 1634; was also Palatine of Hungary.

Ref.: *Picc.* 2054, 2133.

PESTALUTZ, a captain under Terzky, but reported to have joined the conspirators.

Ref.: *Death* 3282 ff., 3309.

PICCOLOMINI, Max, a fictitious character invented by Schiller. Perhaps suggested by Max von Waldstein (Wallenstein), a favorite nephew and heir of Wallenstein.

PICCOLOMINI, Octavio, one of Wallenstein's generals, member of an old Italian family. At the close of the war he was made Duke of Amalfi.

PROKOP, name of two leaders of the Taborites in the Hussite wars, Prokop the Great and Prokop the Small. The former, for years a victorious general, was defeated and slain at Lipau in 1434.

Ref.: *Picc.* 2104.

PYRRHUS, a king of Epirus, who ruled and warred against the Romans in the first half of the third century B.C.

Ref.: *Death* 287.

THE QUEEN OF HUNGARY, wife of Ferdinand III, the Spanish Infanta Mary, sister of Queen Anne of France.

Ref.: *Picc.* 634, 671.

QUESTENBERG, QUESTENBERGER, member of the Imperial Privy Council and a staunch friend of Wallenstein. Schiller has rather curiously selected his name to stand in place of several of Wallenstein's enemies.

Appears: *Picc.* I, II. Ref.: *Camp* 71; *Picc.* 72, 116, 1007, 2481; *Death* 885, 1371, 1660.

QUIROGA, a Capuchin monk, confessor to the Queen of Hungary. It was he who, on January 5, 1634, brought to Wallenstein at Pilsen the request for the detail of 6,000 men to escort the Cardinal Infante to the Netherlands. His role at this point is assigned in the play to Questenberg.

Ref.: *Camp* 173 ff.; *Picc.* 2127.

THE RHINEGRAVE, Otto Ludwig von Salms, Count of the Rheingau, took a prominent part in the war after the arrival of Gustavus. Commanded in Alsace in 1633 and made conquests in Breisgau. At the time of Wallenstein's death he was on the upper

Rhine. In the play he is assigned a considerable share of the role historically played by Bernhard of Weimar. (See BERNHARD.)

Ref.: *Picc.* 1034; *Death* 332, 2633, 2665, 3040, 3066, 3070, 3638.

RUDOLPH II, the Emperor who preceded Ferdinand II. It was he who originally granted the Bohemians their charter of religious toleration in 1609.

Ref.: *Picc.* 2090.

SCHAFGOTSCH, Count Ulrich, member of an ancient Silesian family. Though a Lutheran, one of Wallenstein's most trusted generals. Was commissioned in February 1634 with the command in Silesia. The only one of Wallenstein's officers who tried to resist after the ban had been pronounced against his chief. He was captured and executed in 1635.

Ref.: *Picc.* 2371.

SCHERFENBERG, Wallenstein's High Steward, a loyal adherent. After Wallenstein's death he was sentenced to death, then to life imprisonment.

Ref.: *Death* 2022.

SECKENDORF, name of a distinguished Austrian general and diplomat of the first part of the 18th century; also a young poet who was a friend of Schiller; neither has any connection with the Swedish command of 1634.

Ref.: *Death* 3082.

SENI (Senno), Wallenstein's astrologer.

Appears: *Picc.* II; *Death* II, V, 2. Ref.: *Camp* 372; *Picc.* 1348, 1581 ff.

SESINA, SESIN (Sesyma Raschin), a Bohemian employed by Terzky as messenger in negotiations with the Swedes. He was not captured at all, but after Wallenstein's death purchased his own safety by a detailed confession of all his transactions.

Ref.: *Picc.* 812, 1337, 2564, 2576, 2596; *Death* 40 ff., 98 ff., 392.

SLAWATA, Wilhelm von, a prominent Bohemian noble who took the part of Austria against the Protestant Estates of Bohemia. He was one of the three men "defenestrated" in Prague in 1618. In spite of the fall of eighty feet the men were not seriously injured, and escaped with the aid of friends. Wallenstein's second wife was connected with the Slawata family. (See MARTINEZ.)

Ref.: *Picc.* 151, 1919, 2109.

STERNBERG, Adam von, chief burggrave of Bohemia, one of the

imperial regents, and father-in-law of Martinitz. He was present at the defenestration, but, being less aggressively imperialistic, was not assailed.

Ref.: *Picc.* 1920.

SUYS, a colonel under Wallenstein, was in charge of four regiments in Upper Austria. Historically he did precisely the opposite of what he is represented as having done in the play: he did not obey the Emperor and disobey Wallenstein by advancing, but refused to advance as the Emperor ordered. For this he was severely reprimanded by the Emperor. Later, however, Suys was put in charge of Prague when the Emperor assumed command.

Ref.: *Picc.* 1196 ff.; *Death* 2660.

TERZKY, TERSCHKA, TERZKA, Count Adam, one of Wallenstein's officers, brother-in-law of the Duchess Wallenstein. For dramatic purposes Schiller has greatly magnified the relatively slight conspiratorial role that Terzky had in history.

Appears: *Picc.* II, III, IV; *Death* I; II, 1; III, 1, 2; IV, 1. Ref.: *Camp* 84, 1017; *Picc.* 17, 904, 1690, 1717, 1914, 2051, 2372, 2574; *Death* 63, 1739, 1820, 2740, 3300, 3520, 3767.

COUNTESS TERZKY, daughter of Count Harrach and sister of the Duchess Wallenstein. In history she knew little of Wallenstein's plans. In the drama she takes over the historical role of Terzky's *sister*, the Countess Kinsky, who *was* an intriguer. Her character has about it something of the character of Terzky's mother, "the old Countess" (referred to in *Picc.* 1915, 2037, 2146–2148), but in larger part she derives from Lady Macbeth.

Appears: *Picc.* II, III; *Death* I; III, 1, 2; IV, 2; V, 2. Ref.: *Picc.* 1379, 2146.

THURN, Count Matthias, a Bohemian noble and leader of the Protestant opposition to the Austrian encroachments. After the Protestant loss of Bohemia in the early stages of the war he fought under Bethlen Gabor, and under Gustavus Adolphus at Leipzig and at Lützen. In October 1633 he was captured by Wallenstein together with his force of allied Protestants. Wallenstein set him free in return for certain guarantees to evacuate Silesia, a move which would favor the imperial armies but which aroused bitter criticism of Wallenstein at court. Thurn died soon afterward.

Ref.: *Picc.* 814, 1095, 1119, 1336, 2111; *Death* 50.

TIEFENBACH, a Moravian colonel who served in the imperial army as early as 1618 but not mentioned in connection with Wallenstein's closing career.

Appears: *Picc.* II, IV. Ref.: *Picc.* 17, 879, 2047; *Death* 964, 1268, 1577, 1862, 2250.

TILLY, Johann von, after Wallenstein, the most famous Catholic general in the Thirty Years War. A Walloon by birth, he served under many flags; was made field marshall of the Catholic League; won the battle of White Hill, 1620; was made Count, 1623; defeated the King of Denmark in the battle of Lutter, 1626; succeeded Wallenstein as imperial generalissimo, 1630. He met his first great defeat at the hands of Gustavus Adolphus in the battle of Breitenfeld, 1631, and was mortally wounded April, 1632 in the battle on the Lech.

Ref.: *Camp* 273, 343; *Picc.* 112; *Death* 1798.

TOSKANA (Tuscany), a representative of the decaying house of the Dukes of Tuscany.

Ref.: *Death* 1267, 1861.

WALLENSTEIN (Waldstein), Albrecht von, Duke of Friedland, generalissimo of the Catholic armies, central character in Schiller's drama.

born 1583 at Hermanitz, in Bohemia, of Lutheran parents.

educated first by the Bohemian (Moravian) Brothers, then by the Jesuits at Olmütz, where he was converted to Catholicism, then at the University of Altdorf (near Nürnberg).

travelled in Europe with a friend of Kepler, from which time dates his interest in astrology.

military service against the Turks; application for a position at the court of Austria; service, for Austria, against Venice; marriage to a wealthy and elderly widow; ennoblement (1617); second marriage to Count Harrach's daughter, a lady with important connections at court.

1618, outbreak of war; he raised a regiment of Walloons for the Emperor and led them with distinction. In the early stages of Catholic victories he bought up, at low prices, the confiscated lands of the Protestant Bohemian nobles.

1623 made Prince of Friedland.

1625 he voluntarily recruited and paid for an army to serve the Emperor; rewarded by being made Duke of Friedland and "Capo d'Armada" of the new army.

1626 defeated the Protestant General Mansfeld; made Duke of Sagan.

1627 totally defeated Denmark; given the Duchy of Mecklenburg temporarily.

1629 made Duke of Mecklenburg outright and hereditary prince of the empire.

1630 removed from command upon complaints from the Emperor's advisors.

1631–1632 was repeatedly urged to resume command and finally did so in April of 1632 after having received almost the powers of an independent ruler; defeat of the Swedes under Gustavus Adolphus at the battle of Lützen, Nov. 16, 1632.

1633 carried on peace negotiations, with the approval of the court; new victory in Silesia; Bernhard of Weimar invaded Bavaria, but Wallenstein failed to attack him.

1634, February 21, received news that he had been declared a traitor.

February 23, fled to Eger with a small force.

February, 25 assassinated.

Assessment of his motives and actions has been a subject of unending controversy, depending on the religious and political attitudes of historians, who have portrayed him as everything from a common traitor to a visionary, ahead of his time, who sought to end the Thirty Years War and establish the principle of religious toleration in Europe.

WALLENSTEIN, ELIZABETH (her real name was Isabella Katherina), second wife of the generalissimo, daughter of Count Harrach, Duchess of Friedland. She was a devoted wife but she was not present at either Pilsen or Eger, nor was she aware of her husband's plans.

Appears: *Picc.* II; *Death* III, 1, 2; IV, 2. Ref.: *Camp* 57; *Picc.* 32, 269; *Death* 1301, 1338 ff., 3769, 3819.

WERDENBERG, a member of the imperial council, several times employed on commissions to Wallenstein.

Ref.: *Picc.* 116.

WRANGEL, Gustav, a famous Swedish general and admiral who was only thirty-one years old at the time of Wallenstein's death. His father, Hermann Wrangel, led the Swedish forces in Poland, but was not at Stralsund.

Appears: *Death* I. Ref.: *Death* 95, 132, 481, 643, 657, 845 ff.

ZISKA, a famous Hussite general, leader of the extreme Taborite party. He lost one eye in youth and the other in battle, yet continued to command.

Ref.: *Picc.* 2140.

CHARLES E. PASSAGE

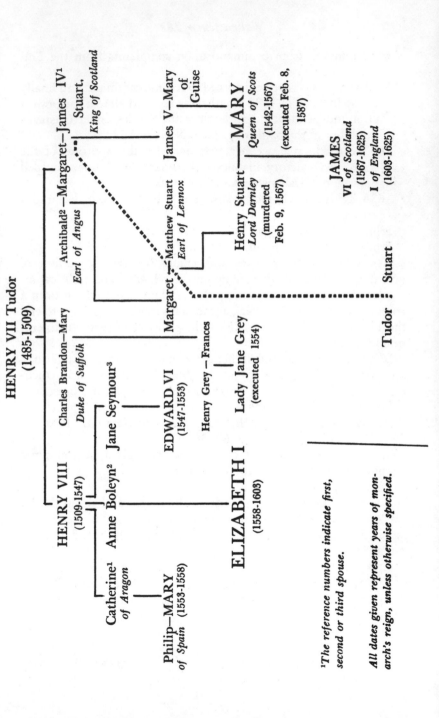

HENRY VII Tudor
(1485-1509)

Margaret—James IV[1] Stuart, *King of Scotland*

Archibald[2]—Margaret *Earl of Angus*

James V—Mary *of* Guise

MARY *Queen of Scots* (1542-1567) (executed Feb. 8, 1587)

Margaret—Matthew Stuart *Earl of Lennox*

Henry Stuart *Lord Darnley* (murdered Feb. 9, 1567)

JAMES VI of Scotland (1567-1625) I of England (1603-1625)

Charles Brandon—Mary *Duke of Suffolk*

Henry Grey — Frances

Lady Jane Grey (executed 1554)

HENRY VIII (1509-1547)

Catherine[1] *of Aragon*

Anne Boleyn[2]

Jane Seymour[3]

EDWARD VI (1547-1553)

ELIZABETH I (1558-1603)

Philip—MARY *of Spain* (1553-1558)

Tudor   Stuart

[1]The reference numbers indicate first, second or third spouse.

All dates given represent years of monarch's reign, unless otherwise specified.

MARY STUART

A Tragedy

The Historical Background of *Mary Stuart*

It was from a province of obscurity and fear that Elizabeth Tudor found herself unexpectedly summoned forth in 1558, at age twenty-five, to become the Queen of England. As recently as the beginning of the decade of the 1550s her succession to the throne had been merely a remote possibility, and since that time she had passed close to the brink of death by either execution or assassination. In 1553 her half-brother, King Edward VI, had died childless after a reign of only six years. As the sole male heir of Henry VIII he had been his father's fond preference over two daughters, though he was the offspring of Henry's third marriage. Moreover, that third marriage had been solemnized under the new Protestantism, Edward was himself necessarily Protestant, and the powerful Protestant leaders of the country supported him as the mainstay of their cause. At his death without children to succeed him they were seized with consternation, because the throne had then unquestionably to revert to the elder of Henry's daughters, Mary Tudor, the intensely Catholic child of Henry's Catholic first marriage to the Spanish Princess Catherine of Aragon. In desperation, the Protestant leaders had precipitated civil war and attempted to place Henry's Protestant grandniece, Lady Jane Grey, upon the throne of England.

Amid cruelties of that civil disorder Mary Tudor ascended the throne in 1553. She suppressed the rebellion with harshness. Lady Jane Grey, after a nominal queenship of nine days, was apprehended, committed to prison, and eventually beheaded. As yet unmarried, Mary Tudor now selected for her spouse none other than King Philip II of Spain, the most powerful monarch in Catholic Christendom and militant foe of Protestantism everywhere. The English people, however, who had loyally taken her as their rightful Queen and who were acceding to her reconversion of the country to the old Faith, would not brook rule from the alien King, and Philip, to his discomfiture, was coldly accepted as the Queen's consort but icily refused the title of King of England. In the process of eradication of Protestantism from the realm Mary met strong opposition. The severity of her persecutions won her the hateful name of "Bloody Mary" and a memory forever tainted in the history of her country. Yet objective critics just judge her as a woman understandably embittered and sincerely dedicated to a supremely difficult task.

Her young womanhood had endured atrocious humiliation. As royal Princess of England she had been suddenly relegated to an indeterminate position between legitimacy and illegitimacy by Henry VIII's belated divorce of her mother. The divorce itself was a monstrous sin in her eyes, and the sin was increased hundredfold when the divorce served as the pretext for Henry's removal of all England from the Roman Catholic religion and his institution of the new Protestant order. The final humiliation came with her father's second marriage to the upstart Anne Boleyn. It was understandable, therefore, that she should bear small affection to the half-sister Elizabeth that was born of that union. By the time of her accession in 1553 the human agents in the drama of religious conflict had, by the working of Providence it seemed, been removed from the scene of life. The erring King and father was in his grave; the Protestant Edward VI had died without issue; Anne Boleyn had long since perished on the scaffold publicly disgraced as an adulteress and condemned to death with her royal husband's consent; four additional Protestant wives of Henry were also dead. Her mission to turn England back to the old religion seemed expressly indicated by the Deity in the disposition of human events. There remained to be dealt with only the unwanted half-sister Elizabeth. For a time Queen Mary Tudor had her committed to the Tower of London, from which prisoners often emerged only to the place of execution. Subsequently she caused her to be removed from there and installed in

Woodstock House under surveillance, wresting from her an overt profession of Catholicism.

Nevertheless all things conspired to frustrate her great mission. The love of her subjects withered away in the searing sun of fanaticism, projects did not advance, her husband bore her almost a contemptuous aversion, and, worst of all, her womanhood was blighted with childlessness. In her final illness, after a mere five years of reign, she realized that she had failed on every count she deemed important and that Elizabeth, as her successor, would prove false to the Catholic cause. And so it proved. Childless and defeated Queen Mary Tudor died in 1558, and Elizabeth, summoned from obscurity and the shadow of death, lost no time in proclaiming herself and England Protestant.

The action was all but mandatory for the new Queen. Catholic law could not countenance Henry VIII's divorce, still less his remarriage to Anne Boleyn according to rites unhallowed by the Catholic religion. Before Catholic law, therefore, Elizabeth was a mere illegitimate offspring of her royal father and without any rightful claim to the throne of England. Before Protestant law the reverse was true, and the tide of national feeling was also running strong in the direction of Protestantism. Her personal convictions reinforced the choice.

What, then, must have been the young Queen's feelings when, in the very year of her accession, her right to rule was publicly and spectacularly challenged by her first cousin once removed, Mary Stuart, heiress to the throne of Scotland! As granddaughter of Margaret Tudor, a sister of Henry VIII, Mary Stuart considered herself the only legitimate heir to the English throne. That she was next in line after Elizabeth, in case the latter had no issue, no one denied; it was her assertion of rightful queenship *now* that offered such galling offense. Mary's maternal relatives, the Dukes and Cardinals of Guise, had taught her to look upon Protestantism as a work of devils, upon Protestant law as no law at all, and upon Elizabeth as a bastard and usurper. The occasion for the public challenge was the resplendent marriage in Paris between Mary Stuart and Prince Francis, heir to the crown of France. In the solemn procession Mary displayed the royal emblems of Scotland, of France, and of England, as though she were already Queen of all three realms. With defiance thus proclaimed, the struggle was to continue between the two women for almost thirty years. It was to end with Elizabeth's sending Mary to her death in 1587.

Unglamorous duty proved to be Elizabeth's lot for many years, while glamorous adventure and misadventure befell Mary time and again. During the next quarter of a century Elizabeth worked as a dedicated servant of a nation that was lifting itself into greatness, herself hardly existing as a private individual apart from her Queenship, while Mary ranged freely through life as a personage of independent destiny. The story and the romance are hers, and even the most skeptical and antipathetic cannot help but be struck by her brilliant and tragic course of existence.

The deaths of kings formed the milestones of her career, the first of these being the death of her father, King James V of Scotland, which occurred only a few days after her birth. Already a Queen in her infancy, she was sent abroad to France at age three to be betrothed to the equally young heir to the throne of France. Her rearing was that of a French Princess amid the sophistication and elegance of the Parisian court, and there, as an uncommonly lovely girl in her teens she fell fondly in love with her husband-to-be. Their tender mutual devotion was a rare phenomenon in the life of courts. It could not but promise a happy future, was the common opinion. Their marriage in 1558 was the occasion for that provocative display of the English royal emblems whereby her English cousin was so gravely offended, but the action must be construed as sinister inspiration from other parties and accepted by Mary's naiveté. Within a year the princely couple was thrust into the position of reigning monarchs by a bizarre and tragic coincidence. In 1559 the French King, while participating in one of those mediaeval tournaments which he fondly perpetuated in the midst of the Renaissance, galloped in a joust against a visiting knight and received his opponent's lance-thrust through his visor and died instantaneously as the weapon pierced his eye and brain. As Queen of France, Mary reached all too early and all too briefly the apogee of her life's good fortunes. The health of King Francis II was precarious. A year later he died, and once again Mary's fate was radically altered. From Queen she was relegated over night to the ambiguous position of widow of the late monarch, the mere sister-in-law of the new King Charles IX, and subject to the unwelcome control of the ambitious Queen Mother, Catherine of Medici, who overshadowed her sons. The situation was intolerable. Moreover, Mary's own mother had recently died in Scotland, and thus all events joined to make it imperative that she return to her native land, which, as viewed from Paris, seemed remote and drab indeed. The return itself was fraught with perils. In that same year, 1560, representatives of England, Scotland and France had attempted to draft the Treaty of Edinburgh, wherein it was stipulated that Mary should renounce all claim to the English throne as long as Elizabeth lived, but Mary perversely refused to agree to that article. Now, as she prepared to sail from France to Scotland, English naval forces vowed they would intercept her ship if they encountered it and take her captive. Amid her own tears and amid tributes from famous poets she did set sail, however, and by good luck arrived safely in Scotland. She was not yet twenty years of age.

Her Scottish subjects received her very well at first, captivated by her youthful beauty and charm, although the radical adherents of the new Prebyterian faith recently imported into the country by John Knox were less enthusiastic than the Catholics. For a time Mary sought to rule effectively, yet even from the beginning her political obtuseness made significant mistakes. The feudal clans of Scotland could not be managed by methods patterned on those of the French court. It was also Mary's decided policy now to conciliate her English cousin. Solicitously she consulted her "dear sister" Elizabeth,—for Queens addressed each other as "sisters,"—asking her advice in the matter of choosing a second husband. She herself proposed Don Carlos, son of Philip II and Infante of Spain, but Elizabeth frowned on the politically dangerous alliance of Spain and Scotland. The counterproposal was Robert Dudley, Earl of Leicester, Elizabeth's own lover. What devious plan underlay such a proposal is hard to imagine. When the suggestion was declined, Elizabeth made a new suggestion, namely their common cousin Henry Darnley, the only remaining descendant of the Tudor family and therefore the only possible heir, other than the two women themselves, to the throne of England. Mary agreed to receive Lord Darnley as a suitor. Accordingly, Darnley came to Edinburgh, a handsome, petulant youth, his good looks temporarily masking his petulance, and to the amazement of all inspired Mary with a sudden and vehement passion so that she presently married him. Directly his disagreeable nature became manifest, his paramount concerns being the outward show of kingship and morbid jealousy of his beautiful wife. Soon Mary's passion turned to cordial dislike; the dislike turned to active hatred when Darnley burst into her apartments one night with a band of assassins and before her eyes slew her favorite court singer, David Rizzio. Three months later, in June of 1566, she bore Darnley's child, the future James I of England.

At this point there came into Mary's life the man who was to decide her destiny. He was James Hepburn, Earl of Bothwell, a forceful and possessive man with great power in the complex political life of the kingdom. Their headlong passion could not long be kept secret, yet Darnley's folly seems to have been dark suspicion of Rizzo when suspicion was unwarranted and now a total underestimation of Bothwell. For Bothwell now planned nothing less than the assassination of Darnley and kingship of Scotland through marriage with Mary. Whether Mary herself actively or passively was engaged in the murder plan is one of history's unresolved mysteries. Proof of her guilt or non-guilt rests with the famous "Casket Letters," which, if genuinely hers, demonstrate her full involvement in the scheme to kill her detested husband. In any case, Darnley, returning from a trip to Glasgow, was prevailed upon by his wife to spend the night of February 9, 1567 in a lonely house outside of Edinburgh rather than cover the last short lap of his journey back to the capital. During the night the house was blown up by an explosion of gunpowder and Darnley's body was discovered next morning, strangled to death, in the garden. Bothwell was accused of murder and brought to trial. Mary insisted on standing aloof from the proceedings and Bothwell was acquitted. Almost immediately thereafter Bothwell seized Mary and carried her off a prisoner to his castle at Dunbar. He now announced his intention of divorcing his wife and keeping the Queen in his castle until she agreed to marry him. This was too much even for Mary's staunchest friends, while her enemies, political, religious, and personal, had long vowed her ruin. Civil war broke out; the forces of Bothwell and Mary were defeated; Bothwell fled abroad; Mary was imprisoned in the castle of Loch Leven; her infant son was proclaimed King of Scotland, while Mary's illegitimate half-brother, the Earl of Murray, was named regent until the child should come of age. Not the least fantastic of Mary's adventures was her romantic escape in disguise from her prison on Loch Leven, but her brief effort to regain her crown met with fresh defeat. Escaping anew, she fled to the west coast and took ship with a small company of friends. Return to France now seemed more of a humiliation than an escape; Spain was distant and the voyage there hazardous around the English coasts. She determined to stop at the nearest English port and announce herself as a temporary visitor in Elizabeth's country. She landed at Carlisle, proclaimed her presence there, and asked to proceed to an interview with the English Queen. She was informed that she was being temporarily detained. It soon became apparent that the detention was outright captivity.

For nineteen years she remained Elizabeth's prisoner, now at one castle, now at another. The situation was at a complete impasse. Elizabeth was well aware that she had no legal right whatsoever to hold Mary captive, much less to bring her before a court for trial. Yet she dared not let her go. Neither did she dare confront her, knowing herself to be legally in the wrong. And the longer the state of affairs continued, the more difficult it became to take any step at all. In 1570 the Pope excommunicated Elizabeth, thereby absolving her Catholic subjects from their allegiance to her. This action, together with an armed Catholic uprising in the north of England, only served to prompt Parliament to pass stricter laws against the Catholic religion and to debar Mary permanently from succession to the English throne. Conspiracies were repeatedly organized to liberate the imprisoned Queen. All such attempts failed. In 1572 the Duke of Norfolk was executed for such a treasonable attempt, while his confederate, the Bishop of Ross, was banished. The Spanish ambassador Mendoza was implicated in the conspiracy of James Throckmorton in 1584. After the unsuccessful attempt by Dr. Parry in 1585 Parliament passed an Act which would hold the prisoner herself responsible in the event of a further plot. Murder of Elizabeth was repeatedly discovered to be one of the plotters' objectives, and such was the avowed plan of Babington and Savage, who paid with their lives for the next attempt. To enforce the Parliamentary Act, a commission of forty-two judges was sent down to Castle Fortheringhay, the last of Mary's prisons, to bring her to trial for conspiracy against the life of the English monarch. At first, the captive refused to answer before the court; then, changing her mind, she pleaded her cause with admirable dignity. Nevertheless the commission found her guilty and condemned her to death. Reluctantly Elizabeth signed the necessary warrant for execution, then entrusted it to her secretary Davison with ambiguous directions as to how he was to proceed with it. Her ministers, acting in urgency and in fear of prolonged hesitations on the part of their sovereign, proceeded to have the warrant carried out. Mary Stuart was accordingly beheaded at Fotheringhay Castle on February 8, 1857.

CHARLES E. PASSAGE

MARY STUART

CHARACTERS

ELIZABETH, QUEEN OF ENGLAND
MARY STUART, QUEEN OF SCOTLAND, a prisoner in England
ROBERT DUDLEY, EARL OF LEICESTER
GEORGE TALBOT, EARL OF SHREWSBURY
WILLIAM CECIL, BARON OF BURLEIGH, Lord High Treasurer
THE EARL OF KENT
WILLIAM DAVISON, State Secretary
AMIAS PAULET, KNIGHT, Mary's jailer
MORTIMER, his nephew
COUNT AUBESPINE, the French Ambassador
COUNT BELLIÈVRE, Ambassador extraordinary from France
O'KELLY, Mortimer's friend
DRUGEON DRURY, Mary's second jailer
MELVIL, her chief steward
BURGOYN, her surgeon
HANNA KENNEDY, her nurse
MARGARET KURL, her lady-in-waiting
The Sheriff of the shire
An Officer of the Bodyguard
French and English gentlemen
Guards
Court servants of the Queen of England
Male and female servants of the Queen of Scotland

ACT I

In Fotheringhay Castle. A room.

Scene 1

Hanna Kennedy, the Queen of Scotland's nurse, in a vehement dispute with Paulet, who is in the act of opening a cabinet. Drugeon Drury, his assistant, with a crowbar.

KENNEDY: What are you doing, Sir? More insolence!
  Get back from there!
PAULET: How did this jewel get here?
  It had been thrown down from the upper storey;
  The gardner was supposed to have been bribed
  By means of this—A curse on women's wiles!
  For all my watchfulness, my sharp-eyed search,
  More precious items yet, *more* hidden treasures!
                    (*going to work on the cabinet*)
  Where that was hidden there are more!
KENNEDY: Get back you reckless man!
  Here lie my Lady's secrets!
PAULET: Those are just
  What I am looking for.
                    (*taking out papers with writing*)
KENNEDY: Mere harmless scraps
  Of paper, exercises of the pen
  To make the prison's dreary time more short.
PAULET: The Devil thinks up work for idle hands.
KENNEDY: The writing is in French.
PAULET: So much the worse!
  That is the tongue of England's enemies.
KENNEDY: Rough drafts of letters to the Queen of England.
PAULET: I will deliver them.—What glitters here?
      (*He has opened a secret compartment and takes out
                jewels from a hidden drawer.*)
  A royal tiara, rich with precious stones
  And in-wrought with the fleur-de-lys of France!
                    (*He gives it to his companion.*)
  There, take it, Drury. Put it with the others!
                    (*Exit Drury.*)
KENNEDY: Outrageous violence that we endure!
PAULET: While she owns anything she can do harm,
  For anything in her hands is a weapon.
KENNEDY: Be kind, Sir. Do not take the last adornment
  Out of our lives. The piteous creature finds
  Delight beholding the magnificence
  Of old, for you have robbed us of all else.

PAULET: It will be in good hands. And in due time
  It will be scrupulously given back.
KENNEDY: Would anyone who looked at these bare walls
  Guess that a queen resided here? Where is
  The canopy above her chair? Must she
  Not set her tender, soft-accustomed foot
  Upon the rough and common floor? And at
  Her table she is served from ugly tin,—
  The humblest noblewoman would disdain it.
PAULET: She served her spouse that way at Sterling Castle
  While she drank with her lover out of gold.
KENNEDY: We even lack the mirror's small requirement.
PAULET: As long as she beholds her vain reflection
  She will not cease to hope and venture plans.
KENNEDY: We lack for books to entertain the mind.
PAULET: She has been left her Bible to improve
  Her heart.
KENNEDY: Her very lute has been removed.
PAULET: Because she played her wanton songs upon it.
KENNEDY: Is this a fate befitting one soft-reared,
  Who was a queen already from her cradle,
  Who at the sumptuous court of Catherine
  Of Medici grew up in joy's abundance?
  It should have been enough to take away
  Her power; must you begrudge her these poor trinkets?
  A noble heart enures itself to *great*
  Misfortune finally, but it is painful
  To be deprived of life's small ornaments.
PAULET: They only turn toward vanity the heart
  That should, by turning inward, learn repentance.
  A wanton, crime-stained life can be atoned
  In deprivation and abasement only.
KENNEDY: If tender youth in her once trespassed, let
  Her settle that with God and with her heart.
  There is no judge in England over her.
PAULET: She will be judged where she did her misdeeds.
KENNEDY: Bonds much too tight bind her from all misdoing.
PAULET: And yet from those tight bonds she has been able
  To stretch her arm into the world to hurl
  The torch of civil war into the realm
  And to equip assassin-packs with weapons
  Against our Queen, whom God preserve from harm!

Did she not from these very walls stir up
That scoundrel Parry and that Babington
To the accursed deed of regicide?
And did these iron bars deter her from
Ensnaring Norfolk's noble heart with love?
The best head in our island fell beneath
The headsman's ax in sacrifice for her—
And did that woeful spectacle scare off
The madmen striving to outdo each other
In plunging into the abyss for her sake?
The scaffolds are filled up because of her
With new and ever newer death-doomed victims,
And this will never end till she herself,
The guiltiest of all, is slaughtered there.
—Cursed be the day when the coasts of this country
With hospitality received this Helen.
KENNEDY: England, you say, showed hospitality?
To this unfortunate, who since the day
When she set foot within this country and
As suppliant, as exile dispossessed,
Came seeking harborage with relatives,
Sees herself captive in defiance of
The dignity of kings and laws of nations,
Forced to waste lovely years of youth in prison—
Who after all she has gone through, and all
The bitter things imprisonment entails,
Must now like common criminals be haled
Before the bar of judgment and accused
Disgracefully, on pain of death—a Queen!
PAULET: She came here as a murderess, expelled
By her own people, driven from a throne
She had dishonored with a deed of horror.
She came, conspiring against England's welfare.
To bring the times of Spanish Mary back,
Those bloody times, make England Catholic
Again, and then betray it to the Frenchman.
Why should she have disdained to sign the Treaty
Of Edinburgh abandoning her claim
To England, which with one stroke of the pen
Would have directly opened her a way
Out of this prison? She preferred to stay
A captive and mistreated rather than

Renounce the empty glory of that title.
And why did she do that? Because she trusts
Intrigues and vile arts of conspiracy,
Because she hopes with woven wiles of mischief
To conquer this whole island from her prison.

KENNEDY: You mock us, Sir.—To harshness you add further
Your bitter scorn! Such dreams as these you claim
She fosters, living walled up here alive,
No sound of comfort reaching her, no voice
Of friendship from her homeland coming through,
Beholding this long time no human face
Except the sombre mien of jailers, lately
Receiving one more spying watcher in
The uncouth person of your relative,
Perceiving new bars hemming her about—

PAULET: No iron bars protect us from her cunning.
How do I know these bars are not filed through,
Or that this floor, these walls, apparently
Quite sound, have not been followed out inside
To let in treason while I am asleep?
O what a cursed task to fall to me
To guard this mischief-plotting, cunning creature.
Fear starts me up from slumber; in the night
I wander like a ghost in torment, testing
The bolts of doors and loyalty of guards,
And trembling see each morning come, lest it
Should make my fears come true. But happily
For me, there is hope that this soon will end.
For I would rather have a post beside
The gate of hell and guard the legions of
The damned, before this wily, scheming Queen.

KENNEDY: Ah, here she comes!

PAULET: With Christ clasped in her hand,
And pride and worldly pleasure in her heart.

Scene 2

Enter Mary in a veil and with a crucifix in her hand.

KENNEDY (*hurrying toward her*):
O Queen! They trample us beneath their feet,

Of tyranny and harshness there will be
No limit, each new day heaps newer sorrows
And shame on your crowned head.
MARY: Compose yourself!
  Now tell me, what new thing has happened?
KENNEDY: Look!
  Your desk is broken open, and your papers,
  Your only prize that we had salvaged with
  Such pains, the last of all your bridal jewels
  From France,—all those are in his hands. You now
  Have nothing royal left. All has been stolen.
MARY: Compose yourself, Hanna. All those trinkets do
  Not make the Queen. We can be treated basely
  But they cannot debase us. I have learned
  How to put up with many things in England;
  This, too, I can get over. Sir, you have
  Appropriated forcibly what I
  Today intended to surrender to you.
  Among those papers you will find a letter
  Which was to be sent to my royal sister
  Of England.—Give me now your word that you
  Will faithfully deliver it to her
  And not put it in Burleigh's treacherous hand.
PAULET: I will consider what to do about it.
MARY: Sir, you shall know the contents. In that letter
  I make request of a tremendous favor—
  I ask her for an interview in person,
  With her whom I have never seen.—I have
  Been summoned up before a court of men
  Whom I do not acknowledge as my peers,
  In whom I cannot put my confidence.
  Elizabeth is of my family
  And of my sex and rank—to her alone,
  The sister, queen, and woman, can I speak.
PAULET: My Lady, you have very often trusted
  Your honor and your destiny to men
  Who were less worthy of your high esteem.
MARY: I make request of still another favor.
  Sheer inhumanity alone would fail
  To grant it. I have been in prison this
  Long time without the Church's consolation,
  The benison of sacraments, and she who has

Robbed me of crown and freedom and now threatens
My life itself, will not close Heaven's gate
To me.

PAULET: The local Dean at your request will—

MARY (*interrupting him sharply*):
I will have nothing of the Dean. It is
A priest of my own Church that I demand.
—I also ask for clerks and notaries
To draw up my last will and testament.
Affliction and long misery of prison
Are gnawing at my life. My days are numbered,
I fear, and I now look upon myself
As on a dying woman.

PAULET: You do well
To do so. Those are views befitting you.

MARY: How do I know but that a sudden hand
Will hasten the slow business of my sorrow?
I want to draw my will, make disposition
Of everything that I possess.

PAULET: You have
That liberty. The Queen of England does
Not wish enrichment gained from plundering you.

MARY: I have been separated from my loyal
Servants and chamberladies. Where are they?
What is their fate? Their services I can
Forego; but I wish reassurance that
These loyal persons shall not want and suffer.

PAULET: Your servants are provided for.
                    (*He starts to leave.*)

MARY: You leave me, Sir? You leave me once again
Without discharging my tormented heart
Of its dread anguish of uncertainty?
I am, thanks to your spiers' vigilance,
Cut off from all the world; no information
Can penetrate these prisons walls to reach me;
My enemies hold my fate in their hands.
A painfully long month has now gone by
Since I was taken by surprise by forty
Commissioners who came into this castle,
Set up their court, and with unseemly haste
Called me, without attorney's aid, unready,
To come before a tribunal unheard of,

And made me speak off-hand, from recollection,
To grave and deviously worded charges
While I was flustered with surprise and stunned.—
Like ghosts they came and disappeared again.
Since that day every mouth has maintained silence.
I seek in vain to read your looks and tell
Which has prevailed: my innocence, and zeal
Of my friends, or evil counsel of my foes.
At long last, break your silence—let me know
What I may have to fear, or have to hope for.

PAULET (*after a pause*):
Settle your account with Heaven.

MARY: Sir,
I have hopes in its mercy—and hopes in
The strict uprightness of my earthly judges.

PAULET: You shall have justice. Have no doubt of that.

MARY: Has my case been decided?

PAULET: I don't know.

MARY: *Am* I condemned?

PAULET: My Lady, I know nothing.

MARY: They like to do things quickly here. Am I
To be *surprised* by my assassins too,
As by my judges?

PAULET: Think of it that way,
And they will find you more prepared than did
The latter.

MARY: Nothing will amaze me, Sir,
That a Westminster court of justice, guided
By Burleigh's hatred and by Hatton's zeal,
Might now presume to judge.—I do know, though,
What England's Queen is bold enough to *do*.

PAULET: England's rulers need have fear of nothing
Except their consciences and parliaments.
What Justice has pronounced, Might will perform,
And fearlessly, for all the world to see.

Scene 3

*Enter Mortimer, Paulet's nephew. Without paying any
attention to the Queen, he says to Paulet:*

MORTIMER: They want you, Uncle.

(*He withdraws in the same manner. The Queen notices
it with annoyance and turns to Paulet, who is on the
point of following him.*)

MARY: Sir, one more request.
  If *you* have anything to say to me—
  I will bear much from you, revering your
  Old age. I will not bear this stripling's brashness.
  Spare me the spectacle of his rude manners.
PAULET: What makes you loathe him so, makes me esteem him.
  He is indeed not one of those weak fools
  Whom a false woman's tear will melt.—And he
  Is traveled. He has been to Rheims and Paris,
  But he brings back his good old English heart:
  My Lady, you will waste your wiles on him.

(*Exit.*)

Scene 4

Mary. Kennedy.

KENNEDY: O, does the brute dare say that to your face!
  O, that is hard.
MARY (*lost in thought*):
  Back in the days of our magnificence
  We lent our flatterers an ear too willing;
  It is but just, good Kennedy, that we
  Now harken to Reproach's solemn voice.
KENNEDY: So daunted, so dispirited, dear Lady?
  You used to be so cheerful, used to comfort me;
  I used to have to scold you more about
  Frivolity than melancholy.
MARY: I know him.
  It is the gory shadow of King Darnley
  That rises menacing up from his tomb,
  And he will never make his peace with me
  Until misfortune's measure has been filled
  For me.
KENNEDY: What kind of thoughts—
MARY: Hanna, you forget—
  But I possess a faithful memory—

Today the anniversary of that
Unholy deed has once again come round,
And that is what I keep with prayer and fasting.
KENNEDY: Dismiss that evil ghost to rest at last.
  You have atoned for that deed by long years
  Of heart's remorse and grievous acts of penance.
  The Church, which holds the key of absolution
  For every sin, has pardoned you, and Heaven as well.
MARY: The long forgiven sin fresh-bleeding
  Has risen from its lightly covered grave!
  My husband's vengeance-seeking spirit will
  Not be dismissed into its tomb by any
  Priest-raised Host or bell of acolyte.
KENNEDY: You did no act of murder! Others did!
MARY: I knew of it. I let the deed be done,
  And lured him smiling to the toils of death.
KENNEDY: Youth mitigated your misdeed. You were
  Still of such tender years.
MARY: Such tender years—
  Yet burdened my young life with grievous guilt.
KENNEDY: You were provoked to it by brutal outrage
  And by the arrogance of a man whom
  Your love had elevated as a god's
  Hand elevates out of obscurity,
  Whom you led through your bridal chamber to
  A throne, and favored with your lovely self
  And with your own hereditary crown.
  Could he forget his splendid lot was only
  The generous creation of your love?
  And yet he did forget, unworthy wretch!
  And with his base suspicion and rude manners
  Committed outrage on your tenderness
  And made himself quite odious to your sight.
  The spell was broken that deceived your gaze,
  You fled in anger from the shameless creature's
  Embrace and then consigned him to contempt.—
  And he—did he try to regain your favor?
  Or did he sue for mercy? Did he fall
  Repentant at your feet and promise to
  Improve? The worthless wretch defied you—who
  Created him—and tried to play the King.

Before your eyes he had your favorite murdered,
The handsome singer Rizzio.—You merely
Took bloody vengeance for that bloody deed.
MARY: And bloodily it will avenge itself
On me. Consoling me, you speak my doom.
KENNEDY: When you consented to that action, you
Were not yourself, not mistress of yourself.
Blind frenzy of desire swept you away
And held you subjugated to the dread
Seducer, ill-starred Bothwell.—Over you
With arrogant male will that artful man
Held sway, inflaming you with magic philtres
And hellish tricks that throw the mind into
Confusion—
MARY: His tricks were never anything more than
His masculinity and my own weakness.
KENNEDY: Oh no, say I! He had to summon all
The spirits of perdition to his aid
To weave those fetters over your clear senses.
For your friend's voice of warning you no longer
Had ears, nor any eyes for what was seemly.
Your delicate respect for men's opinion
Deserted you. Your cheek, which once had been
The seat of bashful, blushing modesty,
Was flushed with nothing but the fire of passion.
You cast aside the veil of secrecy.
The brazen vice of that man overcame
Your timid shyness; with defiance you
Exposed your shame before the general view.
You caused the royal sword of Scotland to
Be carried through the streets of Edinburgh
Triumphantly in front of you by that
Assassin, in whose wake the people's curses
Resounded; then you ringed your Parliament
With weapons, and within the very temple
Of justice forced the judges in a farce
To clear the guilty man of murder.—Yes
You went still further—God in heaven—
MARY: Say it!
And I gave him my hand before the altar!
KENNEDY: O let an everlasting silence cloak

That deed! It is revolt, horrible,
It suits a woman wholly lost—But you are no
Lost woman—I know you, I was the one
Who supervised your childhood. Your heart is
Of tender kind, accessible to shame,
And indiscretion is your only crime.
Again I say it: there are evil spirits
Which momentarily in man's unguarded
Bosom make their habitation and
Within us perpetrate these monstrous things,
Then, making their escape to hell, leave horror
Behind them in the heart they have polluted.
Since that deed which put blackness on your life,
You have done nothing reprehensible.
I am a witness to your betterment.
Therefore take courage! Make peace with yourself!
Whatever you have to repent, in England
You are not guilty; neither England's Queen
Nor England's Parliament can be your judge.
What overwhelms you here is force. To that
Presumptuous court you may present yourself
With all the courage lent by innocence.

MARY: Who comes?

               (*Mortimer appears at the door.*)

KENNEDY: It is the nephew. Go inside.

Scene 5

Enter Mortimer timidly.

MORTIMER (*to the nurse*):
  Withdraw, and keep a watch outside the door.
  I have things I must speak of to the Queen.

MARY (*with authority*):
  Jane, you will stay.

MORTIMER: Have no fear, my Lady. Learn to know me.
               (*He hands her a card.*)

MARY (*looks at it and falls back startled*):
  Ha, what is this?

MORTIMER (*to the nurse*):   Go, Mistress Kennedy,

Take care my uncle does not take us by
Surprise.

MARY (*to the nurse, who is hesitating and looking questioningly at the Queen*):
Go! Go! Do as he says.
(*The nurse withdraws with signs of astonishment.*)

Scene 6

Mortimer. Mary.

From France,
And from the Cardinal of Lorraine, my uncle!
(*reading*)
"Trust in Sir Mortimer who brings you this,
You have no friend more loyal in all England."
(*looking at Mortimer in astonishment*)
Can it be possible? Not some delusion
That dazzles me? I find a friend so near
And thought myself abandoned totally—
Find him in you, the nephew of my jailer,
Whom I took for my direst enemy—

MORTIMER (*throwing himself at her feet*):
Forgive me, Queen, this odious disguise
Which I have had to fight enough to wear
And yet which I must thank for being able
To get to you and bring you help and rescue.

MARY: Stand up—You take me by surprise, Sir—I
Cannot arise so fast out of the depths
Of wretchedness to hope—Speak, Sir—Explain
This stroke of luck to me, so that I may
Believe it.

MORTIMER (*rises*):   Time is running short. My uncle
Will soon be here. An odious man is with him.
Before you are surprised by their dread errand,
Hear first how Heaven sends you rescue.

MARY: Heaven's
Omnipotence has wrought this miracle!

MORTIMER: Allow me to begin first with myself.

MARY: Speak, Sir!

MORTIMER: I had achieved the age of twenty, Queen,
  I had grown up amid stern obligations,
  Been bred to grim hate for the papacy,
  When irresistible desire impelled me
  To travel to the continent. I left
  The gloomy sermon-rooms of Puritans,
  I left my native land behind me, and
  In rapid journey crossed through France in search
  Of much-praised Italy with hot desire.
    It was the great time of the jubilee,
  The roads were teeming with the throngs of pilgrims,
  Every image wore a wreath, it was
  As if mankind were travelling together
  Upon a pilgrimage to heaven—I
  Myself was caught up in the faithful throng
  And borne along into the realm of Rome—
    What feelings swept me, Queen,
  When to my sight arose the splendor of
  Triumphal arch and column, when amazement held me
  Enthralled amid the Colosseum's majesty,
  And when the lofty soul of art enclosed
  Me in a cheerful world of wonders. I
  Had never sensed the power of the arts.
  The church that reared me hates the senses' charms,
  It tolerates no image, reverences
  The fleshless Word alone. What feelings swept me
  When entering the churches. Heaven's music
  Descended, and a plenitude of forms
  Arose luxuriant from wall and ceiling,
  And the supreme sublimity was borne
  Quite tangibly past my enraptured senses;
  And then when I beheld those things divine—
  The Angel's Salutation, Our Lord's Birth,
  The Blessed Mother, the Transfiguration
  In glory, the descending Trinity—
  And when I saw the Pope himself in splendor
  Say Mass and give the nations benediction!
  O what is the magnificence of gold
  And jewels which adorn the kings of earth!
  Divinity encircles *him* alone.
  A realm of heaven is his house, indeed,

For those forms surely are not of this world.
MARY: O spare me! Speak no more of these things! Cease
    Unfurling the fresh tapestry of life
    Before me—I am wretched and a captive.
MORTIMER: And so was I, my Queen! And then my prison
    Sprang open, and my spirit suddenly
    Felt free and welcomed life's resplendent day.
    I vowed to hate the narrow, gloomy book,
    To wreathe my temples with fresh garlands, and
    To mingle joyously among the joyous.
    Many noble Scotsmen thronged to me,
    And jolly companies of Frenchmen too.
    And then they took me to your noble uncle,
    The Cardinal of Guise—O what a man!
    How clear, assured, and manly great!—How wholly
    Born to be ruler over human minds!
    The model of a royal priest, a Prince of
    The Church, the like of which I never saw!
MARY: You have beheld his cherished countenance,
    The face of that sublime and much-loved man
    Who was the mentor of my tender youth.
    O speak of him! Does he still think of me?
    Does Fortune love him? Does his life still flower?
    And does he still stand as the Church's rock?
MORTIMER: The excellent man himself deigned to expound
    To me the lofty doctrines of the Faith
    And to dispel the doubts that filled my heart.
    He showed me how Reason with its quibbles
    Must everlastingly lead man astray,
    How human eyes have need of seeing what
    The heart is to believe, how the Church must
    Present a visible head, how the Spirit
    Of Truth dwelt in the Councils of the Fathers.
    How the illusions of my childish soul
    Were all dispelled by his triumphant mind
    And by the suasion of his mouth. Thus I
    Returned into the bosom of the Church
    And there into his hands renounced my error.
MARY: You are one of those thousands, then, whom he,
    Like that sublimest Preacher on the Mount,
    Has seized on by his eloquence from heaven

And brought back to salvation everlasting.
MORTIMER: When duties of his office soon thereafter
  Called him to France, he sent me up to Rheims,
  Where the Society of Jesus in
  Its pious diligence trains priests for England.
  And there I found the noble Scotsman Morgan,
  Your faithful Lessley too, the learned Bishop
  Of Ross, who are all living joyless days
  Of banishment upon the soil of France.—
  I joined those worthy men in close alliance
  And strengthened myself in the Faith.—One day
  While looking through the Bishop's residence,
  A woman's picture fell upon my eyes
  Of wondrously affecting charm. It moved
  Me powerfully to the depths of my soul,
  And there I stood with feelings uncontrolled.
  The Bishop said to me: You do quite right
  To dwell upon that portrait with emotion.
  For that most beautiful of living women
  Is also the most miserable of all.
  It is for our Faith's sake that she endures
  And it is your home country where she suffers.
MARY: That upright man! No, all has not been lost.
  When such a friend is left in my misfortune.
MORTIMER: Then he began describing to me with
  Heart-rending eloquence your martyrdom
  And the bloodthirstiness of all your foes.
  And he referred me to your family tree
  And showed me your descent from the high House
  Of Tudor and convinced me you alone
  Should properly be ruler here in England,
  Not this pretender of a Queen, conceived
  In an adulterous bed, repudiated
  By Henry, her own father, as a bastard.
  I would not trust his testimony only,
  I sought advice from all the learned jurists,
  Poured over many books of heraldry,
  And all the experts whom I found to ask
  Confirmed to me your claim's validity.
  By now I realize that your good right
  To England constitutes your only wrong,

That this realm is your rightful property
In which you languish as a guiltless captive.

MARY: Alas, that right is my misfortune! It
Is the sole cause of all my sufferings.

MORTIMER: Just at that time the information reached me
That you had been removed from Talbot's castle
And been committed to my uncle's charge—
In that contingency I thought I saw
Miraculous deliverance from heaven.
It seemed as though Fate clearly summoned me
And made choice of *my* arm to set you free.
My friends with joy agreed, the Cardinal
Gave me his blessing and his counsel and
Taught me the hard art of dissimulation.
The plan was soon contrived, and I set out
Upon my homeward journey to my country
Where, as you know, I landed ten days since.

(He stops.)

Then, O my Queen, I saw you—you yourself!
Not just your picture!—O, what treasure is
Kept in this castle! This is not a prison!
This is a hall of gods more splendid than
The royal court of England—O how lucky
The man who may breathe this same air with you!
    O she does well to hide you so completely!
For all the youth of England would rise up,
No sword would be left idle in its sheath,
Rebellion with gigantic head would stalk
This peaceful island, if the Briton were
To see his Queen!

MARY: And it is well for her,
If every Briton saw her through your eyes.

MORTIMER: If they, like me, were witness to your sorrows,
And to your meekness, and the noble calm
With which you here endure unworthiness.
For do you not emerge from all your trials
Of sorrow like a Queen? Does prison's shame
Deprive you of the glory of your beauty?
You lack all things that make life beautiful,
Yet light and life are ever shed about you.
I never set my foot upon this threshold

But that my heart is torn with torments and
Enraptured with the joy of looking at you!—
Yet fearsomely decision nears, and danger
Becomes more menacing with every hour.
I must postpone no longer—must no longer
Conceal the dread news from you—

MARY: Is my sentence
Pronounced? Disclose it frankly. I can hear it.

MORTIMER: It is pronounced. The forty-two high judges
Have brought their verdict: *Guilty;* and the House
Of Lords, the House of Commons, and the City
Of London urgently demand the sentence
Be carried out; the Queen alone is still
Delaying—craftily, so they will force her,
Not from compassion or from humane feelings.

MARY (*with composure*):
Sir Mortimer, you do not take me by
Surprise nor frighten me. For such news I
Have long since been prepared. I know my judges.
After the mistreatment I have suffered,
I realize they cannot grant me freedom—
I understand what they are driving at.
They mean to hold me prisoner forever
And thus to bury my revenge and all
My rights and claims in prison darkness with me.

MORTIMER: No, Queen—no, no! They will not stop at that.
This tyranny will not be satisfied
To do its work half way. As long as you
Still live, the Queen of England's fear still lives.
No prison can inter you deep enough,
Your death alone can make her throne quite safe.

MARY: But would she ever dare to lay my crowned
Head down in shame upon the headsman's block?

MORTIMER: She will so dare. Make no mistake about it.

MARY: Would she hurl her own majesty into
The dust and all kings' majesty as well?
Does she not fear the vengeance France might take?

MORTIMER: She is now making lasting peace with France
And gives the Duc d'Anjou her throne and hand.

MARY: And will the King of Spain not take up arms?

MORTIMER: She would not fear the whole world up in arms

As long as she has peace with her own people.

MARY: Would she give Britons such spectacle?

MORTIMER: This country has, in recent times, my Lady,
Witnessed several royal women step
Down from the throne to mount upon the scaffold.
This same Elizabeth's own mother trod
That path, and Katherine Howard, and the Lady
Jane Gray wore a crown likewise on her head.

MARY (*after a pause*):
No, Mortimer! Vain fear has made you blind.
It is your loyal heart's concern for me
That now gives rise to these vain terrors in you.
Sir, it is not the scaffold that I fear.
There are quite different means, more quiet ones,
To which the Queen of England can resort
To rid herself of my disturbing claims.
Before a headsman can be found for me,
A paid assassin will be found and hired.
—And *that,* Sir, is what makes me tremble. Never
Do I raise any cup's brim to my lips
But that a shudder courses through me lest
My sister's love should have prepared it for me.

MORTIMER: Assassination shall not touch your life
By either public means or secret ones.
Have no fear! Everything has been prepared.
Twelve noble young men of this country are
In league with me; this very morning they
Took their oath on the sacrament to set
You free by force and take you from this castle.
Count Aubespine, the French ambassador,
Knows of the plan and lends us help himself;
We have our place of meeting in his palace.

MARY: You make me tremble, Sir—but not with joy.
My heart is touched with evil premonition.
What have you undertaken? Do you know?
Do Babington's and Tichburn's bloody heads
Nailed up on London Bridge not terrify you?
Not yet in the ruin of the countless ones
Who in like risky hazard found their deaths
And only made my chains the heavier?
Unfortunate, misguided youth—flee now!

Flee while there still is time—if that spy Burleigh
Is not already on your track, has not
Already set a traitor in your midst.
Flee swiftly from this kingdom! Mary Stuart
Has yet to be fought for without disaster.

MORTIMER: No, Babington's and Tichburn's bloody heads
Nailed up on London Bridge affright me not,
Nor yet the ruin of the countless ones
Who in like risky hazard found their deaths;
They found undying fame as well, and it
Is happiness to perish for your rescue.

MARY: All futile! Neither force nor craft can save me.
The foe is sleepless and the power is his.
Not only Paulet and his host of spies
But all of England guards my prison doors.
The free will of Elizabeth alone
Can open them.

MORTIMER: O do not hope for that!

MARY: There does live one man who can open them.

MORTIMER: O name that man to me—

MARY: Count Lester.

MORTIMER (*falls back astonished*):   Lester!
Count Lester—your bloodthirstiest opponent,
The favorite of Elizabeth—By that—

MARY: If I can be saved, only he can save me.
—Go to him. Speak your purpose frankly.
As surety that it is I who send you,
Give him this letter. It contains my picture.
       (*She takes a paper from her bosom. Mortimer steps
              back and hesitates to accept it.*)
Take it. I long have carried it about me
Because your uncle's steady vigilance
Has barred all means of access to him.—You
Were sent by my good angel—

MORTIMER: Queen—this riddle—
Explain—

MARY: Count Lester will resolve it for you.
If you trust him, he will trust you—Who comes here?
                (*Enter Kennedy in haste.*)

KENNEDY: Sir Paulet with a gentleman from court.

MORTIMER: It is Lord Burleigh. Queen, compose yourself!

Hear what he says with equanimity.
(*He goes out by a side door. Kennedy follows him.*)

Scene 7

*Enter Lord Burleigh, Lord High Treasurer of England,
and Sir Amias Paulet.*

PAULET: You wished today for certainty about
  Your fate. His Excellency, my Lord of Burleigh,
  Brings you that certainty. Bear it with meekness.
MARY: With dignity, I trust, befitting innocence.
BURLEIGH: I come as the court's representative.
MARY: Lord Burleigh lent the court his mind before,
  He now obligingly lends it his mouth.
PAULET: You speak as if you knew the verdict now.
MARY: Because Lord Burleigh brings it, I do know.
  —Come to the point, Sir.
BURLEIGH: Lady, you submitted
  Yourself before the court of forty-two—
MARY: Forgive my interrupting you, my Lord,
  Right at the start—You say that I submitted
  To judgment by the court of forty-two?
  I never did submit myself to them.
  I could not do so—I could not impugn
  My rank and dignity so much, nor those of
  My people, or my son, or of all monarchs.
  It is decreed in English law that any
  Person brought to trial shall be tried
  By sworn men chosen from among his equals.
  And who on that Commission is my equal?
  Kings are my only peers.
BURLEIGH: You listened to
  The articles of accusation and
  In court submitted to examination—
MARY: I let myself be lured by Hatton's cunning,
  Merely for my honor's sake and trusting
  The winning power of my arguments,
  To hear those articles of accusation
  And demonstrate their groundlessness.—I did so

Out of respect for the Lords' worthy persons,
Not for their office, which I must reject.

BURLEIGH: Acknowledge it or not, my Lady, that
Is only meaningless formality
Which cannot hamper the court's operation.
You breathe the air of England and enjoy
The blessings and protection of its laws,
And you are subject to its sovereignty!

MARY: I breathe the air inside an English prison.
Is that in England known as living and
Enjoying benefaction of its laws?
I hardly know them. And I never gave
Consent to keep them. I am not a subject
Of this realm, but a free Queen from abroad.

BURLEIGH: And do you think your royal name can serve
As patent to sow with impunity
Blood-stained dissension in a foreign country?
What would become of the security
Of states if the just sword of Themis could
Not reach the guilty brows of royal guests
As certainly as it does beggars' heads?

MARY: I do not seek escape from justice but
From judges whom I do not recognize.

BURLEIGH: From judges! What, my Lady? Are they some
Dredged-up and outcast scourings from the rabble,
Some shameless shysters for whom truth and justice
Are cheap, who willingly allow themselves
To be hired out as tools of crass oppression?
Are they not the first men of this country,
And of sufficient independence to
Be upright and be elevated far
Above base bribery and fear of Princes?
And are they not the very ones who rule
A noble people freely and with justice,
Whose names need but be named to silence all
Suspicion and all doubt immediately?
To head the list there is the people's shepherd,
The pious primate of Canterbury,
Wise Talbot, Keeper of the Privy Seal,
And Howard who directs the nation's fleet.
Now tell me, could the Queen of England do

More than she has done, to select the noblest
From all her monarchy and to appoint
Them to be judges in this royal quarrel?
Even if it were thinkable that hatred
Of parties could bribe individuals,—
Could forty chosen men agree upon
A verdict that involves such passion?

MARY (*after a silence*):
I stand amazed to hear the vehemence
Of lips which always have brought me misfortune—
How shall I, a woman and unlearned,
Compete against a speaker of such skill!—
Ah! if those Lords were such as you describe them,
I should be forced to silence; my case would
Be lost and hopeless if they found me guilty.
But those names which you mention with such praise,
Which are supposed to crush me with their weight,
My Lord, I see them play quite different roles
Down through the course of annals of this country.
I see those high aristocrats of England
And that majestic senate of this kingdom
Act like seraglio slaves in flattering
The Sultan's whims of my great-uncle Henry
The Eighth—I see that noble Upper House,
As venal as the venal House of Commons,
Enact laws and revoke them, now dissolve
A marriage, now enforce it, at the mighty
Man's bidding, disinherit England's Princesses
Today and shame them with the name of bastards,
And then again tomorrow crown them Queens.
I see those worthy peers with swiftly changed
Convictions *four times* alter their religion
Under *four* regimes.

BURLEIGH: You claim that you
Are unfamiliar with the laws of England
But you are well informed on England's woes

MARY: Such are my judges!—Lord High Treasurer!
I want to be quite fair with you! Be so
Likewise with me.—They say that you are well
Intentioned toward this state, that with your Queen
You are alert, unbribeable, and tireless—

I shall believe that. You are governed not
By your advantage but by what is of
Advantage to your Sovereign and your country.
Do not therefore, my noble Lord, mistake
For justice what is useful to the state.
I do not doubt that other noble men
Are seated there with you among my judges.
But they are *Protestants*, men filled with zeal
For England's welfare, and they sit in judgment
On me, the Queen of Scotland and a Papist!
The Englishman can not be just in judging
The Scotsman, goes an ancient saying.—Hence
Tradition has it since times of our fathers:
No Englishman shall testify in court
Against a Scot, nor any Scot against him.
Necessity occasioned that strange law.
Deep meaning lies in those old usages,
And one must honor them, my Lord.—These two
Fierce nationalities were cast by Nature
Upon this plank in ocean; this she parcelled
Unequally and bade them fight for it.
The narrow Tweed is all that separates
Those fiery tempers; often in its waves
The blood of fighting men has been commingled.
With hand on sword, they have looked threateningly
Across from both those shores these thousand years.
No enemy has menaced England yet
But that the Scotsman joined him as a helper;
No civil war has kindled Scotland's cities
But that the Englishman provided tinder.
Nor will the hatred ever die until
One parliament joins them in brotherhood,
Until one sceptre rules throughout the island.

BURLEIGH: And I suppose a Stuart would afford
    The realm that blessing?
MARY: Why should I deny it?
    Yes, I confess that I had cherished hopes
    Of unifying these two noble nations
    Freely in the shadow of the olive.
    I never thought I would become the victim
    Of these two peoples' hatred. I had hoped

To quench forever their long jealousy,
The wretched passion of their ancient quarrel,
And, as my forebear Richmond once united
Both roses after bloody struggle, wed
In peace the crowns of Scotland and of England.

BURLEIGH: Then you pursued that goal by evil ways
When you sought to enflame the kingdom and
Ascend the throne through fires of civil war.

MARY: That I did not seek, by the living God!
When did I seek that? Where are proofs of that?

BURLEIGH: I did not come to argue here. The matter
Is past the point of disputation now.
Decision has been made by forty votes to two
That you have violated last year's Act
Of Parliament and have incurred the forfeit.
It was enacted into law last year:
"In case disorder shall arise within
The kingdom in the name and to the vantage
Of any person claiming rights upon
The throne, that person shall be prosecuted
By law and, if found guilty, put to death."—
And since it now is proved—

MARY: My Lord of Burleigh!
I do not doubt but that a law, expressly
Drawn up against me, written to destroy me,
Will be invoked and used against me.—Woe
To the poor victim, when the very mouth
That made the law pronounces sentence also!
Can you deny, my Lord, that that same Act
Referred to was devised for my destruction?

BURLEIGH: It was intended as a warning to you,
You have yourself turned it into a snare.
You saw the pit that opened up before you,
And yet, despite fair warning, you plunged in,
For you were in collusion with the traitor
Babington and his accomplices;
You were informed of everything, and from
Your prison guided the conspiracy.

MARY: When do you claim I did that? Let them show
Me documents to prove it.

BURLEIGH: Those were laid

Before you only recently in court.

MARY: The copies, written by an unknown hand!
But let proof be adduced that I dictated
Those documents myself, and that I did so
In that precise form in which they were read.

BURLEIGH: Before his execution Babington
Acknowledged them as those he had received.

MARY: And why was he not brought before my eyes
Alive? And why were they in such a hurry
Despatching him out of the world before
He was produced before me, face to face?

BURLEIGH: Your secretaries also, Kurl and Nau,
Confirmed on oath those were the very letters
That they had written down from your own mouth.

MARY: I am condemned, then, on the testimony
Of my domestics! On the basis of
The faith and trust of those men who betrayed me,
Their Queen, who broke their faith that very moment
When they bore witness there against me?

BURLEIGH: You once declared the Scotsman Kurl yourself
To be a man of virtue and of conscience.

MARY: I knew he was—And yet the hour of danger
Alone can test the virtue of a man.
It may be that the rack so terrified him
That he confessed to things he did not know!
False witness, he imagined, might save him,
Yet not harm me, a Queen, so very much.

BURLEIGH: He gave his evidence with a free oath.

MARY: He did not give it in my presence!—What, Sir?
Here are two witnesses, both still alive!
Let them be brought before me, and have them
Repeat their testimony to my face!
Why should a favor be refused to me,
A right, in fact, not kept from murderers?
I know from Talbot's lips, my former jailer,
That under date within this very reign
An Act of Parliament was passed requiring
Accused to be confronted with accuser.
What? Or did I not hear aright?—Sir Paulet!
I always have found you an honest man.
Now prove that. Tell me on your conscience: Is

That not so? Is there no such law in England?

PAULET: My Lady, it is so. That is our law.

   I must speak what is true.

MARY: Well then, my Lord!

   If I must be so strictly treated by

   Your English law when that law does me harm,

   Why circumvent that very law when it

   Can operate to help me!—Answer me!

   Then why was Babington not brought before

   My eyes, as the law stipulates? Why not

   My secretaries, who are still alive?

BURLEIGH: Do not get angry, Lady. Your collusion

   With Babington was not the only thing—

MARY: It is the only thing that lays me open

   To the law's sword, and of which I must clear me.

   My Lord! Stick to the point. Do not evade.

BURLEIGH: It has been proved that you had dealings with

   Mendoza, the ambassador of Spain—

MARY (*agitatedly*):

   Stick to the point, my Lord!

BURLEIGH: —that you laid plots

   To overthrow the state religion here,

   That you had stirred up all the kings of Europe

   To war with England—

MARY: And what if I did?

   I did not do so—Yet supposing that

   I did! My Lord, I am held captive in

   Defiance of all international law.

   I did not come into this country with

   A sword, I came here as a suppliant,

   Asked for asylum, threw myself into

   A Queen's arms who is my blood-relative—

   Force apprehended me, put me in chains

   Where I had sought protection.—Tell me now!

   Do I owe anything in conscience to

   This state? Am I in duty bound to England?

   I practice nothing but the sacred right

   Of self-defense in trying to shake off

   These bonds, in turning force by force,

   In stirring up all states to my defense.

   I may quite rightly exercise whatever

Is right and chivalrous in a just war.
Murder alone, the secret deed of blood,
My conscience and my pride forbid my doing.
I would be stained by murder and dishonored.
I said: dishonored—but in no respect
Condemned, subjected to a legal sentence.
For the concern between me here and England
Is not with justice, but with force alone.

BURLEIGH (*pointedly*):
Do not invoke the fearful right of strength,
My Lady! for it does not favor prisoners.

MARY: I am the weak one, she the mighty one—
So be it! Let her use force, let her kill me,
Let her slay this victim for her safety.
But let her then acknowledge that she had
Recourse to force alone, and not to justice.
Let her not borrow the law's sword to rid
Herself of her detested enemy,
Let her not clothe in holy garb the bloody
Audacity of naked violence.
Deceit like this must not deceive the world!
She can assassinate me, but not judge me!
Let her give up combining fruits of crime
With the external holy look of virtue,
And let her seem to be just what she *is!*
                    (*Exit.*)

Scene 8

Burleigh. Paulet.

BURLEIGH: So she defies us—will defy us, Paulet,
Right to the scaffold steps!—That haughty heart
Cannot be broken.—Did the sentence take
Her unawares? Or did you see her shed
One single tear? Or even change her color?
She did not play upon our sympathy,
She knows the indecision of the Queen
Of England, and our fear makes her courageous.

PAULET: My Lord High Treasurer! This vain defiance will
  Soon vanish if the pretext is removed.
  There were some improprieties, if I
  May be allowed to say so, in this trial.
  They should have brought that Babington and Tichburn
  To her in person, and her secretaries
  Should likewise have confronted her.
BURLEIGH (*quickly*):   No, no,
  Knight Paulet! That was much too great a risk.
  Her power over people's feelings is
  Too great, as is her woman's force of tears.
  Her secretary Kurl, if he should face her,
  And if it came to speaking that one word
  On which her life depends, he would back down
  Faint-hearted and retract his testimony—
PAULET: But this way England's enemies will fill
  The world with their malicious rumors, and
  The solemn ceremony of the trial
  Will look like nothing but a bold-faced outrage.
BURLEIGH: That is precisely what disturbs our Queen—
  Oh, if this instigator of misfortune
  Had only died before she ever set
  Her foot on English soil!
PAULET: To that I say Amen!
BURLEIGH: If she had died of illness while in prison!
PAULET: That would have saved this country lots of trouble.
BURLEIGH: Yet if some accident of Nature had
  Despatched her—we would still be called assassins.
PAULET: Quite true. For people cannot be prevented
  From thinking what they will.
BURLEIGH: At any rate it could
  Not have been proved, and would have caused less talk that
    [way—
PAULET: Well, let it cause talk if it will! It is
  Not loud but righteous blame that can do harm.
BURLEIGH: O! justice in its holiness will not
  Escape blame either, for opinion holds
  With the unfortunate, and envy always
  Pursues the fortunate amid their triumph.
  The sword of judgment, which adorns a man,
  Is odious in a woman's hand. The world

Does not believe in justice from a woman
When a woman is the victim. All
For naught we judges answered by our conscience!
She has a Queen's prerogative of mercy
And she must use it! If she lets the law
Take its strict course, it is intolerable!

PAULET: And so—?

BURLEIGH *(interrupting)*: So she must go on living? No!
She must not go on living! Never! That
Is just the thing that makes our Queen so anxious—
The thing that drives sleep from her couch—I read
The struggle of her spirit in her eyes,
But her lips do not dare pronounce her wishes.
Her silent glances meaningfully ask:
Is there not one of all my servants who
Will save me from the loathesome choice of living in
Eternal fear upon my throne, or else
Condemning cruelly this Queen, my own
Blood-relative, to death?

PAULET: Necessity will have it so, it can't be helped.

BURLEIGH: The Queen feels that it might indeed be helped
If only she had more attentive servants.

PAULET: Attentive?

BURLEIGH   Who could take an unexpressed
Command from her.

BURLEIGH: An unexpressed command?
Who, if a poisonous snake were given them
To keep, would not preserve that enemy
As if it were a sacred precious jewel.

PAULET *(pointedly)*:
A good name is a precious jewel, and
The unsmirched reputation of the Queen,
Sir, cannot be too carefully protected.

BURLEIGH: When they removed the Lady from the keeping
Of Shrewsbury and put her in the care
Of Paulet, the idea was—

PAULET: I hope,
Sir, the idea was to trust the task
That was most difficult to hands most clean.
By God! I never would have taken over
This bailiff's office if I had not thought

That it required the best man in all England.
Do not give me the notion that I owe it
To anything but my good reputation.
BURLEIGH: It is reported she is in decline,
   Then she gets worse, and finally just dies.
   That way she dies in people's memories—
   While you have your name clear.
PAULET: But not my conscience.
BURLEIGH: If you decline to lend your own hand to it,
   You surely won't object to someone else's—
PAULET (*interrupting him*):
   No murderer shall step across her threshold
   As long as gods of my roof shelter her.
   Her life is sacred to me; the Queen of England's
   Head is not any more so in my sight.
   You are the judges! Judge her! Break the staff!
   And when the time comes, have the carpenter
   Come up here with his ax and saw and build
   The scaffold.—For the sheriff and the headsman
   You will find that my castle gates are open.
   But now she is entrusted to my keeping,
   And you may be assured I will protect her
   From doing harm or letting harm affect her.
                            (*Exeunt.*)

ACT II

The palace of Westminster.

Scene 1

Enter the Earl of Kent and Sir William Davison, meeting.

DAVISON: My Lord of Kent? Back from the tournament
   Already? Is the festival all over?
KENT: Why, didn't you attend the knightly games?
DAVISON: My duties kept me.
KENT: You have missed the finest
   Spectacle that taste has yet devised
   Or noble grace has executed.—For,
   You see, they represented the chaste Fortress

Of Beauty under siege there by Desire;
And the Lords Marshal and Chief Justice and
Chief Steward and ten more knights of the Queen
Were there to hold the Fortress's defense
While cavaliers of France rode to attack.
A herald came up first and bade the castle
Surrender in a madrigal he sang,
And from the walls the Chancellor replied.
Then the artillery came into play
And precious perfumes and bouquets of flowers
Were fired from pretty mimic cannon. But
To no avail; Those making the attack
Were beaten off; Desire had to retreat.

DAVISON: A sign of evil omen, my Lord Earl,
Regarding the French match-making.

KENT: Oh well, all that was in fun.—In earnest
I think, the Fortress will surrender in
The end.

DAVISON: You think so? I cannot believe it.

KENT: The articles that were most difficult
Are settled now and France accedes to them.
Monsieur will be content to have his own
Religious services in private chapel
And honor and protect the state religion
In public.—O you should have heard the jubilation
Of people when that information was made known.
That was this country's constant fear, that she
Might die and leave no issue of her body,
And England would again wear Papal fetters
If Mary Stuart should succeed her on
The throne.

DAVISON: *That* fear can be dismissed.—*She* goes
To marriage, while the Stuart goes to death.

KENT: The Queen is coming!

Scene 2

Enter Elizabeth on the arm of Leicester, Count
Aubespine, Bellièvre, the Earl of Shrewsbury, Lord
Burleigh, together with other French and English
gentlemen, come in.

ELIZABETH (*to Aubespine*):
    Count, I regret these noble gentlemen,
    Whom gallant zeal has brought here from across
    The sea, should have to miss the splendor of
    The Court of Saint Germain while at my court.
    I am unable to devise such gorgeous
    Feasts of the gods as does the royal mother
    Of France.—An orderly and happy people
    Who throng with benedictions round my
    Sedan-chair when I show myself in public,—
    Such is the spectacle that I can show
    With my own pride to foreign eyes. The glory
    Of noble maidens who in Catherine's Garden
    Of Beauty show their loveliness would only
    Eclipse me and my own unlustrous merit.
AUBESPINE: Westminster Court shows but one lady to
    Astonished foreigners,—but everything
    About the charming sex that gives delight
    Is gathered and assembled in that one.
BELLIÈVRE: Will Sublime Majesty of England grant
    Permission for us to take leave of her
    And go to bring Monsieur, our royal master,
    The joyous tidings for which he so yearns?
    The hot impatience of his heart would not
    Let him remain in Paris; he is waiting
    In Amiens for messengers of his
    Good fortune, and his post extends right to
    Calais to carry the consent which will
    Be spoken by your royal lips, with all
    The speed of wings to his enchanted ear.
ELIZABETH: Count Bellièvre, do not press me further.
    The present moment, I repeat, is not
    The proper time to light the torch of Hymen.
    Black hang the skies above this country, and
    The mourner's veil of crape would suit me better
    Than pomp and finery of bridal raiment.
    A grievous blow is threatened close at hand,
    Aimed at my heart and at my family.
BELLIÈVRE: Give us no more, Queen, than your promise, and
    Fulfillment will ensue in happier days.
ELIZABETH: Monarchs are mere slaves of their condition,

They may not follow as their own hearts bid.
My wish has always been to die unwed,
And my choice would have been to have my fame
Consist of this: that on my gravestone people
Should some day read: "Here lies the Virgin Queen."
And yet my subjects will not have it so.
Already they are thinking of the time
When I shall be no more.—It will not do
For them to have prosperity right now;
I must be sacrificed for future welfare
As well, I must give up my virgin freedom,
My highest treasure, for my people also,
And have a lord and master forced upon me.
They show me in this way that I am only
A woman in their eyes, while I thought I
Had ruled them like a man and like a king.
I realize that God is not well served
When Nature's order is abandoned, and
Those who ruled here before me merit praise
For having closed the monasteries and
Returned a thousand victims of a wrongly
Conceived devotion to the obligations
Of Nature. But a Queen who does not spend
Her days in idle, useless contemplation,
Who prosecutes the hardest of all tasks
Undaunted and unwearying, *she* ought
To be excepted from that goal of Nature
Which has the one half of the human race
Subordinated to the other. . . .

AUBESPINE: You have exalted every virtue, Queen,
   Upon your throne, and nothing is left wanting
   Except to shine as paragon before
   The sex whose glory you embody, in
   Its unique merits. Actually, there is
   No man alive on earth who would be worthy
   Of having you renounce your freedom for him.
   But if nobility, and birth, heroic
   Virtue, and male comeliness have ever
   Made any mortal worthy of that honor,—

ELIZABETH: There is no doubt, my Lord Ambassador,
   But that a bond of marriage with a royal

Son of France would do me honor. Yes,
I frankly say, if it *must* be—if there
Is no way but yield to my people's pressure—
And they will prove, I fear, more strong than I—
I do not know of any Prince in Europe
To whom I would with less reluctance yield
My freedom, my most treasured jewel. Let
That statement be sufficient for you now.

BELLIÈVRE: It is a *glorious* hope. But it is only
A *hope*. My master wishes something *more*—

ELIZABETH: What does he wish?

(*She takes a ring from her finger and looks at it
pensively.*)

The Queen has no advantage
Over the wives of common citizens!
An equal token marks an equal duty,
An equal servitude.—From rings come weddings,
Rings also finally make up a chain.
—Accept this gift and take it to His Highness.
It is not *yet* a chain, does not yet bind me;
And yet it can become a bond to bind me.

BELLIÈVRE (*kneels and receives the ring*):
In his name I accept this gift, great Queen,
And kneel as I receive it, pressing also
The kiss of homage on the hand of my new Princess.

ELIZABETH (*to the Earl of Leicester, at whom she has been
looking fixedly during the last speech*):
My Lord, permit me!

(*She takes the blue sash from him and puts it on
Bellièvre.*)

With this decoration
Invest His Highness as I here invest
You and accept you in the duties of my Order.
Honi soit qui mal y pense!—Between
Two nations let suspicion disappear,
And let a bond of confidence henceforward
Entwine the crowns of England and of France.

AUBESPINE: Exalted Queen, this is a day of joy!
May it be such for all, and further, may
No sufferer in all this island grieve!
Now mercy gleams upon your countenance.

O! if a glimmer of its cheerful light
Might fall upon a Princess in misfortune
Whose destiny concerns both France and England
Alike—

ELIZABETH: No further, Count! Let us not mingle
Two wholly incompatible affairs.
If France sincerely wishes my alliance,
Then it must also share my cares with me
And not be friendly to my enemy—

AUBESPINE: In your own eyes France would be acting basely
If she forgot in this alliance that
Unhappy Queen, her co-religionist,
The widow of her King.—Humanity
And honor both require—

ELIZABETH: In that sense I
Esteem her intercession as its due.
France will fulfill her duty as a friend;
Grant me, however, to act as a Queen.
          (*She bows to the French gentlemen, who withdraw
          respectfully with the other Lords.*)

Scene 3

Elizabeth. Leicester. Burleigh. Talbot.
(*The Queen sits down.*)

BURLEIGH: Illustrious Queen! Today you crown the ardent
Wishes of your people. Not till now
Have we enjoyed the prosperous days which you
Confer upon us, for we look no more
With anxious dread into the stormy future.
One fear alone besets this country still,
There is one victim whom all voices cry for.
Grant us this one thing more, and this day will
Have founded England's welfare for all time.

ELIZABETH: What more is it my people ask for? Speak,
My Lord.

BURLEIGH: They want the Stuart's head.—If you
Wish to assure your people's precious freedom
And the so dearly purchased light of truth,

Then *she* must be no more.—If we are not
To tremble for your precious life forever,
This enemy must perish!—You well know
That not all Englishmen hold like opinions.
The Romish idol-cult still numbers many
A secret worshipper within this island.
And all of them still cherish hostile thoughts;
Their hearts are for this Stuart, and they are
In league with the two brothers of Lorraine,
Irreconcilable foes of your name.
A grim war of annihilation has
Been vowed against you by that rabid party
To be waged with false instruments of hell.
At Rheims, the Cardinal-bishop's see, they have
Their arsenal where they forge thunderbolts.
There regicide is taught—and busily
The missions destined for this island are
Sent out from there, those resolute fanatics
Disguised in every sort of garb.—From there
The third assassin has already come,
And inexhaustibly, forever new
In that abyss breed hidden enemies.
—In Castle Fotheringhay there sits the Atè
Of that eternal warfare, who is using
The torch of love to set this realm on fire.
For her sake, who cajoles them all to hope,
Young men devote themselves to certain death—
Their watchword is: To liberate her, and
Their purpose is to place her on your throne.
Your sacred right is not acknowledged by
The family of Lorraine; in their eyes you
Are merely a usurper, crowned by chance!
They were the ones who led that foolish woman
To sign herself "the Queen of England." There
Can be no peace with her or with her clan!
You must endure the blow or deal it. Her
Life is your death, and her death is your life!

ELIZABETH: My Lord: It is a dreary post you hold.
I know the upright impulse of your zeal,
I know that sterling wisdom speaks in you.
Yet when that wisdom bids that blood be shed,

I hate it from the bottom of my soul.
Invent a milder counsel.—Noble Lord
Of Shrewsbury! Now tell us *your* opinion.
TABLOT: You paid a fitting tribute to the zeal
    That stirs in Burleigh's loyal heart.—I too,
    Although my mouth has eloquence less ready,
    Have in my bosom a heart no less loyal.
    May you live on, O Queen, a long time yet
    To be your people's joy and to extend
    The bension of peace upon this kingdom.
    Such prosperous days this island never has
    Beheld since it was ruled by its own rulers.
    Let it not purchase happiness at fame's
    Expense! Let Talbot's eyes at least have closed
    Before a thing like that occurs!
ELIZABETH: Now God forbid that we should stain our fame!
TALBOT: Well, in that case you will devise some other means
    To save this kingdom,—for the execution
    Of Mary Stuart is an unjust means.
    You cannot judge *her* and pass sentence on her
    Who is not subject to you.
ELIZABETH: Then my Council
    Of State and Parliament are wrong, and all
    This country's courts are equally in error,
    When they agree that I do have that right—
TALBOT: Majorities are no proof of the right,
    England is not the world, your Parliament
    Is not a union of the human races.
    This England of today is not that of
    The future, nor the past one either.—Just
    As inclination shifts, so also rises
    And falls the changeful wave of world opinion.
    Do not say that you were compelled to follow
    Necessity and pressure of your people.
    Whenever you so wish, at any moment
    You can discover that your will is free.
    Just try it! Say that you revolt at bloodshed
    And that you *want* your sister's life preserved.
    To those who would advise you otherwise
    Reveal the truth of your most queenly wrath
    And you will quickly see Necessity

Displaced and Right converted into Wrong.
And you yourself must judge, and you alone.
You cannot lean upon that shaky reed.
Be guided by your natural clemency.
God did not give severity to woman's
Gentle heart.—The founders of this kingdom,
Who also gave the reins of government
To women, meant that rulers of this country
Were not to make severity a virtue.

ELIZABETH: An ardent advocate is my Lord Talbot
For mine and for this country's foe. But I
Prefer the counsellors who love my welfare.

TALBOT: No advocate has been allowed her; no one
Dares to expose himself to your great ire
By pleading her defense.—Allow me then,
An old man near his grave, who cannot be
Seduced by any hopes this world can offer,
To speak up in behalf of this doomed woman.
O let it not be said that selfishness
And passion had their voices in your Council
Of State while only mercy held its tongue.
Against her everyone united stands,
You never have beheld her countenance,
And nothing in your heart speaks for this stranger.
—Her misdeeds I do not excuse. They say
She had her husband murdered. It is certain
She took the murderer as second husband.
A heinous crime! But it occurred back in
A sinister and evil-fortuned time,
Amid the anxious stress of civil war,
When she was weak and saw herself surrounded
By urgently demanding vassals, and
She threw herself into the strongest, bravest
Man's arms—compelled by what devices, who
Can tell? For woman is a fragile creature.

ELIZABETH: Woman is not weak. There are strong souls
Among the sex.—I will not tolerate
Talk of that sex's weakness in my presence.

TALBOT: Misfortune was a rigorous school to you.
Life did not turn its joyous side to *you*.
You did not see a throne far up ahead,

You only saw the grave before your feet.
In Woodstock and the Tower you were trained
For solemn duty by affliction at
This country's gracious Father's own behest.
You were not sought by flatterers. While young,
You went untroubled by the world's vain pomp
And learned by thought and self-communion how to
Esteem the true possessions of this life.
—No god saved that poor creature. As a tender child
She was removed to France and to the court
Of thoughtless pleasure and frivolity.
There in the constant giddy festival
She never heard the solemn voice of Truth.
With glittering vice she was bedazzled there
And swept away by the stream of destruction.
The futile gift of beauty was her portion,
Her loveliness eclipsed all other women,
And in her body no less than her birth—
ELIZABETH: Come to your senses, my Lord Earl of Shrewsbury!
Recall: we sit here in a solemn council.
Those must indeed be charms beyond compare
To stir such ardor in an aged man.
—My Lord of Lester! You alone are silent?
What makes him eloquent has tied your tongue?
LEICESTER: Queen, I am silent from astonishment
To think that they should fill your ear with terrors
To think these fairy tales, which in the streets
Of London scare the credulous, should rise
Up to the cheerful air of your State Council
To occupy the thoughts of serious men.
Amazement seizes me, I must confess,
To think this stateless Queen of Scotland, she
Who was incapable of holding on
To that small throne she had, the mockery
Of her own vassals, outcast from her country,
Should suddenly in prison terrify you!
—By God Almighty! What should make you fear her?
Because she claims this kingdom? Or because
The Guises won't acknowledge you as Queen?
How can this opposition from the Guises
Invalidate what birth has given you

And Parliament confirmed by resolution?
In Henry's last will was *she* not passed over
In silence? And will England, which rejoices
In the new light with so much satisfaction,
Throw itself into the Papist's arms?
Will they go running off from you, the monarch
Whom they adore, to Darnley's murderess?
What do these clamorous people want, that they
Should so torment you while alive about
An heir; who cannot have you married fast
Enough, to save the State and Church from danger?
Are you not in the flower of your youth
While each day she is withering to her grave?
By God! You will, I hope, walk on her grave
For many years to come, without your ever
Needing to plunge her into it yourself.—

BURLEIGH: Lord Lester did not always think this way.

LEICESTER: It is quite true my vote was given in
Support of her death sentence at the *trial*.
—In this State Council I speak otherwise.
Expediency, not right, is here in question.
Is this the time to fear a threat from her,
When France abandons her, her sole protector,
When you are going to bestow your hand
Upon the royal Prince, and hope arises
For a new line or rulers in this country?
Why kill her then? She is already dead!
To be despised is death in fact. God save us
From letting pity bring her back to life!
So here is my advice: we let the sentence
That dooms her to the headsman, stand in full
Force; let her live—but let her live beneath
The headsman's ax. As soon as any hand
Takes up a weapon for her—let it fall.

ELIZABETH (*rising*):
My Lords, I have heard your opinions now,
And thank you cordially for all your zeal.
With God's assistance, who sheds light and guidance
On rulers, I shall test your reasons and
Select the one which seems to me the best.

Scene 4

Enter Knight Paulet and Mortimer.

ELIZABETH: Here comes Sir Amias Paulet. Noble Sir,
  What news have you?
PAULET: Illustrious Majesty!
  My nephew, not long since returned from journeys
  Abroad, desires to cast himself before
  Your feet and swear to you his youthful oath.
  May you receive it graciously and let
  Him flourish in the sunlight of your favor.
MORTIMER (*genuflecting on one knee*):
  Long live my royal Lady, and may fame
  And happiness sit crowned upon her brow!
ELIZABETH: Arise. And welcome back to England, Sir.
  You have made the grand tour, have been to France,
  And Rome, and spent some time in Rheims.
  Now tell me what our foes are up to now.
MORTIMER: May some god send confusion on them and
  Turn back the arrows on their marksmen's hearts
  Whom they have dared to send against my Queen!
ELIZABETH: Did you see Morgan and the treason-hatching
  Bishop of Ross?
MORTIMER: I made acquaintance with
  All of the Scottish exiles who at Rheims
  Are forging plots against this island and
  I wormed my way into their confidence
  To see what I could learn about their schemes.
PAULET: And they entrusted him with secret letters
  In cipher for the Queen of Scotland, which
  He loyally delivered here to *us*.
ELIZABETH: Well, tell me now, what are their latest plans?
MORTIMER: They were all struck as by a thunderbolt
  That France had cast her off and was allying
  Herself with England. Now their hopes are turning
  Toward Spain.
ELIZABETH: So Walsingham has written me.
MORTIMER: Then, too, a bull which recently Pope Sixtus
  Has hurled against you from the Vatican

Had just arrived at Rheims as I was leaving.
By the next boat it will come to this island.

LEICESTER: England no longer trembles at such weapons.

BURLEIGH: They can be frightful in fanatics' hands.

ELIZABETH (*looking searchingly at Mortimer*):
It has been claimed that while at Rheims you went
Into the schools and disavowed your faith?

MORTIMER: I did give that appearance, I will not
Deny,—so far went my desire to serve you!

ELIZABETH (*to Paulet, who hands her some papers*):
What are you giving me?

PAULET: It is a letter
Directed to you by the Queen of Scotland.

BURLEIGH (*reaching for it quickly*):
Give me that letter.

PAULET (*gives the paper to the Queen*):
                    Pardon me, my Lord
High Treasurer! Into my Queen's own hands
She ordered that this letter be delivered.
She always says I am her enemy.
I only hate her crimes. Whatever is
In keeping with my duty, I will gladly
Perform for her.
      (*The Queen has taken the letter. While she is reading
      it, Mortimer and Leicester secretly exchange a few
      words.*)

BURLEIGH (*to Paulet*):   What can the letter say?
Unfounded protestations which should be
Kept from afflicting the Queen's tender heart.

PAULET: She made no secret of its contents. She
Requests the privilege of speaking with
The Queen.

BURLEIGH (*quickly*):   O that must never be allowed!

TABLOT: Why not? What she entreats is not unjust.

BURLEIGH: For her, the favor of the royal presence
Is forfeit, the assassination-plotter
Who thirsted for the Queen's own blood. And no
Man whose intentions toward the Queen are loyal
Could offer such false, treasonable advice.

TALBOT: But if the Monarch wants to make her happy,
Would you hinder mercy's gentle impulse?

BURLEIGH: She has been sentenced! Her head lies beneath
 The ax. It is not seemly Majesty
 Should see the head that has been doomed to death.
 The sentence can no longer be fulfilled
 Once she has thus approached the Queen, because
 The royal presence is a sign of mercy—
ELIZABETH (*drying her tears after reading the letter*):
 O what is man! And what is earthly fortune!
 How low this Queen has fallen now, who once
 Began with such proud hopes, who once was called
 To the most ancient throne in Christendom,
 And who at one time had it in her mind
 To set three royal crowns upon her head!
 How different is her language now from then,
 When she assumed the coat-of-arms of England,
 And by the flatterers of her court allowed herself
 To be named Queen of both Britannic isles!
 —Forgive me, Lords, it cuts me to the heart,
 A sadness seizes me, and my soul bleeds
 To think that earthly things do not stand with
 A greater firmness, that the monstrous fate
 Of man should pass so close to my own head.
TALBOT: O Queen! God has reached down to touch your heart;
 Obey that heavenly emotion! She
 Has gravely expiated her grave guilt
 And it is time her hard ordeal ended!
 Extend your hand to her, the deeply fallen!
 Go like an angel's form of shining light
 Down to the tomb-like darkness of her prison—
BURLEIGH: Great Queen, be steadfast. Do not let yourself
 Be misled by a laudable and human
 Emotion. Do not rob yourself of freedom
 Of action to perform the necessary.
 You *cannot* pardon her, you *cannot* save her,
 So do not heap yourself with hateful censure
 For having feasted your eyes on your victim
 In a scene of cruelly mocking triumph.
LEICESTER: Let us remain within our bounds, my Lords.
 The Queen is wise, and she does not require
 Advice from us to choose the worthiest thing.
 An interview between the Queens has nothing

In common with the course of legal justice.
The law of England, not the Monarch's will,
Has sentenced Mary. It is worthy of
The great soul of Elizabeth that *she*
Should follow where the lovely impulse of
Her heart leads her, while law takes its strict course.

ELIZABETH: Leave me, my Lords. We shall find seemly ways
Whereby both things,—what is required by mercy
And what necessity enjoins upon us,—
Can be combined. Now—go.

> (*The Lords withdraw. At the door she calls Mortimer back.*)
>
> Sir Mortimer!

A word!

Scene 5

Elizabeth. Mortimer.

(*after she has scrutinized him searchingly for several minutes*)

ELIZABETH: You showed courageous daring and
A self-control rare for one of your years.
One who has practiced young the hard art of
Deception is of age before his time
And has cut short the years of his probation.
—I prophesy that Destiny will call you
To a high course, and, happily for you,
I can myself fulfill my oracle.

MORTIMER: Illustrious Sovereign, all I am and can
Perform is dedicated to your service.

ELIZABETH: You came to know the enemies of England.
Their hatred of me is implacable,
Their schemes of murder inexhaustible.
Almighty God has saved me up to now.
And yet the crown upon my head will always
Be shaky while *she* lives who lends the pretext
And feeds the hopes of her fanatic zealots.

MORTIMER: As soon as you so bid, she lives no more.

ELIZABETH: Ah, Sir! I thought I saw myself close to

That goal, and am no further than when I
Began. I meant to have the law proceed
And keep my own hand clean of blood. The sentence
Has been pronounced. And yet, what have I gained?
It must be *executed*, Mortimer!
And I must order such an execution.
The odium of the deed must fall on me.
I must acknowledge it and cannot save
Appearances. That is the worst of it.

MORTIMER: What do you care about appearances
In a just cause?

ELIZABETH: You do not know the world, Sir.
What one *appears* to be, all people judge;
But none judge what one *is*. No one will be
Convinced that I am in the right, hence my
Concern lest my part in her death be always
In doubt. With deeds like this of double form
There can be no defense except in darkness.
The worst step is the one that one confesses;
What one does not give up, was never lost.

MORTIMER (*sounding her out*):
The best thing, then, would be—

ELIZABETH (*quickly*):   That *would* be best!
—O my good angel speaks in you. Go on
And do it, worthy Sir! You are in earnest,
You get right to essentials, and you are
A man entirely different from your uncle—

MORTIMER (*struck*):
Have you disclosed your wishes to the Knight?

ELIZABETH: I did, and I regret it.

MORTIMER: You must pardon
The aged man. The years have made him leery.
So hazardous an undertaking needs
The daring verve of youth—

ELIZABETH (*quickly*):   Then I may count
On you to—

MORTIMER: I will lend my hand to you,
Your name you must save as you can—

ELIZABETH: Sir! If
You could some morning wake me with the news:
Your deadly adversary, Marty Stuart,

    Last night took leave of life!, then—
MORTIMER: Count on me.
ELIZABETH: When will my head lie down to sleep in peace?
MORTIMER: The next new moon shall lay your fears to rest.
ELIZABETH: Farewell, Sir! Do not be aggrieved because
    My gratitude is forced to borrow Night's
    Dark veil.—Remember: Silence is the god
    Of happy men.—It is the closest bond—
    And tenderest—that secrecy creates!
                    (*Exit.*)

Scene 6

MORTIMER (*alone*):
    Go, hypocritical, false Queen! As you
    Deceive the world, so I will you. It is
    Quite proper to betray you,—a good deed!
    Do I look like a murderer? Did you
    Read villainous adeptness on my brow?
    Trust *my* arm only, and hold *your* arm back.
    Assume the falsely pious look of mercy
    Before the world, while secretly you go
    On hoping I will help you by this murder,
    We shall gain breathing time that way for rescue!
    So you would elevate me—From afar
    You hinted at some previous reward—perhaps
    Your very self, your favor as a woman!
    Who are you, wretch, and what can you give me?
    Ambition lures me not to Glory's height!
    With her alone is life's delight—
    In choirs of joy, gods float eternally
    Around her, gods of grace and youthful pleasure,
    And at her bosom heavens yield their treasure,
    While you hold only lifeless gifts in fee!
    The one supreme thing life confers, when plighted
    Heart gives to heart, delighting and delighted,
    Its very self in sweet forgetfulness,
    That womanly crown you never did possess,
    No loving man have you with love requited!
    —I must wait for Lord Lester and deliver
    Her letter to him here. A hateful errand!

I have no stomach for that courtier.
Her rescue I alone can realize,
Be mine the peril, mine the fame and prize!
(*As he is on the point of leaving he encounters Paulet.*)

Scene 7

Mortimer. Paulet.

PAULET: What was the Queen discussing with you?
MORTIMER: Nothing,
  Sir. Nothing—of importance.
PAULET (*fixing an earnest gaze upon him*):
                        Mortimer!
  It is a smooth and slippery path on which
  You have set foot. There is a lure in monarchs'
  Favor; youth craves honors.—Do not let
  Ambition carry you astray!
MORTIMER: Was it not you who brought me to the court?
PAULET: I wish I had not done so now. At court
  The honor of *our* house was not achieved.
  Stand fast, my nephew. Do not buy too dear!
  Do nothing to offend your conscience!
MORTIMER: What are you thinking of? Such apprehensions!
PAULET: However great the Queen may promise now
  To make you—do not trust her flattery.
  She will deny you after you obey her,
  And then, to wash her own name clean, she will
  Avenge the bloody deed that she commanded.
MORTIMER: Did you say "bloody deed"—
PAULET: Enough pretending!
  I know what the Queen expects of you.
  She hopes your youth in its desire for fame
  Will be more pliant than my stiff old age.
  Did you consent to do it? Did you?
MORTIMER: Uncle!
PAULET: If you have done so, I shall curse you,—and
  May God renounce you—
              (*Enter Leicester.*)
LEICESTER: Worthy Sir, will you

Allow me one word with your nephew? Our
Great Queen is well disposed toward him and she
Desires the person of the Lady Stuart
Be unreservedly committed to him.—
She will rely upon his probity—
PAULET: Rely on—Good!
LEICESTER: What were you saying, Sir?
PAULET: The Queen relies on him, and I, my Lord,
  Rely upon myself and my two eyes.
                     (*Exit.*)

Scene 8

Leicester. Mortimer.

LEICESTER (*astonished*):
  What is the matter with the Knight?
MORTIMER: I couldn't say—This confidence the Queen
  Has placed in me so unexpectedly—
LEICESTER (*looking at him searchingly*):
  Do you deserve to be confided in?
MORTIMER (*likewise*):
  I ask the same of you, my Lord of Lester.
LEICESTER: You wished to tell me something secretly.
MORTIMER: Assure me first that I may dare to do so.
LEICESTER: And who gives me a guarantee for you?
  —Take no offense at my mistrust! I have
  Seen you display two different faces at
  This court.—And of these, necessarily,
  One must be false. But which one is the real one?
MORTIMER: I have observed the same of you, Lord Lester.
LEICESTER: Then which of us will start the confidences?
MORTIMER: The one who has the lesser stake to risk.
LEICESTER: Well, that is you?
MORTIMER: No, you! *Your* testimony
  As mighty Lord whose word is of great weight,
  Can strike me down, where *mine* is powerless
  In opposition to your rank and favor.
LEICESTER: You are mistaken, Sir. In all else I
  Am mighty, but on this one tender point

With which I am supposed to trust you now,
I am the weakest man in all this court;
One wretched testimony can destroy me.
MORTIMER: If the all-powerful Lord Lester stoops
And condescends as low as to confess
A thing like this to me, then I may think
A little higher of myself and set him
Example by my generosity.
LEICESTER: Your secret first, and I will follow suit.
MORTIMER: (*suddenly producing the letter*):
The Queen of Scotland sends you this.
LEICESTER (*startled, reaches for it hastily*):   Speak softly,
Sir—What is this I see! Her picture! Ah!
          (*He kisses it and gazes at it with rapture.*)
MORTIMER (*who has been watching him sharply while he read*):
My Lord, I now believe in you.
LEICESTER (*after running quickly through the letter*):
You know this letter's contents, Mortimer?
MORTIMER: No, I know nothing.
LEICESTER: Well, she doubtless has
Confided to you—
MORTIMER: She confided nothing
To me. She said that *you* would solve this riddle.
To me it is a riddle that the Earl
Of Lester, favorite of Elizabeth,
Vowed foe of Mary and one of her judges,
Should be the man from whom the Queen hopes for
Deliverance in misfortune.—All the same,
It must be so, because your eyes express
Too plainly what your feeling for her is.
LEICESTER: First tell me how it happens that you take
This ardent interest in her destiny,
And what won you her confidence.
MORTIMER: My Lord,
That I can tell you in a few brief words.
In Rome I disavowed my faith and I
Am in alliance with the Guises. Letters
Sent by the Archbishop of Rheims gained me
Accreditation with the Queen of Scotland.
LEICESTER: I know about your changing your religion;
That was what roused my confidence in you.

Give me your hand. Forgive me for my doubt.
I cannot overdo the use of caution,
For Walsingham and Burleigh hate me, and
I know that they are laying snares for me.
You could well be their creature and their tool
To lead me to their net—

MORTIMER: What little steps
So great a Lord must measure in this court!
Lord Earl, I pity you.

LEICESTER: I throw myself
With joy upon the bosom of a friend,
Where I at last can lay aside the long
Constraint. You are amazed, Sir, that I have
Had such a sudden change of heart toward Mary.
I never hated her in fact,—the pressure
Of the times made me her adversary.
For long years she had been intended for me,
You know, before she gave her hand to Darnley
While sovereignty still smiled in glory on her.
I coldly thrust that happiness aside,
But now in prison, at the gates of death,
I seek her, and at peril of my life.

MORTIMER: I call that acting generously!

LEICESTER: —The shape
Of things has altered in the meantime, Sir.
It was ambition made me feelingless
Toward youth and beauty. Mary's hand I then
Considered was too slight for me, I hoped
For the possession of the Queen of England.

MORTIMER: It is well known that she preferred you over
All men—

LEICESTER: It seemed so, noble Sir.—Now after ten
Lost years of indefatigable wooing
And odious constraint—O Sir, my heart
Cries out! I must vent my long indignation—
I am called lucky—If they only knew
What chains these are for which they envy me—
Now after sacrificing ten long, bitter
Years to the idol of her vanity,
Submitting with a slave's humility
To every change of her Sultana's whims,

The toy of petty, whimsical caprices,
Cajoled at one time by her tenderness
And then again repulsed by proud reserve,
Tormented by her favor and her harshness
Alike, by Argus-eyes of jealousy
Watched like a prisoner, now taken like
A boy to task, now scolded like a servant,—
O, language does not have a word for this
Especial hell!

MORTIMER: I pity you, Lord Earl.

LEICESTER: To have the prize elude me at the goal!
  Another comes to rob me of the fruits
  Of this dear wooing. To a younger husband
  I lose the rights that I have long possessed!
  I am supposed to go down from the stage
  Where I have shone so long as leading man.
  Not just her hand, her favor too, this new
  Arriver threatens to deprive me of.
  She is a woman, he is lovable.

MORTIMER: He is a son of Catherine. He has learned
  The arts of flattery in a good school.

LEICESTER: My hopes are foundering—and now amid
  This shipwreck of my fortunes I am seeking
  A spar to which I can cling fast—My eye
  Turns back again to its first lovely hope.
  Then Mary's image in the splendor of
  Its charms stood once again before me; beauty
  And youth then reasserted their full claims;
  The heart, not cold ambition, now compared,
  And I felt what a treasure I had lost.
  With terror I saw her plunged into deepest
  Misery, and plunged there by my fault.
  Then hope awoke within me and I wondered
  If I could yet deliver and possess her.
  Thanks to a loyal hand I was successful
  In opening to her my altered heart.
  And now this letter that you bring me here
  Assures me she forgives and will bestow
  Herself as prize upon me if I save her.

MORTIMER: And yet you have done nothing toward her rescue!
  You let it come about that she was sentenced

And even gave your vote that she should die!
It took a miracle—the light of Truth
Had to touch me, the nephew of her jailer,
And Heaven in the Vatican in Rome
Had to pick out her unexpected savior,
Or she would not have found a way to you.

LEICESTER: Ah, this has cost me torments, Sir, enough!
At just that point she was removed from Talbot's
Castle up to Fotheringhay and placed
Beneath the stern surveillance of your uncle.
All access to her was closed off, I had
To go on persecuting her before
The world. But do not think I would have let her
Go passively to death! No, I hoped then,
And still hope to prevent the ultimate,
Till means are found of liberating her.

MORTIMER: That means, Lord Lester, has been found. Your noble
Secret merits a response. I mean
To set her free. That is why I am here.
Arrangements have been made. Your powerful
Assistance will assure us of success.

LEICESTER: What's that you say? You frighten me. Could you—

MORTIMER: I mean to open up her jail by force.
I have companions, everything is ready—

LEICESTER: You have accessories and confidants!
Into what hazard are you dragging me!
And do they also know about *my* secret?

MORTIMER: O have no fear. The plan was made without you,
Without you it would have been carried out,
Had *she* not asked to thank *you* for her rescue.

LEICESTER: Can you assure me then quite certainly
My name has not been mentioned in this group?

MORTIMER: You may depend on that! So dubious,
Lord Earl, at hearing news that brings you aid?
You want to save and to possess the Lady,
You suddenly find friends when least expected,
The readiest means drop to you from the sky,—
And you show more embarrassment than joy?

LEICESTER: It is no good, this use of force. The risk
Is far too dangerous.

MORTIMER: So is delay!

LEICESTER: I tell you, Sir, it is not to be risked.

MORTIMER (*bitterly*):

    No, not for you, you want to *possess* her!
    We only want to *save* her, hence are not
    So scrupulous—

LEICESTER: Young man, you are too rash
    In such a dangerous and thorny matter.

MORTIMER: You—too discreet in such a case of honor.

LEICESTER: I see the nets that are laid out around us.

MORTIMER: I feel the strength to rip them all asunder.

LEICESTER: Your courage is foolhardiness and madness.

MORTIMER: This prudence is not bravery, my Lord.

LEICESTER: Perhaps you long to end like Babington?

MORTIMER: You don't, to follow Norfolk's noble action.

LEICESTER: Norfolk did not live to marry her.

MORTIMER: He proved that he deserved to do so, though.

LEICESTER: If we are ruined, she is ruined with us.

MORTIMER: If we are chary, she will not be saved.

LEICESTER: You do not think or listen, you will ruin
    Everything with blind impetuousness
    That had been started on such a good path.

MORTIMER: On the good path, perhaps, that *you* had cleared?
    O, when have you done anything to save her?
    —Besides, if I had been enough the scoundrel
    To *murder* her, as I was ordered by
    The Queen just now, as at this moment she
    Expects of me,—declare the steps to me
    You would have taken to preserve her.

LEICESTER (*astonished*):

    Did the Queen give you such a fatal order?

MORTIMER: She was mistaken in me, as was Mary
    In you.

LEICESTER: And you agreed to do it? Did you?

MORTIMER: To see that she did not hire other hands,
    I offered mine.

LEICESTER: And you were wise to do so.
    This will give us a chance. She will rely
    Upon your bloody service, the death sentence
    Remains unexecuted, we gain time—

MORTIMER (*impatiently*):

    No, we lose time.

LEICESTER: She will be counting on you,
    She will be that much less afraid of making
    A show of mercy out before the world.
    Perhaps by cunning I can talk her into
    Seeing her opponent's countenance;
    A step like that would surely tie her hands.
    Burleigh is right. The sentence can no longer
    Be executed once she has beheld her.
    —Yes, I will try, I will make every effort—
MORTIMER: And what will that accomplish? If she sees
    Herself deceived in me, if Mary goes
    On living—will not everything be as
    Before? She never will be free. The least
    She can expect is life imprisonment.
    You still will have to end by a bold deed,
    So why not start with such immediately?
    The power is in your hands, you can assemble
    An army if you just agree to arm
    The nobles stationed at your many castles!
    And Mary still has many hidden friends;
    The noble houses of the Howards and
    The Percys, though their chiefs have fallen, still
    Are rich in heroes, they are merely waiting
    For some high Lord to set them an example!
    Stop this dissimulation! Act in public!
    Defend your loved one like a paladin,
    Fight a noble fight for her! Whenever
    You like, you are the master of the Queen
    Of England's person. Lure her to your castles,
    She often followed you there. Show yourself
    A man! Speak as her master! Keep her guarded
    Until she sets the Lady Stuart free!
LEICESTER: I am astonished, horrified—Where has
    Your madness brought you?—Do you know this land?
    Or how things stand here at this court, how straitly
    This distaff-rule holds minds in bondage here?
    Go seek for that heroic spirit which
    Once stirred throughout this country.—Everything
    Is now subdued beneath a woman's key,
    The springs and coils of courage have gone slack.
    Take my advice. Risk nothing indiscreet.

—Go! I hear someone coming.

MORTIMER: Mary hopes!
Shall I go back to her with empty comfort?

LEICESTER: Take her my vows of everlasting love!

MORTIMER: Take them yourself! I volunteered to be
Her means of rescue, not your love-note bearer!
                    (*Exit.*)

Scene 9.

Elizabeth. Leicester.

ELIZABETH: Who left you here just now? I heard some talking.

LEISCESTER (*turning around swiftly, startled at seeing her*):
It was Lord Mortimer.

ELIZABETH: What is the matter?
You look so startled.

LEICESTER (*getting control of himself*):
                By the sight of you!
I never saw you look so fascinating.
I stand here dazzled by your beauty.—Ah!

ELIZABETH: Why do you sigh?

LEICESTER: Do I not have good reason
To sigh? When I consider all your charm,
The nameless sorrow is renewed within me
Of my impending loss.

ELIZABETH: What are you losing?

LEICESTER: I stand to lose your heart, your lovely self.
You presently will come to happiness
Within an ardent husband's youthful arms,
And he will own your undivided heart.
He is of royal blood, as *I* am not.
But I defy the entire world to find
A man alive upon this earthly globe
Who feels more adoration for you than
Do I. The Duc d'Anjou has never seen you,
He must love only your renown and splendor,
While I love *you*. Had you been born the poorest
Shepherdess and I the greatest Prince
In all the world, I would stoop to your station

And lay my diadem before your feet.

ELIZABETH: Don't scold me, Dudley, pity me!—I could
   Not ask my heart. It would have chosen elsewhere.
   And how I envy other women who
   Can elevate the one they love. Ah, *I*
   Am not so fortunate that I can place
   The crown upon the man who is the dearest
   Of all to me!—The Stuart was permitted
   To give her hand as inclination willed.
   She took all kinds of liberties; she drank
   The brimming cup of pleasure to the lees.

LEICESTER: And now she drinks the bitter cup of sorrow.

ELIZABETH: She paid no heed to anyone's opinion.
   She found life easy, never once did she
   Assume the yoke beneath which *I* have bent.
   Yet I too might have made my claims to taste
   The joy of life and pleasures of the earth,
   But I chose the stern duties of a monarch.
   And yet she won the favor of all men
   Because she only strove to be a woman,
   And young and old are always courting her.
   Men are like that. Voluptuaries all!
   Frivolity they will pursue, and pleasure,
   And set no store by what they must revere.
   That Talbot, didn't he talk like a youngster
   When he got on the topic of her charm!

LEICESTER: Forgive him. He was once her jailer. She,
   The sly one, fooled him with her flattery.

ELIZABETH: And is it true she is so beautiful?
   I've had to hear so much about that face
   I'd really like to know what to believe.
   Descriptions falsify and paintings flatter,
   I would put faith in no eyes but my own.
   —Why do you look at me so strangely?

LEICESTER: I
   Was thinking of you side by side with Mary.
   —I won't deny that I would like the pleasure,
   Provided it could be arranged in secret,
   Of seeing you confronted with the Stuart!
   Then you might taste your total victory!
   I would not grudge her the humiliation

Of seeing for herself—for jealousy
Does have sharp eyes—and proving to herself
How utterly in nobleness of form
She is surpassed by you, to whom she must
Give way in every other worthy virtue.

ELIZABETH: In years, however, she is younger.

LEICESTER: Younger!
She doesn't look it. Suffering, of course!
She may well have grown old before her time.
And what would make her sorrow bitterer
Would be to see you as a bride to be!
She has her lovely hopes for life behind her.
She would see you approaching happiness,
Betrothed, what's more, to France's royal Prince,
While she has always been so proud about
And was forever flaunting her French marriage,
And even now touts France's mighty aid.

ELIZABETH (*remarking carelessly*):
They keep tormenting me to see her.

LEICESTER (*eagerly*):   She
Demands it as a favor; grant it as
A punishment! Though you can send her to
The scaffold, that will grieve her less than seeing
Herself obliterated by your charms.
By that means you will kill her, as she once
Wished to kill you.—Once she has glimpsed your beauty,
By modesty close guarded, set in glory
By reputation for a saintless virtue
Such as *she* cast away for wanton loves,
Exalted by the splendor of the crown
And now adorned with bridal winsomeness,—
Destruction's hour will have struck for her.
Yes,—when I cast my eyes upon you now—
You never have been better armed for triumph
In beauty than right now.—When you stepped into
The room just now, you shed a radiance
Upon me like an apparition of
Celestial light.—If you stepped up to her
Right now,—you will not find a better hour—

ELIZABETH: Not now—No—Not now, Lester—I must think
It over first—discuss with Burleigh—

LEICESTER (*eagerly interrupting*):   Burleigh!
  He only thinks of your political
  Advantage! Womanhood has its rights too.
  That tender point befits your own tribunal
  And not the statesman's.—Statecraft also wants
  To have you see her and gain public favor
  By this display of generosity!
  Though afterwards you may dispose of this
  Detested foe in any way you please.
ELIZABETH: To see my relative in shame and want
  Would not be seemly for me. I have heard
  That her establishment is not quite royal;
  The sight of her in want would be reproachful.
LEICESTER: You will not need to cross her threshold.
  Here is my plan. Coincidence has managed
  Things perfectly. The great hunt is today,
  The route leads right past Castle Fotheringhay,
  There in the park the Stuart takes a stroll,
  And you come riding over quite by chance;
  Let nothing seem to have been planned beforehand;
  And if it is repugnant to you, do not
  So much as speak to her—
ELIZABETH: If I commit
  A folly, Leicester, it is yours, not mine.
  I shall deny no wish of yours today,
  Because of all my subjects I have done
  The most today to cause you pain.
                    (*looking at him tenderly*)
  Let it be no more than a whim of yours.
  Affection shows itself when it is moved
  To grant requests which it has disapproved.
               (*Leicester throws himself at her feet.*
                    The curtain falls.)

ACT III

Region in a park. The foreground is planted with trees; at the rear a distant prospect.

Scene 1

Enter Mary running swiftly up from beyond the trees.
Hanna Kennedy follows slowly.

KENNEDY: You rush as if you had wings on your shoulders.
   I can't keep up with you. Wait, wait for me!
MARY: Let me delight in freedom new-found
   And be as a child,—O be one too!
   And on the meadows' greensward round
   Let my winged foot now dance on the dew.
   Have I from dark and the grave now arisen,
   Am I no longer a captive in there?
   Let me drink full and a-thirst from my prison,
   Full of the free and the heavenly air.
KENNEDY: O my dear Lady! Close-confining prison
   Is widened for you only by a little.
   You merely do not see the walls that hem
   Us in, because the trees' dense branches hide them.
MARY: O thanks, thanks for this friendly green of trees
   That hide my prison walls by their profusion!
   I want to dream myself to happy ease,
   Why would you wake me from my sweet illusion?
   I rest upon the broad lap of the sky,
   Unfettered now and free, my eye
   Roves through its vast immensities.
   And yonder where the grey mist-mountains rise
   The borders of my realm advance,
   And yonder cloud that toward the south-land flies
   Is searching for the distant shores of France.
   Hastening cloud, you sailer in air!
   Happy are they who with you may fare!
   Greet for me the land of my youth.
   I am a captive, in bondage I lie.
   No other messenger have I,
   Free in air is your highway,
   You are not held under this Queen's sway.
KENNEDY: Dear Lady! You are quite beside yourself,
   This long-lost freedom carries you away.
MARY: A fisherman brings in his skiff down there.
   It could mean my rescue, that wretched thing,
   Swiftly to friendly towns we could fare.
   It barely offers the man a living.
   I would heap on him the richest of treasures,
   He would draw such a draft as he never drew,
   In his nets he would find all fortunes and pleasures,
   If his rescuing boat would take me too.

KENNEDY: A waste of wishes! Don't you see that we
   Are followed from afar by steps of spies?
   A cruel prohibition frightens every
   Sympathetic creature from our path.
MARY: No, my good Jane. Believe me, not for nothing
   Have they unbarred my prison doors for me.
   This little favor is the harbinger
   Of greater fortune. I am not mistaken.
   It is love's active hand I have to thank.
   I recognize Lord Lester's mighty arm.
   My prison will be widened gradually,
   I will progress from lesser things to greater
   Until I finally see the face of one
   Who will set loose my bonds for evermore.
KENNEDY: I cannot make sense of this contradiction.
   Just yesterday death was proclaimed for you,
   Now suddenly today they give this freedom.
   The chains are loosed, I have heard tell, for those
   Whom everlasting liberty awaits.
MARY: That hunting-horn! Do you hear it sounding
   Mighty of call through field and grove?
   O for a steed of spirit bounding
   To join the gladsome throng as they rove!
   Still more! O, that familiar voice
   Full of memories painfully sweet.
   Often my ear has heard it with joy,
   As when hunters on heaths of the upland deploy
   And the race of the hunt is wild and fleet.

Scene 2

Enter Paulet.

PAULET: Well, have I finally acted right, my Lady?
   Do I deserve your thanks for once?
MARY: What, Sir?
   Are you the one who got me this reprieve?
   You?
PAULET: Why should I not be the one? I was
   At court, and I delivered what you wrote—

MARY: You did deliver it? You really did?
  And so the freedom that I now enjoy
  Is a fruit of that letter—
PAULET (*significantly*):   More than that!
  Prepare yourself for something greater yet.
MARY: For something greater, Sir? What do you mean?
PAULET: Well, you have heard those horns—
MARY (*startled with premonition*):   You frighten me!
PAULET: The Queen is hunting in this region.
MARY: What!
PAULET: In a few minutes she will stand before you.
KENNEDY (*hurrying to Mary, who is trembling and on the verge of
  fainting*):
  What is the matter, Lady? You look pale.
PAULET: Well! Was it not right? Was that not your wish?
  It has been granted sooner than you thought.
  You always used to be so quick of tongue,
  Why do you not bring on your speeches now?
  Now is the time to speak!
MARY: O, why did no one give me any warning!
  I am not ready for that now, not now.
  What I requested as the highest favor
  Now seems quite dreadful, horrible—Come, Hanna,
  Take me into the house until I can
  Compose myself—
PAULET: You must wait here for her.
  You may well be alarmed, I understand,
  At coming up before your judge.

Scene 3

Enter the Earl of Shrewsbury.

MARY: O not on that account! My feeling is
  Quite different—Noble Shrewsbury! You come
  Sent to me like an angel down from Heaven!
  —I cannot see her! Save me, save me from
  The sight which I detest—
SHREWSBURY: Control yourself, Queen! Gather up your courage.
  This is indeed the hour of decision.

MARY: O, I have waited for this—For years on end
I have prepared, said over everything
And written it upon my memory,
How I was going to move her, touch her pity.
Now everything is suddenly forgotten,
Nothing lives within me at this moment
Except the burning sense of sufferings.
My heart within me turns against her in
Fierce hatred, all my good thoughts flee away,
And with their heads of serpent-locks all shaking,
The evil spirits up from hell surround me.

SHREWSBURY: Control your frantic blood in its revolt,
Restrain your bitterness of heart! Good fruit
Will never come of hatred meeting hatred.
However much your inner heart rebels,
Obey the time and the law of the hour!
She is the one in power—so be humble!

MARY: In front of her! No!

SHREWSBURY: Do it anyway!
Speak deferentially, with calm! Invoke
Her generosity, do not insist
Upon your rights now, now is not the time.

MARY: Alas, I have implored my own destruction,
And as a curse my plea is being granted!
We never should have seen each other, never!
No good can ever, ever come of it!
Sooner could fire and water meet in love
And sooner could the tiger kiss the lamb—
I am too deeply hurt—she has offended
Too grievously—No peace is possible!

SHREWSBURY: But see her first from face to face!
You know, I saw how she was shaken by
Your letter, and her eyes were wet with tears.
She is not feelingless, but you must cherish
More trust in her.—That is the reason why
I hurried on ahead so that I could
Forewarn you and induce a state of calm.

MARY (*grasping his hand*):
O Talbot! You have always been my friend—
Would I had stayed in your mild custody!
I have been hardly treated, Shrewsbury!

SHREWSBURY: Forget all that now. Only think of how
  You will receive her with complete submission.
MARY: Is Burleigh with her too, my evil angel?
SHREWSBURY: No one is with her but the Earl of Lester.
MARY: Lord Lester!
SHREWSBURY: Have no fear of him. He does
  Not seek your ruin.—It is his work that
  The Queen has now consented to this meeting.
MARY: O, I was sure it was!
SHREWSBURY: What are you saying?
PAULET: The Queen is coming!
      (*They all step aside; only Mary remains, leaning on*
          Kennedy's bosom.)

Scene 4

Enter Elizabeth, the Earl of Leicester, and retinue.

ELIZABETH (*to Leicester*):
  What castle is this?
LEICESTER: Castle Fotheringhay.
ELIZABETH (*to Shrewsbury*):
  Send our hunting party on ahead
  To London. People throng the roads too much.
  We shall seek shelter in this quiet park.
      (*Talbot dismisses the retinue. She fixes her eyes on*
         Mary while she goes on talking to Leicester.)
  My people love me far too much. Their joy
  Is quite immoderate, idolatrous.
  God may be honored so, but not mere mortals.
MARY (*who all this time has been leaning on the nurse's bosom,
rises now, and her eye encounters the intent gaze of Elizabeth.
She shudders and throws herself back on the nurse's bosom*):
  O God, no heart speaks from that countenance!
ELIZABETH: Who is the Lady?
             (*General silence.*)
LEICESTER: —You are at Castle Fotheringhay, my Queen.
ELIZABETH (*pretends to be surprised and astonished and fixes a
dark look on Leicester*):
  Who has done this to me? Lord Lester!

LEICESTER: Well, it has happened, Queen—And so, now that
    Your footsteps have been guided here by Heaven,
    Let generosity and mercy triumph.
SHREWSBURY: Allow us to entreat you, royal Lady,
    To cast your eye on this unfortunate
    Here overwhelmed before your gaze.
        (*Mary collects herself and starts to walk towards*
        Elisabeth, then stops half way with a shudder; her
        gestures express the most vehement struggle.)
ELIZABETH: What's this, my Lords?
    Who was it then that told me of a woman
    In deep humility? I find a proud one
    No wise subdued by adverse fortune
MARY: Be
    It so! I shall submit even to this.
    Hence, impotent pride of the noble soul!
    I shall forget now who I am and what
    I have endured; I shall bow down before her
    Who thrust me down to this ignominy.
              (*She turns toward the Queen.*)
    Heaven has decided for you, Sister!
    Crowned with triumph is your happy brow,
    And I adore the deity that raised
    You up.
                (*She kneels before her.*)
        Be generous in turn, my Sister!
    Let me not lie here in ignominy.
    Stretch forth your hand, your royal right hand give
    Me now, to raise me up from my deep fall!
ELIZABETH (*stepping back*):
    Lady Mary, you are in your place!
    And thankfully I praise the favor of
    My God, who did not will that I should lie
    At your feet as you now lie here at mine.
MARY (*with rising emotion*):
    Think of the change that comes to all things human!
    Gods do exist who punish arrogance!
    Revere them, dread them, they are terrible,
    And they have cast me down before your feet—
    For the sake of these stranger witnesses,
    Respect yourself in me! Do not dishonor

Or put to shame the Tudor blood that flows
In my veins as in yours—O God in Heaven!
Do not stand there so inaccessible
And rugged, like a cliff that shipwrecked men
Vainly strive and struggle to attain.
My life, my destiny, my all, now hangs
Upon the power of my words and tears.
Release my heart so that I may touch yours!
When you look at me with that icy glance,
My heart shrinks shuddering and closes shut,
The stream of tears is stopped, and frigid horror
Chokes my words of entreaty in my bosom.

ELIZABETH (*coldly and severely*):
What do you have to tell me, Lady Stuart?
You wished to speak to me. I disregard
My Queenship, my profoundly outraged Queenship,
So I may do my duty as a sister.
I grant the solace of beholding me.
My generous impulse leads me on, and I
Expose myself to righteous censure by
Such low descending—for, as you
Well know, you did attempt to have me murdered.

MARY: Where shall I start, how shall I prudently
Contrive my words so that they may have their
Effect upon your heart, yet not offend it!
O God, lend power to my speech and take
From it all thorns that could cause any wounds!
I cannot any way plead for myself without
Accusing you, and that I do not want.
—You have dealt with me in a way that is
Not proper, for I am, like you, a Queen,
And you have held me as a prisoner.
I came to you a suppliant, and you,
Scorning in me the sacred rights of nations
And sacred laws of hospitality,
Had me shut up in prison walls; my friends
And servants were most cruelly removed;
I was myself left in unseemly hardship;
I was called up to an outrageous court—
No more of that! Oblivion shall forever
Enshroud the cruel things I have endured.

—See! I shall term those things of fate's contriving,
You are not guilty, nor am *I* to blame.
An evil spirit rose from the abyss
To kindle hot the hatred in our hearts
That had already split our tender childhood.
It grew with us, and wicked people fanned
The wretched flame and blew their breath upon it;
Insane fanatics armed with sword and dagger
Officious hands that had no right to meddle—
For this is the accursed fate of rulers,
That once they are at odds, they rend the world
And set at large the Furies of all discord.
—There is no alien mouth to come between
Us now,
    (*approaching her trustingly and with caressing tone*)
        we stand here in each other's presence.
Now, Sister, speak! Name my offense to me
And I will render total satisfaction.
If only you had given me a hearing
When I so urgently besought your eye!
Things never would have gone so far, nor would
There now be taking place in this sad spot
This sorry and unfortunate encounter!
ELIZABETH: My lucky star protected me from putting
The adder in my bosom.—You should not
Accuse the fates, but rather your black heart,
The wild ambition of your family.
Between us nothing hostile had occurred.
And then your uncle, that ambition-crazed
Proud priest that stretches out his impious hand
To seize all crowns, threw down his challenge to me,
Befooled you till you took my coat-of-arms,
Till you assumed my royal title, till
You entered with me into battle to
The death— Whom did he not enlist against me?
The tongues of priests, the swords of nations, and
The frightful weapons of religious frenzy;
Here in the peaceful seat of my own kingdom
He blew the flames of revolution up—
But God is with me, and that haughty priest
Has not maintained the field—The blow was aimed
At my head, but it is your head that falls!

MARY: I stand here in the hands of God. You will not
  Presume so brutally upon your power—
ELIZABETH: Who is to hinder me? Your uncle set
  The model for all monarchs of this world
  Of *how* to make peace with one's enemies.
  The Saint Bartholomew shall be my school!
  What is blood-kinship, or the law of nations,
  To me? The Church absolves all bonds of duty
  And blesses breach of faith and regicide;
  I practice only what your own priests teach.
  What pledge would guarantee you for me if
  I were so generously to set you free?
  What lock would I put on your loyalty
  Without Saint Peter's key unlocking it?
  The only safety lies with force, for with
  The breed of serpents can be no alliance.
MARY: That is your sorry, sinister suspicion!
  You always looked upon me only as
  An enemy and stranger. If you had
  Proclaimed me as your heir, as was my due,
  Then gratitude and love would have retained
  A loyal friend and relative in me.
ELIZABETH: Out yonder, Lady Stuart is your circle
  Of friends, your home is with the Papacy,
  Your brother is the monk—Proclaim you as
  My heir! A treacherous, deceiving snare!
  So that you might seduce my people in
  My lifetime, so that like a sly Armida
  You might entice the young men of my kingdom
  By cunning to your nets for paramours—
  So everyone could turn to the newly rising
  Sun, while I meanwhile should—
MARY: Rule in peace!
  All claims upon this kingdom I renounce.
  Alas, my spirit's pinions have been lamed,
  I am no longer lured by greatness.—You
  Have gained your end. I now am but the shadow
  Of Mary. Prison's shame has broken my
  Proud spirit.—You have done your uttermost
  To me, you have destroyed me in my bloom!
  —Now, Sister, make an end! Pronounce those words
  Which you have come here to pronounce. For never

Will I believe that you have come here to
Make cruel mockery of me as victim.
Pronounce those words! Say to me: "Mary, you
Are free! My power you have felt, but now
You shall revere my generosity."
Say that, and from your hand I shall accept
My life, my freedom, as a gift.—One word,
And all will be as if it never happened.
I wait. O let me not await too long!
And woe to you if you do not close with
Those words! For if you do not leave me now
With blessing, grandly, like a goddess,—Sister!
Not for this whole rich island, not for all
The countries that the sea surrounds, would I
Stand here before you as you stand with me!

ELIZABETH: Do you admit at last that you are beaten?
Are your plots done? No other murderer
Is on his way? Will no adventurer
Attempt his sorry chivalry for you?
—Yes, Lady Mary, all is over. You
Will tempt no more. The world has other cares.
No one is anxious to be your—fourth husband,
Because you kill your suitors as you kill
Your husbands!

MARY (*flaring up*):   Sister! Sister!
O God! God! Give me self-control!

ELIZABETH (*looks at her with a long look of proud contempt*):
So these, my Lord of Lester, are the charms
Which no man with impunity has seen,
With which no other woman dares to vie!
Indeed! *This* fame was cheap to come by: it
Costs nothing to become the world-wide beauty
But to have all the world hold one in common!

MARY: That is too much!

Elizabeth (*with a sneering laugh*):
                              You show your true face now.
    Till now we only saw the mask.

MARY (*with burning anger, though with noble dignity*):
I erred, but in a human, youthful way.
I was seduced by power. I did not
Conceal or make a secret of it. With
A royal candor I disdained false seeming.

The world has known the worst of me, and I
Can say that I am better than my name.
But woe to you if from your deeds they once
Rip off the cloak of honor which you use
To hide the wild heat of your secret lusts.
It was not chastity your mother left you;
We all know what the virtue was for which
Anne Boleyn climbed the scaffold to the block.

SHREWSBURY (*stepping between the two Queens*):
O God in Heaven! Must it come to this!
Is this your self-control and your submission,
Lady Mary?

MARY: Self-control! I have
Endured all that a mortal can endure.
Hence and be gone, lamb-hearted resignation!
Fly up to Heaven, patient tolerance!
Burst from your bonds at last, and from your cavern
Come forth, you long-suppressed resentment now!
And you who gave the angered basilisk
His murderous glance, lay now upon my tongue
The poisoned dart—

SHREWSBURY: She is beside herself!
Forgive this mad and deeply injured woman!
          (*Elizabeth, speechless with anger, is darting furious*
                    looks at Mary.)

LEICESTER (*in the most vehement agitation, tries to lead Elizabeth*
away): Do not listen to this frenzied woman! Come
Away from this unhappy place.

MARY: A bastard has profaned the throne of England,
The noble-hearted British people has
Been cheated by a crafty, cheap imposter.
—If right prevailed, you would be lying in
The dust before me for *I* am your King.
          (*Elizabeth swiftly leaves. The Lords follow her in the*
                    greatest dismay.)

Scene 5

Mary. Kennedy.

KENNEDY: What have you done! She goes away in fury!
Now all is lost, and all our hopes have vanished.

MARY (*still completely beside herself*):
  In fury! And she bears death in her heart!
                    (*falling on Kennedy's neck*)
  O Hanna, how glad I feel! At last, at last,
  Now after years of this humiliation
  And grief, one moment of revenge, of triumph!
  A mountain's load is taken from my heart,
  I plunged the dagger in my foeman's heart!
KENNEDY: Unhappy woman! Madness sweeps you on,
  You have offended the implacable.
  She wields the lightning bolt, she is the Queen,
  You mocked her in the presence of her lover!
MARY: Before Lord Lester's eyes I shamed her! And
  He saw it, he was witness to my triumph!
  He stood there when I struck her from her height,
  It was his presence that gave me the strength!

Scene 6

Enter Mortimer.

KENNEDY: O, what an outcome, Sir—
MORTIMER: I heard it all.
  (*He gives the nurse a sign to go to her post, then comes
      closer. His entire being expresses a vehement and
                  passionate mood.*)
  You won, you won! You trod her in the dust!
  You were the Queen, and *she* the criminal.
  I am enraptured by your spirit, I
  Adore you, great and splendid like a goddess
  You now appear to me.
MARY: You did speak with
  Lord Lester, and you did deliver to him
  My letter and my gift—O tell me, Sir!
MORTIMER: O how your noble royal anger shone
  About you, how your charms were all transfigured!
  Most beautiful of women on this earth!
MARY: I beg you, Sir! Allay my great impatience.
  What did he say? Tell me, do I dare hope?
MORTIMER (*looking passionately at her*): Who? He? That

wretched coward! Hope for nothing
From him. Despise him and forget him!
MARY: What!
  What are you saying?
MORTIMER: He save you, possess you!
  He, you! Just let him try it! He! With me
  He'd have to fight first, fight me to the death!
MARY: You did not give my letter to him then?
  —Then all is lost!
MORTIMER: That coward loves his life.
  Whoever saves you and then claims your charms
  Must doughtily clasp Death within his arms.
MARY: He will do nothing for me then?
MORTIMER: No more
  Of him! What can *he* do? What need of him
  When I shall save you, I alone?
MARY: O what can you do?
MORTIMER: Do not dream that matters
  Still stand as they stood with you yesterday!
  The way the Queen took leave of you just now,
  The way that conversation ended, all
  Is lost, all avenues of pardon blocked.
  We now need *action*. *Boldness* must decide.
  Let all be risked for all in a bold fight,
  You must be free before the morning light.
MARY: What's this? Tonight! How is that possible?
MORTIMER: Hear what has been decided. I have gathered
  All my confederates in secret chapel.
  A priest heard our confessions and absolved
  Us of all sins we ever may have done
  And gave us absolution in advance
  For any that we might commit henceforth.
  And we received the final sacraments
  And thus are ready for the final journey.
MARY: O, what a fearful preparation, Sir!
MORTIMER: This castle we shall scale this very night.
  I have the keys in my possession. We
  Shall slay the guards and wrest you from your chamber
  By force. At our hands everyone must die
  So not a living soul is left behind
  Who might betray the fact of your abduction.

MARY: And Drury, Paulet, and my other jailers?
  O they will shed their final blood before—
MORTIMER: My dagger will begin by killing them!
MARY: What? Kill your uncle, kill your second father?
MORTIMER: He shall die by my hand. Yes, I will kill him.
MARY: O monstrous crime!
MORTIMER: All crimes are pardoned in
  Advance. I can commit the worst of crimes,
  And I intend to do so.
MARY: Monstrous, monstrous!
MORTIMER: And even if I have to stab the Queen,
  I took my oath upon the Host to do it.
MARY: No, rather than shed so much blood for me—
MORTIMER: What is the whole of life compared to *you*
  And to my love? Let all the bonds of all
  The worlds dissolve, and let a second deluge
  Roll in engulfing everything that breathes!
  —I value nothing any more! Before
  I give you up, the end of time may come.
MARY (*falling back*):
  My God! What language, Sir!—the way you look!
  —You terrify me, frighten me away.
MORTIMER (*with wild looks and with the expression of quiet
  madness*):   Life is
  One instant only; death, too, only one!
  —So let them drag me off to Tyburn, tear
  Me limb from limb with red-hot iron tongs,
      (*advancing toward her vehemently with wide-open
                  arms*)
  If I embrace you, ardently beloved—
MARY (*falling back*):
  Away from me, you madman!—
MORTIMER: If I clasp
  You to this bosom, to this love-breathing mouth—
MARY: In Heaven's name, Sir, let me go inside!
MORTIMER: A man is mad not to clasp happiness
  In close and indissoluble embrace
  When once a god had put it in his hand.
  I'll save you though a thousand lives should stand
  To fall. I will, I will, as surely as
  God lives! I swear it, and possess you too.

MARY: O, will no god or angel shield me through
    My peril? O monstrous fate, to fling
    Me on from ghastly thing to ghastly thing.
    Was I born to have madness wakened by me?
    Do love and hate conspire to terrify me?
MORTIMER: Yes, ardently, the way they hate, I love you!
    Their will is to behead you and to sever
    With a sharp ax that neck of dazzling white.
    O vow unto the god of life's delight
    What you must sacrifice to brutal hate!
    With all these charms that are no longer yours
    Confer joy on your fortunate beloved!
    These lovely locks, these locks of silken hair
    Are doomed unto the dismal powers of the grave,
    Entwine me in them timelessly, your slave!
MARY: O Sir, what language do I hear from you!
    To you my grief and my misfortune should
    Be holy if my royal head is not.
MORTIMER: The crown has fallen from your royal head,
    Of earthly majesty you have no more,
    So try it, let your queenly word be said,
    And see if any savior is in store.
    Nothing but your alluring form remains,
    The beauty that with god-like power reigns,
    It makes me dare and undertake all things,
    It drives me toward the ax the headsman swings—
MARY: O, who will save me from his frenzied will?
MORTIMER: Audacious service claims audacious cost!
    In what cause would you have a brave man spill
    His blood? Is life not life's supreme worth still?
    Whoever squanders it for naught, is mad!
    But I want first to rest on its warm breast—
                 (*He presses her vehemently to him.*)
MARY: O, must I call for help against the man
    Who wants to rescue me?
MORTIMER: You do have feelings;
    The world does not report you as severe
    Or cold; the hot appeal of love can sway
    Your heart; you made the singer Rizzio happy,
    And you let Bothwell carry you away.
MARY: How dare you!

MORTIMER: He was nothing but your bully!
  You trembled in his presence when you loved him!
  If only terror can control you fully,
  Then by the god of hell, you—
MARY: Let me go!
MORTIMER: Shall tremble in my presence too!
KENNEDY (*rushing in*):
  Quick! there are people coming! The whole garden
  Is full of men with weapons.
MORTIMER (*starting up and reaching for his sword*):
                    I'll protect you!
MARY: Hanna, save me from his hands! I am afraid!
  Where can I find a place where I can hide?
  To what saint can I turn to plead for aid?
  Out here is terror, murder waits inside.
       (*She flees to the house; Kennedy follows.*)

Scene 7

*Mortimer. Paulet and Drury rush in in great
excitement. The retine hurry across the stage.*

PAULET: Lock up the gates. And hoist the draw-bridge up!
MORTIMER: Uncle, what's wrong?
PAULET: Where is the murderess?
  Down with her to the darkest dungeon cell!
MORTIMER: What is it? What has happened?
PAULET: It's the Queen!
  Accursed hands! Devilish audacity!
MORTIMER: The Queen? What Queen?
PAULET: The Queen of England, Sir!
  She has been murdered on the road to London!
         (*He rushes into the house.*)

Scene 8

Mortimer, immediately followed by O'Kelly

MORTIMER: Am I insane? Did someone not come by
  Just now and cry: the Queen was murdered? No,

No, I was only dreaming. To my mind
A fever dream presents as true and real
The very thing that fills my ghastly thoughts.
Who comes? It is O'Kelly. So distraught!

O'KELLY (*rushing in*):
Flee, Mortimer! Flee! Everything is lost.

MORTIMER: What has been lost?

O'KELLY: Don't ask too many questions.
Think of swift flight!

MORTIMER: What is the matter?

O'KELLY: Savage
Has dealt the blow, the madman.

MORTIMER: Then it's true?

O'KELLY: True, true! Make your escape!

MORTIMER: She has been murdered,
And Mary now ascends the throne of England!

O'KELLY: Murdered? Who said that?

MORTIMER: Why, you yourself!

O'KELLY: She is alive! And you and I are dead men.

MORTIMER: She is alive?

O'KELLY: The blow glanced off, her mantle caught it,
And Shrewsbury disarmed the murderer.

MORTIMER: She is alive!

O'KELLY: Alive, to send us all to death!
Come, they are cordoning off the park already.

MORTIMER: Who did this crazy thing?

O'KELLY: The Barnabite,
That friar from Toulon that you saw sitting
Sunk in thought there in the chapel when
The monk was spelling out the bull in which
The Pope pronounced anathema on the Queen.
He wanted to seize on the quickest means
And liberate the church of God with one
Bold stroke and win himself a martyr's crown.
But only to the priest did he confide
His act, and did it on the road to London.

MORTIMER (*after a long silence*):
A cruelly malicious fate pursues you,
Unhappy woman! Now—now you must perish,
Your very angel broaches your disaster.

O'KELLY: Which way will you direct your flight? I shall

Go hide amid the forests of the north.
MORTIMER: Go on and flee, and may God guide your flight!
I stay,—in spite of all to save her head,
Or else upon her coffin make my bed.
                  (*They leave in opposite directions.*)

ACT IV

An anteroom.

Scene 1

Count Aubespine, Kent, and Leicester.

AUBESPINE: How are things with Her Majesty? My lords,
You see me still beside myself with terror.
How did it happen? How could it have happened
Right in this loyal nation's midst?
LEICESTER: Our people
Did not do it. The perpetrator was
A Frenchman and a subject of your King.
AUBESPINE: A madman surely!
KENT: No, it was a Papist,
Count Aubespine!

Scene 2

Enter Burleigh in conversation with Davison.

BURLEIGH: The execution warrant
Must be drawn up immediately and have
The royal seal affixed.—When it is ready
It should be brought directly to the Queen
For signing. Go! There is no time to lose.
DAVISON: It shall be done.
                    (*Exit.*)
AUBESPINE (*approaching Burleigh*):
                  My Lord, my loyal heart
Shares in this island's justified rejoicing.
Praise be to Heaven that the murderer's

Blow was averted from that royal head!
BURLEIGH: Praise be to Heaven that the malice of
Our enemies was put to shame!
AUBESPINE: May God
Condemn the doer of this cursed deed!
BURLEIGH: The doer and the shameless man who planned it.
AUBESPINE (*to Kent*):
Lord Marshal, will Your Highness deign to take
Me to Her Majesty so that I may
Lay the congratulations of my Lord
And King most dutifully down at her feet?
BURLEIGH: Don't bother, Count Aubespine.
AUBESPINE: (*formally*):   I know my duty,
Lord Burleigh.
BURLEIGH: Sir, your duty is to leave
This island just as soon as possible.
AUBESPINE (*falling back in astonishment*):
What! What is this?
BURLEIGH: Your sacred title will
Protect you yet today, but not tomorrow.
AUBESPINE: And may I ask what is my crime?
BURLEIGH: If I
Gave it a *name,* it could not be forgiven.
AUBESPINE: I trust my right as an ambassador—
BURLEIGH: Will not protect a traitor.
LEICESTER AND KENT: What was that!
AUBESPINE: My Lord,
Consider well—
BURLEIGH: A passport, written by
Your hand, was found in the assassin's pocket.
KENT: Is it possible?
AUBESPINE: I issue many passports.
I cannot know a person's inner thoughts.
BURLEIGH: The murderer went to confession in
Your house.
AUBESPINE: My house is open.
BURLEIGH: To the foes
Of England.
AUBESPINE: I demand investigation.
BURLEIGH: Beware of one.
AUBESPINE: My King is outraged in

My person. He will break off the alliance.
BURLEIGH: The Queen has broken it already. There
   Will be no marriage now of France with England.
   My Lord of Kent, you will assume the task
   Of furnishing the Count safe conduct to
   The sea. The outraged populace have stormed
   His mansion, where an arsenal of weapons
   Was found; and they are threatening to tear him
   To pieces if he shows himself. Conceal him
   Until their rage is calmed.—You answer for
   His life!
AUBESPINE: I go, I quit this country where
   They trample under foot the rights of nations
   And toy with treaties.—But my King will ask
   A stern accounting—
BURLEIGH: Let him come and get it!
                (*Exeunt Kent and Aubespine.*)

Scene 3

Leicester and Burleigh.

LEICESTER: So you are now dissolving the alliance
   Which you officiously arranged yourself.
   You have deserved but little thanks from England,
   My Lord, you might have saved yourself the trouble.
BURLEIGH: I meant well. God disposed things otherwise.
   Lucky the man aware of nothing worse.
LEICESTER: We all know Cecil's brow of mystery
   When he is on the hunt for criminals
   Of state.—These are good times for you, Sir, now.
   A monstrous outrage has occurred; as yet
   A mystery surrounds its perpetrators.
   A court of inquisition can now be
   Set up. Now words and glances can be weighed
   And thoughts themselves made to appear in court.
   Now *you* will be the all-important man,
   The Atlas of the state, with all of England
   Upon your shoulders.
BURLEIGH: I acknowledge you

My master, Sir. Such triumph as you won
With your fine talk, was never won by mine.
LEICESTER: What do you mean by that?
BURLEIGH: It was you, was it not, who lured the Queen
Behind my back to Castle Fotheringhay?
LEICESTER: Behind your back? When have my actions ever
Shrunk from your sight?
BURLEIGH: Did I say you conducted
The Queen to Castle Fotheringhay? Oh, no!
In this case there was nothing of the sort!
You did not take the Queen!—It was the Queen
Who was so kind as to conduct *you* there.
LEICESTER: What do you mean by that, my Lord?
BURLEIGH: And what
A noble rôle you had the Queen perform down there!
A splendid triumph you arranged for her,
That guileless, trusting lady.—Kindly Princess,
They mocked you with such shameless impudence,
They victimized you so relentlessly!
—That generosity and clemency
That suddenly came over you at Council!
So that was why the Stuart was so weak,
So insignificant a foe that it
Was not worth while to be stained with her blood!
A clever plan! And sharpened to a point!
A shame it was so sharp the point snapped off!
LEICESTER: You scoundrel! Follow me at once! Before
The Queen's throne you shall answer me for this.
BURLEIGH: You'll find me there.—My Lord, see to it that
Your eloquence does not desert you there!
                         (*Exit.*)

Scene 4

Leicester alone, afterwards Mortimer enters.

LEICESTER: I am discovered, they see through me.—But
How did that wretched man get on my traces!
And woe to me if he has proof! If once

The Queen discovers there had been an understanding
Between myself and Mary—God! How guilty
I stand before her! How deceitful my
Advice will seem, and my unfortunate
Concern with getting her to Fotheringhay!
She will see herself cruelly mocked by me,
Betrayed to her detested enemy!
O, she can never, never pardon that!
Now everything will look premeditated,
The bitter turn that conversation took,
Her rival's victory and mocking laughter,
Yes, she will think I even put the weapon
In the assassin's hand that intervened
As unexpected, monstrous act of fate!
Escape is nowhere to be seen! Who comes here!
>   (*Enter Mortimer at the peak of excitement; he looks*
>   *anxiously about.*)

MORTIMER: Lord Lester! Is it you? Are we alone?

LEICESTER: Unhappy man, away! What have you come for?

MORTIMER: They have got on our track, on yours as well;
Be on your guard!

LEICESTER: Away! Away!

MORTIMER: They know
That at Count Aubespine's there was a secret
Meeting—

LEICESTER: What do I care!

MORTIMER: And that the assassin
Was present at it—

LEICESTER: That is your affair!
You reckless fool! Are you presuming to
Get *me* involved in your audacious crime?
Defend your evil actions for yourself!

MORTIMER: At least hear what I tell you.

LEICESTER (*in violent anger*):   Go to hell!
Why cling to my heels like an evil spirit!
Begone! I do not know you, I have nothing
In common with cheap murderers like you.

MORTIMER: You will not listen. I have come to warn you;
Your actions are betrayed as well, and—

LEICESTER: Ha!

MORTIMER: The Lord High Treasurer came to Fotheringhay

Directly after the unhappy deed had happened.
The Queen's rooms were minutely searched, and they
Discovered—

LEICESTER: What?

MORTIMER: A letter which the Queen
Had started to write you—

LEICESTER: The wretched woman!

MORTIMER: In which she urges you to keep your word,
Renews the promise of her hand to you,
Speaks of the picture which—

LEICESTER: Death and damnation!

MORTIMER: Lord Burleigh has the letter.

LEICESTER: I am lost!

> (*During the following speech of Mortimer he keeps
> walking back and forth in desperation.*)

MORTIMER: Seize the moment now! Anticipate him!
Save both yourself and *her*.—Swear your way out,
Invent excuses, and avert the worst!
I can do nothing more myself. All my
Confederates are scattered and our whole
Alliance has been broken. I shall hurry
To Scotland to enlist new friends up there.
It's up to you now. Try and see what your
Bold front and influence can do!

LEICESTER (*stops with a sudden resolve*): I will!

> (*He goes to the door, opens it, and calls.*)

Ho, guards!

> (*to the officer who comes in with armed men*)
>   Arrest this traitor to the state

And guard him well! A plot has been discovered,
A plot of the most shameful kind, and I
Shall bring the Queen the news of it myself.

> (*Exit.*)

MORTIMER (*at first stands frozen with astonishment, then gets
control of himself, and with a look of supreme contempt
watches Leicester disappear*):
The vile deceiving cur!—But I deserve it!
Who ever bade me trust the jackanapes?
And so he walks away above my neck,
My fall builds him a bridge and he escapes.
—Make your escape, then! My lips shall be true.

You will not be involved in my transgression.
I would not even be allied with you
In death. Life is a bad man's sole possession.
  (*to the officer of the guard who steps forward to arrest*
                                    him)
What do you want, cheap slave of tyranny?
I ridicule you, I am free!
            (*He draws a dagger.*)
THE OFFICER: He has a weapon!—Take away his dagger!
          (*They close in on him; he wards them off.*)
MORTIMER: And freely in this final moment I
  Shall open up my heart and loose my tongue!
  A curse and ruination on you, you
  Who have traduced your God and your true Queen!
  Who from the earthly Mary faithlessly
  Have turned away, as from the one in Heaven,
  And sold yourselves unto this bastard Queen—
THE OFFICER: You hear his blasphemy! Go and seize him!
MORTIMER: Beloved! I have failed to set you free
  But I set an example by my love
  Holy Mary, pray for me
  And take me with you to your life above!
        (*He stabs himself with the dagger and falls into the*
                  arms of the guards.)

The Queen's apartments.

Scene 5

Elizabeth, with a letter in her hand. Burleigh.

ELIZABETH: To take me down there! Make such mockery
  Of me! The traitor! To parade me there
  Triumphantly before his paramour!
  O Burleigh, never was a woman so deceived!
BURLEIGH: I cannot understand it yet,
  What power, what magic arts he could have used
  To take my Queen's sagacity so wholly unawares.
ELIZABETH: O, I shall die of shame!

O, how he must have ridiculed my weakness!
I wanted to shame *her*, and was myself
The object of her mockery!
BURLEIGH: You now see *I* had loyally advised you!
ELIZABETH: O, I have been severely punished for
   Departing from your sage advice! But was
   I not to trust in him? Was I to fear
   A snare in his vows of the truest love?
   Whom can I trust if *he* deceives me so?
   Whom I made great above all other great,
   Who always was the closest to my heart,
   Whom I allowed to act as if he were
   The King, the very master of this court!
BURLEIGH: And all the time he was deceiving you,
   Betraying you to that false Queen of Scotland!
ELIZABETH: O she shall pay me for this with her blood!
   —Has the death warrant been drawn up?
BURLEIGH: It is
   Laid ready, as you ordered.
ELIZABETH: She shall die!
   He shall behold her death, then die himself.
   I have expelled him from my heart, my love
   Is gone and vengeance occupies it wholly.
   Let his fall be as deep as he stood high,
   A monument to my severity
   As he was an example of my weakness!
   Conduct him to the Tower. I shall name
   The peers to sentence him. Let him be subject
   To the full rigor of the law
BURLEIGH: He will
   Force his way to you, justify himself—
ELIZABETH: How can he justify himself? The letter
   Incriminates him, does it not? His crime
   Is clear as day!
BURLEIGH: But you are kind and gracious;
   The sight of him, before his mighty presence—
ELIZABETH: I will not see him. Never, never! Have
   You issued orders to refuse him entrance
   If he should come?
BURLEIGH: The orders have been issued.
                (*Enter a page.*)

THE PAGE: My Lord of Lester.

THE QUEEN: O, the shameless scoundrel!
  I will not see him. Tell him that I will not see him.

THE PAGE: I would not dare say that to
  The Lord, and he would not accept the statement.

THE QUEEN: This is the way I raised him up, until
  My servants fear his orders more than mine!

BURLEIGH (*to the page*):
  Tell him the Queen forbids him to come near!
                    (*The Page goes out hesitantly.*)

THE QUEEN (*after a pause*):
  But what if it were possible—What if
  He still could justify himself?—Tell me,
  Might it not be a trap that Mary set
  To make me quarrel with my truest friend?
  She is an arrant ruthless jade! What if
  She wrote the letter just to cast suspicion
  Into my heart and plunge him whom she hates
  Into disaster—

BURLEIGH: But my Queen, Consider—

Scene 6

The former. Leicester.

LEICESTER: (*Leicester wrenches open the doors by force and enters
  with an imperious step.*) I want to see the shameless man who
    would
  Forbid me access to my own Queen's room.

ELIZABETH: Audacious man!

LEICESTER: To turn me from the door!
  If she can be seen by a Burleigh, then
  She can be seen by me!

BURLEIGH: You are most bold, my Lord,
  To storm your way in here without permission.

LEICESTER: And you most insolent, my Lord, to speak
  At all. Permission? What! At this court there
  Is no one by whose lips the Earl of Lester
  Can be forbidden or allowed!

(*as he humbly approaches Elizabeth*)
Now from
My Queen's own lips I want to hear what she—
ELIZABETH (*without looking at him*):
Out of my sight, unworthy, graceless wretch!
LEICESTER: This is not my own kind Elizabeth
I hear; I hear the Lord, my enemy,
In these ungracious words.—But I appeal
To *my* Elizabeth.—You granted *him*
Your ear, now I ask for the same.
ELIZABETH: Speak, wretch!
And make your outrage worse! Deny you did it!
LEICESTER: Let this unwanted party first retire—
Withdraw, my Lord.—The things I have to settle
Here with my Queen do not require a witness.
Leave us.
ELIZABETH (*to Burleigh*):
Stay here. I order you to stay.
LEICESTER: What business have third parties here between us?
These matters have to do with no one but
My worshipped Monarch.—I demand the rights
That suit my station.—These are sacred rights,
And I insist upon it that the Lord
Withdraw!
ELIZABETH: This haughty language well befits you!
LEICESTER: It does indeed. I am the lucky man
To whom your favor gave high preference.
That lifts me over him and over all!
Your heart conferred this haughty rank upon me,
And what love gave, I will maintain, by God!
And will defend it with my very life.
Now have him go—and it will take two minutes
For me to reach an understanding with you.
ELIZABETH: You need not hope to get around me by
Sly talk.
LEICESTER: The chatterer might get around you,
But I am going to talk straight to your heart,
And what I dared, relying on your favor,
That I will justify before your heart
Alone.—And I will recognize no other
Tribunal over me but your affection!

ELIZABETH: You shameless man! That is the first to damn you.
My Lord, show him the letter.

BURLEIGH: Here it is!

LEICESTER (*runs through the letter without losing countenance*):
This is the Stuart's hand.

ELIZABETH: Read and be speechless.

LEICESTER (*quietly, after reading*):
Appearance is against me! but I trust
That I shall not be judged on mere appearance!

ELIZABETH: Can you deny you had an understanding
In secret with the Stuart, that you had
Her picture, that you gave her hope for freedom?

LEICESTER: It would be simple for me, were I guilty,
To disallow the evidence that is
Presented by an enemy. My conscience
Is clear, however. I acknowledge that
She writes the truth.

ELIZABETH: Well, then?

BURLEIGH: His own mouth damns him.

ELIZABETH: Out of my sight! And to the Tower,—Traitor!

LEICESTER: That I am not. I erred in that I made
A secret of the step and kept it from you.
And yet my purpose was sincere. I did it
To sound the enemy and to destroy her.

ELIZABETH: Absurd evasion!

BURLEIGH: What, my Lord? You think—

LEICESTER: I played a daring game, I realize,
And no one but the Earl of Lester could
Have ventured such an action at this court.
The world well knows how much I hate the Stuart,
The rank I occupy, the confidence
With which the Queen has honored me, can not
Help but refute all doubt of my good motives.
The man who is above all others marked
By your good favor may strike out upon
His own way to achieve his duty!

BURLEIGH: Why,
Though, if the cause was good, did you keep silent?

LEICESTER: My Lord, your habit is to talk before
You act, you are your actions' trumpet. *That*
Is *your* way, Sir, of doing things. Mine is to

Act first, and then to talk.

BURLEIGH: You're talking now because you must.

LEICESTER (*measuring him with his eyes proudly and scornfully*):
                                        And you

Are boasting that you managed to achieve
Some great fantastic deed in rescuing
Your Queen and in unmasking treachery.—
You fancy you know everything, that nothing
Can get past your keen eye.—Poor, empty boaster!
Despite your keenness Mary Stuart would
Be free today if *I* had not forestalled it.

BURLEIGH: You claim that you—

LEICESTER: Yes, I, my Lord. The Queen

Had placed her trust in Mortimer, she opened
Her inmost heart to him, she went so far
As to give him a bloody charge against
The Stuart, since his uncle had rejected
A similar commission with abhorrence—
Now, is that not the case?

        (*The Queen and Burleigh look at each other in
                        astonishment.*)

BURLEIGH: How did you find
    That out?

LEICESTER: But is it not true?—Well, my Lord,
    Where were your thousand eyes that you should fail
    To see that Mortimer was fooling you?
    And that he was the Guises' tool, a frantic
    Papist, and a creature of the Stuart,
    A bold fanatic with determination,
    Who came to set the Stuart free and murder
    The Queen—

ELIZABETH (*with the utmost astonishment*):
                This Mortimer!

LEICESTER: It was through him that Mary
    Was able to communicate with me.
    It was in that way that I came to know him.
    She was to be abducted from her prison
    This very day, so his own lips revealed
    To me just now. I had them place him under
    Arrest, but in despair at seeing all
    His work undone and frustrate, and himself

Unmasked, he killed himself.

ELIZABETH: O, I have been betrayed
  As no one ever was.—This Mortimer!

BURLEIGH: This happened just now, after I had left you?

LEICESTER: I must, for my part, very much regret
  That things turned out this way with him. If he
  Had lived, his testimony would have cleared
  Me fully and relieved me of all guilt.
  That's why I turned him over to his judges.
  The strictest processes of law should state
  My innocence before the world and prove it.

BURLEIGH: He killed himself, you say? Is that so? Or did you
  Kill him?

LEICESTER: A base suspicion! Let the guard
  Be heard into whose hands I turned him over.
       (*He goes to the door and calls. The officer of the
                bodyguard comes in.*)
  Inform Her Majesty about the way
  This Mortimer came to his death.

THE OFFICER: I was on guard
  Out in the hall when suddenly the door
  Was opened by my Lord, who ordered me
  To seize the knight as traitor to the state.
  Thereat we saw him fly into a rage
  And draw his dagger with a furious curse
  Upon the Queen; before we could prevent him,
  He plunged it in his heart, so that he fell
  Dead to the floor and—

LEICESTER: That will do. You may
  Withdraw now, Sir. The Queen has heard enough.
               (*The Officer leaves.*)

ELIZABETH: O what abysses of atrocities!

LEICESTER: Who was it now that rescued you? Was it
  My Lord of Burleigh? Did he know the danger
  Surrounding you? Did *he* avert it from you?
  —Your ever loyal Lester was your angel!

BURLEIGH: Lord Earl! This Mortimer died most opportunely
  For you.

ELIZABETH: I don't know what to say. I do
  Believe you and I don't. I think you're guilty
  And yet are not. That wretched woman, she

Is causing all this trouble!
LEICESTER: She must die.
   I now vote for her death myself. I once
   Advised her sentence be left in abeyance
   Until a hand was raised again to help her.
   That now has come about—and I insist
   The sentence be invoked without delay.
BURLEIGH: You would advise that! You!
LEICESTER: As much as I
   Recoil before recourse to extreme measures,
   I see now and believe the welfare of
   The Queen requires this bloody sacrifice.
   Therefore I now propose that the command
   For execution be applied at once.
BURLEIGH (*to the Queen*):
   Then since my Lord appears to be in earnest,
   I move the execution of the sentence
   Shall be assigned to him.
LEICESTER: To me!
BURLEIGH: To you.
   There is no better way for you to counter
   All the suspicion that still weighs upon you
   Than by your having *her* beheaded whom
   You are yourself accused of having loved.
ELIZABETH (*fixing her eyes on Leicester*):
   My Lord gives good advice. So shall it be.
LEICESTER: The highness of my rank should really free me
   From a commission of such dismal nature,
   Which would in every sense be more becoming
   To Burleigh than to me. A man who stands
   Thus closely to his Queen ought not to be
   Asked to perform such grim unhappy things.
   However, to affirm my readiness
   To give my Queen full satisfaction, I
   Shall waive the privilege of my rank and shall
   Assume this dire responsibility.
ELIZABETH: Lord Burleigh shall divide it with you.
                 (*to the latter*)   Have
   A care the order is enforced at once.
        (*Exit Burleigh. A tumult is heard outside.*)

Scene 7

Enter the Earl of Kent.

ELIZABETH: What is amiss, my Lord of Kent? What tumult
  Disturbs the town? What is the matter?
KENT: Queen,
  The populace are all around the palace
  Urgently insisting they shall see you.
ELIZABETH: What do my people want?
KENT: There is alarm
  Abroad in London that your life is threatened
  And that assassins are afoot sent by
  The Pope. The Catholics are said to be
  Conspiring to abduct the Stuart from
  Her prison and proclaim her Queen. The mob
  Believes it and is wild. The Stuart's head
  Alone, that must fall yet today, can calm them.
ELIZABETH: Is violence to be employed against me?
KENT: They are determined not to yield until
  You sign the warrant for her execution.

Scene 8

Reenter Burleigh with Davison, the latter with a document in his hands.

ELIZABETH: What do you bring me, Davison?
DAVISON (*approaching solemnly*):   You ordered
  Me, Queen,—
ELIZABETH: What is it?
      (*As she is about to take the document she shudders and
                        shrinks away.*)
              O my God!
BURLEIGH: Obey
  The people's voice, it is the voice of God.
ELIZABETH (*indecisive, struggling with herself*):
  My Lords! Who will assure me whether I

Am really hearing my whole people's voice,
The whole world's voice? O, I am very much
Afraid that once I have obeyed the people's
Desire, a wholly different voice will then
Be heard—and that precisely those who now
Urge me so vehemently to the deed
Will sharply blame me when the deed is done!

Scene 9

Enter the Earl of Shrewsbury in great agitation.

SHREWSBURY: My Queen, they're hurrying you unduly! O,
Stand firm, be steadfast!
        (as he perceives Davison with the document)
            Or is it all over?
Has it already happened? I perceive
A sorry document there in his hand.
Do not allow that in my Queen's sight now.
ELIZABETH: O noble Shrewsbury! They're forcing me!
SHREWSBURY: Who can force you? You are the mistress here.
Now is the time to show your majesty!
Command those brutish voices to be silent
Who dare to offer violence against
Your royal will and govern your high judgment.
Fear and blind error agitate the people,
You are yourself exasperated, hurt,
You are but human, you can not judge now.
BURLEIGH: This was judged long ago. There is no sentence
To *pass*, but one to *carry out*.
KENT (*who withdrew at Shrewsbury's entrance, now comes back*):
The uproar grows, the mob can not be held
In check much longer.
ELIZABETH (*to Shrewsbury*):   See how they compel me!
SHREWSBURY: I only ask postponement now. This pen-stroke
Decides your whole life's peace and happiness.
You have been pondering this for years; then shall
The moment carry you away by storm?
Just brief postponement. Gather up your thoughts
And wait for a more tranquil hour, my Queen.

BURLEIGH (*vehemently*):
  Yes, wait, postpone, delay, until the kingdom
  Is all a-flame, until the enemy
  Succeeds at last in really dealing her
  Death-blow. Three times a god has kept you from it;
  It touched you *close* today; to hope for one
  More miracle yet would be tempting God.
SHREWSBURY: The God who has four times preserved you by
  His wondrous hand, and who today gave strength
  To the old man's weak arm to overwhelm
  A raging madman—He deserves your trust!
  I shall not seek to raise the voice of justice,
  This is not the time for that, nor could
  You hear it for the fury of this tempest.
  But hear just this one thing! You tremble now
  Before this living Mary. Have no fear
  Before the living one. But tremble at
  The dead one, the beheaded one. She will
  Rise from her grave and stalk your kingdom as
  Avenging ghost and goddess of contention
  To turn your people's hearts away from you.
  The Briton *hates* this woman whom he fears,
  He will *avenge* her when she is no more.
  Once he feels pity, he no longer will
  Look on her as the adversary of
  His faith, but only as his King's granddaughter
  And victim of harsh jealousy and hatred.
  You soon will find out what a change there is.
  Cross London when the deed of blood is done,
  Show yourself to the people who once thronged
  About you in their jubilation, and
  You will behold another England and
  Another people, for that splendid justice
  That won all hearts for you, will not invest you;
  Before you, Fear, that dread concomitant
  Of tyranny, will walk with quaking step
  And empty every street through which you pass.
  You will have done the uttermost; what head
  Is safe when once this sacred one has fallen?
ELIZABETH: Ah, Shrewsbury! You saved my life today,
  Averted the assassin's dagger from me,—

Why did you not let him pursue his course?
Then all contention would be over, and,
Free from all doubts, unstained by any guilt,
I would be lying in my quiet tomb!
For I am weary of my life and rule!
If one of us two Queens *must* die so that
The other one may live—and I perceive
It cannot well be otherwise—can I
Not be the one to yield? I'll give my people
Their choice, I'll give them back their sovereignty.
God is my witness I have not lived for
Myself, but only for my people's good.
If from this flattering Stuart, and if from
This younger Queen, they hope for better days,
Then I will step down gladly from this throne
And go back to the quiet solitude
Of Woodstock where my unambitious youth
Was lived, where far from trifles of this earthly
Greatness, I found greatness in myself.—
I was not made to be a ruler! Rulers
Have to be stern; my heart is soft. I have
Long ruled this island happily because
I only needed to give happiness.
Now comes the first hard duty of a king,
And I perceive my weakness—

BURLEIGH: Well, by Heaven!
When I hear words as totally unroyal
As these now spoken by my own Queen's lips,
It would be treason to my fatherland
And duty to keep silent any longer.
—You say you love your people more than self.
Then show that now! Do not choose peace now for
Yourself and leave your kingdom to the tempests.
—Think of the Church! Shall the old misbelief
Be reimported to us by this Stuart?
And shall the monk rule here anew? and shall
The Legate come from Rome to close our churches
And to unseat our kings from their own thrones?
—The souls of all your subjects, I demand
Them from you.—Whether they are saved or lost
Depends on how you act on this occasion.

This is no time for wishy-washy pity.
The people's welfare is your highest duty.
Shrewsbury may have rescued you today,
But I shall rescue England.—That is more!

ELIZABETH: Let me be left now to myself. With human beings
Is neither peace nor counsel in this matter.
I shall refer it to a higher Judge.
As he instructs me, I shall do.—Withdraw,
My Lords!

(*to Davison*)
You, Sir, are to remain near by.
(*The Lords withdraw. Shrewsbury alone remains a few
minutes yet before the Queen with a meaningful look,
then slowly goes out wearing an expression of deepest
sorrow.*)

Scene 10

ELIZABETH (*alone*):
O, slavery of the people's service! Bondage
Of shame.—How tired I am of flattering
This idol that my inmost heart despises!
O, when am I to stand free on this throne!
I must respect opinion, court the mob's
Approval, satisfy a populace
Who can be pleased with charlatans alone.
O, no one is a king who has to please
The world! The only king is he who in his actions
Need ask approval of no man alive.
   To what end have I practiced justice, hated
Capricious despotism all my life,
To find that I have tied my hands in this
First unavoidable deed of sheer force!
The model I myself have set condemns me!
Were I a tyrant like the Spanish Mary,
My predecessor on this throne, I now could shed
The blood of kings without the fear of censure.
But was it, then, my own free choosing to
Be just? Omnipotent Necessity,
Which also forces the free will of kings,
Constrained me to this virtue and compelled me.

Hemmed in by foes, the people's favor is
All that stays me on this disputed throne.
The continental powers are all trying
To ruin me. Implacably the Pope
In Rome hurls his anathema at my head,
With false fraternal kiss I am betrayed
By France, and on the sea the Spaniard frankly
Prepares a mad war of annihilation.
Thus I, defenseless woman, stand embattled
Against a world! I am compelled to clothe
In lofty virtues my claim's nakedness
As well as that stain on my princely birth
Which my own father cast to my disgrace.
I covet it in vain.—The hatred of
My foes has laid it bare and sets this Stuart
Up as a ghost to threaten me forever.

    No, no, this fear shall have an end!
Her head shall fall. I must and will have peace!
—She is the Fury of my life, a plague
Of torment fastened on to me by Fate.
Wherever I have planted joy or hope,
There lies that serpent out of hell upon
My path. She takes away my lover from me,
She steals my very bridegroom! All misfortunes
That strike me bear the name of *Mary Stuart!*
Once *she* is driven from among the living
I shall be free as air upon the mountains.

                  (silence)
With what scorn she looked down on me, as if
Her glance should strike me to the ground like lightning!
Poor, helpless creature! I wield better weapons,
Their stroke is deadly, and you are no more!

        (walking with rapid step to the table and seizing the
                         pen)
In your eyes, then, I am a bastard?—Wretch!
I am such only while you live and breathe.
The doubt as to my princely birth will be
Wiped out as soon as I have wiped you out.
As soon as no more choice is left for Britons,
My birth shall have been in a bed of wedlock!

        (With a quick, firm stroke of the pen she writes her

signature, then drops the pen and steps back with an
expression of horror. After a pause she rings.

Scene 11

Elizabeth. Davison.

ELIZABETH: Where are the other lords?
DAVISON: They went out to
  Bring the excited populace to order.
  Their turbulence was quieted as soon
  As my Lord Earl of Shrewsbury appeared.
  "He is the one," a hundred voices shouted,
  "Who saved the Queen! So listen to him now,
  The bravest man in England!" Noble Talbot
  Then started talking and in gentle words
  Reproved the people for their violent
  Intention; he spoke so convincingly
  That everyone was pacified and stole
  Away in silence.
ELIZABETH: O this fickle mob
  That shifts with every wind! And woe to any
  Who lean upon that reed!—That will do now,
  Lord Davison. You may withdraw again.
             (when he has turned toward the door)
  O, and this paper—Take it back—I place
  It in your hands.
DAVISON *(casts a glance at the paper and starts with alarm)*:
               My Queen! Your signature!
  You did decide?
ELIZABETH: I was supposed to sign.
  I did so. A mere piece of paper does
  Not make decisions, names don't kill.
DAVISON: But *your* name, Queen, upon this document
  Decides all matters, kills, and is a bolt
  Of lightning winging to its prey.—This piece
  Of paper orders the commissioners
  And sheriff to betake themselves at once
  To Fotheringhay and to the Queen of Scotland
  And to announce to her her execution
  And to perform it with the coming dawn.

Here there is no postponement: she has lived,
Once I release this paper from my hands.

ELIZABETH: Yes, Sir. God lays a weighty destiny
In your weak hands. Implore Him now in prayer
That He may shed His light of wisdom on you.
I go and leave you to your duty now.

(She starts to leave.)

DAVISON *(intercepting her)*:
O no, my Queen! I beg you, do not leave me
Before you have made your will clear to me.
Is any other wisdom needed here
Than following your orders to the letter?
—You place this paper in my hands for me
To forward with despatch to execution?

ELIZABETH: Be guided by your *own* discretion—

DAVISON: *(responding immediately and frightened)*: Not
By mine! O God forbid! Obedience
Is my entire discretion. Nothing should
Be left here for your servant to decide.
A tiny error might mean regicide,
A monstrous and immeasurable disaster.
Allow me in so great a matter to
Be your blind instrument without a will.
Declare your meaning in clear words: What is
To be done with this fatal order now?

ELIZABETH: —Its name makes that quite plain.

DAVISON: Then you wish it to be fulfilled at once?

ELIZABETH *(hesitating)*:
I did not *say* that, and I shudder at
The thought.

DAVISON: You wish me to hold on to it?

ELIZABETH *(quickly)*:
O, at your peril! You will answer for
The consequences!

DAVISON: I? My God! —Speak, Queen!
What is your wish?

ELIZABETH *(impatiently)*: I wish no further mention
Be made of this unhappy subject, I
Wish to have done with it for evermore.

DAVISON: It will cost you a single word. O tell me,
Decide what is to be done with this paper!

ELIZABETH: I told you. Do not bother me again.

DAVISON: You say you told me? You have told me nothing.
O, may it please my Queen to recollect.

ELIZABETH (*stamping her foot*):
This is intolerable!

DAVISON: I beg you to have patience
With me! I have been only a few months
In office here. I do not know the language
Of courts and monarchs.—I grew up amid
Plain ways and simple customs. Therefore please
Have patience with your servant! Do not be
Regretful for a word that will instruct me
And set me clear as to my duty—

        (*He approaches her in a posture of supplication; she
        turns her back to him. He stands in despair, then says
                in a decisive tone*):
Take back this paper! Take it back again!
It turns to burning fire between my hands.
Do not choose me to serve you in so fearful
A business.

ELIZABETH: Do the duty of your office!
                (*Exit.*)

Scene 12

Davison, immediately followed by Burleigh.

DAVISON: She goes. She leaves me helpless and in doubt
With this dread document.—What shall I do?
Am I to keep it? Or deliver it?
                (*Addressing Burleigh who enters.*)
O good, good that you come, my Lord! You were
The person who appointed me to office.
Release me from it now! I undertook it,
Unconscious of what it entailed. Let me
Return to the obscurity where you
Once found me, I do not belong in this post—

BURLEIGH: What is the matter, Sir? Compose yourself.
Where is the warrant? The Queen summoned you.

DAVISON: She left me in great anger. O advise me!

Help me! Save me from this anguished hell
Of doubt! Here is the warrant—it is signed.
BURLEIGH (*hastily*):
It is? Then give it here!
DAVISON: I must not.
BURLEIGH: What?
DAVISON: She has not made her wishes plain to me—
BURLEIGH: Not plain! She signed it. Let me have it then.
DAVISON: I am supposed to execute it—yet
Not execute it—God! What *shall* I do?
BURLEIGH (*pressing more urgently*):
You execute it right away. So let
Me have it. You are lost if you delay.
DAVISON: I will be lost if I am over-hasty.
BURLEIGH: You are a fool, and mad! Give it to me!
(*He snatches the document from him and hurries off
with it.*)
DAVISON (*hurrying after him*):
What are you doing? Stop! You'll ruin me!

ACT V

The scene is the same room as in Act I.

Scene 1

Hanna Kennedy, dressed in deep mourning, her eyes red from weeping, and with great but silent sorrow, is busy sealing packages and letters. Grief frequently interrupts her in her task, and intermittently she is seen praying silently.
Enter Paulet and Drury, likewise in black garments. They are followed by numerous servants carrying gold and silver vessels, mirrors, paintings, and other valuables, with which they fill up the rear of the room. Paulet hands the nurse a jewel-box together with a paper, and indicates to her by gestures that it contains an itemization of the things he has brought. At the sight of these luxuries the nurse's grief is renewed. She sinks into profound sorrow, while the former silently withdraw again.
Enter Melvil.

KENNEDY (*utters a cry as she catches sight of him*):
  Melvil! You! I see you once again!
MELVIL: Yes, loyal Kennedy, we meet again.
KENNEDY: And after such a long, sad separation!
MELVIL: This is a sad, unhappy meeting, too!
KENNEDY: O Lord, then you have come—
MELVIL: To bid my Queen
  A last farewell for all eternity.
KENNEDY: At last, now, on the morning of her death
  She is allowed the long-missed presence of
  Her people.—O dear Sir, I will not ask
  How things have fared with you, nor will I name
  The grievous things that we have suffered here
  Since you were wrested from among our midst.
  Ah, some day there will come the hour for that!
  O Melvil! Melvil! Why must we have lived
  To see the drawing of this day!
MELVIL: Let us
  Not make each other weak! As long as I
  Have life within me, I shall weep; no smile
  Shall ever cheer these cheeks of mine again,
  Nor shall I ever lay aside this garment
  Of night. I shall mourn everlastingly!
  But for today I shall be steadfast.—Promise
  Me too, to moderate your grief as well.—
  If all the others inconsolably
  Give way to their despair, let *us* proceed
  Before her with a nobly calm composure
  And be her staff along this path to death.
KENNEDY: Melvil, you are mistaken if you think
  The Queen has any need of our assistance
  In order to walk steadily to death!
  She sets us the example of a noble
  Composure. Have no fear, Sir. Mary Stuart
  Will perish as a Queen and heroine.
MELVIL: Did she receive the death announcement with
  Composure? They say she was not forewarned.
KENNEDY: No, she was not. But other terrors did
  Distress my Lady. Mary did not tremble
  At death but at her would-be liberator.
  —We had been promised freedom. Mortimer

Vowed he would take us out of here last night,
And thus between her hope and fear, in doubt
If she should trust her princely person and
Her honor to that reckless youth, the Queen
Had waited for the coming of the morning.
—Then came a tumult in the castle; pounding
Struck fright into our ears, and hammer blows.
We thought we heard the liberators coming,
Hope beckoned, and the sweet impulse of life
Involuntarily and strongly stirred—
And then the door was opened—and it was
Lord Paulet to announce—that—carpenters
Were putting up the scaffold at our feet.

> (*She turns aside, seized by violent grief.*)

MELVIL: Just God! O tell me, how did Mary bear
  The revelation of that dreadful change?
KENNEDY (*after a pause during which she has somewhat regained
  her composure*):
  One does not gradually let go of life.
  All of a sudden, swiftly, instantly
  The change must be made from the temporal
  To the eternal. To my Lady God vouchsafed
  The power at that moment to reject
  The hopes of earth with a decisive soul
  And to grasp Heaven with abundant faith.
  No sign of fear, no word of lamentation
  Dishonored my Queen then.—And not until
  She heard about Lord Lester's treachery,
  About the wretched fate of that esteemed
  Young man who sacrificed his life for her,
  And saw that old knight's deep distress for whom
  The final hope had died because of her,
  Then her tears flowed; it was not her own fate, however,
  That forced them from her, but the grief of strangers.
MELVIL: Where is she now? Can you take me to her?
KENNEDY: She passed the night in vigil and in prayer,
  Wrote letters of farewell to cherished friends,
  And drew up her last will in her own hand.
  This last sleep will refresh her.
MELVIL: Who is with her?
KENNEDY: Burgoyn, her house physician, and her women.

Scene 2

Enter Margaret Kurl.

KENNEDY: What word now, Mistress? Has the Lady wakened?
KURL (*drying her tears*):
   She is already dressed—and asks for you.
KENNEDY: I'll come directly.
           (*to Melvil who starts to accompany her*)
                  Do not follow me
  Till I prepare the Lady for your coming.
             (*She goes inside.*)
KURL: Melvil! Our old steward!
MELVIL: It is I.
KURL: O, this house needs no steward any more!
  —Melvil, you come from London; can you tell
  Me anything about my husband?
MELVIL: He will be set at liberty, they say,
  As soon—
KURL: As soon as the Queen is no more!
  O, the detestable, the shameless traitor!
  He is this dear Lady's murderer.
  They say it was his testimony that
  Condemned her.
MELVIL: So it was.
KURL: O, may his soul
  Be damned to hell! He gave false testimony—
MELVIL: My Lady Kurl! Consider what you say!
KURL: I will swear to it at the bar of justice,
  I will repeat it to his very face,
  I will proclaim it to the entire world
  That she dies innocent—
MELVIL: God grant she may!

Scene 3

Enter Burgoyn followed by Hanna Kennedy.

BURGOYN (*catching sight of Melvil*):
  O Melvil!

MELVIL (*embracing him*):
      Burgoyn!
BURGOYN (*to Margaret Kurl*):   Go prepare a cup of wine
  For our dear Lady, Mistress Kurl. And hurry!
             (*Exit Kurl.*)
MELVIL: Why, is the Queen not well?
BURGOYN: She feels quite strong.
  She is deceived by her heroic spirit
  And thinks that she requires no sustenance.
  A heavy struggle still awaits her, and
  Her enemies shall not boast that her cheeks
  Grew pale before the fear of death, not even
  If nature does succumb out of sheer weakness.
MELVIL (*to the nurse, who has come back in*):
  Will she see me?
KENNEDY: She will be here directly.
  —You seem to look about with wonderment
  And your eyes ask me what are all these things
  Of splendor doing in this place of death.
  —O Sir, we suffered want while we still lived,
  But now with death this superfluity returns.

Scene 4

*Enter two other of Mary's ladies-in-waiting, likewise
dressed in mourning. At sight of Melvil they burst into
loud weeping.*

MELVIL: O, what a sight is this! And what a meeting!
  Gertrude, Rosamund!
SECOND LADY: She sent us out.
  She wishes to communicate alone
  With God this one last time.
      (*Enter two more female servants, dressed in mourning
      like the former ones. They express their grief in mute
      gestures.*)

Scene 5

*Enter Margaret Kurl. She is carrying a cup with wine
which she sets on the table; pale and trembling she
steadies herself at a chair.*

MELVIL: What is the matter? What affrights you so?

KURL: O God!

BURGOYN: What is the matter?

KURL: What I saw!

MELVIL: Compose yourself, and tell us what it was.

KURL: As I was carrying this cup of wine
    Just now up the great stair that leads down to
    The lower hall, the door was opened—I
    Glanced in—I saw—My God!

MELVIL: What did you see?

KURL: I saw the walls all draped in black, and from
    The floor a mighty scaffold rose, hung with
    Black cloth, and in the middle a black block,
    A cushion and a gleaming whetted ax
    Laid there beside it.—And the hall was full
    Of people thronging round that fatal platform
    With lust of blood hot in their eyes, awaiting
    The sacrifice.

THE LADIES-IN-WAITING: O God, have mercy on our Lady!

MELVIL: Be calm. She comes.

Scene 6

> *Enter Mary. She is magnificently dressed in white;
> upon a chain of little beads an Agnus Dei hangs at her
> throat; a rosary is suspended from her girdle; she has a
> crucifix in her hand and a diadem in her hair, and her
> great black veil is thrown back. At her entrance, those
> present step back on both sides and give expression to
> the most vehement grief. Melvil, with an involuntary
> movement, has fallen to his knees.*

MARY (*surveying the whole circle with serene dignity*):
    Why are you weeping? Why are you lamenting?
    You should be glad with me because my goal
    Of grief is reached at last, my fetters fall,
    My prison opens, and my joyous soul
    On angel wings soars up to everlasting
    Liberty. When I was in the power
    Of my haughty enemy, enduring

Indignities unseemly for a great
Free Queen, then was the time to weep for me!
—Benignly, healingly, Death comes to meet me,
My earnest friend. And he bedecks my shame
With his black wings.—A human being is
Ennobled by his last, his lowest fate.
I feel the crown upon my head again
And in my noble soul a worthy pride.
         (*as she advances a few steps forward*)
What? Melvil here?—No kneeling, noble Sir!
Arise! You have come here to witness your
Queen's triumph, not her death. Such happiness
Has fallen to my lot as I had never
Hoped for, because report of me is not
In the hands of my enemy entirely,
But one friend, a professor of my faith,
Shall stand as witness to my hour of death.
—Now tell me, noble Sir, how have you fared
In this ungracious, hostile country since
The time when you were wrested from my side?
Concern for you has often grieved my heart.
MELVIL: No want afflicted me except my sorrow
  For your sake, and my powerlessness to serve you.
MARY: And what of Didier, my old chamberlain?
  O, but that faithful man must long be sleeping
  Eternal sleep, for he was far in age.
MELVIL: God has not granted him that mercy. He
  Is still alive to bury your fair youth.
MARY: O, if before my death the happiness
  Had fallen to me to embrace just one
  Beloved head of my dear relatives!
  But I must perish in the midst of strangers
  And see no tears but yours shed for me here.
  —Melvil, my last wishes for my kinsmen
  I shall lay to your true heart's charge:—I now
  Bless the Most Christian King, my brother-in-law,
  And all the royal house of France;—I bless
  The Cardinal of Guise, my holy uncle,
  And Henry, Duke of Guise, my noble cousin.
  I also bless the Pope, the sacred Vicar
  Of Christ, who will return his blessing to me,

And that Most Catholic King who nobly offered to
Become my rescuer and my avenger.—
They all are cited in my will, and they
Will not set slight store by the gifts of my
Affection, be those gifts however poor.

                        (*turning to her servants*)

You I have recommended to my royal
Brother of France; he will look after you
And find another fatherland for you.
And if you prize my last request at all,
Do not remain in England for the Briton
To glut his haughty heart on your misfortune
And see *those* in the dust who once served *me*.
Now swear to me upon the image of
The Crucified that you will leave this wretched
Country just as soon as I am dead.

MELVIL (*touches the crucifix*):
  I swear it in the name of all here present.

MARY: Whatever I, impoverished and despoiled, still own
  And over which they grant me disposition,
  I have divided up among you, and
  I trust that they will honor my last will.
  What I now wear upon my path to death
  Shall be yours also.—Grant me once again
  My earthly splendor on my way to heaven.

                        (*to the young women*)

  To you, my Alix, Gertrude, Rosamund,
  I give my pearls and all my dresses, for
  Your youth still takes delight in fine adornment.
  You, Margaret, have the highest claim
  Upon my generosity because
  I leave you most unhappy of them all.
  That I do not avenge your husband's guilt
  On you, my will will testify.—But you,
  My faithful Hanna, find no charm in the value
  Of gold or in the worth of splendid jewels;
  Your jewel is the memory of me.
  Take, then, this cloth. I worked it with my own
  Hand for you in the hours of my sorrow,
  And wove my burning tears into its pattern.
  With this cloth you will bind my eyes for me

When we shall come to that.—That final service
I wish to have performed by my own Hanna.
KENNEDY: O Melvil, I can't bear it!
MARY: Come now all
Of you, come and receive my last farewell.
    (She holds out her hands; one after another falls at her
       feet and kisses her extended hands amid intense
            weeping.)
Farewell now, Margaret—Alix, too, farewell—
Thanks, Burgoyn, for your loyal services—
Your lips burn hot, my Gertrude—I have been
Much hated, but I have been much loved also.
O, may a noble husband make my Gertrude
Happy, for this fervent heart needs love.—
Bertha, you have chosen what is best,
You wish to be the unstained bride of Heaven.
O, hasten to fulfill that vow! The goods
Of this earth are deceptive, as you learn
From the example of your Queen! —No more!
Farewell! Farewell! For all of time, farewell!
    (She turns quickly away from them. All except Melvil
          withdraw.)

Scene 7

Mary. Melvil.

MARY: I have set all things temporal in order
  And hope to leave this world the debtor of
  No human being.—But there is one thing
  Yet, Melvil, which prevents my burdened soul
  From rising up with freedom and with joy.
MELVIL: Disclose it to me and relieve your heart,
  Confide your sorrow to your loyal friend.
MARY: I stand at the brink of eternity;
  Soon I shall step before the Judge Supreme,
  And still I have not made my peace with God.
  A priest of my own Church is still denied me,
  And I disdain to take the Sacrament's
  Angelic food from false priests' hands. I want

To die within the Faith of my own Church,
For it alone can make one blessed.

MELVIL: Set
Your heart at rest. The fervent pious wish
Without the deed will be enough for Heaven.
The tyrant's might can only bind the hands,
The heart's devotion rises free to God.
The word is dead, belief brings us to life.

MARY: The heart unaided, Melvil, cannot be
Sufficient; faith requires an earthly sign
In order to perceive the High Divine.
For that, God took the form of man and closed
Invisible, celestial gifts in mystic
Fashion in the body visible.
—It is the Church, the lofty, holy Church
That builds the ladder for us up to heaven;
Its name: the universal Catholic Church,
For only by the faith of all is Faith
Confirmed. Where thousands worship and adore,
There fervor turns to flame, and there the wingèd
Spirit soars aloft to all the heavens.
—Ah, happy they, whom joyous prayer in common
Assembles in the temple of the Lord!
The altar is adorned, the candles shine,
The bell is sounded, incense is poured forth,
The Bishop stands in stainless vestments clad,
He takes the chalice, blesses it, proclaims
The miracle of transsubstantiation,
And there before the present God the people
Sink down in the conviction of their faith.—
Alas, I am excluded, I alone,
No sign from Heaven penetrates my prison.

MELVIL: Oh, but one does! And it is close at hand.
Trust the Omnipotent.—The withered staff
Can put forth branches in the hand of faith.
And he who struck the water from the rock
Can set an altar for you in your prison,
He can transform *this* chalic and this earthly
Refreshment speedily into divine ones.
       (*He picks up the cup which stands on the table.*)

MARY: Melvil! Do I grasp your meaning? Yes!

I do! There is no priest here, and no church,
No Eucharist.—But the Redeemer says:
Where two of ye are gathered in *my* name,
I shall be present there among them also.
What consecrates a priest to be the Lord's
Own mouth? A pure heart and a sinless life.
—Thus *you* for me are, though unconsecrated,
A priest, God's messenger, who brings me peace.
To you I now will make my last confession,
And your lips shall pronounce my absolution.
MELVIL: If you feel such a mighty impulse in
    Your heart, my Queen, then to your comfort know
    That God can work a miracle as well.
    You say that there is no priest here, no church,
    No body of the Lord?—You are mistaken.
    There is a priest here, and God is here present.
        (*At these words he uncovers his head; at the same time
            he shows her a Host in a gold case.*)
    —I am a priest. To hear your last confession,
    And to pronounce peace over you upon
    Your path to death, I have myself received
    The seven holy orders on my head,
    And from the Holy Father, who himself
    Pronounced the consecration, I bring you
    This Host.
MARY: O, must such happiness of heaven
    Befall me at the threshold of my death!
    As an immortal comes on golden clouds
    Descending, as once the Apostle was
    Led by an angel out of prison bonds,
    No bars preventing him, no keeper's sword,
    And walking mightily through bolted doors
    Until he stood there radiant in the dungeon,
    Just so am I surprised by Heaven's herald
    Where every earthly rescuer has failed me!
    —And you, *my* servant once, are now the servant
    Of Most High God,—you are His holy mouth!
    As your knee formerly was bent to *me,*
    So I now lie before you in the dust.
        (*She falls on her knees before him.*)

MELVIL (*as he makes the Sign of the Cross over her*):
  In the name of the Father, of the Son,
  And of the Spirit! Mary, Queen! Have you
  Searched in your heart, and do you swear and promise
  To speak the truth before the God of Truth?
MARY: My heart is open here to you and Him,
MELVIL: Of what sin does your conscience call you guilty
  Since you were reconciled last time to God?
MARY: My heart was filled with jealous hatred, and
  Thoughts of revenge have raged within my bosom.
  I, as a sinner, hoped for God's forgiveness
  While I could not forgive my enemy.
MELVIL: Do you repent this sin, and is it your
  Sincere resolve to leave this world atoned?
MARY: As truly as I hope, may God forgive me.
MELVIL: What other sin does your heart find upon you?
MARY: Ah, not through *hate* alone, through sinful love
  I have still more offended Highest God.
  My foolish heart felt drawn in its affection
  To one who broke his faith in vile deception.
MELVIL: Do you repent that sin, and has your heart
  Turned from the foolish idol back to God?
MARY: It was the hardest battle I have won,
  But that last earthly bond is now undone.
MELVIL: What further guilt lies still upon your conscience?
MARY: Alas, an early blood-guilt, which I had
  Long since confessed, returns in frightening power
  Now in the reckoning of this final hour
  And blackly washes toward the gates of heaven.
  I caused the King, my husband, to be murdered
  And gave my heart and hand to the seducer.
  I did harsh penance for it by church laws,
  Yet in my soul the conscience-worm still gnaws.
MELVIL: Does your heart still complain of other sin
  Which you have not confessed or yet atoned for?
MARY: You now know all that weighs upon my heart.
MELVIL: Think of your nearness to Omniscient God!
  Think of the punishments which Holy Church
  Imposes for an incomplete confession.
  That is a sin unto eternal death,
  For it offends against His holy spirit.

MARY: Eternal Mercy grant me triumph then
    In this last struggle, as I withhold nothing when
    I speak to you.
MELVIL: What? Will you hide from God
    The very crime for which mankind condemns you?
    You tell me nothing of your bloody share
    In Parry's and in Babington's high treason?
    For that deed you die temporal death; will you
    Die everlasting death for it as well?
MARY: For God's world I am ready. Be it known:
    Before the minute-hand in its progression
    Moves, I shall stand before my Judge's throne;
    But I repeat that I have finished my confession.
MELVIL: Weigh this with care. The heart is a deceiver.
    Perhaps with cunning ambiguity
    You have got round the *word* that makes you guilty,
    Though the *intention* shared in the misdeed.
    Be sure that trickery will not deceive
    The eye of flame that looks into the heart!
MARY: I did appeal to all the potentates
    To set me free from my unworthy bonds,
    But never by intention or by deed
    Did I plot harm to my opponent's life!
MELVIL: Your secretaries bore false witness, then?
MARY: As I said, so it is. May God be judge
    Of what they testified!
MELVIL: You mount the scaffold
    In the assurance of your innocence?
MARY: God deems me worthy to atone for youthful grievous
    Blood-guilt by a death unmerited.
MELVIL (*makes the Sign of the Cross over her*):
    Go, then, and by your death atone for it!
    Fall as assenting victim at the altar!
    Blood can atone for what blood once transgressed.
    Only woman's frailty erred in you,
    The weaknesses of flesh will not pursue
    The blessed soul to its transfigured rest.
    But I, by virtue of the power which
    Is vested in me to remit and bind, proclaim
    Remission of your sins in God's high name.
    According to your faith, so be it with you.

(*He gives her the Host.*)
Receive the body, for you it was slain.
    (*He takes the chalice which is standing on the table,
consecrates it with silent prayer, and then hands it to
her. She hesitates to take it and pushes it back with her
hand.*)
Receive the blood, for you it was poured forth.
Receive, I say; the Pope grants you this favor.
At death you are to exercise this highest,
This priestly function of the kings of old.
    (*She receives the chalice.*)
As you now in your earthly body are
Bound mystically together with your God,
So, yonder in His kingdom of pure joy,
Where there is no more sin and no more weeping,
You will, as a transfigured angel,
Be joined with God in His eternal keeping.
    (*He sets the chalice down. At a noise that is heard, he
covers his head and goes to the door. Mary remains on
her knees in silent reverence.*)
MELVIL (*coming back*):
You still have one hard fight to undergo.
Do you feel strong enough to conquer any
Impulse now of bitterness and hatred?
MARY: I do not fear relapse. My hate and love
Together I have sacrificed to God.
MELVIL: Prepare yourself, then, to receive the Lords
Of Lester and of Burleigh. They are here.

Scene 8

*Enter Burleigh; also Leicester and Paulet. Leicester
remains standing way off to one side without raising
his eyes. Burleigh, who observes his self-possession,
steps between him and the Queen.*

BURLEIGH: I have come, Lady Stuart, to receive
Your last commands.
MARY: I thank you, noble Lord.
BURLEIGH: It is the will of my great Queen that nothing
Within the bounds of reason be denied you.

MARY: My will contains the list of my last wishes.
  I have put it into Lord Paulet's hands
  And ask that it be followed faithfully.
PAULET: Rely upon it.
MARY: I ask that all my servants be released
  To go unharmed to Scotland or to France,
  Wherever they themselves wish and desire.
BURLEIGH: It shall be as you wish.
MARY: And since my corpse
  Is not to rest in consecrated ground,
  Permit this faithful servant here to carry
  My heart to France and to my family.
  —Ah, it was always there!
BURLEIGH: It shall be done.
  Have you a further—
MARY: To the Queen of England
  Take my sisterly salute.—Tell her
  That I forgive her for my death with all
  My heart, and that I beg her pardon for
  My violence of yesterday.—May God
  Protect her and grant her a happy reign!
BURLEIGH: And have you still not chosen better counsel?
  You still disdain to have the Dean's assistance?
MARY: I have been reconciled to God.—Lord Paulet!
  I have unwittingly caused you much grief,
  Deprived you of the prop of your old age—
  O, let me hope you won't remember me
  With hatred—
PAULET (*gives her his hand*):
  May God be with you, Lady. Go in peace.

Scene 9

*Enter Hanna Kennedy and the Queen's other women
with expressions of horror. They are followed by the
Sheriff with a white staff in his hand; behind him,
through the opened door, are seen armed men.*

MARY: What is the matter, Hanna?—Yes, it is time.
  Here comes the Sheriff to lead us to death.

It is the time to part. Farewell! Farewell!
> (*Her women cling to her with violent grief.*
> *To Melvil*):

You, worthy Sir, and you, my faithful Hanna,
Shall now accompany me on this last walk.
My Lord, do not deny me this last kindness.
BURLEIGH: I do not have authority for that.
MARY: What, Sir? You would refuse me that small wish?
Have some consideration for my sex!
Who is to do these final services
For me? It cannot be my sister's will
To see offense done to my sex through me
And that rude hands of men should touch me now!
BURLEIGH: No woman is permitted to ascend
The scaffold steps with you.—Their cries and wailing—
MARY: She shall not wail! I shall be guarantee
For my Hanna's self-possession and calm spirit.
Be kind, my Lord! Do not divide me in
My death from my true nurse and foster-mother!
She bore me into life upon her arms,
Let her lead me with gentle hand to death.
PAULET (*to Burleigh*):
Let it be done.
BURLEIGH: So be it.
MARY: I have nothing
More in this world.—
> (*She takes the crucifix and kisses it.*)
>   My Saviour! My Redeemer!

As on the Cross thou didst spread wide Thy arms
Of mercy, spread them to receive me now.
> (*She turns to go. At this moment her eye encounters*
> *the Earl of Leicester who had involuntarily started up*
> *at her departure and looked at her.—Mary trembles to*
> *behold him, her knees falter, she is on the verge of*
> *collapse; whereupon the Earl of Leicester seizes her*
> *and takes her into his arms. She looks at him solemnly*
> *for a time in silence; he cannot bear her glance. Finally*
> *she speaks.*)

You keep your word, Lord Earl of Lester.—You
Once promised me your arm to lead me from
This prison, and you lend it to me now.

(*He stands as though annihilated. She goes on speaking
in a mild tone.*)

Yes, Lester, and not merely
My freedom did I wish to owe to you.
You were supposed to make my freedom *precious;*
At your hand, and made happy by your love,
I wanted to rejoice in my new life.
And now, when I am on the path departing
From this world to become a blessed spirit
Whom no affection of this earth can tempt,
Now, Lester, now, without the blush of shame
I may confess to you my conquered weakness.—
Farewell, and if you can, live happily.
It was your privilege to woo two Queens:
You have disdained a tender loving heart,
Betrayed it so that you could win a proud one.
Go kneel before Elizabeth! May your
Reward not prove a punishment in store!
Farewell!—On earth I now have nothing more!
(*She walks out, the Sheriff preceding her, her nurse at
her side. Burleigh and Paulet follow; the others,
wailing, watch her out of sight, then they withdraw
through the other two doors.*)

Scene 10

LEICESTER (*remaining behind alone*):
And I am still alive! I still endure
Existence! Will this roof not fall on me!
Will no abyss cleave open to consume
The wretchedest of creatures! *What* have I
Lost here! And what a pearl I cast away!
What happiness of heaven I have squandered!
—She goes, already a transfigured spirit,
And leaves *me* to the lost hope of the damned.
—But where is that resolve with which I came,
To stifle my heart's voice relentlessly?
To watch the falling of her head unflinchingly?
Does sight of her revive my withered shame?
—Must she in death snare me in love's captivity?
It will henceforth be an ill-suited aim,

You wretch, for any pity to be shown;
Love's happiness lies now beyond your claim;
Let armor made of bronze be made to frame
Your breast, and let your brow be made of stone.
Lest the prize of your shameful deed be lost,
You must see it fulfilled at any cost.
Be silent, Pity! Turn to stone, my eye:
I will be witness, I will see her die.

> (*He walks with determined step toward the door
> through which Mary has passed, but stops midway in
> his course.*)

In vain! In vain! Hell's anguish seizes me!
I cannot, cannot force myself to see
The ghastly sight, I cannot watch her die—
Hark! What was that?—They are downstairs already—
The dreadful business is now under way
Beneath my feet—I hear their voices—Out!
Out of this house of horror and of death!

> (*He starts to flee by another door but finds it locked
> and reels back.*)

Has some god chained me to this floor? Must I
Hear what I shudder to behold? That is
The Dean's voice now—He is exhorting her—
—She interrupts him—Hark!—She prays aloud—
With a firm voice—Now silence—total silence!
I only hear the women sobbing now—
They are undressing her—They shove the stool up—
She kneels upon the cushion—lays her head—

> (*After he has spoken these last words with mounting
> anguish and stopped for a time, he is seen to shudder
> suddenly with a convulsive motion and collapse
> fainting. Simultaneously the muffled sound of voices
> rises from below and continues for a long time.*)

The Queen's apartments, as in Act IV.

Scene 11

*Elizabeth emerges from a side door; her gait and gestures
express the most intense uneasiness.*

ELIZABETH: No one here yet—No news yet—Will it never
  Be evening? Does the sun stand firmly placed
  In its celestial course?—Am I to go
  On waiting on my rack of expectation!
  —Has it been done? Or has it *not?*—I shudder
  In either case, yet do not dare inquire!
  Lord Lester does not come, nor Burleigh either,
  Whom I had named to carry out the sentence.
  If they are gone from London—then it has
  Been done. The arrow has been shot, it flies,
  It strikes, it has already struck. Not for
  My kingdom can I hold it back.—Who's there?

Scene 12

Elizabeth. A Page.

ELIZABETH: You come back alone—Where are the Lords?
THE PAGE: My Lord of Lester and the High Treasurer—
ELIZABETH (*in the utmost suspense*):
  Where are they?
THE PAGE: They are not in London.
ELIZABETH: No?
  Then where are they?
THE PAGE: No one was able to inform me.
  Before the break of day both of the Lords
  Had left the city secretly and in Great haste.
ELIZABETH (*blurting out*): I am the Queen of England, then!
      (*pacing back and forth in extreme agitation*)
  Go, call—No, better stay here—She is dead.
  Now I have room at last upon this earth.
  —Why am I trembling? Why does terror seize me?
  The grave will cover up my fear, and who
  Can say I did it? I shall never lack
  For tears to shed for the dead woman's sake!
          (*to the Page*)
  Are you still here?—Send instantly and have
  My secretary Davison come here.
  Send for the Earl of Shrewsbury.—Ah, here
  He is!
          (*Exit the Page.*)

Scene 13

Elizabeth. Enter the Earl of Shrewsbury.

ELIZABETH: Welcome, noble Lord! What do you bring?
   It cannot be a trifling matter that
   Directs your step this way so late.
SHREWSBURY: Great Queen,
   My anxious heart, concerned about your fame,
   Forced me today to journey to the Tower,
   Where Mary's secretaries, Kurl and Nau,
   Are kept in prison; for I wished to test
   Once more the truth of what they had deposed.
   Dismayed, embarrassed, the Lieutenant of
   The Tower refused to show the prisoners.
   By threats alone I managed to get entry.
   O Heaven, what a sight I there beheld!
   With hair dishevelled, with the eyes of madness,
   Like one tormented by the Furies, lay
   The Scotsman Kurl upon his cot.—The wretch
   Had barely recognized me when he threw
   Himself down at my feet, and shrieking, clutched
   My knees; in desperation like a worm
   That writhed before me—he kept begging me
   And conjuring me to tell him his Queen's fate.
   For a report that she had been condemned to death
   Had got in through the Tower's crevices.
   When I confirmed the rumor as the truth
   And added that it was *his* testimony
   That caused her death, he jumped up frantically,
   Attacked his fellow-prisoner, pulled him
   Down to the floor with madman's giant-strength
   And tried to strangle him. We barely wrenched
   The wretched creature from his frenzied hands.
   And then he turned his rage against himself
   And beat his breast with frenzied fists, and cursed
   Himself and his companion to all devils.
   He said he gave false evidence; the letters
   To Babington that he called genuine,
   Were false; he had put down quite different words

From what the Queen was dictating to him;
The rascal Nau had led him on to do it.
Then he ran to the window, threw it open
By raging force, and screamed down to the streets
For everybody to come up and hear
That he was Mary's secretary and
The scoundrel who had falsely called her guilty,
That he was cursed, that he had borne false witness.

ELIZABETH: You said yourself that he was not in his
Right mind. The words of raving lunatics
Prove nothing.

SHREWSBURY: But this madness of itself
Proves all the more. O Queen, let me entreat
You to do nothing in excessive haste.
Command them to investigate anew!

ELIZABETH: I shall do so—because you wish it, Sir,
Though not because I think my Peers have moved
With too great haste to judgment in this matter.
But for your peace of mind let them reopen
The trial.—Fortunately there is still
Time left. Not so much as the shadow of
A doubt shall rest upon our royal honor.

Scene 14

Enter Davison.

ELIZABETH: The warrent, Sir, which I entrusted to
Your hands—where is it?

DAVISON (*in the utmost astonishment*):
                              Warrant?

ELIZABETH: Which I gave
You yesterday to keep—

DAVISON: Gave me to keep!

ELIZABETH: The people importuned me so to sign it
That I was forced to do their will, and did so,
Under duress I did so, and then gave it
To you to keep. I wanted to gain time.
Oh, you know what I said!—Well, let me have it!

SHREWSBURY: Do, worthy Sir! Things now stand otherwise,
  We must reopen the investigation.
DAVISON: Reopen?—Everlasting Mercy!
ELIZABETH: Do
  Not take so long. Where is the document?
DAVISON (*in despair*):
  I am undone, I am a dead man!
ELIZABETH (*interrupting quickly*):   Sir,
  Do not lead me to think that—
DAVISON: I am lost!
  I do not have it.
ELIZABETH: What? What?
SHREWSBURY: God in heaven!
DAVISON: It is in Burleigh's hands—since yesterday.
ELIZABETH: Unhappy man! Then you did not obey me?
  Did I not strictly order you to keep it?
DAVISON: Oh no, you gave me no such order, Queen.
ELIZABETH: Will you call me a liar, wretch? When did
  I bid you give the document to Burleigh?
DAVISON: Not in so many words—but—
ELIZABETH: Worthless creature!
  Do you presume to read interpretations
  Into my words? to put your own blood-thirsty
  Construction on them?—Woe to you if any
  Misfortune has come of your arbitrary
  Action! You'll pay me for it with your life.
  —Lord Earl of Shrewsbury, you see how they
  Misuse my name.
SHREWSBURY: I do see—O my God!
ELIZABETH: What did you say?
SHREWSBURY: If this squire has presumed
  To undertake this step at his own peril,
  If he has acted here without your knowledge,
  He must be summoned up before the judgment
  Seat of the Peers, because he has delivered
  Your name to the abhorrence of all ages.

Last Scene

Enter Burleigh, at last Kent.

BURLEIGH (*bending on one knee before the Queen*):
  Long live my royal Lady, and may all

This island's enemies so perish as
This Stuart perished!
> (*Shrewsbury covers his face. Davison wrings his hands*
> *in despair.*)

ELIZABETH: Tell me now, my Lord!
Did you receive this execution order
From *me?*

BURLEIGH: Why, no, my Sovereign. I received it
From Davison.

ELIZABETH: Did Davison deliver
It to you in *my* name?

BURLEIGH: No, he did not.

ELIZABETH: But you went on in haste to execute it
Without first ascertaining my intention?
The sentence was a just one, and the world
Can not blame us. But you improperly
Forestalled our clemency of heart—and for
This action you are banished from our sight!
> (*to Davison*)

A sentence more severe shall fall on you
For overstepping your authority
And for abusing a most sacred trust.
Let him be taken to the Tower. I ask
That he be charged with penalty of death.
—My noble Talbot! You alone among
My counsellors have I found to be just,
And you shall henceforth be my guide, my friend—

SHREWSBURY: O do not banish your most loyal friends,
Do not throw them in prison, who have acted
On your behalf and now keep silent for you.
—But as for me, great Queen, permit me to
Give back into your hands the seal with which
You have entrusted me for these twelve years.

ELIZABETH (*taken aback*):
No, Shrewsbury! You will not leave me now,
Not now—

SHREWSBURY: Forgive me, but I am too old,
And this hand is too stiff and straight to set
The seal upon your newer policies.

ELIZABETH: Can it be that the man who saved my life
Would leave me now?

SHREWSBURY: It was a small thing that
I did.—I was not able to preserve
Your better part. Live and reign happily!
Your enemy is dead. From now on you
Have nothing more to fear, no further scruples.

                (*Exit.*)
          (*Enter the Earl of Kent.*)

ELIZABETH (*to Kent*):
Send in the Earl of Lester.

KENT: The Lord begs
To be excused, he has set sail for France.

      (*She controls herself and stands with quiet self-*
                possession.
             The curtain falls.)

              Translated by Charles E. Passage